The Truth Abou

The Truth About Denial

Bias and Self-Deception in Science, Politics, and Religion

ADRIAN BARDON

OXFORD

UNIVERSITY PRESS

OXFORD
UNIVERSITY PRESS

Oxford University Press is a department of the University of Oxford. It furthers
the University's objective of excellence in research, scholarship, and education
by publishing worldwide. Oxford is a registered trade mark of Oxford University
Press in the UK and certain other countries.

Published in the United States of America by Oxford University Press
198 Madison Avenue, New York, NY 10016, United States of America.

© Oxford University Press 2020

Library of Congress Cataloging-in-Publication Data
Names: Bardon, Adrian, author.
Title: The truth about denial : bias and self-deception in science,
politics, and religion / Adrian Bardon.
Description: New York : Oxford University Press, 2019.
Identifiers: LCCN 2019021041 | ISBN 9780190062262 (hbk) |
ISBN 9780190062279 (pbk) | ISBN 9780190062286 (etext) |
ISBN 9780190062293 (etext) | ISBN 9780190062309 (online)
Subjects: LCSH: Truthfulness and falsehood. | Denialism. |
Deception. | Disinformation.
Classification: LCC BJ1420 .B37 2019 | DDC 177/.3—dc23
LC record available at https://lccn.loc.gov/2019021041

Paperback printed by Bridgeport National Bindery, Inc.,
United States of America

Contents

Preface

Eighteenth-century philosopher David Hume is justly celebrated for treating the mind as part of nature, rather than as something that belongs to some spiritual realm separate from the material world. "Naturalism" about the mind just means that the mind's operations are natural phenomena that obey rules like any other phenomenon described by science. According to naturalism, the proper study of our mental operations is through natural sciences like biology, neuroscience, and psychology. In offering explanations for various phenomena, the sciences center on the search for causal regularities. In seeking to understand belief as a naturally occurring phenomenon, Hume therefore decided to focus on what *causes* one to hold a given belief, rather than on what *justifies* one in holding a belief. This might seem the wrong approach if one felt that (a) one's beliefs about the world are typically well grounded in reasons, and (b) the process of arriving at—and acting on—those beliefs is accurately described as one that involves a dispassionate weighing of evidence before reaching a conclusion. But human beings generally do not operate this way, if ever. Hume argued that reason is an essential tool for achieving our ends, but it remains a "slave" to the passions, in that our actions are ultimately explained by our *motives*—and reason by itself does not motivate.

The often-insidious influence of unconscious motives on our actions is most apparent in the area of ideology. Philosophers, historians, psychologists, political scientists, and other students of human nature have long noted that we exhibit an enormous susceptibility to unconscious bias in our beliefs. Our interests and emotional needs affect not just our values and choices but also our factual picture of the world around us. In his book on self-deception, psychologist Harry Triandis discussed the many reasons to conclude that "people often see what they wish to see, and believe what they wish to believe."[1] Our picture

---

[1] Harry Triandis, *Fooling Ourselves: Self-Deception in Politics, Religion, and Terrorism* (Westport, CT: Praeger, 2009).

of the world is distorted by self-interest, peer influence, prejudice, fear, and favoritism, and we are often not aware of the influence our motives have on our factual understanding of the evidence for our conclusions. Triandis described how we tend to prefer (again, often without self-awareness) explanations of phenomena that conform to our favored view of things. We seek out evidence and opinions that tend to confirm our prejudices; we ignore or avoid unwanted information. At the same time, we routinely view ourselves as more objective in our judgments than our ideological opponents.

An approach to understanding the mind's operations that focuses on motives seems particularly apt when our subject of study is ideological or doctrinal belief. Political, religious, and other worldviews include certain ideals and prescriptions, but such worldviews themselves rest on a bedrock of factual claims about the world. Because we are not dispassionate about our ideological commitments, it is exceedingly difficult (indeed, almost unheard of) to be entirely dispassionate in the way we account for them using facts and evidence. The justifications we offer for our ideological positions are suffused by unconscious, implicit bias, and are maintained by selective attention to evidence. "Denial" is a word we sometimes use in describing the psychological state of those who are self-deceived about the real causes for the beliefs they hold. Any economist will tell you that human behavior is all about incentives. We are increasingly coming to understand that *factual belief* can work much the same way.

Those with an interest in manipulating public opinion are happy to exploit this aspect of human nature by spinning the truth in ways that appeal to existing prejudices. As a result, ideological partisans wind up disagreeing not just on policy preferences but even on basic facts.

Of late, observers of the U.S. political landscape have been commenting more and more on the alarming ways in which Americans of different political persuasions and cultural, racial, and other identity groups seem not just to disagree on issues but also to be living in different realities. One area where this situation has significant consequences is in the way people can interpret reports of scientific consensus differently, depending on their prejudices and allegiances. Different people, for example, may hear about the science on the human causes of climate change and—sincerely—perceive either certainty, uncertainty, or outright hoax. This phenomenon undercuts public discourse on matters where public policy grounded in solid science has never been more essential.

This phenomenon is on a continuum with the way in which different people can look at those living in poverty, and see them either as victims of unfair circumstances or as people who are complicit in a culture of irresponsibility and dependency. Different people will consider a given refugee population, and see either an alien threat to our way of life or deserving potential members of our society. Different people will see a video of a police shooting; some will see justification and others will see murder.

An environment of polarization, prejudice, bias, and willful self-deception, combined with an often misleading political and media environment, is toxic for political discourse. Polarization on matters of *fact* is affecting progress on matters of critical public importance, such as action on climate.

Research on denial has exploded over just the last few years. This includes game-changing work from social, political, cognitive, and evolutionary psychology, as well as from sociology, communication studies, political science, history, and philosophy. My goal has been to bring this diverse work together for the reader while, I hope, convincing readers of the urgent importance of gaining a better understanding of unconscious bias and self-deception. Denial concerns all of us—both as victims and as perpetrators—and so this work is intended not just for an academic audience; it is for everyone.

Acknowledgments

This wide-ranging project would have been impossible without the contributions of others. I benefited from discussions with Emily Austin, Mark Bedau, Melissa Harris-Perry, Ana Iltis, Justin Jennings, Ralph Kennedy, Win-Chiat Lee, Christian Miller, Naomi Oreskes, Keith Payne, Jedediah Purdy, Maura Tumulty, and Alan Wilson. A 2015 seminar here at Wake Forest on "The Science of Science Denial" allowed me to have extremely productive interactions with Peter Ditto, Heather Douglas, Erin Hennes, Neil Van Leeuven, Aaron McCright, Mark Navin, Brendan Nyhan, Jay Odenbaugh, Vanessa Schweizer, Elizabeth Suhay, and Sara Yeo. A number of these scholars read portions of my manuscript and made really helpful comments. (Peter Ditto and Elizabeth Suhay need to be given special mention as providing comments, advice, and guidance above and beyond the call of duty.) The amazing Alex Madva read drafts of several chapters and made many great suggestions.

I would like to thank Oxford University Press executive editor Peter Ohlin for his support and advice. I also benefited greatly from the comments and suggestions made by six anonymous referees for Oxford University Press. Peer review is a time-consuming job with little reward, yet it is of absolutely central importance to research and scholarship.

Jacque Acierno helped with research work for the project, and Kathryn Dillin and Ally Howell each provided editorial assistance. Tyler Pruitt rendered the two charts in chapter 3 using data I supplied.

I am grateful for the support I received, over the final year of this project, as a Fellow with the Humility and Conviction in Public Life project at the University of Connecticut.

I have been very fortunate to be able to discuss the issues covered in this book with my wife, Janna Levin; she also checked the manuscript for errors. Dr. Levin made many sacrifices so I could have the time to work on this project over the last few years. This book is dedicated to her, as well as to my two wonderful boys, Zev and Max.

The Truth About Denial

1
Bias and Belief

1.1 What Is Denial?

In his 1689 book *An Essay Concerning Human Understanding*, English philosopher John Locke laments the human tendency to close the mind off to unwanted conclusions:

> Let ever so much probability hang on one side of a covetous man's reasoning, and money on the other; it is easy to foresee which will outweigh. Earthly minds, like mud walls, resist the strongest batteries: and though, perhaps, sometimes the force of a clear argument may make some impression, yet they nevertheless stand firm, and keep out the enemy, truth, that would captivate or disturb them. Tell a man passionately in love that he is jilted; bring a score of witnesses of the falsehood of his mistress, it is ten to one but three kind words of hers shall invalidate all their testimonies. *Quod volumus, facile credimus*; what suits our wishes, is forwardly believed, is, I suppose, what every one hath more than once experimented: and though men cannot always openly gainsay or resist the force of manifest probabilities that make against them, yet yield they not to the argument.[1]

This observation about human nature is pretty uncontroversial. Indeed, as social psychologist Peter Ditto puts it, the pervasive influence of our hopes and fears on our judgment "would likely seem so obvious to the average person as to defy the need for empirical confirmation."[2] Individual factual beliefs often derive not from a cold assessment of probabilities but, rather, from a psychological phenomenon sometimes simply called **denial**. Denial involves the emotionally motivated rejection (or embrace) of a factual claim in the face of strong evidence to the contrary. Easily recognizable examples include denying one's spouse is being unfaithful despite ample evidence that he or she is cheating; denying that one has a terminal illness despite diagnoses to that effect; or denying one is an alcoholic despite a history of heavy drinking with destructive consequences. In such cases we colloquially describe the person as being "in denial." (The word "denial" suggests disbelief rather than a positive assertion, but as a misrepresentation of reality, denial can be expressed in terms of either denying something true or affirming something false: The person denying he is an alcoholic may say "I am not an alcoholic," or, affirmatively, "I can stop drinking anytime I like." The candidate down 20 points in the polls who privately insists that she can still win the election may be in denial.[3])

We may find applications of the concept of being "in denial" most familiar in cases of personal difficulties like those just mentioned.[4] But such cases are structurally identical to many instances of belief of much more public import. One pressing example of tendentious belief in the face of contrary evidence is the sincere denial of the reality, severity, and/or urgency of anthropogenic global warming (AGW). Given adequate information about the clear scientific consensus on the overall situation, no one should be denying AGW with confidence. Just as in the more common, more personal instances of denial, the selective representation of the climate consensus is based on a preexisting, affective attachment to a particular conclusion. Another significant example is the not uncommon belief in the inherent superiority of one's own race or ethnicity—or in the inferiority of another's. When sincerely articulated by someone who is sane and moderately well informed, this sort of denial of reality—just as in the case of someone who wants to disbelieve one's spouse has been unfaithful, or who wants to believe he or she has many more years to live—derives from wanting the world to be a certain way that it evidently isn't. Any sincere statement like "My husband would never do that to me," or "The Armenian genocide is a myth," or "Vaccines frequently cause injury," or "President Obama was born in Kenya," or "My financial success has had nothing to do with my inheritance," or "The Cowboys are definitely going to win the Super Bowl this year" is an indication that sincere speaker is in denial when the speaker (a) has little reason, all things considered, to believe the claim; (b) has been exposed to good reasons, all things considered, to doubt it; and (c) has some emotional need to believe it that accounts for the belief (i.e., if the emotional need weren't there, the belief wouldn't be either).

Beliefs like these are not purely self-generated. Powerful political or economic elites, through their paid agents or media surrogates, may be motivated to deliberately misinform the public on various issues. Such efforts are no doubt helped along by ignorance. Many Americans are uninformed about science, the economy, and many other issues relevant to social and economic policy. Obviously, many Americans deny the reality and severity of climate change. A majority deny the evolution of human beings by natural selection.[5] When U.S. adults are asked what percentage of the federal budget goes to foreign aid, the median response is 25% (the real foreign aid figure is less than 1%); Americans also grossly overestimate how much those from the U.S. middle class pay in federal income taxes.[6] Despite the fact that violent crime in the United States has fallen by over 50% since 1992,[7] year after year a majority of Americans report an overall increase in violent crime.[8] When asked, in a 2016 Ipsos-MORI poll, what percentage of wealth is held by the bottom 70% of Americans, U.S. respondents guessed 28%, whereas the actual figure is about 7%.[9] In the same poll, the average U.S. respondent's guess as to the Muslim population in the United States was 17%, whereas the actual figure is about 1%. Survey after survey shows that voters know very little about political party platforms, and yet voters' own policy preferences are heavily influenced by what the party elites favor.

But to bring the public along, lies and demagoguery need to find fertile ground. Hitler's claims that the Jews were responsible for Germany's economic problems were only effective because they catered to a baseline anti-Semitism on the part of a substantial portion of the German population. False claims about climate science by vested interests and their allies find a receptive audience in those with preexisting anti-government inclinations. Doctrines upholding the special, divinely chosen status of some particular religious or ethnic group persist because they satisfy powerful emotional needs for affirmation, status, security, and/or meaning. This is why the study of problems caused by the public and private misunderstanding of reality needs to look not just at misinformation but also at the murky psychological processes that allow bias and self-deception to thrive.

The purpose of this book is to examine the pervasive human tendency to deny uncomfortable truths and to discuss how this tendency affects public discourse—as well as private life—on an exceedingly wide range of important topics. The phenomenon of denial, as we shall see, is dependent on **motivated cognition**. "Motivated cognition" refers to the "unconscious tendency of individuals to process information in a manner that suits some end or goal extrinsic to the formation of accurate beliefs."[10] Motivated cognition happens behind the scenes, but is closely tied to the more overt **rationalization** of belief, which I shall define as the process of retroactively inventing defensive justifications for holding those beliefs formed via motivated cognition. Motivated cognition is about belief formation, whereas rationalization is about maintaining and defending beliefs. Rationalization is thus a kind of second stage for motivated cognition. Unlike motivated cognition, explicit rationalization is a conscious process, though we are often not consciously aware of our motives when we engage in it. (I shall use the familiar phrase **motivated reasoning**—the popular use of which doesn't generally distinguish between initial motivated cognition and the second-stage rationalization of that way of thinking—to denote the whole process wherein implicit, motivated cognition is followed by the generation of spurious reasons to maintain those sincerely held beliefs formed via motivated cognition.)

Let's get a little clearer on exactly what "denial" does and does not include, for purposes of this discussion. It does not refer, for instance, simply to being misinformed. I wish to examine denial strictly in that sense of being "in denial" wherein the denier is exhibiting a kind of emotionally self-protective self-deception. (Denial is often misattributed to ignorance; as I shall discuss further, there is good reason to think that the real issue is motivated reasoning.) Denial, in this context, presumes some exposure to relevant—and unwelcome— facts and constitutes a kind of reaction to them. This sort of self-deception is different from **mendacity**, wherein one purposefully lies to others about the existence of evidence for something, or deliberately misrepresents the evidence. One might know perfectly well, for example, that one's oil company is responsible for a toxic spill, and respond by actively and consciously engaging in a cover-up and public denial of responsibility.[11]

Neither am I talking about "spin," or what philosopher Harry Frankfurt has termed **bullshit**.[12] The bullshitter's intent is not to lie but, rather, to influence or to create a certain reality, and is simply indifferent as to whether his or her claims are true or false. The job of the trial attorney, the political operative, or the commercial advertiser is neither to uphold the truth nor to lie; rather, the job is to represent one's client in the best light possible.

Being in denial is also to be distinguished from **wishful thinking**. What wishful thinking has in common with denial is that each fulfills an emotional need of some kind. However, with wishful thinking, there is a belief without solid evidence for a conclusion one way or the other. You might wishfully believe, for example, that an acquaintance is romantically interested in you, despite having no clear positive indication of this. This becomes denial only if you come to discredit strong evidence to the contrary, such as the knowledge that the object of your affections is romantically involved with someone else, or is only attracted to members of a different sex, and so on. Unlike beliefs arising from denial, beliefs arising from wishful thinking can even become what philosopher Neil Van Leeuven calls "self-fulfilling beliefs": An otherwise unwarranted confidence in, say, romantic or athletic prospects can sometimes contribute to the actual fulfillment of those prospects.[13] These are also sometimes called "positive illusions," and a tendency to experience them may be adaptive, in that a stubborn disposition to maintain a particular belief in the face of contrary evidence might sometimes work in one's favor.[14] Negative emotions can hamper our ability to function, and some ability to automatically discount the factual sources of some negative emotions may be adaptive. As psychologist Timothy Wilson puts it, people are "equipped with powerful psychological defenses that operate offstage, rationalizing, reinterpreting, and distorting negative information in ways that ameliorate its impact."[15] (He calls this our "psychological immune system.") A tendency to unrealistically positive self-appraisal may give us the confidence to overcome daunting challenges. Undue discounting of the odds against us when faced with, say, an external threat, may expedite a productive response by heading off paralyzing fear. Belief in a benevolent higher power may solidify group member-ship, or provide the comfort we need to endure loss. Unfortunately, what in some contexts might be an adaptive—even charming—facet of human nature can have very bad consequences. Wishful thinking can easily morph into denial when the evidence turns against you, at which point the failure to respond appropriately to the facts can be destruc-tive on a personal, societal, or global scale.

We sometimes use the word "delusional" as a derogatory term for people who we think are in the grips of motivationally biased thinking, but there is an important distinction between denial and **delusion**. Delusions arise from illness or psychiatric disorder (like schizo-phrenia), or from injury (e.g., phantom limb syndrome), rather than from emotional need.[16] Neurologist Robert Burton describes known delusional conditions like Cotard's syndrome (in which a person suffers from an unshakeable conviction that he or she is already dead) or Capgras syndrome (in which one suffers from an unshakeable con-viction that a loved one has been replaced by an imposter), that often directly result from acute brain-related events like stroke or viral men-ingitis.[17] In such cases, we may rarely happen also to find some dis-tinct, accompanying emotional need to believe such things, but even if so, we would not attribute the delusion to that need. Further, a de-lusional belief need not be based on a rationale the believer actually expects everyone else to accept. In cases of delusion, the victim may not even attempt to rationalize the delusional belief.[18] Someone with Capgras, or who suffers from the delusion that he is in communication with aliens, may not necessarily also believe that others ought to be able to come to the same conclusion by considering publicly available evidence. By contrast, the person in denial is rational in the sense that evidence still matters. Typically, as psychologist Ziva Kunda argued in an influential essay on motivated reasoning, even those who are "motivated to arrive at a particular conclusion attempt to be rational and to construct a justification of their desired conclusion that would persuade a dispassionate observer."[19] Motivated reasoners are neither divorced from nor indifferent to reality; their perception of reality is just motivationally skewed in nonconscious ways. Nor do we think of people in denial as literally incapable of revising their beliefs, unlike people whose false beliefs can be traced to acute brain injury. Delusion is unusual, abnormal, and pathological, whereas denial is common, normal, and requires no malfunction.

People are motivated to deny reality for many different reasons, including self-interest, a desire to avoid feelings of insecurity or loss of control, or a desire to defend one's cultural or political identity. **Cognitive dissonance** is the state of mind one experiences when one encounters information that is inconsistent with one's beliefs. This is *cognitively* disruptive simply because it forces a reassessment of some accustomed representation of reality. Groundbreaking studies on dissonance and dissonance resolution were executed by Leon Festinger in the 1950s, wherein he studied the psychological effects of new, inconsistent information on one's existing beliefs or worldview.[20] He observed a natural, psychological resistance to belief revision as a result of dissonant information. One likely explanation for some of this resistance is an evolved cognitive heuristic telling us that, other things being equal, mental representations of the world built up over time are more likely to be accurate, and so should be favored over new information up to a point. But Festinger noted an *emotional* component in subjects' responses. Cognitively dissonant information can also be experienced as personally disruptive—undermining the comfort one feels in thinking one has a good grasp of things—and therefore be anxiety inducing. This discomfort spurs an unconscious drive to resolve the dissonance by discounting or otherwise dismissing information that contradicts existing beliefs. In important confirming studies of subjects in an induced dissonant state, social psychologists Andrew Elliot and Patricia Devine demonstrated that "dissonance is experienced as psychological discomfort."[21] Further studies by psychologist Eddie Harmon-Jones tested whether the dissonance itself causes the discomfort, or rather simply by some perception of the consequences of being wrong. He confirmed that "dissonance is associated with increased feelings of negative affect even in situations void of aversive consequences."[22]

Most dissonant information one encounters is not particularly emotionally threatening in terms of its content (e.g., "I was sure that only Australia had marsupials, but now I hear that American opossums are marsupials," or "I thought that low-fat diets were better for losing weight than low-carb diets, and now this magazine article is saying that's not true"). Such new information just spurs brief confusion, followed, in some cases, by dismissal of the new claim or, in others, a not terribly disruptive update of one's obsolete beliefs and/or behaviors. In his original studies, however, Festinger found that cognitive dissonance can produce intense emotional discomfort, when the particular change in thinking demanded by the dissonant information threatens a representation of reality to which the subject is emotionally attached. Information can be threatening to the self because it conflicts with one's desires, expectations, sense of control, or cultural or political identity (e.g., "I was expecting the Rapture on this day, but it didn't happen," or "I was sure Hillary Clinton was going to win the election, but she didn't").[23] In other words, cognitive dissonance can refer either to the "plain vanilla" dissonant effect of unexpected information or to the "extra spicy" dissonance experienced upon receiving un*wanted* information. The effects of the latter feelings of dissonance are much more dramatic than the effects of the former. It is when it represents some sort of threat to a state of affairs the individual prefers to believe in, or to some system of thought with which the individual identifies, that dissonant information will frequently lead to outright denial. (The cultists Festinger was studying chose to believe not that they had been wrong about the apocalypse but, rather, that they had headed off the apocalypse by their devotion. After the 2016 U.S. presidential election, Hillary Clinton supporters called for recounts in the states they unexpectedly lost, and blamed foreign interference for electoral losses—while at the same time, Donald Trump denied that he had lost the popular vote, insisting that millions of people voted illegally for his opponent.) What is quite clear is that, when dissonance arises, the extent to which one is emotionally committed to maintaining a certain belief or worldview now under threat both increases the negative response to the dissonance and affects how the discrepancy is resolved.[24] (The ancient Greek word *amathia* ["not-learning"] is sometimes taken to refer specifically not to ignorance but to the state of unwillingness to learn—typically, when one is motivated to maintain a certain belief or worldview in the face of recalcitrant evidence.[25])

It might be helpful here also to mention **compartmentalization**, which is a way of doing a kind of cognitive judo move on dissonant beliefs and feelings: When we compartmentalize, we somehow manage—at least temporarily—simply to avoid thinking about one side of the inconsistency in our beliefs and behavior. For example, consider the environmental activist who blithely makes flight reservations, thinking only about the vacation destination and not about his or her knowledge of the contribution passenger jet travel makes to global warming. The liberal opposing unfair labor practices overseas can walk into Walmart and think only about the low prices; someone who is revolted by factory farming practices can grab a burger at a fast-food restaurant without the inconsistency this decision represents ever coming to mind. Mere moments after sincerely avowing a duty to the poor, a devout Christian exiting his church can stroll right by a homeless beggar without giving it a thought. Though it is also an unconscious defensive response to distressing cognitive dissonance, I would distinguish compartmentalization from denial in that, with compartmentalization, the inconvenient information in question is suppressed rather than denied; dissonance is thus avoided rather than defeated. The compartmentalizer's beliefs do not change; there is simply a temporarily unrecognized, hypocritical inconsistency between his or her avowed beliefs and his or her behavior. It is a different story when we twist our representation of the facts to suit our needs (e.g., "I'm sure Apple has fixed the labor practices in their factories by now," or "That guy probably just wants money for drugs").[26] This sort of manipulation is characteristic of denial. The compartmentalizer might change his or her behavior when called out on the inconsistency, but the person in denial has eliminated inconsistency by altering his or her (perceived) reality. The denier is harder to dislodge because he or she has devoted cognitive resources to eliminating dissonance, rather than just ignoring it.

Denial manifests itself in a wide spectrum of contexts, both private and public. Believing in fate or luck, in supernatural powers, in the fidelity of one's spouse, or in one's own competence at auto repair can (depending on circumstances) be examples of denial. In a forthcoming book, sociologist Keith Kahn-Harris suggests a further distinction between denial and **denialism**:

> Denialism is an expansion, an intensification, of denial. At root, denial and denialism are simply a subset of the many ways humans

have developed to use language to deceive others and themselves. Denial can be as simple as refusing to accept that someone else is speaking truthfully. Denial can be as unfathomable as the multiple ways we avoid acknowledging our weaknesses and secret desires. Denialism is more than just another manifestation of the humdrum intricacies of our deceptions and self-deceptions. It represents the transformation of the everyday practice of denial into a whole new way of seeing the world and—most important—a collective accomplishment. Denial is furtive and routine; denialism is combative and extraordinary. Denial hides from the truth, denialism builds a new and better truth.[27]

Denialism is the (usually collective) building of a worldview that both derives from and supports the denial of some inconvenient truth. Some forms of denialism have significant public policy implications: for example, holding a belief—despite having good reason not to— in inherent racial superiority, in the status of others as dangerous nonbelievers or apostates, in the efficacy of destructive authoritarian policies, in the claims of vaccine opponents, or in the claims of anthropogenic global warming deniers. These forms of denialism will typically be linked to the believer's **ideology**, or ideological worldview.

"Ideology" is another general term without a fully agreed-upon meaning. Roughly, it refers to a set of factual beliefs—together with some evaluative attitudes pertaining to those facts—that give rise to some broader social, cultural, political, economic, or religious viewpoint. An ideology combines a kind of factual, explanatory theory of (some aspect of) the world, with some prescriptive conclusions based on the factual picture presented by the theory. For example, one might believe that (a) self-interested bankers exert disproportionate control over the world economy, and that (b) this control has proven harmful to the interests of much of the world's population. This picture, in turn, is the (alleged) factual basis for the broader evaluation that unregulated globalized capitalism is a problem, and therefore we ought to have greater governmental control over international banking.

There is nothing inherently wrong with having an ideology. However, in practice, ideology is often tied up with denial, and denial is a primary reason for the intractability of ideological conflict: Someone in denial, by definition, is not receptive to disconfirming evidence or argument, and is highly resistant to change or compromise. This is why "ideologue" tends to be used as a pejorative term, equivalent to characterizing someone as closed-minded. Denial can be a *cause* of ideological positions, or a *product* of an emotional attachment to such a position. It is interesting to note that the most influential early discussion of ideology was that of Karl Marx, who saw ideology primarily as a vehicle for *mis*conceptions on the part of the majority as to where its economic interests lie. (Friedrich Engels' famous term "false consciousness" was coined in reference to this phenomenon.[28])

It has been much lamented in recent years that opposing political factions in the United States seem increasingly unable to agree on basic facts, such as the fact that the Earth's surface is warming due to human activity.[29] Ideological conflict is often thought of as primarily a matter of conflicting value systems. Yet, it is a dispute over factual claims, rather than a difference in values, that should be *expected* to be the primary arena for ideological disagreement in liberal democratic contexts. The defining feature of a liberal democracy, in the Lockean, "classical" sense, is that individual rights trump any particular, sectarian conception of the good (i.e., what way of life and/or belief system is best). By contrast, in, say, an authoritarian communist or theocratic context, the state claims the authority to impose a particular conception of the greater good on its citizens; these latter kinds of regime are thus "illiberal" in the classical sense.* In an open society, mainstream public policy positions at least ostensibly rely on factual claims about the expected benefits of certain social, economic, or foreign policies, rather than explicitly relying on sectarian or doctrinal claims as justifications in themselves.[30]

The boundaries between factual beliefs and moral values can be fuzzy, partly due to some mutual dependence of one on the other.[31] Yet, ideological debates over right and wrong (in liberal democratic contexts) almost always involve some disagreement over factual

---

* To the list of illiberal social systems I would add the libertarian's ideal free market capitalist regime. Such a regime would claim the moral authority to enforce a morally indefensible system of natural and absolute property rights on individuals, to the detriment of their capacity to pursue their own conception of the good. But more on this in chapter 3.

claims. Consider opposition to marriage equality for same-sex couples. Clearly, some oppose marriage equality because they evaluate homosexuality as wrong, as immoral. But which comes first—value or fact? This moral evaluation of homosexuality is predicated on a set of factual claims, including (a) that God exists and (b) that God condemns homosexuality. In the public sphere we hear the claim that marriage equality would undermine the institution of marriage and/or that "traditional" heterosexual marriages provide a more stable environment for children.[32] These are claims of fact, and appeal to these alleged facts in opposing any expansion of the legal definition of marriage implies an appeal to *shared* evaluative beliefs: that marriage is a positive social institution and that stable families are best for children. Even genocide/ Holocaust denial can be understood as resting on factual beliefs about the innate qualities of members of other races: Genocide apologists value peace and humanity while excluding some inconvenient group, such as the Jews or Kurds, from the ranks of the fully human.

Or consider the mid-2000s debate over the morality of the Bush administration's "enhanced interrogation" techniques, as practiced on insurgents captured in Afghanistan and elsewhere. Most members of each side would quickly agree with the evaluative statement that "torture is wrong." The primary dimension of public disagreement was on historical and legal precedents as to what constitutes torture. The Bush administration produced lawyers who were willing to claim that causing physical pain does not constitute torture, so long as it falls short of pain associated with "serious physical injury, such as organ failure, impairment of bodily function, or even death."[33] Under this definition of torture, the U.S. government could argue that waterboarding is not torture, even though, after World War II, Japanese officers were executed by representatives of the U.S. government for having used waterboarding as an interrogation tactic.[34]

Nothing exemplifies ideological "fact polarization" like the debate over economic policy. During the last few decades in the United States, this debate has revolved around whether taxation and spending policies should reflect Keynesian demand-side economics or small-government supply-side economics. Proponents of the former emphasize fairness and equality of opportunity; proponents of the latter emphasize liberty and personal responsibility. Yet each side typically would agree that, strictly speaking, these are *all* positive values; the main issue is the factual, empirical question as to what is lost or gained by relatively high taxation and a strong social safety net, versus the reverse policy of low taxation and limited social spending.[35]

In each of these cases, ideological conflict has centered on a disagreement over facts, not values. Sociologist John Levi Martin writes:

> [D]ifferences in ideology seem to correlate much more strongly with differences in *descriptive* statements than they do with differences in purely *prescriptive* ones. . . . And this is because . . . the thing about values is that they are all good, considered singly. It's only in trade-offs that people begin to distinguish themselves. So people can agree with one another in their value commitments, while still having diametrically opposed opinions.[36]

In one respect, this is an optimistic view of ideological conflict: If ideological conflict is a matter of irreducible and irreconcilable value systems, there is no possible resolution but for one side to suppress or dominate the other; by contrast, factual disputes are resolvable, in principle, without violence. So there is a puzzle here: In the face of roughly the same available information, how is it that different individuals or groups can come to such wildly different conclusions about reality? If most ideological differences rest on factual disputes, and if factual disputes can (in principle) be resolved by appeal to evidence and reasoning, then most ideological disputes should be resolvable simply by study and debate among reasonable and open-minded persons. Yet in practice this is not what happens. Why not? A vast amount of—mostly quite recent—evidence from social psychology, sociology, political science, and allied fields points to the answer: motivated reasoning and denial. Answering the following questions is therefore essential: (a) What are the motivators behind motivated reasoning? and (b) What are the psychological mechanisms that can turn a defensive emotional impulse into a sincere factual representation?

Much of the academic, philosophical literature on belief has focused on the necessary and sufficient conditions of a belief's being justified. The phenomenon of denial spotlights the ways in which evidence and justification can be effectively irrelevant as to whether someone believes something or not. In this context, then, the correct line of inquiry (as David Hume proposed) would seem to be one directed at what *causes* or *explains* belief, rather than one examining technical questions surrounding what theoretically constitutes adequate evidence and warranted belief.*

An inquiry into the motivational underpinnings of denial and denialism demands an extensive dive into the interdisciplinary study of noncognitive bias. Psychologists and social scientists from various subfields have examined a number of nonrational factors that can influence information processing in ideologically heated contexts; and researchers have identified a wide variety of mechanisms by which—once motivation is activated—bias explains belief.

1.2 "Hot Cognition"

The naïve account of reasoning is that the process of human judgment is entirely conscious, and is primarily motivated by accuracy (with some additional consideration given to balancing the need for precision with the need for efficiency in expenditure of resources). A conscious, *willful* blindness to the truth would seem paradoxical: This implies simultaneously knowing and not knowing the truth.[37] The concept of motivated cognition suggests a process by which evidence known to undermine a preferred result is ignored or discounted, with the intention of producing a false, or at least unwarranted, belief. But if the processes leading to belief are always transparent, then self-deception would involve believing the result of motivated cognition

---

* The problem of establishing precise, necessary and sufficient conditions for an assertion being justified (or refuted) is extremely difficult and very technical. This is a central concern of the fields of epistemology and philosophy of science, and the relevant philosophical literature is extensive. For purposes of this text I am taking for granted that there are some clear-cut cases of overwhelming evidence and/or settled scientific issues, the denial of which—under certain circumstances—is patently unjustified. I am therefore appealing to an intuitive notion of having (overwhelmingly) good reasons to believe something, and conversely lacking good reason to deny it. It would otherwise be impossible to proceed to an examination of motivated reasoning and denial. My focus is on examining why we form the (often irrational) beliefs we have, rather than on giving a general, theoretical account of rationality itself.

while knowing you don't have reason to believe it, and/or consciously intending to self-deceive—but how can you deceive yourself if you are aware of your intention to do so? The answer is that reasoning is *not* a self-transparent process. René Descartes assumed that, if I have a thought or belief, I am necessarily aware of my own role in producing it.[38] Modern psychological science has not been kind to this assumption. Self-deception, and thus motivated cognition, is possible because of unconscious bias in accessing and/or assessing evidence.[39]

In adding to many other lines of investigation pointing away from the reasoning-as-transparent model, social scientist Daniel Kahneman and his collaborators have identified a routine role in judgment for an "implicit cognition" system of spontaneous, unconscious, "gut" processes that can have as much to do with belief formation as conscious processes.[40] This system can be responsible for many helpful shortcuts and processing successes, but also innumerable individual and systemic errors. Psychologist Timothy Wilson has explained some of the ways in which nonconscious processing is vital to our making sense of the world: There is far too much incoming information, moment to moment, for us to consciously handle; if it weren't for nonconscious heuristics, selective attention, and implicit processing, effective interaction with the world would be impossible.[41] This is about making quick, efficient decisions. The world would leave us behind in short order if we constantly questioned everything.

Obviously, how we process information affects decision-making and behavior. Philosopher Tamar Gendler introduced the term **alief** to refer to propensities to judge and act based on implicit, automatic association:

> To have an alief is . . . to have an innate or habitual propensity to respond to an apparent stimulus in a particular way. It is to be in a mental state that is . . . *a*ssociative, *a*utomatic and *a*rational. As a class, aliefs are states that we share with non-human *a*nimals; they are developmentally and conceptually *a*ntecedent to other cognitive attitudes that the creature may go on to develop. Typically, they are also *a*ffect-laden and *a*ction-generating.[42]

Gendler goes on to claim, quite plausibly, that these aliefs are responsible for much of the moment-to-moment management of our behavior.[43] Implicit associations—and the emotional values they carry—allow us to react to situations much more quickly and efficiently than if we always thought everything through. If you see a snake on the path, you jump back; you don't need to think about what to do.

But this helpful, cognition-bypassing mechanism also opens the door to innumerable unconscious motivational influences on belief. Political scientists Milton Lodge and Charles Taber have shown in great detail how automatic, affective responses to stimuli can have a significant short- and long-term influence on political opinion, even when the individual in question takes the time to carefully weigh reasons for and against.[44] Implicit bias is the general term for "relatively unconscious and relatively automatic features of prejudiced judgment and social behavior."[45] Lodge and Taber found that unconscious emotional associations can sharply bias our evaluations of situations, persons, and evidence (they call this phenomenon "affect transfer"), as well as our automatic processes of retrieval of considerations relevant to a conclusion ("affective contagion"), to the point where even conscious and considered processing of information about political candidates and public policy issues is deeply influenced by unconscious valences.[46] It is clear this is a precognitive effect: Subjects asked about polarizing political figures will execute a measurable "like–dislike" judgment on the politician in milliseconds, whereas it takes longer to report the most basic cognitive associations, such as that the politician is male or a Democrat. "Affect," Lodge and Taber conclude, "precedes and contextualizes cognition."[47]

Stephen Colbert introduced the term "truthiness" on the first episode of his television show *The Colbert Report* in 2005.[48] Editors at Wikipedia define "truthiness" as "a quality characterizing a 'truth' that a person making an argument or assertion claims to know intuitively 'from the gut' or because it 'feels right' without regard to evidence, logic, intellectual examination, or facts."[49] Critically, what our "gut" tells us has a lot to do with our background and with our peer group. That's where many of our gut reactions come from. If most people I trust think something is true, that becomes part of what

I judge to be true—guided by the automatic, affective associations that "precede and contextualize" decision-making in so many contexts.

Human beings are demonstrably bad at figuring out the reasons for our own decisions, preferences, and the like. Study after study has shown that people will unintentionally invent post hoc "rational" explanations for decisions that were really caused by something else (this is known in the literature as **confabulation**).[50] In fact, it has proven shockingly easy to demonstrate that our decisions are frequently explained by factors of which we are not introspectively aware.[51] People demonstrate more helping behavior when in the presence of pleasant ambient smells, such as the aroma of baking cookies—but will not cite any awareness of the odor or its mood effects as a contributing factor in deciding to help.[52] Shoppers will choose a product simply because of its positioning on the right side of a display of identical products, and then confabulate some quality it has that the others lack.[53] Study participants will report greater relief from a medication if they were told it is more expensive than another, identical one.[54] Significantly, effects like these may extend to expressions of moral and ideological preferences. Multiple studies have indicated that moral judgments are more severe when sensory disgust is induced in study subjects being asked to make a moral assessment.[55] Voting behavior trends more conservative when the polling place is a church and less so in a public school.[56]

Of all the implicit influences on our thinking and our behavior, our emotional needs are the most pervasive and the most persuasive. **Affect bias** is the standard term for the distorting influence of emotion on behavior. ("Affect" and "emotion" are often used interchangeably. "Affect" refers to the positive/negative feelings we have in response to some stimulus, and "emotion" to the same thing—and also to the motives the affective response engenders.[57]) Researchers have identified a wide range of unconscious effects of emotion on those particular behaviors directly involved in belief acquisition and maintenance. For example, we know that one's emotional state can affect how much attention is paid to aspects of a situation. A subject's feeling angry can result in greater attention being paid to evidence of blameworthiness; feeling fear can lead him or her to focus more on evidence of risk.[58] Such changes in attention can lead to different assessments of evidence, and thus to different conclusions.

The influence of emotion on belief is particularly insidious, thanks to the nature of emotion itself. As psychologists Gerald Clore and Karen Gasper put it,

> [E]motions are believable. Because emotional feelings are directly experienced, and arise from within, the personal validity of the information they appear to convey seems self-evident to the person experiencing them. One can argue with logic, but not with feeling.[59]

(One is reminded of the all-purpose excuse for unwise romantic liaisons, using language appropriated from Emily Dickinson: "The heart wants what it wants.") Psychologists Nico Frijda and Batja Mesquita describe ways that strong feelings or desires have been shown to influence belief, and even to induce new beliefs.[60] A strong desire that one's romantic love be reciprocated can all too easily develop into a belief that, in fact, it *is* reciprocated. It's not unusual for love for one's child to grow into a conviction that he or she is especially or uniquely talented. Fear of death may explain a belief in the afterlife, and an emotional commitment to religious dogma can incite a dogmatic rejection of counterevidence (just ask Galileo!). Frijda and Mesquita note also the special emotional valence of conversion experiences, veneration, inspiration, and the like, where the emotional intensity of these experiences—along with the feelings of longing, despair, or guilt that cause the believer to seek out such experiences—seems to validate the associated belief.[61] (Blaise Pascal famously proposed immersing oneself in ritual and enthusiasm in order to engender a genuine belief in God not otherwise supported by reason and evidence.) By contrast, cognitive biases employed as mere heuristics by automatic information-processing systems—even if difficult to avoid—lead to judgments that are relatively easy to correct after the fact when pointed out. This is because, in most such cases, only "plain vanilla" cognitive dissonance is at issue, so *the reasoner is not motivated to remain in the wrong.* It is a different story when the individual is experiencing the "extra spicy" dissonance that derives from emotional needs.

Hume pointed out the artificiality of separating emotion from cognition. Reason is "slave to the passions," he argued, in that reason alone cannot account for motivation.[62] Reason supplies the means to achieve some end, but not the end itself. "'Tis not contrary to reason," Hume wrote, "to prefer the destruction of the whole world to the scratching of my finger." Even the so-called dispassionate reasoning motivated exclusively by an interest in accuracy depends on one's *caring* about being accurate. It is impossible to discuss rational deliberation in abstraction from the emotional bases of motivation.* Neurologist Antonio Damasio studied patients who had, through accident or disease, suffered damage to their brains that eliminated their emotional processing while leaving their so-called higher-order reasoning skills entirely intact.[63] He found that these subjects' very ability to make decisions was crippled.

Further—as Damasio argues—the notion that we must always be aware of the factors involved in our beliefs and decisions is an unfounded holdover from the Cartesian view of the self (a view inspired by the substance dualism of major strains of Christianity), according to which we are composed of essentially distinct material bodies and immaterial minds. For Descartes, all thoughts are conscious thoughts: The essence of the mind or "soul" is only to think; and so the mind's activity must necessarily always be transparent to the mind.[64]

Neuroscientists have concluded that the circuitry of cognitive processing heavily overlaps with the circuitry of affect in the embodied beings that we are, and that emotion influences sensory processing, language, and memory functions basic to cognitive processing.[65] Emotion, in short, is itself an inextricable aspect of information processing.[66] In addition to supplying the motivation to act (as Hume described), emotions are directly implicated in belief formation. Key brain areas are involved in both social judgment and emotional processing.[67] Some have gone so far as to state that the brain does not "respect" the affective–cognitive distinction, and that any apparent

---

* Though being motivated by accuracy is importantly different, in that such motivation applies not to the content of the belief but, rather, to its correspondence with reality.

difference between affect and cognition is merely phenomenological.[68] Cognitive scientists George Lakoff and Mark Johnson summarize the point:

> Reason is not disembodied, as the tradition has largely held, but arises from the nature of our brains, bodies, and bodily experiences. . . . The same neural and cognitive mechanisms that allow us to perceive and move around also create our conceptual systems and modes of reason. . . . Reason is not a transcendent feature of the universe or of disembodied mind. Instead, it is shaped crucially by the peculiarities of our human bodies, by the remarkable details of the neural structure of our brains, and by the specifics of our everyday functioning in the world.[69]

We are biological organisms whose nervous system evolved to serve bodily needs. Our reasoning skills are inseparable from somatic and emotional responses; and accuracy in reasoning is secondary in importance, from an evolutionary perspective, to issues like survival and fecundity (two accomplishments that often importantly rest on successful social integration with one's tribe).[70] Under this understanding of cognition, any expectation that human beings would or could characteristically reason in complete independence from their motivations seems unrealistic.

The developmental psychologist Alison Gopnik describes an innate "theory formation system" in children that mimics in some respects the process of theory formation and revision in science.[71] The evolutionary purpose of this system, she argues, is to help us develop reasonably accurate, explanatory "causal maps" of the world that allow us to operate in our environment more effectively. Built into this system are rewards for producing explanations. Gopnik compares this link to the rewards for sexual activity. Thanks to the evolutionary process, nature has provided us with reasons to associate sexual activity with pleasure. The pleasure of sex would serve the purpose of encouraging activities that often lead to reproduction, which obviously is a positive development from an evolutionary standpoint. Thanks also to the evolutionary process, Gopnik argues, nature has similarly provided us with a motivational phenomenology that encourages theory formation—namely, the emotion of curiosity and the joys of discovery and sudden understanding.

From our phenomenological point of view, it may seem to us that we construct and use theories to achieve explanation or that we have sex to achieve orgasm. From an evolutionary point of view, however, the relation is reversed, we experience orgasms and explanations to ensure we make babies and theories.[72]

Just as Hume insisted, emotion is essential to agency, and this is true even for the (allegedly) coldly dispassionate activity of assembling factual beliefs about the world. It is, perhaps, the long shadow of the traditional, naïve separation of emotion and cognition that has caused many students of human nature to overlook the function of certain emotions within cognition, or what Gopnik calls, simply, "cognitive emotion."[73]

However, Gopnik continues, the fact that the existence of the sex drive is explained by its past success in stimulating reproduction doesn't mean that reproduction occurs in all cases or that the sex drive is operational only in contexts where reproduction is even possible. We explain the presence of the sex drive in terms of reproduction even though, for example, people have sex while using contraception and women continue to enjoy sex after menopause.[74] With someone who always uses contraception because he or she wants to avoid having children, or who is only attracted to a person or persons with whom he or she cannot reproduce, or is only motivated to have sex with non-human animals, we may see orgasms without any connection to reproduction. Similarly, someone who is motivated by factors other than accuracy in forming his or her judgments about the world may hold any number of theories about the world (and normative conclusions based on those theories) that are disconnected from the evidence. As Gopnik puts it,

> The function of theory formation may be to obtain veridical causal maps, in general and over the long run . . . but this is perfectly compatible with the idea that the products of theory formation are often not veridical. . . . [G]enuine explanation, and indeed genuine theory

formation, can take place whose outcome is normatively deficient, even, very deficient much of the time.[75]

And indeed, the evidence from social psychology has strongly indicated that information processing is quite often motivated by emotions other than accuracy, and that such distorted processing is largely unconscious and driven by nonrational attitudes and dispositions.

Commercial advertising is often designed specifically to generate emotions through images and associations that have little or nothing to do with any actual advantages of a product; the purpose of these affective proddings is to lead us to believe that a given product is the best of its kind or will improve one's life in some way. The influence of emotion on belief is also exploited in political propaganda, where scapegoating, demonization, or dehumanization of political opponents is so common as to be ubiquitous; tying members of other nationalities, racial groups, or other subgroups to crimes, economic collapse, and the like generates affective associations that in turn seem to validate convictions of superiority and the justice of one's cause.[76]

Motives permeate even paradigm cases of "cold" scientific reasoning, where investigators truly feel no personal stake in the outcome. As philosopher Heather Douglas has stressed, any inquiry requires decisions about what questions to investigate, which hypotheses to test, and what margin of error is permissible.[77] Motives and values need to be brought in at some level to explain such choices. Consider an inquiry into the effects of certain gun laws. Certain private or public institutions need to have decided that this topic is worth studying; they need to decide exactly which questions to ask; and the level of risk they already believe to be posed by guns (or gun laws) will help determine when they feel they have enough information to draw a conclusion. We therefore should speak not of unmotivated reasoning but, rather, of relatively unmotivated reasoning. Some reasoning is motivated mainly by some combination of curiosity and a widely shared sense of the importance of the topic. By contrast, some reasoning is characterized by distinctively personal/political interests; an individual may feel threatened by some factual claim or worldview, and thus has an intense desire to find some particular result. The question is, Does the topic of gun control trigger certain self- or worldview-protective responses specific to the issue of gun control? Are these motives un-consciously affecting the inquiries launched, the methods used, and the conclusions drawn?

In sum, the real explanations for our preferences and decisions, and for the factual beliefs on which they are based, often are not in-trospectively transparent, and thus our various evaluations and representations of reality are frequently—even routinely—subject to factors of which we are unaware. ("The heart has its reasons of which reason knows nothing," as Pascal insightfully asserted.) And this phenomenon not only is implicated in narrowly circumscribed per-sonal situations but also plays a hidden role in the formation of broad, ideology-defining worldviews.

Emotion, at both the psychological and neurological levels, is an integral part of judgment, motivation, and belief. Which emotions are specifically implicated in denial? We have already discussed cog-nitive dissonance: at root, the experience of a discrepancy between how one expects—or wants—the world to be and how it appears to be.[78] Dissonance, especially when it represents a threat to one's emo-tional needs, spurs discomfort or anxiety, which in turn unconsciously influences how we handle evidence; the resulting biased informa-tion processing empowers us in rejecting unwanted beliefs and in instigating new beliefs that we anticipate will make us happier.[79] *This response is, in general terms, the phenomenon that characteristically underlies denial.*

Perhaps the most obvious emotional/attitudinal factor that can im-plicitly bias information processing is self-interest.[80] Bias based on self-interest can take several forms. One is the unconscious motive to maintain beliefs conducive to one's individual self-interest, as when a tobacco company executive sincerely maintains the belief that the health impacts of tobacco remain unproven.* (This phenomenon is the subject of Upton Sinclair's famous quip, "It is difficult to get a man to understand something when his salary depends on his not under-standing it.") Another **self-serving** motive is that of maintaining beliefs that validate our moral worthiness, intelligence, and/or competence

---

* This is to be distinguished from the case in which the executive is *insincere* in pub-licly maintaining this position; that would be a case of mendacity rather than denial.

(see, for example, evidence for the Dunning-Kruger effect, wherein individuals tend to overestimate their knowledge or abilities[81]).

Next there is **group-serving** motivation, wherein individuals are motivated to maintain beliefs and worldviews that favor the social group with which they identify.[82] For various reasons, people come to identify with cultural, racial, religious, political, and other communities or subgroups. To the extent that one's self-concept is tied up with one's membership in a group, then, evidence working either for or against the status of that group should be expected to trigger, respectively, a positive or negative emotional response.[83] There is a strong psychological motivation to view one's own group, or **in-group**, as special and privileged, and thus by contrast other groups, or **out-groups**, as inferior in various respects. This partisanship motivates biased information processing in the wide variety of contexts where the status of one's group is at issue. Furthermore, as political psychologist Elizabeth Suhay has shown, conformity to group norms can enhance one's standing in one's in-group, while deviation can lead both to social exclusion and to personal feelings of shame and alienation; these effects can function as powerful influences on ideological belief.[84]

In a similar vein, psychologist Jonathan Haidt has found associations between ideological partisanship and biased information processing. He characterizes our reasoning regarding moral or ideological matters in terms of individual "righteousness" and group- or system-serving "tribalism," stemming from a pervasive, nonrational "intuition" coloring our assessment of information.[85] Journalist David Roberts summarizes this perspective:

> In fact, human beings are not primarily rational creatures. We are primarily *social* creatures. We are born into specific social contexts, overlapping tribes from which we absorb our worldviews and values. We stitch our identities together out of those tribal affiliations. Most of what we believe, we do not conclude. We do not reason to it at all. We *inherit* it. Those inherited beliefs are often tribal markers, conditions of approbation, even acceptance, among our tribes. Because belonging to tribes is fundamental to our well-being, those markers become very important to us. Protecting them is adaptive behavior, among our most basic instincts.[86]

In cases where our social identity is under threat, reasoning is a tool to assert and defend ourselves, rather than primarily a tool to develop accurate beliefs. In such contexts, as Haidt puts it, "the reasoning process is more like a lawyer defending a client than a judge or scientist seeking truth."[87]

This sort of factual "partisan cheerleading" is context dependent, as recent studies have found subjects to be somewhat more accurate on politically charged factual issues when they are given a monetary reward for accuracy. This just goes to show how one's interests, motivations, social context, and threat context affect one's view of the world from moment to moment.[88]

Our tribalistic, "us versus them" tendencies are exacerbated by **group polarization**, which is the well-recognized tendency for groups of predominately like-minded individuals to form more extreme positions as a result of the in-group dynamic. Opinions can feed off each other, as individuals starting out with more nuanced views are influenced by the group consensus; the result is that the members of the group tend to collectively move in the direction of a more steadfast and doctrinal way of thinking. After interacting, groups of like-minded individuals will arrive at more extreme, one-sided views about, for example, race, punishment, public policy, and/or the threat posed by out-groups.[89] Group polarization thus can play a part in exacerbating preexisting ideological differences.

Political psychologist John Hibbing and his collaborators have highlighted evidence that polarizing ideological identification may be rooted in measurable personality traits.[90] There is a modest, but very consistent, correlation between identifying as a conservative and getting a high score on the "conscientiousness" dimension in personality tests. Political liberals have a modest, but consistent, tendency to score higher on the "openness" dimension. High levels of conscientiousness indicate a stronger interest in security, predictability, and authority; a high score on openness indicates a greater comfort with uncertainty, complexity, and novelty.[91] These personality dimensions can be used effectively to predict motivated assessments of evidence either confirming or undermining one's political views.[92] Further, researchers have found that certain differences in physiological responses can also be associated with ideological positions.

People who are more physiologically sensitive to negative or threatening stimuli—like images of spiders, or of people who have been
assaulted—are more likely to support "socially protective policies" like
"greater military spending, harsher punishment for criminals, and re-
strictive immigration."[93] Some people are measurably more reactive
to disgusting stimuli—such as being exposed to the idea of touching
feces or eating worms. It turns out that there is a strong correlation between having a high sensitivity to disgust and a conservative attitude
toward gay marriage.[94] Several studies have linked disgust sensitivity
to various kinds of negative attitudes toward out-groups.[95] In fact,
heightened sensitivity to disgusting images (as directly measured in
terms of neural responses via MRI) is strongly predictive of a conservative political orientation overall.[96] Results like these have led Hibbing,
along with the other proponents of what they call **biopolitics**, to suggest that ideology is heavily influenced by inner psycho-physiological
dispositions.[97]

   System justification theory agrees that "dispositional variables"
like openness and conscientiousness "co-vary with ideological self-
placement," and adds that "situational variables" like "system threat
and mortality salience" are also partly determinative of ideological
stance.[98] According to this theory, the combination of personality
and situation goes a long way toward explaining an individual's ideological positions—in particular, with respect to ideological positions
defending the status quo. Evidence from many subdisciplines shows
that, just as Marx and Engels suspected, "citizens often think and
act in ways that maintain existing social, economic, and political arrangements (i.e., the status quo)—even if alternatives might
be better for them as individuals or as members of social groups."[99]
Conscientiousness, as noted by dispositionalists like Hibbing, is partly
predictive of a conservative, pro–status quo belief system. Further,
some situations prime "epistemic needs to reduce uncertainty, existential needs to manage threat, and relational needs to achieve shared
reality with others"; such situations can trigger a compelling bias in
favor of existing social, economic, political, or theological systems.[100]
For example, multiple studies have shown that reminders of terrorism
or other mortal threats increased approval of conservative political
leaders and pro–status quo attitudes.[101] This bias, in turn, can explain

selective, unconscious motivated responses to *informational* threats to accustomed systems of thought or social arrangements. The system of thought with which one identifies is strongly associated with how one assesses information that either supports or threatens that system.[102]

System justification theorists see self-, group-, and system-serving motives often blending together in practice:

> For example, an individual's (false) belief that President Obama is a Muslim or was born outside of the United States may simultaneously reflect a self-serving desire to maintain and justify prior attitudes and behaviors, a group-serving desire to believe that Republicans are superior to (or more honest than) Democrats, and a system-serving desire to maintain the traditional racial hierarchy, whereby African-Americans are denied powerful leadership roles. Most likely, such beliefs reflect some combination of these (and perhaps other) motives and purposes.[103]

All these motives may themselves derive from a combination of innate personality traits, developmental environment, and situation, leading to what is likely to be a complex web of causes underlying any particular instance of denial.

The **cultural cognition thesis** proposes that factors surrounding cultural identity are central to ideological bias, and are associated with motivated cognition and denial. As defined on law professor and social scientist Dan Kahan's Cultural Cognition Project webpage, "cultural cognition refers to the tendency of individuals to conform their beliefs about disputed matters of fact (e.g., whether global warming is a serious threat; whether the death penalty deters murder; whether gun control makes society more safe or less) to values that define their cultural identities."[104] On the cultural cognition model, persons can be effectively classified according to where they fall on a two-dimensional ideological spectrum: hierarchicalism versus egalitarianism, and individualism versus communitarianism. People who self-identify as political conservatives tend to be more accepting or approving of nonegalitarian social arrangements; they tend also to respond more favorably to social policy favoring individual rights and responsibilities over community rights and obligations. The views of political liberals or progressives, by contrast, are exemplified by what Kahan calls "egalitarian-communitarianism": Liberals tend to prioritize equality and community in their value judgments.[105] Research has repeatedly shown that the cultural-value identifications of subjects are significantly correlated with their assessment of contested *factual* claims in ideological contexts.[106] For example, this sort of value group membership has been shown to be effectively predictive of beliefs about the cancer-preventing efficacy of the HPV vaccine;[107] the risks and benefits of nanotechnology;[108] and the scientific consensus on global warming, nuclear waste disposal, and the effects of concealed handgun laws.[109] A strong individualist may reject evidence of the efficacy of government regulation because of his or her ideological opposition to government interference in personal freedoms; a strong egalitarian may reject evidence of the benefits of markets because of their inegalitarian outcomes. Hierarchicalists are suspicious of cultural elites and their perceived attempts to undermine the status quo economic order, while egalitarian-communitarians are suspicious of corporations, and so are more ready to believe their activities are harmful.[110] These sorts of automatic responses are examples of what Kahan calls "identity-protective" cultural cognition, wherein assessments of factual claims (such as risk assessments) underlying policy positions are colored by the individual's motives to maintain his or her identity as a member of a cultural group defined by its values.

Of course, most people don't use technical terms like "individualist" or "communitarian" to describe themselves. More familiar identifiers like "Christian evangelical," "environmentalist," "conservative Republican," or "Latino/a child of undocumented immigrant" can correlate with certain value prioritizations like the above. Such identifiers also can be effectively predictive of what sources of information and opinion a given person turns to in drawing conclusions about the actual relationship between religiosity and divorce rates, or between immigration and crime.

Cultural identifications like these say a lot about who one typically associates with. Sociologist Kari Marie Norgaard sees cultural identity and peer pressure as key to the kinds of informational selectivity inherent in denial. She cites Evitar Zerubavel's concept of the "social organization of denial," according to which we get our cues from social interaction about not only what is important but also what information to ignore and what topics to avoid.[111] These "norms of attention" can serve the protective function of protecting cultural identity, reducing dissonance, and alleviating negative emotions like guilt and insecurity. As individuals increasingly self-segregate into like-minded geographical[112] and online[113] communities, group polarization effects only intensify the level of ideological agreement, as well as the confidence expressed in the factual beliefs bolstering the group's ideological commitments. As John Zaller argued in his influential 1992 book *The Nature and Origins of Mass Opinion*, most of the general public lack fixed or systematic views about ideology, as opposed to a vague sense of loyalty to some identity group. Most people, most of the time, rely on signals from elites (through mass media) and peers (through personal interactions and social media) about what views (and thus what *facts*) are acceptable.[114] And so, the greater the fragmentation into separate identity groups, the more the individual's existing views are confirmed by the group's thought leaders and are reinforced by interactions with peers.

Unconscious bias based on cultural-group identification likely works in parallel with self-serving bias, personal dispositions, and situational factors. A close cultural-group identification could mean that threats to one's in-group could register as emotionally indistinguishable from threats to oneself. Further, one's values, and the value community with which one identifies, are likely influenced both by one's personality and by situational factors; for example, someone who is highly sensitive by nature to external threats, and who lives in a context where, say, violent crime or terrorism is particularly salient, could thereby be especially attracted to an ideology that values hierarchy and order over openness and tolerance. And this works in the other direction: The community in which one is raised—and the value system it endorses—is likely to influence the kinds of emotional responses one is disposed to exhibit in different situations.

Whatever the source of the motive to deny, the proximate trigger leading to denial appears to be, once again, the emotional distress brought on by the conflict between what one wants to believe and some incoming inconvenient information.[115] We work, self-protectively and unconsciously, to resolve this uncomfortable dissonance by any means necessary. The need to mitigate anxiety brought on by unwanted information is the cause of motivated cognition. Dissonance reduction is thus implicated in much ideological thinking. This is unconscious, affectively laden **hot cognition**, as contrasted with the "cold" cognition of reasoning mainly motivated simply by curiosity and accuracy.[116]

We are now in a better position to understand motivated cognition and denial. Motivated cognition is the sincere confounding of an emotional need—usually of a self-serving, self-protective, and/or social identity-defining sort—to hold a certain view of things with having good reasons to hold that view. To be in denial, then, is to engage in a kind of psychological projection—that is, *to unconsciously mistake the emotional value of denying something for actually having good reasons to deny it.*

The opponent of scientific consensus need not be a victim of bad information. An early hominid who thought the earth was the unmoving center of the universe was not in denial; a reasonably well-educated creationist in a contemporary industrialized society who sincerely maintains this belief probably is. Someone like the latter person *ought to know better.* We have noted that there are always motives present, even in the context of rigorous scientific inquiry. In this case, however, the individual is unduly affected by nonepistemic motives specific to the issue: The evolution-denying creationist is emotionally threatened by this particular conclusion in a way likely to color his or her assessment of the evidence. The fact that the creationist doesn't "know better" is explained not by the individual's ignorance but by his or her motives; in the absence of those motives, the individual would accept the truth. We often think of people in denial—however unaware of their motivations they may be—as at fault in some way, or even complicit. Thus the seemingly paradoxical term "willful ignorance." Denial is willful in a way, but indirectly. The person in denial is complicit in that we can distinguish between people who are (relatively) "epistemically responsible" and those who are unconsciously influenced by nonepistemic motives specific to the subject matter. Someone who is epistemically irresponsible is intellectually capable of avoiding bias in acquiring beliefs, and/or getting at the root causes of his or her existing beliefs, but doesn't really want to. Imagine two persons who regularly lose their temper. We can distinguish between the person who makes an effort to understand the roots of her out-of-control aggression and the person who does not. The second person is perfectly sincere in attributing his outbursts to the chronic failings of others, but also has avoided taking steps—such as seeking therapy or engaging in serious self-reflection—to determine whether the conflicts he keeps getting into are sometimes his fault. Alternatively, consider a parent who is disturbed at the prospect of having her child subjected to multiple painful and invasive vaccine injections, containing substances the parent does not understand. She then selectively seeks out websites that question the safety of vaccines, and attends only to media figures who do the same. She neither seeks out nor attends to authoritative medical information or advice, even as she tells herself she is doing her due diligence as a concerned parent. Finally, imagine two scientists, each of whose research is funded by a pharmaceutical company that wants to see if its new drug is effective. One scientist makes sure she is using a controlled, double-blind process in testing the efficacy of the drug; the other does not. The latter scientist—unaware of the subtle ways his personal stake in positive results has influenced his conclusions—may sincerely believe the glowing reports he returns to his corporate patrons, even though he knows by training that the methods he is using are deficient.

1.3 Mechanisms of Motivated Reasoning

Identifying motives to believe something in the face of evidence to the contrary is only part of the puzzle of denial. What are the mechanisms by which these motives determine belief? How, exactly, is information processing affected by unconscious bias?

A person in a state of denial is, by definition, motivated to *stay* in denial: The whole point of denial is that it allows us to maintain beliefs that are emotionally satisfying. It is therefore all too easy to continue on this path by treating incoming information in a biased manner. **Confirmation bias** refers to the tendency to seek out only confirming evidence for our beliefs and expectations, rather than impartially considering all the evidence from neutrally selected sources. ("Disconfirmation bias" refers to the complementary tendency to ignore evidence disconfirming our beliefs.) In his groundbreaking seventeenth-century treatise on the scientific method, the *Novum Organum*, Francis Bacon eloquently described this habit of mind:

> The human understanding, when any proposition has been once laid down (either from general admission and belief, or from the pleasure it affords), forces everything else to add fresh support and confirmation; and although most cogent and abundant instances may exist to the contrary, yet either does not observe or despises them, or gets rid of and rejects them by some distinction, with violent and injurious prejudice, rather than sacrifice the authority of its first conclusions. It was well answered by him who was shown in a temple the votive tablets suspended by such as had escaped the peril of shipwreck, and was pressed as to whether he would then recognize the power of the gods, by an inquiry, But where are the portraits of those who have perished in spite of their vows? All superstition is much the same, whether it be that of astrology, dreams, omens, retributive judgment, or the like, in all of which the deluded believers observe events which are fulfilled, but neglect and pass over their failure, though it be much more common. But this evil insinuates itself still more craftily in philosophy and the sciences, in which a settled maxim vitiates and governs every other circumstance, though the latter be much more worthy of confidence. Besides, even in the absence of that eagerness and want of thought (which we have mentioned), it is the peculiar and perpetual error of the human understanding to be more moved and excited by affirmatives than negatives, whereas it ought duly and regularly to be impartial; nay, in establishing any true axiom the negative instance is the most powerful.[117]

As Bacon here observes, it is a common error in reasoning to go about trying to confirm an existing conviction (a "settled maxim") by looking exclusively for confirming evidence. Suppose you have run across a lot of white swans, and you subsequently form the hypothesis that all swans are white. Now, which would be a better way to explore the hypothesis that all swans are white: by looking for more white swans in places where they are known to congregate, or by looking for *non*-white swans in places you haven't looked yet? Finding more white swans doesn't tell you anything you don't already know—namely, that at least some swans are white. Finding a non-white swan, by contrast, would tell you something new, as would the failure of a reasonably comprehensive search for non-white swans.* Unconsciously favoring confirming evidence is an easy cognitive shortcut wherein we assume we can generalize from what experience we have; this heuristic allows us to form working theories of the world more quickly and efficiently. ("I saw a bunch of white swans. I guess swans are white.") It makes sense as a strategy built in by evolution: Beings whose cognitive systems insisted on a full and proper examination of every generalization about the world would get completely bogged down; we wouldn't be able to function if we were that thorough all the time. In inquiry there are always trade-offs and individual preferences. The value of the scientific method (including invaluable institutions like peer review, publication, and replication) lies in its built-in protections against confirmation bias.

So human beings characteristically exhibit confirmation bias anyway, just because it makes things easier. But when we find a factual worldview either comforting or socially helpful, we now have not only a *tendency* (a cognitive bias) but also a *motive* (a noncognitive bias) in favor of seeking out confirmation for that worldview and, further, to avoid sources that might undermine that worldview. This emotional motivation piggybacks on the existing cognitive bias and makes confirmation bias "hot"—potentially very much so, if the motive is strong. This sort of motivation can operate unconsciously at the level of forming desirable beliefs (motivated cognition), or at the level of defending existing beliefs (rationalization).

Motivationally distorted information gathering and processing are the fundamental mechanisms of denial. Researchers have identified and observed a number of ways such distortion can happen; roughly, these fall under the categories of biased search for information, selective assimilation and recall of information, and biased interpretation of evidence.[118]

When affectively inclined to confirm a particular belief or worldview, individuals often prefer information sources of a sympathetic

---

* FYI, Australian swans are generally black.

ideological bent. This phenomenon is sometimes called **selective exposure**.[119] As sociologist Robert Brulle puts it, "Individuals want to maintain their self-identity and self-image. They're not going to read something that challenges their values, their self-worth, their identity, their belief system."[120] Such selectivity maximizes comforting feelings of reassurance while minimizing uncomfortable exposure to dissonant information. The fragmentation of contemporary media facilitates the self-reinforcing process of confirmation bias via selective exposure to sources that will corroborate existing beliefs. Attending to ideologically friendly sources is a more *pleasant* experience, just because those sources provide more confirmation of desirable beliefs and less by way of dissonant, anxiety-inducing views. In the United States, political conservatives strongly prefer Fox News as a news source; liberals are less monolithic, but gravitate away from Fox and are more likely to make use of the left-leaning MSNBC.[121]

Online information search is also demonstrably influenced by confirmation bias.[122] Social media enables selective exposure by providing platforms where individuals can selectively limit their online encounters to interactions with like-minded people, even as the media service itself algorithmically tailors its "news feed" to articles those individuals are predicted to "like," based on past indicators of interest. In this way, the current media landscape allows individuals automatically to fill their days almost exclusively with ideologically friendly inputs across multiple platforms.

Further, as psychologist Peter Ditto and fellow researchers have shown, in many contexts individuals will be lax in examining evidence confirming a cherished belief, but will expend more time and energy trying to recheck or disconfirm evidence dissonant with their preferred beliefs. For example, subjects will reliably accept a negative diagnosis of disease without further investigation, but will question the test, examine it longer, and/or request further tests when a positive diagnosis is indicated. The **quantity of processing view**[123] is the idea that confirmation bias characteristically expresses itself via the unconscious application of what psychologist David Dunning calls "differential stopping rules" in assessing evidence.[124] John Locke was familiar with the idea that we may conveniently halt our inquiries before they get too uncomfortable: "Not but that it is the nature of the understanding constantly to close with the more probable side; but yet a man hath a power to suspend and restrain its inquiries, and not permit a full and satisfactory examination, as far as the matter in question is capable, and will bear it to be made."[125] On Ditto's view, what we call motivated reasoning is primarily the issue of a biased allocation of cognitive resources with regard to unwelcome information: We unconsciously allocate more resources to disconfirm the conclusions we wish to shun.[126] Elsewhere in the social science literature, **information avoidance** is the term for the familiar phenomenon of actively avoiding information that would be unwelcome because it would force the individual to relinquish a cherished belief or worldview, would force an unwelcome change in behavior, or would simply cause unpleasant emotions.[127] A classic example is failing to go through with a recommended medical test for fear of a frightening result; but so is, say, avoiding news sources when something dissonant to one's ideological worldview has occurred. It is patently the case that such avoidance, just like selective exposure or biased evidence collection, can sometimes be unconscious, and be bolstered by self-deceptive rationalization.

Individuals will also predictably demonstrate selective assimilation and recall of evidence. Test subjects with an established viewpoint on, say, the effectiveness of the death penalty as a deterrent have demonstrated a reliable tendency to take particular note of confirming evidence, and to disregard disconfirming evidence, when presented with empirical findings on the subject.[128] Subjects will demonstrate better recall of evidence confirming their beliefs and poorer recall of discomforting information.[129]

Finally, individuals will *interpret* evidence differently depending on whether it is consonant or dissonant with their preferred beliefs. Studies over the last few decades have shown again and again that subjects will assess the reliability of evidence for or against their views very differently, depending on their prior convictions, on the level of threat posed by the evidence, and/or on their group identification. Subjects have been shown to be predictably biased in assessing evidence regarding the health effects of smoking[130] and caffeine use,[131] and the validity of intelligence tests.[132] Other examples of areas where evidence is predictably given biased treatment include affirmative action, gun control, gay stereotypes, global warming, stem-cell research, nuclear waste disposal, GM food safety, vaccination safety, Saddam Hussein's involvement in 9/11, and WMDs in post-invasion Iraq, just to name a few.[133]

An important respect in which individuals may misinterpret evidence has to do with inflating or discounting probabilities of outcomes, depending on whether one is motivated—by self-interest, system threat, cultural identity protection, and so on—to either inflate or discount estimations of risk. Individuals will assess differently, for example, the level of risk posed by nuclear power or the probability of predicted effects of climate change, quite predictably according to the ideology to which they subscribe.[134]

Frequently, the individual in denial is not the only person involved. Those wishing to manipulate public opinion in service of some agenda are all too happy to exploit humans' emotional needs and biases.[135] All one has to do is to supply the fearful ideologue with information confirming his or her prejudices while disparaging evidence to the contrary. Childhood indoctrination is also highly effective, most prominently with regard to religious belief. Once a worldview is internalized, anxiety in the face of recalcitrant evidence is to be expected; from that point, resistance in the form of biased information processing is all but guaranteed, as the ideologue takes on the task of maintaining his or her emotionally charged beliefs no matter what. As Jonathan Swift put it, "Reasoning will never make a man correct an ill opinion, which by reasoning he never acquired."[136] Reasoned refutation of a prejudice is quite beside the point: Prejudice is based on emotion and is maintained by emotion.

Of course, as Ziva Kunda has noted, the person genuinely in thrall to motivated self-deception does not actually take him- or herself to be irrational. The evidence always looks good from the perspective of the true believer. Subsequently, as a worldview or ideology takes root and continues to affect assessment of evidence, recall, and exposure to sources of information, motivated cognition shades into rationalization, which is a kind of second-order denial, or simply a continuation of the process of denial.

"Rationalization" is a term that fits the sorts of explicit justifications we might offer when called upon to defend our practice of favoring or disfavoring certain pieces of evidence, depending on which fit our favored position. Even though rationalization may sometimes take the form of a more reflective process of explaining why, say, one source is more to be trusted than another, this process is an extension of denial when it is guided by the unconscious, affectively "hot" prejudices of motivated cognition. (Rationalization may also stem from a conscious intent to deceive others, but then it is just an example of mendacity; rationalization representing a venal attempt to spin the truth is just bullshit.)

It is of critical importance to note that emotionally motivated confirmation bias is in no way limited to the uninformed, the careless, or the unsophisticated. It is in the sciences that we find those who have the best grasp of techniques of data collection and analysis, and yet unconscious confirmation bias is a huge issue in scientific research. We may mock those who believe in astrology or mind-reading, but some of the greatest scientists in history were extraordinarily resistant to letting go of their prior commitments. The brilliant Danish astronomer Tycho Brahe was an extremely diligent observer, and he saw that the old Ptolemaic system placing the earth at the center of everything couldn't work. But rather than embrace the Copernican heliocentric model, he crafted a wildly complex theory of the movement of the stars, sun, and planets that allowed him to continue to represent our planet as fixed in place. Another genius-level thinker, Isaac Newton, hung on to the promise of alchemy long after his lack of results should have caused him to question it. The problem, as usual, was confirmation bias: Newton spent many years looking only to *confirm* the principles of alchemy, rather than attending to reasons to reject them. Highly educated anatomists and anthropologists of the eighteenth and nineteenth centuries interpreted anatomical and/or cultural differences between Caucasians and other groups as evidence for polygenism, or the view that different human races are actually different species with different origins—with those of European origin being the superior race. This group-serving search for evidence of superiority included, for example, the supposed "discovery" of racial differences in cranial capacity, physiology, and intelligence invariably confirming the superiority of the researcher's race.[137] At other points in history, various groups such as Sub-Saharan Africans, Highland Scots, and Jews received similar treatment from leading scientists. Some scholars today persist—with ever greater sophistication—in invariably finding a genetic explanation for social differences between ethnic groups experiencing hugely different environmental challenges.[138] The list of prominent intellectuals through history who have found women inherently less intelligent than men is endless.

Scientists are not immune to the ideological implications of their research—and, clearly, entire research programs have been launched with the purpose of validating some worldview. Scientists and researchers want to be right for various other reasons as well: the emotional satisfaction of making a new discovery, or confirming a prior success; the career rewards of publication (the science journals are much more likely to publish reports of positive results than null results); the need to keep your lab operational by pleasing those funding your research into, say, a new drug. Contemporary scientific methodology specifically emphasizes bias avoidance via, for example, directives about identifying falsifying evidence, use of blind and/or randomized studies, and peer review. Yet, even in the context of such guiding principles, it is possible to unconsciously manipulate results. It remains all too easy to fixate on one hypothesis to the exclusion of others, and then keep devising new tests until something comes up that makes that hypothesis look good. Study subjects can be preselected in ways that make a positive result more likely. The way a study is designed and the way the data are collected can also skew the results in the expected or desired direction. Data anomalous to the expected (or desired) result may be discarded as flawed or irrelevant. More time and energy may be spent critically examining unwanted data, so as to find reasons to exclude it. Researchers can halt data collection right at the point where they have found a (marginally) statistically significant result. Looking at huge multivariate data sets can easily lead to finding spurious, but statistically significant, correlations just by chance. The more sophisticated the research and data analysis tools, the more ways information can be massaged—even unconsciously—to yield the positive result the researcher is looking for.[139] Well-trained academic scientists are the most highly attuned to the issue of confirmation bias, but are also in possession of the most sophisticated means to convince themselves they are right. (Indeed, recent, large-scale attempts to replicate certain research findings in psychology and medicine have met with mixed success.[140]) As astrophysicist Saul Perlmutter puts it, "People forget that when we talk about the scientific method, we don't mean a finished product. Science is an ongoing race between our inventing ways to fool ourselves, and our inventing ways to avoid fooling ourselves."[141] Intelligence, specialized training, and responsivity to evidence-based reasoning do not inoculate against self-deception.

1.4 The Origins of Denial

Evidence for chronic, species-wide biases in collecting and processing information might seem quite puzzling. Wouldn't natural selection pressures militate against inaccurate beliefs? How to explain such widespread disdain for accuracy in our belief-forming processes? The field of study sometimes called "evolutionary psychology" is a highly speculative business, but a few options have been proposed that exhibit some prima facie plausibility.

First, as Chris Mooney puts it, it would be highly inefficient to be in the habit of "discard[ing] an entire belief system, built up over a lifetime, because of some new snippet of information."[142] We couldn't function if we exhaustively reviewed the evidence for every belief we have every time something odd comes up. In this respect a certain resistance to change would seem a likely heuristic for any cognitive system. Indeed, there is plenty of evidence that individuals are motivated simply to preserve preexisting beliefs or defend preexisting decisions, whatever they may be, and that this motivation skews processing of evidence contradicting preexisting beliefs or undermining preexisting choices.[143]

Next, one would expect that devoting more cognitive resources to potential physical threats than to nonthreatening stimuli is safer and more efficient; this adaptive selectivity might spill over into devoting more processing time to questioning input that is *emotionally* threatening because it is dissonant with comforting beliefs.[144] Anna Freud asserted that dealing with emotional threat is the main point of selective memory and certain interpretive distortions. As she put it, such distortions can be "ego-protective," allowing individuals to function better because they are less oppressed by emotionally disturbing information.[145] Conversely, positive illusions—say, an inflated notion of one's own competence—can help one maintain the confidence to achieve difficult goals.[146] Positive illusions can even lessen physically damaging stress responses and hasten recovery from illness.[147]

The ability to cooperate and collectively plan for the future is clearly a key adaptive advantage for *Homo sapiens*. In light of this, it is not surprising to find there exists a universal and profound human need for a feeling of belonging. This emotional need may be the single most important factor in motivated cognition. Group membership carries with it a significant sense of kinship, security, and self-affirmation. As system justification theorists John Jost and David Amodio explain, various observers have long argued that "people are drawn to socially shared belief systems for reasons of affiliation": Affiliation with the larger group and its beliefs confers the existential comforts of identity and shared reality.[148] And identifying emotionally with a group clearly means sharing its worldview, at least to some extent. It is hard to imagine feeling part of a group while simultaneously rejecting all the group's most fundamental tenets and traditions.

In addition to these benefits, motivated cognition could be adaptive in that conforming to certain defining group beliefs (regardless of the facts), and thus to in-group culture, can be advantageous—and nonconformity can be disadvantageous. Ideological conformity facilitates cooperation but also can be protective. An individual might be strongly motivated to just "go with the flow" if ostracism or worse (such as execution for heresy) is the alternative. As social scientist Dan Sperber notes, "If an idea is generally accepted by the people you interact with, isn't this a good reason for you to accept it too? It may be a modest and prudent policy to go along with the people one interacts with, and to accept the ideas they accept. Anything else may compromise one's cultural competence and social acceptability."[149] Philosopher Elizabeth Anderson coined the term **expressive rationality**[150] for "forms of information processing that reliably promote the stake individuals have in conveying their commitment to identity-defining groups."[151] As Kahan et al. put it,

> For the ordinary individual, the most consequential effect of his beliefs about climate change is likely to be on his relations with his

peers. A hierarchical individualist who expresses anxiety about climate change might well be shunned by his co-workers at an oil refinery in Oklahoma City. A similar fate will probably befall the egalitarian communitarian English professor who reveals to colleagues in Boston that she thinks the scientific consensus on climate change is a hoax. . . . Given how much the ordinary individual depends on peers for support—material and emotional—and how little impact his beliefs have on the physical environment, he would probably be best off if he formed risk perceptions that minimized any danger of estrangement from his community.[152]

Thus, Kahan concludes, the goals of dissonance reduction *and* maintenance of group standing can work together in favor of denial. Of course, as Sperber points out, this tendency fuels groupthink: "From an epistemological point of view, the fact that an idea is widely shared is not a good reason to accept it unless these people have come to hold it independently of one another."[153] Consensus can result from independent thinkers coming to the same conclusion, or it can result from cultural forces; trusting in the latter sort of consensus is good for getting along, but not so good from the standpoint of actually getting things right.

Further, social groups that share ideological common ground can be expected to show greater cooperation and resilience in the face of external threats. When the group as a whole is more successful, traits shared by group members may be more successfully preserved over the long run. To the extent that group-selection pressures have a role to play in evolutionary adaptation, the cognitive flexibility necessary to consistent ideological conformity could also play a role here.[154]

Nor is it necessarily a bad idea, from an evolutionary standpoint, to be in the habit of placing more trust in members of the group with which you identify: Someone with whom you share cultural values or background is more likely to have your best interests at heart. An innate disposition to conform with your in-group's belief system can work to your advantage because, other things being equal, members of your "tribe" are less likely to be trying to deceive you than would be an outsider. It would then make sense if the statements of those with whom you already feel an ideological kinship have more of that "truthiness" feel to them. And out-group declamations are automatically regarded with some suspicion, or even distaste. A 2017 study in the *Journal of Experimental Social Psychology*, using multiple methodologies, found (a) that participants' interest in hearing about reasons to question their own views about politics was only slightly greater than their interest in, say, having a tooth pulled; and (b) that there was little distinction between political liberals and conservatives with respect to the aversion to hearing about dissonant opinions. The researchers concluded that "People on the left and right are motivated to avoid hearing from the other side for some of the same reasons: the anticipation of cognitive dissonance and the undermining of a fundamental need for a shared reality with other people."[155] Unfortunately, as Dan Sperber points out, this results in a dangerous feedback loop between confirmation bias and the group polarization effect:

> When . . . confirmation bias is not held in check by others with dissenting opinions, reasoning becomes epistemically hazardous, and may lead individuals to be over-confident of their own beliefs, or to adopt stronger versions of those beliefs. In group discussions where all the participants share the same viewpoint and are arguing not so much against each other as against absent opponents, such polarization is common and can lead to fanaticism.[156]

By this route, the innocent, natural human need to feel a connection with others—and to trust those with whom you feel that connection—can be implicated in the worst consequences of ideological thinking. The explosion of "fake news"—often promulgated over social media—during the 2016 U.S. presidential election may be a good example. Many of these items were quite fantastic. Social media posts accused Hillary Clinton of running a child prostitution ring out of a pizza restaurant. Such items were not only read but also reposted, in some cases hundreds of thousands of times. Were these viral nonsense nuggets passed on to friends because people actually believed them to be true? And was anyone's opinion of a politician or policy actually changed by reading them? Did anyone say, "Gosh, I was for Hillary until I found out about her involvement in child trafficking?" Josh Marshall of *Talking Points Memo* has a more plausible account: "In many cases, 'fake news,' the latest manufactured outrage, functions as a kind of ideational pornography ideas and claims that excite people's political feelings, desires, and fears, and create feelings of connection with kindred political spirits."[157] Fake news favoring your side is appealing in exactly the same way that dissonant information can be unappealing.

There is yet more from evolutionary psychology on the possible advantages of a tendency to engage in motivated reasoning. The compelling **argumentative theory** of reasoning states, in short, that a primary evolutionary purpose of the capacity to reason is to justify positions and win arguments rather than to arrive at the truth.[158] This theory focuses on the fact that we evolved in the context of social groups. In a social group, one of the most important factors in reproductive success is social success, and social success means persuasion. In other words, sometimes it is more advantageous to win the argument than to be right.[159] If persuasion plays a central role in evolutionary success, then perhaps we should interpret a tendency to confirmation bias (along with a talent for bullshit) as a *feature* of reasoning rather than as a bug.[160] Relatedly, evolutionary theorist Robert Trivers has argued that self-deception may have an adaptive role, in that it can boost both self-confidence and the projection of that confidence, which in turn can boost social standing and help win mates; in other words, sometimes it is more advantageous to be confident than to be right.[161]

There is a whole cottage industry of evolutionary theorizing specifically about the roots and persistence of religious ideology, where motivated reasoning plays a central role. The primitive, self-protective preference for "false positives" over false negatives when it comes to detecting patterns, and agents behind those patterns, may be behind an interpretive bias in favor of supernatural explanations;[162] religious ideologies promising immortality may facilitate risky, but rewarding activity that otherwise would be hampered by a paralyzing fear of death;[163] shared religious beliefs can enhance reciprocity, adherence to rules, and solidarity against external threats;[164] and, intriguingly, Daniel Dennett has expanded on Richard Dawkins's concept of a genetic "meme" in evolutionary biology[165] in suggesting that religious ideologies may function as cultural memes analogous to viruses—that is, as informational packets that include instructions for their own replication.[166]

So a pervasive tendency to motivated reasoning makes some sense in light of its plausible contributions to personal fortitude, competitive self-promotion in social groups, and social cooperation. As Alison Gopnik argued, accuracy need not be the only factor in the long-term success of your reality-representation strategies. Journalist David Roberts again:

> Motivated reasoning [is] likely what cognition is *for*. After all, why would evolution select for a species of pure reasoning machines? Beyond our ability to successfully navigate our immediate surroundings, we don't really *need* accurate information, certainly not at the level of basic worldviews. It doesn't have a ton of adaptive value. What does have adaptive value is our ability to access the benefits of community, to enter into reciprocal relationships with others around us for mutual benefit. That's what evolutionary pressures are likely to select for—the master to which reasoning is a servant.

Whereas accuracy is essential to survival with regard to particular issues, such as which berries are poisonous or when one can safely cross the street, it is less clear why larger worldviews or ideologies need to be accurate. As long as your beliefs promote your individual well-being (in the context of your social group), it doesn't really matter *why* you hold those beliefs, or what higher-order ideological framework they are part of.

1.5 Pathological Ideology, and Denialism as a Social Phenomenon

When is ideology *non*-pathological? When the ideologue is passionate about his or her values, but dispassionate about his or her assessment of evidence. Ideology is pathological when the factual claims at its center originate in unconscious, self-protective "hot" cognition, and are then selectively rationalized after the fact. Unfortunately, in practice most ideology *is* pathological. Challenges to ideological beliefs are met with anger, avoidance, interpretive bias, fallacious rationalization, and—as a last resort—**conspiracist ideation** (if all the facts seem to be against you, there must a conspiracy of experts to deceive you).[167]

In a democracy, a lack of information and/or education would seem highly relevant to the issue of bad public policy. Over one-third of Americans cannot name a single branch of government.[168] A majority of Americans think that Christianity was written into the U.S. Constitution.[169] Few Americans are able to locate Iraq on a map; two-thirds of Americans estimate the U.S. population as between 750 million and 2 billion.[170] A much-discussed survey conducted by Michael Norton and Dan Ariely showed that most Americans think the wealth distribution in the United States is vastly more egalitarian than it is.[171]

From results like these, it would be easy to jump to the conclusion that ignorance is the root of our problems. Surely, the broad misrepresentation of reality on ideologically charged issues is enabled by a similarly broad failure to understand more basic facts—and it is a short step from blaming denial on apathy and information deficit to a kind of top-down model wherein only the educated elite is qualified to make important decisions. But mightn't it be self-serving, or even dangerous, to think of humanity as divided between the self-deceiving masses and the enlightened few? In the context of his discussion of Marx, Michael Rosen has warned that the identification of ideology with irrationalism is elitist and anti-democratic:

> What is most pernicious, however, is the way the theory of ideology enables those who hold it to divide the world between those who are (presumed to be) and those who are not in ideology's grip. The theory of ideology offers its holders the psychic benefits that come to those who believe that they are part of an elite or vanguard. It licenses that vanguard to ignore the actions, attitudes and even votes of those in whose name they claim to act.[172]

Rosen is not wrong, in that there is indeed room for political elites to appropriate the notion of motivated reasoning, in the way he describes, in the service of rationalizing anti-democratic methods. He continues:

> The Leninist party, the presumed repository of correct policy, acts in pursuit of the interests of the working class, as it understands them;

but it acts *on behalf of* the working class, rather than as its representative, for it follows from the theory of ideology that the working class' own perception of what would further its interests is distorted and inadequate.[173]

And we all know what Leninist thinking led to: massive centralization of power as part of the so-named "dictatorship of the proletariat," and correction of the "distorted thinking" of society through reeducation camps, the Gulag, the Cultural Revolution, and the killing fields of Cambodia.

Yet, social science itself has supplied the corrective to anyone who would utilize evidence of motivated reasoning in order to rationalize elitism. Many studies and meta-analyses have shown decisively that neither ignorance nor lack of intellectual or political sophistication is the cause of denialism.[174] As of 2016, about 24 million Americans continued to believe that President Obama was born outside the United States; and whether the respondent also exhibited overall "high political knowledge" or "low political knowledge" had no bearing whatsoever on the likelihood of responding in this way.[175] In a variety of targeted surveys, polarization over the fact of global warming *increases* according to the respondent's knowledge of politics, science, and energy.[176] Subjects scoring highest on a test for "cognitive reflection" (in other words, showing the greatest tendency to think through problems, as opposed to relying on knee-jerk intuition) show the *greatest* susceptibility to motivated reasoning.[177] Looking at citizens' evaluations of arguments about affirmative action and gun control, Taber and Lodge discovered that the most noteworthy evidence of ideological confirmation bias is found among those with the "highest levels of political sophistication."[178] A recent experiment showed that subjects with the greatest demonstrated abilities in making use of quantitative information were *less* accurate and *more* polarized than less quantitatively inclined subjects when it came to assessing quantitative results of a gun-control study.[179] Further, the evidence shows that a higher level of education can be associated with an increased capacity for science denialism: A 2008 Pew survey[180] showed that "only 19% of college-educated Republicans agreed that the planet is warming due to human actions, versus 31% of non-college educated

Republicans."[181] Vaccine denialism is widely distributed among socioeconomic groups,[182] but there are definitely some elite, very well-educated and politically sophisticated enclaves where it has taken root strongly.[183] As we have discussed, there is plenty of historical evidence of self-deception among highly trained scientists and researchers. This sort of self-deception is nourished by the confidence that comes from feeling like an expert: A 2015 paper reporting on six separate studies found that the more people regard themselves as having expertise in some area, the more closed-minded they become.[184] As columnist Ezra Klein puts it,

> This will make sense to anyone who's ever read the work of a serious climate change denialist. It's filled with facts and figures, graphs and charts, studies and citations. Much of the data is wrong or irrelevant. But it feels convincing. It's a terrific performance of scientific inquiry. And climate-change skeptics who immerse themselves in it end up far more confident that global warming is a hoax than people who haven't spent much time studying the issue. More information, in this context, doesn't help skeptics discover the best evidence. Instead, it sends them searching for evidence that seems to prove them right. And in the age of the internet, such evidence is never very far away.[185]

The transition from fear of change to denial of fact on the part of the well-educated was described in 1937 by the Austrian essayist Robert Musil in his lecture "On Stupidity."[186] In that lecture he decried the "intelligent stupidity" that derives not from ignorance but from a willful blindness to the truth. "Functional stupidity" is that variety of intelligent stupidity in which reasoning is subordinated to interests of party, class, or ideology. This form of intellectual obstinacy, he warned, is "the real disease of culture," and is vastly more dangerous than mere ignorance. Even as personal and cultural pressures make implicit bias more or less universal, greater education and political sophistication give the true believer more ammunition—and more confidence—in justifying his or her position. As Thomas Hobbes observed, "Arguments seldom work on men of wit and learning, when they have once engaged themselves in a contrary opinion."

Further, while most people are aware in principle of the possibility of bias in their judgments, they almost invariably rate themselves as less prone to bias than others. This is known as the **bias blind spot**.[187] Neither education or nor other indicator of sophistication offers protection. An overview of research on the subject indicates that, "while some people are more susceptible to a bias blind spot than others, intelligence, cognitive ability, decision-making ability, self-esteem, self-presentation, and general personality traits were found to be independent characteristics and not related to the bias blind spot."[188] In fact, one study looking at individuals' awareness (or lack thereof) of their own biases found that higher cognitive ability is associated with a *larger* bias blind spot.[189] Once again, we find that bias—in this case, regarding one's own ability to avoid bias—affects everyone.* Only by disregarding the facts about motivated reasoning can the doctrine of ideology as product of motivated reasoning be represented as inherently elitist. Denial is a *human* problem, not just a problem for the uneducated or unsophisticated.

Rosen's critique also doesn't give enough credit to the modern scientific process. Proper scientific practice today is inextricably bound up with transparency, peer review, and replication. While, admittedly, always more or less imperfect in practice, scientific reasoning is, by definition, reasoning that resists confirmation bias and seeks out disconfirmation.[190] Scientists are subject to bias and self-deception, but science itself is systematically and institutionally self-critical; such self-criticism in itself is the best defense against misuse of science—so long, of course, as science is allowed to play its proper role in informing public policy.[191]

The purpose of this book is to examine the psycho-social phenomenon of denialism—and its twin outboard motors, motivated cognition and rationalization—through an analysis of its many contemporary manifestations in both public and private life. Denialism has been in the news a lot lately. Most often we hear about forms of what is specifically characterized as "science denialism"—namely, denial of the science of anthropogenic global warming, creationist denial of the biological sciences, and/or denial of vaccine science. These are important,

---

* Except, of course, the author of this book.

but an exclusive focus on these issues elides the full impact of denial on contemporary society and on the individual person, and obscures its true nature. First, denialism is much, much more pervasive than this focus would suggest. Second, the term "science denialism" is redundant because denial characteristically involves denying science, insofar as to think scientifically just is to take a skeptical, evidence-based approach to forming factual beliefs about reality, on any subject. Advocates for abstinence-only sex education, for example, must deny the social science refuting its effectiveness. Xenophobia and group-serving motivations color the assessment of evidence about employment and crime pertaining to the public policy debate on immigration. Denial is getting in the way of a scientifically informed discussion of the safety of nuclear power and genetically modified foods.

Denial is convenient, comforting, and occasionally even useful; but it also cripples our ability to face urgent public policy issues effectively, and thus stands in the way of essential social, political, and economic changes. It pollutes our culture and retards our individual intellectual and moral development.

There is hope, in that we are evidently capable of relatively dispassionate reasoning in "cold" contexts, and even are able to accept difficult truths under the right circumstances. But to overcome or otherwise mitigate the pernicious effects of denial, we have to understand the phenomenon better—both in its depth and in its breadth. As they say in Alcoholics Anonymous, the first step is to admit that you have a problem. Learning how to make progress as a society on public policy issues requires a better understanding of the roots of ideological conflict, and this in turn requires a better understanding of the causes and mechanisms of denialism regarding matters of public significance. Similarly, learning how people can progress as individuals, and make better decisions for themselves, requires a better understanding of the causes and mechanisms of denial as it manifests itself in the private sphere.

Notes

1. John Locke, *An Essay Concerning Human Understanding* (Book IV, Ch. 20, Sect. 12), p. 715.

2. Peter Ditto, "Passion, Reason, and Necessity: A Quantity of Processing View of Motivated Reasoning," in *Delusion and Self-Deception: Affective and Motivational Influences on Belief Formation*, ed. Tim Bayne and Jordi Fernández (New York: Psychology Press, 2009), p. 23.

3. Jörg Friedrichs distinguishes between "self-deception," which he characterizes as "simulative" (i.e., involving the adoption of inaccurate but desirable beliefs) and "denial," which is "dissimulative" (i.e., involving the rejection of accurate but undesirable beliefs). But I think this distinction breaks down in practice. Friedrichs admits that "it can be very difficult to be in denial about one thing without deceiving oneself about another thing" ("Useful Lies: The Twisted Rationality of Denial," *Philosophical Psychology* 27 [2014], p. 213).

4. The term owes its popularity historically to Sigmund and Anna Freud, who conceived of it as an unconscious "ego"-protective mechanism (see https://www.simplypsychology.org/defense-mechanisms.html). Classic examples of denial in the Freudian sense are included in the broader conception developed here, where group-, system-, and identity-protective cognition are shown to share important aspects of the more personal sorts of denial discussed in Freudian psychoanalysis.

5. Cary Funk and Lee Rainie, "Public and Scientists' Views on Science and Society," Pew Research Center, January 15, 2015, http://www.pewinternet.org/2015/01/29/public-and-scientists-views-on-science-and-society/.

6. Bruce Bartlett, "Voter Ignorance Threatens Deficit Reduction," *The Fiscal Times*, February 4, 2011, http://www.thefiscaltimes.com/Columns/2011/02/04/Voter-Ignorance-Threatens-Deficit-Reduction.

7. Charles C. W. Cooke, "Careful with the Panic: Violent Crime and Gun Crime Are Both Dropping," *National Review*, November 30, 2015, http://www.nationalreview.com/corner/427758/careful-panic-violent-crime-and-gun-crime-are-both-dropping-charles-c-w-cooke.

8. Justin McCarthy, "More Americans Say Crime Is Rising in the U.S.," Gallup, October 22, 2015, http://www.gallup.com/poll/186308/americans-say-crime-rising.aspx.

9. "Perceptions Are Not Reality: What the World Gets Wrong," *Ipsos MORI*, December 13, 2016, https://www.ipsos-mori.com/researchpublications/researcharchive/3817/Perceptions-are-not-reality-what-the-world-gets-wrong.aspx.

10. Dan Kahan, "Neutral Principles, Motivated Cognition, and Some Problems for Constitutional Law," *Harvard Law Review* 125 (2011), pp. 1–77. See also Dan Kahan, "What Is Motivated Reasoning and How Does It Work?," *Science and Religion Today*, May 4, 2011, http://

www.scienceandreligiontoday.com/2011/05/04/what-is-motivated-reasoning-and-how-does-it-work/.

11. See Naomi Oreskes and Erik Conway, *Merchants of Doubt: How a Handful of Scientists Obscured the Truth on Issues from Tobacco Smoke to Global Warming* (New York: Bloomsbury Press, 2010).

12. Harry Frankfurt, *On Bullshit* (Princeton, NJ: Princeton University Press, 2005).

13. Neil van Leeuwen, "Self-Deception," in *The International Encyclopedia of Ethics*, ed. Hugh LaFollette (Hoboken, NJ: Wiley-Blackwell, 2013), p. 8; see also Sean Chris Murphy, William von Hippel, Shelli Dubbs, and Michael Angilletta, "The Role of Overconfidence in Romantic Desirability and Competition," *Personality and Social Psychology Bulletin* 41 (2015), pp. 1036–1052.

14. Ryan McKay and Daniel Dennett, "The Evolution of Misbelief," *Behavioral and Brain Sciences* 32 (2009), pp. 493–561.

15. Timothy Wilson, *Strangers to Ourselves: Discovering the Adaptive Unconscious* (Cambridge, MA: Belknap Press of Harvard University Press, 2002), p. 154.

16. Of course, even the severely delusional experience various motivations themselves, related or not to their illness or injury, so there will often be some interplay between the delusion and emotional influences on belief. Bayne and Fernández, along with some contributors to their volume on delusion, think that bias and motivation play a role in some delusions, but that most will not have a primarily motivational explanation (*Delusion and Self-Deception*, p. 13).

17. Robert Burton, *On Being Certain: Believing You Are Right Even When You're Not* (New York: St. Martin's Griffin, 2008), pp. 15–18.

18. Partly for this reason, there is some controversy over whether delusions, or delusional beliefs, really should count as beliefs at all. See, for example, Maura Tumulty, "Delusions and Not-Quite-Beliefs," *Neuroethics* 5 (2012), pp. 29–37.

19. Ziva Kunda, "The Case for Motivated Reasoning," *Psychological Bulletin* 108 (1990), pp. 480–498. See also van Leeuwen, "Self-Deception," p. 6.

20. Leon Festinger, *A Theory of Cognitive Dissonance* (Stanford, CA: Stanford University Press, 1957).

21. Andrew Elliot and Patricia Devine, "On the Motivational Nature of Cognitive Dissonance: Dissonance as Psychological Discomfort," *Journal of Personality and Social Psychology* 67 (1994), pp. 382–394.

22. Eddie Harmon-Jones, "Cognitive Dissonance and Experienced Negative Affect: Evidence that Dissonance Increases Experienced Negative Affect

Even in the Absence of Aversive Consequences," *Personality and Social Science Bulletin* 26 (2000), pp. 1490–1501.

23. Festinger, *A Theory of Cognitive Dissonance*. See also Kunda, "The Case for Motivated Reasoning."

24. See Eddie Harmon-Jones, "A Cognitive Dissonance Theory Perspective on the Role of Emotion in the Maintenance and Change of Beliefs and Attitudes," in *Emotions and Beliefs: How Feelings Influence Thoughts*, ed. Nico Frijda, Antony Manstead, and Sacha Bem (Cambridge: Cambridge University Press, 2000).

25. Massimo Pigliucci, "How to Be a Stoic," *Howtobeastoic.com*, n.d., https://howtobeastoic.wordpress.com/2016/01/19/one-crucial-word/.

26. See Neeru Paharia, Kathleen Vohs, and Rohit Deshpande, "Sweatshop Labor Is Wrong Unless the Shoes Are Cute: Cognition Can Both Help and Hurt Moral Motivated Reasoning," *Organizational Behavior and Human Decision Processes* 121 (2013), pp. 81–88.

27. Keith Kahn-Harris, "Denialism: What Drives People to Reject the Truth," *The Guardian*, August 3, 2018, https://www.theguardian.com/news/2018/aug/03/denialism-what-drives-people-to-reject-the-truth?CMP=fb_gu.

28. See Denise Meyerson, *False Consciousness* (Oxford: Clarendon Press, 1991); and Brian Leiter, "What Marxist Ideology Can Set in Motion," *3:AM Magazine*, February 7, 2015.

29. See, for example, Farhad Manjoo, *True Enough: Learning to Live in a Post-Fact Society* (Hoboken, NJ: John Wiley, 2008); and Chris Mooney, *The Republican Brain: The Science of Why They Deny Science—and Reality* (Hoboken, NJ: John Wiley, 2012). On "fact polarization," see Dan Kahan, "The Politically Motivated Reasoning Paradigm," *Emerging Trends in Social & Behavioral Sciences* (2016), pp. 1–16.

30. See Dan Kahan's discussion of "Cognitive Illiberalism" in "Motivated Reasoning and Its Cognates," The Cultural Cognition Project at Yale Law School, May 25, 2013, http://www.culturalcognition.net/blog/2013/5/15/motivated-reasoning-its-cognates.html.

31. See Brittany Liu and Peter Ditto, "What Dilemma? Moral Evaluation Shapes Factual Belief," *Social Psychological and Personality Science* 4 (2013), pp. 316–323.

32. "Ten Arguments from Social Science against Same-Sex Marriage," Family Research Council, n.d., http://www.frc.org/get.cfm?i=if04g01.

33. Neil Lewis, "A Guide to the Memos on Torture," *New York Times*, 2005, https://archive.nytimes.com/www.nytimes.com/ref/international/24MEMO-GUIDE.html.

34. Sean Gorman, "Bobby Scott: After WWII U.S. Executed Japanese for War Crimes Including Waterboarding," *PolitiFact Virginia*, January 12, 2015. http://www.politifact.com/virginia/statements/2015/jan/12/bobby-scott/bobby-scott-after-wwii-us-executed-japanese-war-cr/.

35. See Peter Ditto and Spassena Koleva, "Moral Empathy Gaps and the American Culture War," *Emotion Review* 3 (2011), pp. 331–332.

36. From John Martin, "What Is Ideology?," *Sociologia, Problemas e Praticas* 77 (2015), p. 15; ctd. by Milton Rokeach, *Beliefs, Attitudes, and Values: A Theory of Organization and Change* (San Francisco: Jossey-Bass, 1968); David Rumelhart, "Toward a Macrostructural Account of Human Reasoning," in *Similarity and Analogical Reasoning*, ed. Stella Vosniadou and Andrew Ortony (New York: Cambridge University Press, 1989), pp. 289–312; Kenneth Kurtz, Dedre Gentner, and Virginia Gunn, "Reasoning: Handbook of Perception and Cognition," in *Cognitive Science*, ed. Benjamin Martin and David Rumelhart (San Diego: Academic Press, 1999), pp. 145–200.

37. See van Leeuwen, "Self-Deception," on paradoxes of self-deception.

38. See Adrian Bardon, "Descartes, Unknown Faculties, and Incurable Doubt," *Idealistic Studies* 28 (1998), pp. 83–100.

39. Interestingly, Tamar Gendler resolves the paradox of self-deception differently; she proposes that the state resulting from self-deception is not so much a belief state as a kind of imagining or pretense ("On the Relation Between Pretense and Belief," in *Imagination, Philosophy and the Arts*, ed. Dominic Lopes and Matthew Kieran [London: Routledge, 2003], pp. 125–141). I think this has some truth to it but probably goes too far; more on this in chapter 4.

40. Daniel Kahneman, *Thinking, Fast and Slow* (New York: Farrar, Strauss and Giroux, 2011).

41. See Wilson, *Strangers to Ourselves*, esp. ch. 2.

42. Tamar Gendler, "Alief in Action (and Reaction)," *Mind & Language* 23 (2008), p. 557. See Michael Brownstein, "Implicit Bias," *Stanford Encyclopedia of Philosophy*, February 26, 2015, http://plato.stanford.edu/entries/implicit-bias/.

43. Tamar Gendler, "Alief and Belief," *Journal of Philosophy* 105 (2008), pp. 634–663. See Brownstein, "Implicit Bias."

44. Milton Lodge and Charles Taber, *The Rationalizing Voter* (New York: Cambridge University Press, 2013).

45. Brownstein, "Implicit Bias."

46. Lodge and Taber, *The Rationalizing Voter*, p. 20.

47. Patrick Kraft, Milton Lodge, and Charles Taber, "Why People 'Don't Trust the Evidence': Motivated Reasoning and Scientific Evidence," *Annals of the American Academy of Political and Social Science* 658 (2015), pp. 121–133.
48. "Episode 101," *The Colbert Report*, October 17, 2005.
49. "Truthiness," Wikipedia, n.d., https://en.wikipedia.org/w/index.php?title=Truthiness&oldid=680351228.
50. See Wilson, *Strangers to Ourselves*, esp. p. 93.
51. For a classic overview of some experimental demonstrations, see Richard Nisbett and Timothy Wilson, "Telling More than We Can Know: Verbal Reports on Mental Processes," *Psychological Review* 84 (1977), pp. 231–259.
52. Robert Baron, "The Sweet Smell of . . . Helping: Effects of Pleasant Ambient Fragrance on Prosocial Behavior in Shopping Malls," *Personality and Social Psychology Bulletin* 23 (1997), pp. 498–503. Recent concerns about replication of priming studies in social psychology have cast doubt over a number of previously accepted priming effects, but the evidence for effects like the ones mentioned here remains strong. See Christian Miller, *Moral Character: An Empirical Theory* (Oxford: Oxford University Press, 2013), p. 66, for an overview of the demonstrated relationship between positive mood and helping behavior.
53. Wilson, *Strangers to Ourselves*, p. 102.
54. Dan Ariely, *Predictably Irrational: The Hidden Forces that Shape Our Decisions* (New York: HarperCollins, 2008), pp. 235–236.
55. For an overview of the evidence for a connection between disgust and moral judgment, see Cristina-Elena Ivan, "On Disgust and Moral Judgments: A Review," *Journal of European Psychology Students* 6 (2015), pp. 25–36. Daniel Kelly has an extensive discussion of disgust, including its alleged role in moral judgment, in *Yuck! The Nature and Moral Significance of Disgust* (Cambridge, MA: MIT Press, 2011).
56. Jonah Berger, Marc Meredith, and S. Christian Wheeler, "Contextual Priming: Where People Vote Affects How They Vote," *Proceedings of the National Academy of Sciences* 105 (2008), pp. 8846–8849; and Abraham Rutchick, "Deus Ex Machina: The Influence of Polling Place on Voting Behavior," *Political Psychology* 31 (2010), pp. 209–225; ctd. by John A. Hibbing, Kevin Smith, and John Alford, *Predisposed: Liberals, Conservatives, and the Biology of Political Differences* (New York: Routledge, 2014), p. 22.
57. See Michael Spezio and Ralph Adolphs, "Emotion, Cognition, and Belief: Findings from Cognitive Neuroscience," in *Delusion and*

Self-Deception: Affective and Motivational Influences on Belief Formation, ed. Tim Bayne and Jordi Fernández (New York: Psychology Press, 2009), pp. 87–106.

58. Gerald Glore and Karen Gasper, "Feeling Is Believing: Some Affective Influences on Belief," in *Emotions and Beliefs: How Feelings Influence Thoughts*, ed. Nico Frijda, Antony Manstead, and Sacha Bem (Cambridge: Cambridge University Press, 2000), p. 33.

59. Glore and Gasper, "Feeling Is Believing," p. 39.

60. Nico Frijda and Batja Mesquita, "Beliefs Through Emotions," in *Emotions and Beliefs: How Feelings Influence Thoughts*, ed. Nico Frijda, Antony Manstead, and Sacha Bem (Cambridge: Cambridge University Press, 2000), p. 50.

61. Frijda and Mesquita, "Beliefs Through Emotions," pp. 50–51.

62. From David Hume, *A Treatise of Human Nature* (New York: Oxford University Press, 2000), pp. 165–173.

63. Antonio Damasio, *Descartes' Error: Emotion, Reason, and the Human Brain* (New York: G.P. Putnam, 1994).

64. René Descartes, *Meditations on First Philosophy*, trans. John Cottingham (Cambridge: Cambridge University Press 1996).

65. This issue is discussed at length in Lodge and Taber, *The Rationalizing Voter*, esp. pp. 44–48.

66. See Jonathan Haidt, *The Righteous Mind: Why Good People Are Divided by Politics and Religion* (New York: Pantheon, 2012), p. 45.

67. Michael Spezio and Ralph Adolphs, "Emotion, Cognition, and Belief: Findings from Cognitive Neuroscience," in *Delusion and Self-Deception: Affective and Motivational Influences on Belief Formation*, ed. Tim Bayne and Jordi Fernandez (New York Psychology Press 2009), pp. 87–106.

68. Seth Duncan and Lisa Barrett, "Affect Is a Form of Cognition: A Neurobiological Analysis," *Cognition and Emotion* 21 (2007), pp. 1184–1211. (Thanks to Alex Madva for the pointer.)

69. George Lakoff and Mark Johnson, *Philosophy in the Flesh: The Embodied Mind and Its Challenge to Western Thought* (New York: Basic Books, 1999), p. 4, qtd. in Burton, *On Being Certain*, p. 126.

70. See Damasio, *Descartes' Error*, pp. 249–250.

71. Alison Gopnik, "Explanation as Orgasm and the Drive for Causal Knowledge: The Evolution, Function and Phenomenology of the Theory-Formation System," in *Cognition and Explanation*, ed. Frank Keil and Robert Wilson (Cambridge, MA: MIT Press, 2000).

72. Gopnik, "Explanation as Orgasm," p. 300.

73. Gopnik, "Explanation as Orgasm," p. 312.
74. Gopnik, "Explanation as Orgasm," p. 314.
75. Gopnik, "Explanation as Orgasm," p. 315.
76. Frijda and Mesquita, "Beliefs Through Emotions," pp. 47–49.
77. See Heather Douglas, *Science, Policy, and the Value-Free Ideal* (Pittsburgh: University of Pittsburgh Press, 2009).
78. Some early treatments of dissonance treated the motivation to resolve this dissonance as a conscious process, for example, Richard Nisbett and Lee Ross, *Human Inference: Strategies and Shortcomings of Social Judgment* (Englewood Cliffs, NJ: Prentice-Hall, 1980); however, as Kunda and others have argued, the evidence better supports the interpretation that motivated reasoning primarily involves unconsciously biased information search and retrieval. Further, as noted earlier, conscious dissonance remediation suggests a problematically paradoxical *conscious* self-deception.
79. My thanks to Peter Ditto for stressing to me the importance of *anticipated* emotions here.
80. Barbara Lehman and William Crano, "The Pervasive Effects of Vested Interest on Attitude—Criterion Consistency in Political Judgment," *Journal of Experimental Social Psychology* 38 (2002), pp. 101–112. See also John Jost, Erin Hennes, and Howard Lavine, "'Hot' Political Cognition: Its Self-, Group-, and System-Serving Purposes," in *The Oxford Handbook of Social Cognition*, ed. Donal Carlston (Oxford: Oxford University Press, 2013).
81. Justin Kruger and David Dunning, "Unskilled and Unaware of It: How Difficulties in Recognizing One's Own Incompetence Lead to Inflated Self-Assessments," *Journal of Personality and Social Psychology* 77 (1999), pp. 1121–1134. See Kunda, "The Case for Motivated Reasoning," as well for a number of examples.
82. Jost et al., "'Hot' Political Cognition."
83. Henri Tajfel and John Turner, "The Social Identity Theory of Intergroup Behavior," in *Psychology of Intergroup Relations*, ed. Stephen Worchel and William Austin (Chicago: Nelson-Hall, 1986).
84. Elizabeth Suhay, "Explaining Group Influence: The Role of Identity and Emotion in Political Conformity and Polarization," *Political Behavior* 37 (2015), pp. 221–251.
85. Haidt, *The Righteous Mind*.
86. David Roberts, "AP Says to Call Climate Deniers 'Climate Doubters.' Whatever," *Vox*, September 24, 2015, http://www.vox.com/2015/9/24/9393217/ap-climate-doubters-truthers.

87. Jonathan Haidt, "The Emotional Dog and Its Rational Tail: A Social Intuitionist Account of Moral Judgment," *Psychological Review* 108 (2001), pp. 814–834; qtd. in Chris Mooney, "The Science of Why We Don't Believe Science," *Mother Jones*, May/June 2011, https://www.motherjones.com/politics/2011/04/denial-science-chris-mooney/.

88. John Bullock, Alan Gerber, Seth Hill, and Gregory Huber, "Partisan Bias in Factual Beliefs About Politics," *Quarterly Journal of Political Science* 10 (2015), pp. 519–578.

89. See David Myers and George Bishop, "Discussion Effects on Racial Attitudes," *Science* 169 (1970), pp. 778–779; and Daniel Isenberg, "Group Polarization: A Critical Review and Meta-Analysis," *Journal of Personality and Social Psychology* 50 (1986), pp. 1141–1151.

90. Hibbing et al., *Predisposed*. See Mooney, *The Republican Brain*.

91. Hibbing et al., *Predisposed*, p. 142.

92. See Mooney, *The Republican Brain*, ch. 3.

93. Hibbing et al., *Predisposed*, pp. 161 and 170.

94. Hibbing et al., *Predisposed*, p. 163.

95. Ivan, "On Disgust and Moral Judgments: A Review."

96. Woo-Young Ahn, Kenneth Kishida, Xiaosi Gu, Terry Lohrenz, Ann Harvey, John Alford, Kevin Smith, Gideon Yaffe, John Hibbing, Peter Dayan, and P. Read Montague, "Nonpolitical Images Evoke Neural Predictors of Political Ideology," *Current Biology* 24 (2014), pp. 2693–2699.

97. Note that psychological and physiological traits like these likely arise from some quite complex interaction between genetics, experience, and familial and cultural influence. So exactly how this sort of association between personality and ideology relates to other theories about denial, such as the "cultural cognition thesis" discussed later, is a matter for much further study.

98. John Jost, "The End of the End of Ideology," *American Psychologist* 61 (2006), p. 651.

99. Jost et al., " 'Hot' Political Cognition." See also John Jost, Jack Glaser, Arie Kruglanski, and Frank Sulloway, "Political Conservatism as Motivated Social Cognition," *Psychological Bulletin* 129 (2003), pp. 339–375.

100. Jost et al., " 'Hot' Political Cognition."

101. John Jost and David Amodio, "Political Ideology as Motivated Social Cognition: Behavioral and Neuroscientific Evidence," *Motivation and Emotion* 36 (2012), p. 58.

102. See, for example, Jost and Amodio, "Political Ideology as Motivated Social Cognition," pp. 55–64; Michael Petersen, Martin Skov, Søren Serritzlew,

and Thomas Ramsøy, "Motivated Reasoning and Political Parties: Evidence for Increased Processing in the Face of Party Cues," *Political Behavior* 35 (2013), pp. 831–854; and P. Sol Hart and Erik Nisbet, "Boomerang Effects in Science Communication: How Motivated Reasoning and Identity Cues Amplify Opinion Polarization About Climate Mitigation Policies," *Communication Research* 39 (2012), pp. 701–723.

103. Jost et al., "'Hot' Political Cognition," p. 868. (Alex Madva drew my attention to this particular passage.)

104. "The Cultural Cognition Project," Cultural Cognition Project at Yale Law School, n.d., http://www.culturalcognition.net/.

105. Note that, though liberals and conservatives may prioritize certain values over others, in mainstream discourse all these concepts—liberty, equality, community, individuality—are viewed positively across all groups.

106. Dan Kahan and Donald Braman, "Cultural Cognition and Public Policy," *Yale Law & Policy Review* 24 (2006), p. 147.

107. Dan Kahan, Donald Braman, Geoffrey Cohen, John Gastil, and Paul Slovic, "Who Fears the HPV Vaccine, Who Doesn't, and Why? An Experimental Study of the Mechanisms of Cultural Cognition," *Law and Human Behavior* 34 (2010), pp. 501–516.

108. Dan Kahan, Donald Braman, Geoffrey Cohen, John Gastil, and Paul Slovic, "Cultural Cognition of the Risks and Benefits of Nanotechnology," *Nature Nanotechnology* 4 (2009), pp. 87–91.

109. Dan Kahan, Hank Jenkins-Smith, and Donald Braman, "Cultural Cognition of Scientific Consensus," *Journal of Risk Research* 14 (2011), pp. 147–174. See also Aaron McCright and Riley Dunlap, "Cool Dudes: The Denial of Climate Change Among Conservative White Males in the United States," *Global Environmental Change* 21 (2011), pp. 1163–1172.

110. See Dan Kahan, "Three Models of Risk Perception—& Their Significance for Self-Government," The Cultural Cognition Project at Yale Law School, February 23, 2024, http://www.culturalcognition.net/blog/2014/ 2/23/three-models-of-risk-perception-their-significance-for-self.html.

111. Kari Norgaard, *Living in Denial: Climate Change, Emotions, and Everyday Life* (Cambridge, MA: MIT Press, 2011), pp. 5–9; citing Eviatar Zerubavel, *The Elephant in the Room: Silence and Denial in Everyday Life* (Oxford: Oxford University Press, 2006). See also George Marshall, *Don't Even Think About It: Why Our Brains Are Wired to Ignore Climate Change* (New York: Bloomsbury, 2014), pp. 82–84.

112. "The Big Sort," *The Economist*, June 19, 2008, http://www.economist.com/ node/11581447.

113. Amy Mitchell, Jeffrey Gottfried, Jocelyn Kiley, and Kateina Eva Matsa, "Political Polarization & Media Habits," Pew Research Center, October 21, 2014, https://www.journalism.org/2014/10/21/political-polarization-media-habits/. Also see, for example, Sarita Yardi and Danah Boyd, "Dynamic Debates: An Analysis of Group Polarization over Time on Twitter," *Bulletin of Science, Technology and Society* 30 (2010), pp. 316–327.

114. John Zaller, *The Nature and Origins of Mass Opinion* (Cambridge: Cambridge University Press, 1992).

115. Not to discount the importance of *wanting* to believe something (as opposed to *not* wanting to believe something). See Peter Ditto, James Scepansky, Geoffrey Munro, Anne Marie Apanovitch, and Lisa Lockhart, "Motivated Sensitivity to Preference-Inconsistent Information," *Journal of Personality and Social Psychology* 75 (1998), pp. 53–69.

116. Jost et al., "'Hot' Political Cognition." See also Jon Elster, *Making Sense of Marx* (Cambridge: Cambridge University Press, 1985).

117. *Novum Organum*, Aphorism XLVI (Sir Francis Bacon, *Novum Organum*, ed. Joseph Devey, M.A. [New York: P.F. Collier, 1902]).

118. Raymond Nickerson, "Confirmation Bias: A Ubiquitous Phenomenon in Many Guises," *Review of General Psychology* 2 (1998), pp. 175–220; also Jost et al., "'Hot' Political Cognition."

119. William Hart, Dolores Albarracín, Alice Eagly, Inge Brechan, Matthew Lindberg, and Lisa Merill, "Feeling Validated Versus Being Correct: A Meta-Analysis of Selective Exposure to Information," *Psychological Bulletin* 135 (2009), pp. 555–588. See also Manjoo, *True Enough*; Sara Yeo, Michael Cacciatore, and Dietram Scheufele, "News Selectivity and Beyond: Motivated Reasoning in a Changing Media Environment," in *Publizistik und gesellschaftliche Verantwortung: Festschrift für Wolfgang Donsbach*, ed. Olaf Jandura (Berlin: Springer Fachmedien Wiesbaden, 2015); Tom Jacobs, "What's the Appeal of Angry, Polarized Media?," *Pacific Standard*, October. 1, 2013, https://psmag.com/economics/whats-appeal-angry-polarized-media-government-shutdown-politics-67354; and Natalie Stroud, "Polarization and Partisan Selective Exposure," *Journal of Communication* 60 (2010), pp. 556–576.

120. Chelsea Harvey, "Here's How Scientific Misinformation, Such as Climate Doubt, Spreads through Social Media," *Washington Post*, January 4, 2016. https://www.washingtonpost.com/news/energy-environment/wp/2016/01/04/heres-how-scientific-misinformation-such-as-climate-doubt-spreads-through-social-media/.

121. Mitchell et al., "Political Polarization & Media Habits," pp. 316–327.

122. Aaron Scherer, Paul Windschitl, and Andrew Smith, "Hope to Be Right: Biased Information Seeking Following Arbitrary and Informed Predictions," *Journal of Experimental Social Psychology* 49 (2013), pp. 106–112.

123. Ditto, "Passion, Reason, and Necessity"; see also Milton Lodge and Charles Taber, "Motivated Skepticism in the Evaluation of Political Beliefs," *American Journal of Political Science* 50 (2006), pp. 755–769; and Justin Wolfers, "How Confirmation Bias Can Lead to a Spinning of Wheels," *New York Times*, October 31, 2014, https://www.nytimes.com/2014/11/01/upshot/how-confirmation-bias-can-lead-to-a-spinning-of-wheels.html.

124. David Dunning, "Motivated Cognition in Self and Social Thought," in *APA Handbook of Personality and Social Psychology*, ed. Mario Mikulincer and Phillip Shaver (Washington, DC: American Psychological Association, 2015).

125. Locke, *Essay Concerning Human Understanding*, p. 715 (Book IV, Ch. 20, Sect. 12).

126. See Erica Dawson, Thomas Gilovich and Dennis Regan, "Motivated Reasoning and Performance on the Wason Selection Task," *Personality and Social Psychology Bulletin* 28 (2002), pp. 1379–1387. (Thanks to Peter Ditto for the reference.)

127. See Kate Sweeny, Darya Melnyk, Wendi Miller, and James A. Shepperd, "Information Avoidance: Who, What, When, and Why," *Review of General Psychology* 14 (2010), 340–353; and Russell Golman, David Hagmann, David and George Loewenstein, "Information Avoidance," *Journal of Economic Literature* 55 (2017), pp. 96–135.

128. Charles Lord, Lee Ross, and Mark Lepper, "Biased Assimilation and Attitude Polarization: The Effects of Prior Theories on Subsequently Considered Evidence," *Journal of Personality and Social Psychology* 37 (1979), pp. 2098–2109. See Kunda, "The Case for Motivated Reasoning" for many examples of this phenomenon.

129. See Margit Oswald and Stefan Grosjean, "Confirmation Bias," in *Cognitive Illusions: A Handbook on Fallacies and Biases in Thinking, Judgement and Memory*, ed. Rüdiger Pohl (Hove, UK: Psychology Press, 2004), pp. 79–96; see also, for example, Michel J. Dugas, Mary Hedayati, Angie Karavidas, Kristin Buhr, Kylie Francis, Natalie Phillips, "Intolerance of Uncertainty and Information Processing: Evidence of Biased Recall and Interpretations," *Cognitive Therapy and Research* 29 (2005), pp. 57–70.

130. Harold Kassarjian and Joel Cohen, "Cognitive Dissonance and Consumer Behavior," *California Management Review* 8 (1965), pp. 55–64 (see Kunda, "The Case for Motivated Reasoning").

131. Ziva Kunda, "Motivated Inference: Self-Serving Generation and Evaluation of Causal Theories," *Journal of Personality and Social Psychology* 53 (1987), pp. 636–647.

132. Robert Wyer and Deiter Frey, "The Effect of Feedback About Self and Others on the Recall and Judgments of Feedback-Relevant Information," *Journal of Experimental Social Psychology* 19 (1983), pp. 540–559 (see Kunda, "The Case for Motivated Reasoning").

133. Mooney, "The Science of Why We Don't Believe Science."

134. Ellen Peters and Paul Slovic, "The Role of Affect and Worldviews as Orienting Dispositions in the Perception and Acceptance of Nuclear Power," *Journal of Applied Social Psychology* 26 (1996), pp. 1427–1453; Anthony Leiserowitz, "American Risk Perceptions: Is Climate Change Dangerous?," *Risk Analysis* 25 (2005), pp. 1433–1442.

135. See Oreskes and Conway, *Merchants of Doubt.*

136. Jonathan Swift, "Letter to a Young Clergyman" (January 9, 1720).

137. See John Jackson and Nadine Weidman, *Race, Racism, and Science: Social Impact and Interaction* (Santa Barbara: ABC-CLIO, 2004).

138. See, for example, Richard Herrnstein and Charles Murray, *The Bell Curve: Intelligence and Class Structure in American Life* (New York: Free Press, 1994); and Nicholas Wade, *A Troublesome Inheritance: Genes, Race, and Human History* (New York: Penguin, 2014).

139. John Ioannidis, "Why Most Published Research Findings Are False," *Public Library of Science: Medicine* 2 (2005), p. e124. See recent work done by Brian Nosek and collaborators at http://projectimplicit.net/nosek/.

140. Joel Achenbach, "The New Scientific Revolution: Reproducibility at Last," *Washington Post*, January 27, 2015, https://www.washingtonpost.com/national/health-science/the-new-scientific-revolution-reproducibility-at-last/2015/01/27/ed5f2076-9546-11e4-927a-4fa2638cd1b0_story.html; see Ioannidis, "Why Most Published Research Findings Are False."

141. Qtd. in Regina Nuzzo, "How Scientists Fool Themselves—And How They Can Stop," *Nature* 526 (2015), pp. 182–185.

142. Mooney, "The Science of Why We Don't Believe Science"; See Nisbett and Ross, *Human Inference.*

143. For examples, see Kunda, "The Case for Motivated Reasoning"; also Peter Ditto and David Lopez, "Motivated Skepticism: Use of Differential Decision Criteria for Preferred and Nonpreferred Conclusions," *Journal of Personality and Social Psychology* 63 (1992), pp. 568–584; and Lodge and Taber, "Motivated Skepticism in the Evaluation of Political Beliefs," pp. 755–769.

144. Ditto, "Passion, Reason, and Necessity," p. 23.
145. Anna Freud, *The Ego and the Mechanisms of Defence*, trans. Cecil Baines (New York: International Universities Press, 1946). (My thanks to Anna Hundley for drawing my attention to this passage.) Compare Suhay, "Explaining Group Influence," on the personal emotional threats posed by going against one's ideological social group.
146. McKay and Dennett, "The Evolution of Misbelief," pp. 493–561.
147. See, for example, Bruce McEwen, "Central Effects of Stress Hormones in Health and Disease: Understanding the Protective and Damaging Effects of Stress and Stress Mediators," *European Journal of Pharmacology* 583 (2008), pp. 174–185; and Shelley Taylor, Margaret Kemey, Geoffrey Reed, Julienne Bower, Tara Gruenewald, "Psychological Resources, Positive Illusions, and Health," *American Psychologist* 55 (2000), pp. 99–109; ctd. by Paul Biegler, "How We Evolved to Reject Climate Science," *The Conversation*, November 18, 2012, https://theconversation.com/how-we-evolved-to-reject-climate-science-10711.
148. Jost and Amodio, "Political Ideology as Motivated Social Cognition," p. 2.
149. Dan Sperber, Fabrice Clément, Christophe Heintz, Olivier Mascaro, Hugo Mercier, Gloria Origgi, and Deirdre Wilson, "Epistemic Vigilance," *Mind & Language* 25 (2010), p. 380.
150. Elizabeth Anderson, *Value in Ethics and Economics* (Cambridge, MA: Harvard University Press, 1993).
151. Dan Kahan, "Motivated Numeracy and Enlightened Self-Government," September 3, 2013, Yale Law School, Public Law Working Paper No. 307. Again, see Suhay, "Explaining Group Influence," for evidence that "fitting in" can be a significant factor in motivated cognition. Also see Eric Funkhouser, "Practical Self-Deception," *Journal of Philosophical Studies* 20 (2012), pp. 86–97.
152. Dan Kahan, Ellen Peters, Maggie Wittlin, Paul Slovic, Lisa Ouellette, Donald Braman, and Gregory Mandel, "The Polarizing Impact of Science Literacy and Numeracy on Perceived Climate Change Risks," *Nature Climate Change* 2 (2012), pp. 732–735. (My thanks to Jay Odenbaugh for drawing my attention to this passage.)
153. Sperber et al., "Epistemic Vigilance," p. 380.
154. For an overview of a possible relationship between group selection and moral ideology, see Richard Joyce, *The Evolution of Morality* (Cambridge, MA: MIT Press, 2006).
155. Jeremy Frimer, Linda Skitka, and Matt Motyl, "Liberals and Conservatives Are Similarly Motivated to Avoid Exposure to One Another's Opinions," *Journal of Experimental Social Psychology* 72 (2017), pp. 1–12; ctd.

by Brian Resnick, "'Motivated Ignorance' Is Ruining Our Political Discourse," *Vox*, November 23, 2017, https://www.vox.com/science-and-health/2017/5/15/15585176/motivated-ignorance-politics-debate.

156. Sperber et al., "Epistemic Vigilance," p. 379. See Asher Koriat, Sarah Lichtenstein, and Baruch Fischhoff, "Reasons for Confidence," *Journal of Experimental Psychology: Human Learning and Memory* 6 (1980), pp. 107–118; Abraham Tesser, "Self-Generated Attitude Change," in *Advances in Experimental Social Psychology*, 11th ed., ed. Leonard Berkowitz (New York: Academic Press, 1978), pp. 289–338; and Cass R. Sunstein, "The Law of Group Polarization," *Journal of Political Philosophy* 10 (2002), pp. 175–195.

157. Josh Marshall, "Why You're Fooling Yourself About 'Fake News,'" *TPM*, December 27, 2016, http://talkingpointsmemo.com/edblog/why-you-re-fooling-yourself-about-fake-news.

158. Hugo Mercier and Dan Sperber, "Why Do Humans Reason? Arguments for an Argumentative Theory," *Behavioral and Brain Sciences* 34 (2011), pp. 57–111. See also Philip Tetlock, "Social Functionalist Frameworks for Judgment and Choice: Intuitive Politicians, Theologians, and Prosecutors," *Psychological Review* 109 (2002), pp. 451–471; and an extended discussion of this theory in Lee McIntyre's *Respecting Truth: Willful Ignorance in the Internet Age* (New York: Routledge, 2015).

159. Perhaps this explains the enduring popularity of self-help books like Dale Carnegie's *How to Win Friends and Influence People* (New York: Simon & Schuster, 1937).

160. Sperber et al., "Epistemic Vigilance," p. 378. Note that *being* right, and being known for being right, often is the best way to win arguments and gain status. So the argumentative theory need not predict that our reasoning processes evolved without accuracy in mind, so to speak.

161. Robert Trivers, *The Folly of Fools* (New York: Basic Books, 2011).

162. For a good overview of "patternicity," "agenticity," and superstition, see Michael Shermer, *The Believing Brain: From Ghosts and Gods to Politics and Conspiracies—How We Construct Beliefs and Reinforce Them as Truths* (New York: Times Books, 2011).

163. See Ajit Varki and Danny Brower, *Denial: Self-Deception, False Beliefs, and the Origins of the Human Mind* (New York: Hachette, 2013).

164. See, for example, Joyce, *The Evolution of Morality*.

165. Richard Dawkins, *The Selfish Gene* (Oxford: Oxford University Press, 1976).

166. Daniel Dennett, *Breaking the Spell: Religion as a Natural Phenomenon* (New York: Penguin, 2006).

167. See, for example, James Inhofe, *The Greatest Hoax: How the Global Warming Conspiracy Threatens Your Future* (Washington, DC: WND Books, 2012).
168. "Americans Know Surprisingly Little About Their Government, Survey Finds," Annenberg Public Policy Center website, September 17, 2014, http://www.annenbergpublicpolicycenter.org/americans-know-surprisingly-little-about-their-government-survey-finds/.
169. "Most Think Founders Wanted Christian USA," *USA Today*, September 13, 2007, http://usatoday30.usatoday.com/news/nation/2007-09-11-amendment_N.htm.
170. Harry Alsop, "Americans Surveyed: Misunderstood, Misrepresented or Ignorant?," *The Telegraph*, February 15, 2014, http://www.telegraph.co.uk/news/worldnews/northamerica/usa/10640690/Americans-surveyed-misunderstood-misrepresented-or-ignorant.html.
171. Michael Norton and Dan Ariely, "Building a Better America—One Wealth Quintile at a Time" *Perspectives on Psychological Science* 6 (2011), pp. 9–12.
172. Michael Rosen, *On Voluntary Servitude: False Consciousness and the Theory of Ideology* (Cambridge, MA: Harvard University Press, 1996), p. 271.
173. Rosen, *On Voluntary Servitude*, pp. 271–272. One is reminded also of Plato's elitist rejection of democracy in his *Republic*, as decried in Karl Popper's *The Open Society and Its Enemies* (Princeton, NJ: Princeton University Press, 1994).
174. See Matthew J. Hornsey, Emily A. Harris, Paul G. Bain & Kelly S. Fielding, "Meta-analyses of the Determinants and Outcomes of Belief in Climate Change," *Nature Climate Change* 6 (2016), pp. 622–626.
175. Josh Clinton and Carrie Roush, "Poll: Persistent Partisan Divide over 'Birther' Question," *NBCNews.com*, August 10, 2016, https://www.nbcnews.com/politics/2016-election/poll-persistent-partisan-divide-over-birther-question-n627446.
176. Toby Bolsen, James N. Druckman, and Fay Lomax Cook, "Citizens', Scientists', and Policy Advisors' Beliefs About Global Warming," *Annals of the American Academy of Political and Social Science* 658 (2015), pp. 271–295.
177. Dan Kahan, "Ideology, Motivated Reasoning, and Cognitive Reflection," *Judgment and Decision Making* 8 (2013), pp. 407–424.
178. Lodge and Taber, "Motivated Skepticism in the Evaluation of Political Beliefs," pp. 755–69. See Mooney, "The Science of Why We Don't Believe Science."
179. Kahan et al., "Motivated Numeracy and Enlightened Self-Government."

180. "A Deeper Partisan Divide over Global Warming," Pew Research Center, May 8, 2008, http://www.people-press.org/2008/05/08/a-deeper-partisan-divide-over-global-warming/.

181. Mooney, "The Science of Why We Don't Believe Science."

182. Chris Mooney, "The Biggest Myth About Vaccine Deniers: That They're All a Bunch of Hippie Liberals," *Washington Post*, January 26, 2015, http://www.washingtonpost.com/news/energy-environment/wp/2015/01/26/the-biggest-myth-about-vaccine-deniers-that-theyre-all-a-bunch-of-hippie-liberals/.

183. Lessley Anderson, "Vaccine Deniers: Inside the Dumb, Dangerous New Fad," *The Verge*, October 21, 2013, http://www.theverge.com/2013/10/21/4767530/vaccine-deniers-inside-the-dumb-dangerous-new-fad.

184. Victor Ottati, Erika Price, Chase Wilson, and Nathanael Sumaktoyo, "When Self-Perceptions of Expertise Increase Closed-Minded Cognition: The Earned Dogmatism Effect," *Journal of Experimental Social Psychology* 61 (2015), pp. 131–138.

185. Ezra Klein, "How Politics Make Us Stupid," *Vox*, April 6, 2014, http://www.vox.com/2014/4/6/5556462/brain-dead-how-politics-makes-us-stupid.

186. Robert Musil "On Stupidity," in *Precision and Soul: Essays and Addresses*, ed. and trans. Burton Pike and David S. Luft (Chicago and London: University of Chicago Press, 1994), pp. 268–286.

187. See Emily Pronin, Daniel Lin, and Lee Ross, "The Bias Blind Spot: Perceptions of Bias in Self Versus Others," *Personality and Social Psychology Bulletin* 28 (2002), pp. 369–381; and Irene Scopelliti, Carey Morewedge, Erin McCormick, H. Lauren Min, Sophie Lebrecht, and Karim Kassam, "Bias Blind Spot: Structure, Measurement, and Consequences," *Management Science* 61 (2015), pp. 2468–2486.

188. Shilo Rea, "Researchers Find Everyone Has a Bias Blind Spot: Believing You're Less Biased than Your Peers Has Detrimental Consequences," *Carnegie Mellon University News*, June 8, 2015, http://www.cmu.edu/news/stories/archives/2015/june/bias-blind-spot.html.

189. Richard West, Russell Meserve, and Keith Stanovich, "Cognitive Sophistication Does Not Attenuate the Bias Blind Spot," *Journal of Personality and Social Psychology* 103 (2012), pp. 506–519.

190. George Polya, *Mathematics and Plausible Reasoning, Vol. 1: Induction and Analogy in Mathematics* (Princeton, NJ: Princeton University Press, 1954); see Nickerson, "Confirmation Bias."

191. As has been frequently observed, science always takes place in a cultural context, and in practice inevitably imports all kinds of cultural biases and

nonepistemic values. (In fact, Heather Douglas has persuasively argued that nonepistemic values—for example, those pertaining to the relation between margins of error and risk to the public—*should* play a role in scientific investigation ["Inductive Risk and Values in Science," *Philosophy of Science* 67 (2000), pp. 559–579]). Bias, motivated cognition, and rationalization are potential problems for any human knowledge-seeking endeavor. Yet contemporary academic science is the mode of inquiry that—by definition—includes peer review, replication, and other systematic protections against confirmation bias as part of its essential methodology.

2

Science Denial

2.1 Climate Science Denial

A prominent example of contemporary science denial (particularly in the United States) is denial of the scientific consensus on the existence and/or causes of global warming. The fact of dangerous anthropogenic global warming (AGW) is now accepted by all but an insignificant number of climatologists worldwide, by every major national and international scientific society, and by every major nonpartisan humanitarian and economic organization.[1] Given the great complexity of climate systems, many details about the various mechanisms remain only partly understood. Further, a precise estimate of the consequences is impossible because modeling future impact depends not only on the interdependent response of these complex climate systems but also on factors such as future mitigation efforts and social and economic development.[2] But the fundamental nature and reality of the problem are settled.[3]

A 2019 Gallup survey shows that "concern" over global warming has increased modestly since 2001.[4] And yet, a 2015 Pew Research survey found that only 45% of Americans actually accept the reality of AGW. About 7% answer "don't know," with the rest either denying it altogether, denying that the question is settled, or chalking up any warming to natural variations.[5] Results, in other words, have been mixed. But in any event, many Americans continue to deny climate science.

Just in the last few years, an impressive number of books have focused on the failure by large segments of the American public to accept the science of AGW—*Living in Denial*; *Merchants of Doubt*; *Science Under Siege*; *The Inquisition of Climate Science*; *Climate Change Denial: Heads in the Sand*; and *Don't Even Think About It: Why Our Brains Are Wired to Ignore Climate Change* are just a few. Over the same period of time we can find hundreds and hundreds of academic and popular essays and news items decrying AGW denial, as well as dedicated websites like www.skepticalscience.com and the DeSmogBlog. Most people, when told they need antibiotics, don't question medical science. When told they are safer wearing a seat belt, they don't question the laws of physics. What accounts for the remarkable disconnect between public opinion and climate science? The social science discussed in the last chapter gives us the tools to get a good grasp of this phenomenon, and to contextualize it within the larger universe of denial. ·

One obvious approach to the problem of widespread misconceptions about climate is to work on education. Perhaps people just don't know about the causes or the probable effects, or don't know how to interpret the state of the science. In a 2014 survey of members of the American Association for the Advancement of Science, 84% of respondents said that limited public knowledge of science is a "major problem."[6] The idea that the fundamental problem in science denial is a lack of awareness or understanding is sometimes called the **information deficit model**.[7] Surely, if people had a better grasp of the reasons behind the expert consensus, they would be less likely to reject it.

No one would dispute that a well-informed public would, in principle, be in a better position to grasp the reality of the situation— especially in light of the authoritative consensus on the fundamental facts. Upon examination, however, it is not at all clear that ignorance is the main issue in this case. If the problem were a lack of information or understanding, one would expect a major positive correlation between knowledge of science and perception of the risks posed by climate change. Yet, in a large national study, Dan Kahan and colleagues found that science literacy and comprehension is, slightly, *negatively* correlated with perception of climate change risk. Something that really jumps out in the polling on climate science is how one's political ideology so effectively predicts one's beliefs about the facts. In the 2015 Pew survey on AGW, the statement "global warming is caused by human activity" is agreed to by 76% of self-identified liberal Democrats, but by only 15% of self-identified conservative Republicans. Other polling confirms that the political ideology one identifies with is by far the leading factor in whether one accepts AGW.[8] A 2016 meta-analysis of 25 polls and 171 academic studies, covering 56 countries, confirmed that ideological worldview and political orientation are the strongest factors in whether someone accepts the science of climate change.[9] What does one's ideology have to do with believing in the legitimacy of climatology as a research program? Scientific knowledge is not the issue, because one's particular level of climate science literacy completely fails to predict acceptance of the evidence about AGW—whereas one's political views predict one's position on AGW very well indeed (see figure 2.1).[10]

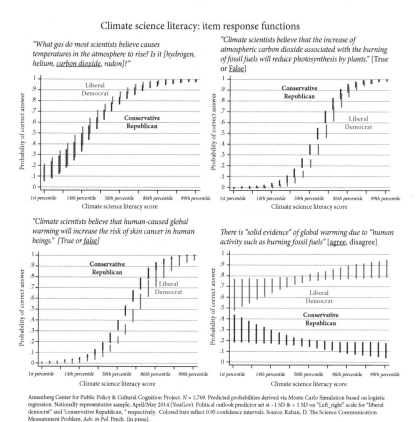

Climate science literacy: item response functions

Annenberg Center for Public Policy & Cultural Cognition Project. N = 1,769. Predicted probabilities derived via Monte Carlo Simulation based on logistic regression. Nationally representative sample, April/May 2014 (YouGov). Political outlook predictor set at −1 SD & + 1 SD on "Left_right" scale for "liberal democrat" and "conservative Republican," respectively. Colored bars reflect 0.95 confidence intervals. Source: Kahan, D. The Science Communication Measurement Problem, Adv. in Pol. Psych. (in press).

Figure 2.1 Scientific Literacy, Political Identification, and Climate Science Denial

Source: From Dan Kahan's "What is the 'Science of Science Communication'?", *Journal of Science Communication* 14 (2015), pp. 1–12. Used by permission of the author.

In fact, as you can see in figure 2.1, increased climate literacy is associated with *greater* denial on the part of conservatives. Most members of the public, liberal and conservative, essentially rely on the testimony of experts—as filtered through media and peer interactions—in making risk assessments and generally in deciding on the truth or falsity of claims that require technical expertise. Political conservatives deny AGW, but not because they lack information that others have. As noted in the last chapter, the highest rate of AGW denial is correlated with higher levels of education in political conservatives. Further, a modest but measurable decline in overall trust in science among conservatives between 1974 and 2010 is exhibited more strongly in those with higher education levels.[11] Neither is there any evidence that the liberals/progressives endorsing climate science have, in the aggregate, a substantially better background in the scientific fields that have generated our current understanding of the relationship between greenhouse gases and climate trends. Few people can go very far in describing how atmosphere affects climate, or how the various factors involved can be expected to cause long-term warming, et cetera. Even fewer have actually looked at the data. On this issue, liberals have simply chosen to accept expert opinion on warming while conservatives, largely, have not.

There are some people who have a direct or indirect financial stake in, for example, energy production companies that are threatened by anti-carbon initiatives and subsidies. In their case, a simple self-serving bias could explain some motivated cognition about expert opinion and subsequent rationalization of AGW denial. Lobbying groups for energy, transportation, and other carbon-intensive industries like meat production are all on record as questioning the science on climate.[12] Paid flunkies troll comment sections on websites in an attempt to create the appearance of controversy. Some of this might originate in motivated cognition, but most of it is undoubtedly just spin. Slightly more interesting from a psychological standpoint are the following quotes from some current and former U.S. congressmen, primarily from oil- and gas-producing states, who each have relied heavily on political contributions from oil and gas producers:

- The former chair of the House Committee on Energy and Commerce, Joe Barton (R-TX), calls global warming "a triumph over good sense and science," as surface temperature is determined by cloud shape. He is against wind power because wind is a "finite resource" and that harnessing wind power would "slow the winds down," which in turn would "cause the temperature to go up."[13]

- Member of the House Committee on Science, Space, and Technology Mo Brooks (R-AL) pushed the narrative that climate scientists were ignoring the effects on sea-level rise of silt and rocks falling into the ocean via erosion.[14]

- John Shimkus (R-IL) was until recently chair of the House Energy and Commerce Subcommittee on Environment and Economy. He claimed that reducing CO_2 emissions would be counter to our interests: "It's plant food. . . . So if we decrease the use of carbon dioxide, are we not taking away plant food from the atmosphere?"[15] He also claimed that neither climate change nor sea-level rise is a possibility, regardless of human activity. Quoting God's promise to Noah in Genesis 8:21–22, he said, " 'Never again will I curse the ground because of man, even though all inclinations of his heart are evil from childhood and never again will I destroy all living creatures as I have done. As long as the Earth endures, seed time and harvest, cold and heat, summer and winter, day and night, will never cease.' I believe that's the infallible word of God, and that's the way it's going to be for his creation. . . . The Earth will end only when God declares its time to be over. Man will not destroy this Earth. This Earth will not be destroyed by a Flood. I do believe that God's word is infallible, unchanging, perfect."[16]

- Oklahoma senator James Inhofe, author of *The Greatest Hoax: How the Global Warming Conspiracy Threatens Your Future*, states that "the claim that global warming is caused by man-made emissions is simply untrue and not based on sound science." Further, "CO_2 does not cause catastrophic disasters— actually it would be beneficial to our environment and our economy."[17]

- Former representative from Texas Steve Stockman disputed that melting ice could cause sea-level rise: "How long will it take for the sea level to rise two feet? I mean, think about it, if your ice cube melts in your glass it doesn't overflow; it's displacement.

I mean, some of the things they're talking about mathematically and scientifically don't make sense."[18]

President Trump's incoming administration included former Environmental Protection Administration director Scott Pruitt, who thinks that the issue of AGW is "far from settled";[19] Secretary of Energy Rick Perry, who has accused climate scientists of falsifying data in order to win grant money;[20] and former Secretary of the Interior Ryan Zinke, who claimed that AGW is "not proven science."[21] These statements could very well be examples of strategic bullshit performances for the sake of moving public opinion and preserving endorsements, donations, and/or party support. There are other varieties of bullshit to be considered here. Dan Kahan has a category within his taxonomy of states of "knowing disbelief" that he calls "FYATHYRIO (Fuck You And The Horse You Rode In On),"

> in which the agent ... merely feigns belief in a proposition she knows is not true for the sake of expressing an attitude, perhaps contempt or hostility to members of an opposing cultural group, the recognition of which actually depends on others recognizing that the agent doesn't really believe it ("Obama was born in Kenya!").[22]

A subcategory of bullshit statements, in other words, is the category of statements that are primarily intended not to fool others but simply to express an attitude (e.g., disapproval, contempt, or solidarity), where the expression of that attitude serves a strategic purpose—such as making your audience feel like you are on their side or whipping up support for some political initiative (a.k.a. "rallying the base"). I call this **expressive bullshit**. This may be a good description of the essential nature of many of the false claims made—on many subjects—by politicians and partisan media elites.

Social psychology is not psychiatry, and it does not concern itself with the mental states of particular individuals. Though attempting to explain what is going on psychologically for any particular individual is unproductive—especially in the absence of a clinical examination by a professional—under the circumstances I feel I cannot avoid briefly addressing the Donald Trump issue. Trump has called AGW a "hoax" for years, and, in general, constantly—seemingly compulsively—makes patently false and self-serving statements about environmental science, as well as most other subjects.* The philosopher Robert Paul Wolff recently offered an insightful assessment, which is worth reproducing at length:

> Here are a number of observations I have made of Trump that set off alarm bells in my head. One: Trump lies about things that are common knowledge to the people he is talking to. He tweets that Meryl Streep is a failure as an actress, for God's sake. This has been so widely commented on that I need not cite examples. Two: Trump is obsessed with issues of *size*. He exaggerates the size of his hands, the size of his genitalia, the size of his fortune, the size of the buildings that bear his name, the size of his election victory, the size of the crowds he draws for his speeches. Three: Trump uses language in primitive ways that reveal an almost complete lack of thought or knowledge behind them. One example that struck me especially powerfully was his bizarre claim, in referring to his speeches, that "I have the best words." Think about that for a moment. What can he possibly have meant by that? Four: Trump makes claims that are absurd and immediately refutable, apparently simply because *at the moment he is making them it feels good to make them*. I am sure many of you could add countless additional examples. What do I make of all this? First, it seems obvious to me that Trump's mental processes are extremely psychologically primitive. They are the thought processes of a child of three or four or five. Now, let us be clear, all of us start out as infants, and if Freud is correct, as I believe he is, we carry along with us throughout our lives the primitive thought processes that develop in us as infants ("primary thought processes," Freud calls them). But in normal adults, reality-tested secondary thought processes have been acquired and overlie the primary processes, which nevertheless live on in the unconscious and never cease affecting our experience of or thought about the world. . . . But some people are psychologically damaged. They never successfully integrate those secondary

---

* In October 2018, Trump claimed that his "natural instinct for science" allowed him to see through the political biases of climate scientists. (Rebecca Morin, "Trump Says He Has 'Natural Instinct for Science' When It Comes to Climate Change," *Politico*, October 17, 2018, https://www.politico.com/story/2018/10/17/trump-instinct-climate-change-910004.)

thought processes with the primary processes and the drives that fuel them.[23]

A playground bully calls a smaller kid a "faggot," not because of some belief he has about the victim's sexual preference, but simply because the bully can temporarily relieve his own painful feelings of insecurity by denigrating others. A proposed subcategory of expressive bullshit, in other words, is a statement that functions to express an attitude, when the primary explanation for that expression is that it provides some sort of noncognitive, visceral satisfaction (or emotional protection) to the bullshitter. This is **infantile bullshit**. My best guess on Trump is that many of his false statements should be interpreted as belonging to this category of expression.

We can't inhabit the hearts and minds of others, so we can't ever definitively say via direct observation whether we are dealing with an instance of denial per se or with bullshit or something even more primitive. Politicians are adept at the strategic use of bullshit. However, the statements mentioned earlier by congressmen and cabinet officials are consistent in terms of content with authentic denialism, and in some of these cases motivated reasoning may be the best explanation for what we are seeing. For example, look at the quote from Stockman. His statement is so embarrassingly off target, so easily refuted—obviously, sea-level rise is a concern, in part, because of the melting of land-based ice, not sea-based ice—that it is hard to imagine his being conscious of what is wrong with his statement while simultaneously believing that this public declamation would constitute an effective piece of political theater. As another example, Congressman Barton has expressed concern that energy production from wind turbines may be harmful because it "slows the winds down."[24] Consider further the infamous February 2015 episode in which Senator Inhofe presented a snowball on the Senate floor, claiming that the presence of snow during wintertime in Washington, D.C., refutes the existence of global warming.[25] This nonsense has been openly mocked by innumerable commentators, such as opinion writers at the *Washington Post*[26] and comedians such as Jon Stewart on *The Daily Show*.[27] Wouldn't opening oneself to such derision only weaken the public perception of the anti-AGW position? Todd Akin was the 2012 Republican candidate for U.S.

Senate from Missouri. He was notorious for having said to a TV interviewer, regarding pregnancies from rape, "It seems to me, from what I understand from doctors, that's really rare. If it's a legitimate rape, the female body has ways to try to shut that whole thing down."[28] This pronouncement was widely derided. If Akin were merely lying, while calculating that this lie would work to his advantage, this would have been a deeply misconceived tactic. Rather, I surmise this alleged medical fact was something he really believed. He heard it somewhere; it fit his own personal and ideological narrative, and confirmation bias kicked in, so there was no need to attend to other sources of information on women's health. I believe that this was a sincere claim. Similarly, none of the above statements about the science of warming from Stockman, Barton, or Inhofe makes sense as a calculated attempt to move public opinion. Like Akin, these politicians appear to be genuinely confused, despite the fact that they are well educated and, in principle, have access to plenty of information that would undermine their rationalizations.

In these cases, the politicians involved have self-serving reasons to selectively focus on bogus arguments for the anti-AGW position favored by their donors. Maintaining such denialist positions sustains standing with ideological supporters, as well as donors. But self-serving motives do not themselves explain the polling data. Most of the main-street, nonelite conservatives who deny AGW, discount the level of certainty about it or otherwise deny its severity or relative importance, do not have an immediate stake in making the whole discussion go away. Most of them are nonpathological and psychologically mature. Further, like all other residents of our biosphere, they face huge, negative consequences from our collective inaction—if not for themselves, then for their cherished descendants. Yet actors with no affiliation with relevant industries deny the science, and even create websites, write opinion pieces, comment on blogs, and so on. They make discredited claims about a lack of scientific consensus, about systemic flaws in temperature measurements, about natural climate variation due to solar activity, and the like.* So why all this denial, and why is it so closely associated with conservative political ideology?

---

* Many of these obfuscators have overt or covert financial support from individuals or corporations with a vested interest in denying AGW; I am here specifically concerned

2.2 Personality, System, and Status Quo

I think that we need to invoke a combination of personality, system justification, identity-protective cultural cognition, in-group thinking, and situational factors to explain the confirmation bias involved in climate science denialism. Frequently, comments by prominent AGW deniers expose political views underlying their denialism. Here's political advisor and columnist George Will:

> Global warming is socialism by the back door. The whole point of global warming is that it's a rationalization for progressives to do what progressives want to do, which is concentrate more and more power in Washington, more and more Washington power in the executive branch, more and more executive branch power in independent czars and agencies to micromanage the lives of the American people—our shower heads, our toilets, our bathtubs, our garden hoses. Everything becomes involved in the exigencies of rescuing the planet.[29]

(Will goes on to accuse his political opponents of their own denialism on climate.[†]) This kind of sentiment is echoed by Senator Inhofe: "Climate alarmists see an opportunity here to tax the American people."[30] Recent House majority leader Paul Ryan saw EPA emissions regulations as "an excuse to grow government, raise taxes and slow down economic growth."[31] Climate science indicates that major changes are needed to national and global economic activity and development, as well as to individual lifestyles, to reduce future warming and associated disastrous externalities. It is difficult to see how this can be accomplished without extensive governmental interventions. A major strain of contemporary political conservatism (a.k.a. "free-market conservatism" or "small-government conservatism") is

with those who do *not*, along with the millions of AGW deniers in the general population who also lack industry ties.

† He continues: "Second, global warming is a religion in the sense that it's a series of propositions that can't be refuted. It's very ironic that the global warming alarmists say, 'We are the real defenders of science,' and then they adopt the absolute reverse of the scientific attitude, which is openness to evidence. You cannot refute what they say."

focused on reducing government interventions in property rights and the economy, including minimizing regulation and keeping taxes as low as possible. The very notion of working to prevent rapid, excessive climate change thus presents a clear and present threat to the heart of this small-government ideology.

Modern political conservatism is also very closely associated with favoring status quo social and economic systems. In the mission statement for the American conservative flagship journal *National Review*, the influential conservative thinker William Buckley described a "conservative" as "someone who stands athwart history, yelling Stop, at a time when no one is inclined to do so, or to have much patience with those who so urge it." In his famous essay, "On Being Conservative," British intellectual (and conservative) Michael Oakeshott characterized conservatism as follows:

> To be conservative, then, is to prefer the familiar to the unknown, to prefer the tried to the untried, fact to mystery, the actual to the possible, the limited to the unbounded, the near to the distant, the sufficient to the superabundant, the convenient to the perfect, present laughter to utopian bliss.[32]

Historian of conservatism Jerry Muller also defines it in terms of an essential resistance to change: "For conservatives, the historical survival of an institution or practice—be it marriage, monarchy, or the market—creates a *prima facie* case that it has served some need."[33] Ideological conservatives, according to this conception, are traditionalists who tend to oppose social experimentation or changes to sociocultural norms, as well as government intervention aimed at changing the existing distribution of wealth and opportunity. A parallel strain of contemporary conservatism is a sort of libertarianism that emphasizes freedom from government interference, rather than the maintenance of traditional social and economic norms; this coexists uneasily with a social conservatism that favors government endorsement of certain social and religious practices, yet dovetails perfectly with the traditionalist conservative's attachment to status quo economic arrangements vis-à-vis the market and the existing hierarchical distribution of wealth.[34] The more the state concerns itself with

the unequal economic outcomes to be expected in an unregulated capitalist context, the more it will try to intervene in the economy in the
form of taxation to fund redistributive programs, plus regulation of
various sorts of economic activity.

Psychological research on ideology mostly concerns the way in
which individual motivational needs can explain both the content
and the persistence of political (as well as religious) ideologies. As we
discussed in chapter 1, psychological studies have found compelling
explanations for the attractiveness of ideologies in the relation between the content of the ideology and the emotional needs of the ideologue. The emotional reward system of motivated reasoning is, in turn,
at the heart of the psychological study of factual belief in politically
charged contexts—in particular, the emotionally satisfying resolution
of the dissonance between how one wants the world to be and how
it actually presents itself. The difference between different ideologies,
on this model, is fundamentally explained in terms of the different
motivations and emotional needs of the individuals and groups involved. As we have seen, the best predictor of what policy positions one
finds *intellectually* most appealing has to do with what alleged truths
one finds *emotionally* most appealing. An ideology has emotional
value when it helps the individual make sense of the world, when it
favors the group with which one identifies, and/or when it reduces fear
and anxiety. In order to understand the one-sided ideological denial of
climate science, we need to look at the particular inclinations and emotional needs of conservatives.

Status quo bias refers to the well-known cognitive bias favoring
inaction over action and the current state of affairs over alternatives.
Other things being equal, most individuals will show some preference
for the status quo no matter what the issue. In various studies where
subjects were given a number of decisions to make about a variety of
hypothetical alternatives, "just describing an option as the status quo
had the effect of increasing the likelihood that it was chosen."[35] These
status quo effects are broad, powerful, and, in many cases, automatic:

> To the extent that deference to the status quo is the native state of
> the organism, then any other set of beliefs or values that is incon-
> sistent with the status quo requires more effort, more energy, and

more attention than other alternatives. Social change is difficult for a wide variety of reasons. It requires expense, it requires leadership, and it can require the consent of the governed. But social change faces another difficulty—it is harder to imagine an alternative universe, and this alternative is likely to feel colder and less appealing than the status quo. There is a wide range of ways that people work in a motivated way to support, justify, and defend the status quo, as system justification theory makes clear. In addition, a wide variety of relatively unmotivated cognitive and affective processes makes the status quo seem more prevalent, more appealing, more correct, more the way things ought to be. Any serious attempt at social change must overcome this initial barrier.[36]

A presumptive bias in favor of the current state of affairs makes sense from an evolutionary standpoint; under ancestral conditions of great day-to-day uncertainty, the rule of thumb "a bird in the hand is worth two in the bush" makes adaptive sense. It's the same for **future discounting**, wherein the value of a future good is subjectively discounted relative to a present one. A large body of evidence supports the persistence of these related biases in both institutional and individual decision-making. This attitude means that human beings characteristically prioritize the short term over the long term in contemplating changes to current patterns of behavior. Psychologists Scott Edelman and Christian Crandall have studied other social and psychological advantages for the status quo that explain the grip of status quo bias. They note the socioeconomic barriers that often stand in the way of change:

> Effecting social change is notoriously difficult. Change can be expensive; it can be risky. There are also many and sundry interests invested in protecting the status quo, and people who profit from the status quo often have significant resource advantages to protect these interests.[37]

But social factors like these are only part of the puzzle, even when it comes to a problem like responding to AGW, where many powerful vested interests are indeed interested in maintaining the status quo.

There is also a whole list of psychological reasons for an overall presumptive bias in favor of status quo maintenance, regardless of overt self-interest. Status quo has proven inherent advantages when it comes to both cognition and evaluation of alternatives. For example, the evidence shows that what is more familiar to us is more cognitively accessible; thinking of alternatives is more effortful and can feel more uncomfortable just because it is not what we are accustomed to. Loss aversion appears to be implicated here. It has been well established in the social sciences that individuals tend to weigh possible losses more than possible gains.[38] Change is, in part, inherently uncomfortable because it raises the specter of losing what we are accustomed to; anchoring refers to the way that familiar ways of doing things can serve as a "start value" in decision-making. What is most familiar and foremost in our mind tends to bias our thinking in favor of our starting point over any alternatives. For example, mock jurors asked to consider the harshest possible penalty first will, on average, eventually recommend harsher penalties than those asked to consider the most lenient penalty first.[39] So human beings inherently have some underlying degree of status quo bias. But, according to system justification theory, conservatives are distinguished by their particular pro–status quo inclinations and an accompanying pro–status quo ideology; this is just what makes them conservatives.

It is unclear whether preexisting emotional needs make an ideology attractive or, alternatively, whether identifying with an ideological group helps determine one's emotional needs. The widely used OCEAN personality test (a.k.a. the "Big Five" test) is a questionnaire that assesses five key personality traits: Openness to experience, Conscientiousness, Extroversion, Agreeableness, and Neuroticism (i.e., emotional stability). Of particular relevance to the study of ideology and denial are the somewhat oppositional traits of openness and conscientiousness. "Openness" refers to the individual's interest in new experiences and his or her willingness to accept difference and uncertainty. Particularly conscientious people appreciate responsibility, structure, order, and predictability. Studies have consistently shown a link between liberalism and open-mindedness; high scores on openness have been found to be predictive of a liberal political identification, with low scores on this measure correlated with conservatism.[40]

The reverse is the case for "conscientiousness"; high scorers on conscientiousness are more likely to identify as political conservatives.*

An intimidating number of studies have consistently indicated that conservatives are more sensitive to risk,[41] to threatening stimuli,[42] and to negative images and messages.[43] Using brain-imaging technology, researchers have found striking differences in brain activity between Republicans and Democrats. When engaged in a risk-taking gambling task,

> Democrats showed significantly greater activity in the left insula region of the brain, a region associated with societal and self-awareness. Meanwhile, Republicans showed significantly greater activity in the right amygdala, a region associated with the body's fight-or-flight system. These results suggest that liberals and conservatives engage different cognitive processes when they think about risk. In fact, brain activity in these two regions alone can be used to predict whether a person is a Democrat or a Republican with 82.9% accuracy. By comparison, the longstanding model in political science, which uses the party affiliation of a person's mother and father to predict the child's affiliation, is only accurate about 69.5% of the time.[44]

Other studies have found differences not only in brain activity but also in brain structure itself. Researchers reported in 2011 that "increased gray matter volume in the anterior cingulate cortex was significantly associated with liberalism" and "increased gray matter volume in the right amygdala was significantly associated with conservatism," to the point that they claimed to be able to distinguish self-reported liberals from conservatives by brain structure alone, with over 71% accuracy.[45] (It is important also to note that brain structure is heavily affected by

---

* Bear in mind that this association does not imply that political leaning is necessarily based on innate personality traits. Personality traits are partly learned. Parents and communities, in teaching values, may prioritize conscientiousness and personal responsibility, or may emphasize empathy and appreciation of differences. Along with family and tribal identification, learned values may play a role in the correlation between the political views of parents and their children.

experience and development.[46] Even if accurate, these results would not suggest that people are "born" liberals or conservatives.)

Societal order, structure, and stability suggest, for both the individual and the community, less vulnerability to uncertainty. (Of possible relevance here are the particular conservative attachments to military spending and gun rights.[47]) Everyone appreciates the comfort of such certainty to some extent. But from the personality studies, we know that conservatives by disposition can be particularly attracted to order, structure, and stability—which would seem to tie in well with the conception of conservatism (whether the social traditionalist or economic laissez-faire variety) as a political ideology centered on defending status quo social and economic systems. In a series of studies and reports, system justification theorists like John Jost,[48] Aaron Kay,[49] and Erin Hennes[50] have determined that individuals with a lesser measured emotional tolerance for loss and uncertainty, and a greater measured emotional need for order and closure, are more likely to hold conservative positions across the board.* Conservatives are more likely, across a wide range of issues, to favor conventional social attitudes and oppose scientific progress.[51]

Political liberals can also be discomfited by uncertainty or societal disruption. Jost and his allies don't claim that only conservatives can think conservatively, or that context is irrelevant: They also explain how emotional needs can vary by **framing**, context, and situation. How a situation or decision is presented, or "framed," can actually spur more conservative thinking. It turns out that individuals generally, when faced with situations that spur feelings associated with threat,

---

* A variety of critics of the "rigidity of the right model" have objected that one can trigger dogmatism and intolerance in leftists by varying survey questions: questions about religion or nationalism trigger more conservative dogmatism, but questions about the environment trigger more liberal dogmatism. (See, for example, Ariel Malka et al., "Rethinking the Rigidity of the Right Model: Three Suboptimal Methodological Practices and Their Implications," in *The Politics of Social Psychology*, ed. Jarret T. Crawford and Lee Jussim [New York: Taylor and Francis, 2018].) Conservatives are threatened by crime; liberals are threatened by pollution. But this is consistent with the idea that context and framing affect emotional needs, which is really the point here—the point is not that conservatives hold a monopoly on either dogmatism or sensitivity. And these concerns do not undermine the association between conservatism and a general affinity for status quo, order, hierarchy, and stability. As we have seen, conservatives literally self-define in terms of these preferences.

uncertainty, or disruption to familiar ways of life ("system instability"), are more likely to support conservative political positions. Jost's results indicate that "framing events in terms of potential losses rather than gains leads people to adopt cognitively conservative, as opposed to innovative orientations"; further, framing situations in a way that reminds individuals of mortality or the threat of death "leads people to defend culturally valued norms and practices to a stronger degree."[52] Jost also claims that, in times of national crisis representing threats to the social and economic order (such as war or economic collapse), "people are more likely to turn to authoritarian leaders and institutions for security, stability, and structure."[53] (When the nation is threated, public approval of government and military institutions increases, as people "rally around the flag.") Finally, Jost presents evidence showing that "threats to the stability of the social system increase politically conservative choices, decisions, and judgments."[54]

So the system justification account attributes conservatism itself to a combination of individual dispositions (as formed either by heredity or by upbringing and experience) and individual and collective situational factors. Indeed, proponents of this analysis claim, meta-analytical studies examining decades of research on the variables associated with different ideologies have "confirmed" that:

> [B]oth situational and dispositional variables associated with the management of threat and uncertainty were robust predictors of political orientation. Specifically, death anxiety, system instability, fear of threat and loss, dogmatism, intolerance of ambiguity, and personal needs for order, structure, and closure were all positively associated with conservatism (or negatively associated with liberalism).[55]

From this we would expect conservatives to exhibit a particular tendency to system justification—that is, they would be especially prone to exhibit motivated cognition when it comes to order- and structure-threatening, system-disruptive information, such as information about the causes and likely consequences of global warming. In the case of political conservatives, scientific conclusions about complex climate systems that seem to mandate aggressive, interventionist policies disruptive to the established social and economic order are likely to instigate substantial dissonance and anxiety. This is fertile ground for denial, where the anti-AGW position just "feels right," regardless of what the experts might say. Republican presidential candidate Chris Christie, when asked why he says he doesn't "buy" that AGW represents a crisis, replied "That's my feeling. I didn't say I was relying on any scientists. I don't see evidence that it's a crisis."[56] Republican strategist and pundit Noelle Nikpour, when asked why she thinks AGW is a "scam," replied, "I think that every American, if they *really* thought about it, would have a gut feeling that some of these numbers that the scientists are putting out are not right."[57] Despite the flood of reasons to accept AGW, the anti-AGW position is sustained by varieties of confirmation bias: Selective attention to anti-AGW claims, selective interpretation and recall of AGW arguments, selective exposure to friendly media sources (facilitated by an increasingly fractured and individualized media environment), and the social reinforcement of one's views via interaction with one's like-minded, largely self-selected cultural community. (Please note that none of this discussion of AGW denialism is intended to discount the importance of intentional deception by elites; denialism on this issue is continuously fed by conscious misinformation by vested interests[58] and their allies in media[59] and politics.[60]) Peer group polarization effects reinforce (and enforce) the hardening of views about what sources to listen to regarding science and policy. One's views become defining cultural markers that inform individuals which facts are acceptable and which must be dissolved via selective rejection of expert opinion. Success means group acceptance and failure means exclusion; the positive feelings associated with group membership are potent, as are the negative feelings associated with ostracism. (Just ask any middle-schooler.)

Those with traits and interests especially conducive to conservatism are more likely to respond to messages threatening to the social and economic order with system-justifying motivated cognition and rationalization. Climate change is a complex problem involving many variables regarding causes, expected effects, and mitigation strategies. It raises issues in terms of loss, threat to life and property, and threat to social order. Any serious attempt at mitigation would upend the status quo in many ways. The doomsday messages of climate change scenarios might thus be expected to have the paradoxical effect for conservatives of hardening their defense of the existing social and economic order.

And what climate change precisely lacks is the set of threat characteristics that would contribute to breaking someone already resistant to change out of an accustomed behavior or worldview. Psychologist Daniel Gilbert uses the acronym PAIN for these characteristics: Personal, Abrupt, Immoral, and Now.[61] Climate change is impersonal in its causes and development; the changes it brings about are too slow to trigger the kind of emotional response that spurs immediate action; the risk presented can't be attributed to a particular actor felt to be immoral or impious; and the worst effects of our current, collective behavior are predicted to arrive only later, down the line. At the same time, thinking about, worrying about, or accepting the reality of long-term environmental degradation generates all kinds of negative emotions, notably fear, helplessness, guilt, and the loss of what sociologist Anthony Giddens calls "ontological security"—that is, the feeling of security that comes from a sense of order and continuity.[62]

As the identification of an ideological community with, say, the anti-AGW stance becomes more definitive, then any new information militating against that position creates more dissonance in the mind of the ideologue; the response is more denial and more rationalization of denial, and ever stronger self-identification as a member of a community of people who do not believe in AGW. The instinctual self- and group-protective response to threatening information is to circle the ideological wagons. Under certain circumstances, with plenty of support in the form of peer interaction and selective media consumption, this can create a sort of self-reinforcing feedback loop of increasing emotional commitment to a (counter-)factual worldview.

Further, conservative politicians naturally will form mutually beneficial alliances with pro–status quo special-interest groups and industries. These politicians and their media allies would then be expected to push an anti-AGW narrative on their constituent communities, thus positively reinforcing the existing emotional need to deny or selectively interpret the threatening information. Certain ideological positions become conditions for membership in one's peer group or cultural community. Failing to conform with the group on, say, its AGW position risks exclusion from a group that provides comforting feelings of affiliation and social support, along with a sense of shared reality. Exclusion from a group when others find you to not share their ideological beliefs threatens self-esteem.[63] There can be direct, practical consequences for failing to toe the ideological line, as Dan Kahan explains in referring to former multi-term South Carolina Republican congressman Bob Inglis. After speaking out against climate science denial, Inglis was promptly booted in his next Republican Party primary race:

> Take a barber in a rural town in South Carolina. Is it a good idea for him to implore his customers to sign a petition urging Congress to take action on climate change? No. If he does, he will find himself out of a job, just as his former congressman, Bob Inglis, did when he himself proposed such action. Positions on climate change have come to signify the kind of person one is. People whose beliefs are at odds with those of the people with whom they share their basic cultural commitments risk being labelled as weird and obnoxious in the eyes of those on whom they depend for social and financial support. . . . People acquire their scientific knowledge by consulting others who share their values and whom they therefore trust and understand. Usually, this strategy works just fine. We live in a science-communication environment richly stocked with accessible, consequential facts. As a result, groups with different values routinely converge on the best evidence for, say, the value of adding fluoride to water, or the harmlessness of mobile-phone radiation. The trouble starts when this communication environment fills up with toxic partisan meanings—ones that effectively announce that "if you are one of us, believe this; otherwise, we'll know you are one of them." In that situation, ordinary individuals' lives will go better if their perceptions of societal risk conform with those of their group.[64]

In this way, one's ideological stances—already attractive because they serve emotional needs—become cultural identifiers: What facts you accept sends a signal to your group as to whether you are with them or against them. And faking it—just going along to get along—will be difficult to sustain over the long term: *What is needed is actual conformity of individual beliefs to the group's preferred interpretation of the facts.* This is what motivated cognition is all about.

Because of the essential emotional components in such ideological groupings—that is, the feelings of security and fellowship in being part of a group, in addition to the emotional needs met by the ideological positions themselves—the distinction between in-group and out-group becomes emotionally charged. In turn, this can contribute to polarization between ideological communities, often expressed in very personal ways: In 1960, only 5% of Republicans, and 4% of Democrats expressed displeasure at the prospect of their child marrying a member of the other party. In 2010, a YouGov poll found that the number is now at least 49% for Republicans and 33% for Democrats.[65] In a poll conducted just before the 2016 presidential election, 60% of Democrats and 63% of Republicans wanted their children to marry someone from the same party.[66]

So conservatives, whose natural status quo bias is enhanced by personality traits that make them big system justifiers by disposition, subscribe to an ideology that is particularly threatened by AGW. And the more strongly conservatism becomes identified with an anti-AGW stance, the more individuals are inclined to signal this position to other members of their cultural and community in-group, and to use this position as a condition of inclusion in the group. Threatening information about climate is avoided via selective exposure and otherwise met with varieties of selective recall, interpretation, and assimilation. Denial is reinforced and encouraged through political messaging, media, and in-group peer interactions.

Climate science threatens the social and economic status quo by revealing the connection between (a) well-established, pervasive human individual and economic behavior, and (b) warming of the Earth that has us on a track catastrophic to human civilization. If ideological stances are fundamentally affected by emotional factors, and if conservatives by disposition are particularly resistant to change with regard to existing social and economic orders, then we have a partial explanation for the reactionary denialism and the—often nonsensical—rationalization of that denialism we see from sincere, well-educated, and scientifically literate anti-AGW conservatives. Many of these climate science deniers (a) have access to the fact of overwhelming expert consensus on the situation; and (b) do not, all things considered, have good reasons to reject this consensus; but (c) have deeply held emotional and self-protective motives—of a sort particularly associated with certain aspects of conservative ideology—to deny the facts.[*]

2.3 The Asymmetry Thesis

It is evident that folks in general are extremely resistant to changing their minds on ideologically charged positions, regardless of what facts or evidence they are presented with. In fact, political scientists Brendan Nyhan and Jason Reifler found that presenting conservatives with information decisively refuting their misconceptions about the presence of WMDs in Iraq or the macroeconomic effects of George W. Bush's tax cuts not only did not get them to change their minds but also— in this test, at least—appeared to *strengthen* their commitment to the misconception.[67] This the authors termed the **backfire effect**. (Liberals proved just as hard to convince, but did not exhibit this backfire effect.) Nyhan and colleagues uncovered a similar backfire effect in a later study, "The Hazards of Correcting Myths about Health Care Reform," on what happened with Sarah Palin supporters who were exposed to corrections of her false claims about "death panels" being part of the Affordable Care Act.[68] The corrections worked for opponents of Palin, as well as for supporters with low political knowledge. However, supporters of Palin with high political knowledge were more likely to believe the death panel myth after being exposed to corrective information. Looking at the answers of more than 11,000 respondents to the 2010–2012 Cooperative Congressional Election Study (CCES) panel survey, social scientists found that Republicans responded to a report about a sharp drop in unemployment (which put the Obama

---

[*] Certainly, consensus is not simply equated with truth. Galileo had good reason to reject the Ptolemaic consensus, Newton had good reason to reject the Aristotelian consensus, Darwin had good reason to reject the Creationist consensus, and Einstein had good reason to reject the Newtonian consensus. But the consensus on the existence and causes of warming is vastly broader, and more rigorously examined under the modern scientific method, than these historical examples of consensus overturned. The heliocentric model of the solar system is not only a consensus position but also settled science; so are the basics of evolution by natural selection or the germ theory of disease.

administration in a positive light) by, on average, *increasing* their estimate of the unemployment rate.[69] In yet another study, professors of communication P. Sol Hart and Erik Nisbet found that messages about the deleterious effects of climate change on foreign populations led to a "boomerang effect" for Republicans, wherein their opposition to mitigation policies grew stronger.[70] The existence of a backfire or boomerang effect might have been expected, given the results of psychological studies on the effects of resisting persuasion. There is some evidence that people who resist being persuaded—especially by strong evidence or argument—self-monitor that resistance and subsequently become more confident. As psychologist Zachary Tormala puts it, "When people perceive that they have done a good job resisting a counter-attitudinal persuasive message, they infer that their attitude is correct (otherwise it would have changed), and this inference manifests as increased attitude certainty."[71]

There are doubts about how robust this alleged backfire response really is—some very recent attempts to find it have met with mixed results, at best[72]—but the issue of apparent asymmetries with regard to resistance to change remains. Alan Gerber and colleagues have found that liberals are more persuadable by political appeals—which isn't surprising if liberals by disposition are more open to new experiences and ideas.[73] A 2015 study by polling data specialist Joshua M. Blank and political scientist Daron Shaw found that, while people of all political persuasions are capable of reacting negatively to ideologically dissonant information, Democrats are more likely to express a willingness to defer to scientific expertise.[74]

These various findings are just what one would expect in light of the personality and system justification evidence. Erik Nisbet identifies (without endorsing it) a position he calls the **intrinsic thesis**, which he defines as the thesis "that political polarization about science is due to fundamental psychological differences between political conservatives and liberals."[75] If conservatives are, by disposition, more resistant to change, and more status quo and system oriented (and liberals more comfortable with uncertainty, and more open to new ideas), then shouldn't we *expect* conservatives to have a greater tendency to deny science and factual evidence than liberals? The idea that conservatives *inherently* have a bigger problem with science and reality has made its way into public discourse. Cognitive scientist and linguist George Lakoff is well known for arguing that conservative political appeals make more—and more effective—use of appeals to emotion, framing, and anecdote. Liberals have largely failed in recent decades, he argues, in thinking that the recitation of facts will win over messages that invoke emotions.[76] According to economist and *New York Times* columnist Paul Krugman:

> The fact that climate concerns rest on scientific consensus makes things even worse, because it plays into the anti-intellectualism that has always been a powerful force in American life, mainly on the right. It's not really surprising that so many right-wing politicians and pundits quickly turned to conspiracy theories, to accusations that thousands of researchers around the world were colluding in a gigantic hoax whose real purpose was to justify a big-government power grab. After all, right-wingers never liked or trusted scientists in the first place.[77]

And *New York* magazine columnist Jonathan Chait:

> The contrast between economic liberalism and economic conservatism . . . ultimately lies not only in different values or preferences but in different epistemologies. Liberalism is a more deeply pragmatic governing philosophy—more open to change, more receptive to empiricism, and ultimately better at producing policies that improve the human condition—than conservatism. . . . What appears to be conservative economic reasoning is actually a kind of backward reasoning. It begins with the conclusion and marches back through the premises.[78]

And blogger Amanda Marcotte:

> The possibility that rationality itself has become a partisan issue is disquieting to many who prefer to believe that "both sides" have topics that they are irrational about and irrationality is evenly distributed among all political stripes. That may have been true in the past, but increasingly, Americans are rearranging their political views and

their views on empiricism so that liberals are putting much more of an emphasis on rationality.[79]

And there are innumerable other examples like this from online media over the last few years. This view of conservative dogmatism is what Stephen Colbert was referring to at the 2006 Washington Correspondents dinner when he said (only semi-jokingly, I think) that "reality has a well-known liberal bias."

And yet a 2019 meta-analysis of 51 experimental studies (led by Peter Ditto) found no significant differences in partisan bias exhibited by liberals or conservatives in the way they assessed information challenging or affirming political beliefs or allegiances.[80] Cultural cognition theorist Dan Kahan rejects what he calls the **asymmetry thesis**: the thesis—itself based on the intrinsic thesis—that science denial in general is to be expected more from the political right than from the left. Contrary to Jost and other system justification theorists, Kahan argues that science denial stems not from a special dogmatic personality particular to conservatives but, rather, from a universal felt need to share a social/cultural identity with a larger, like-minded group:

> The symmetry position (as reflected in cultural cognition and related theories) sees ideologically motivated reasoning as simply one species of *identity-protective cognition*. . . . [I]dentity-protective cognition refers to the dismissive reaction that individuals form toward information that threatens the status of (or their connection to) a group that is important to their identity. "Democrat" and "Republican" (along with hierarchy and egalitarianism, communitarianism and individualism, in cultural cognition) are *both* group affinities of that sort, and so *both* create vulnerability to motivated cognition.[81]

Kahan again:

> People have a big stake—emotionally and materially—in their standing in affinity groups consisting of individuals of like-minded goals and outlooks. When positions on risks or other policy-relevant facts become symbolically identified with membership in and

loyalty to those groups, individuals can thus be expected to engage all manner of information—from empirical data to the credibility of advocates to brute sense impressions—in a manner that aligns their beliefs with the ones that predominate in their group. The kinds of affinity groups that have this sort of significance in people's lives, however, are *not* confined to "political parties." People will engage information in a manner that reflects a "myside" bias in connection with their status as *students* of a particular university and myriad other groups important to their identities.[82]

And this is the reason, he argues, why level of education has nothing to do with acceptance of climate change, or evolution: "Asking whether people believe in evolution doesn't measure science literacy," he says, "it measures whether you're religious. It's an expression of identity."[83] People are against climate science because the kinds of change mandated by these particular facts conflict with their group's cultural values; to accept AGW is to betray their tribe.

This understanding of science denial is echoed, in slightly different terms, by Jonathan Haidt. He thinks that intuitive/emotional responses drive decision-making, with strategic reasoning secondary as a means to justify one's intuitions and convince others. He calls this the **social intuitionist model** of normative judgment (where a "normative judgment" is just any judgment prescribing how people should decide or behave). He identifies six foundational moral priorities that may be emphasized differently, depending on the tendencies of the individual and/or his or her community. Individuals and their social/cultural groups may prioritize "care," "fairness," "loyalty," "authority," and/or "sanctity." According to Haidt's research, U.S. political liberals tend to stress the first two in value judgments, while conservatives draw on all five.[84] But everyone is equal, in his mind, with regard to the fundamental fact that intuitions drive one's evaluations. As he points out, this is really the only way it could be if you subscribe to David Hume's thesis that reason can provide only the means to an end, but not the end itself. For that, you need motivation, on which subject reason is silent.

Once the group defines itself in terms of a particular view of reality, Haidt continues, certain evaluative/ideological positions, and supporting factual claims, become "sacred" to the "tribe." Attacks on these facts are met with a defensive emotional response analogous to the defensive response when one's community is under physical attack. The result is intensely motivated hot cognition, supplemented with reactionary rationalization when the idols of the tribe are challenged. And this description applies to everybody, according to Haidt; thus he rejects the asymmetry thesis for reasons similar to Kahan's.

Kahan argues that the totality of the evidence on motivated cognition shows that people across the ideological spectrum—be they communitarian, egalitarian, individualist, or hierarchicalist—will predictably exhibit motivated reasoning when presented with facts threatening to their identity group's value commitments. If conservatives have a *special* problem with closed-mindedness relating to their particular emotional needs for closure, system stability, and avoidance of uncertainty, then, Kahan argues, they should perform worse than liberals when it comes to **cognitive reflection**—that is, the use of conscious reasoning to overcome intuitive, knee-jerk evaluations.[85] But his research finds no difference between liberals and conservatives with regard to their capacity to engage in careful reasoning, and he shows—as he showed elsewhere with regard to scientific literacy and technical reasoning skills[86]—that greater cognitive reflection skills are, if anything, associated with a *greater* tendency to motivated reasoning, regardless of the subject's ideological standpoint. Kahan has found that liberals and conservatives "are *uniformly* disposed to credit or discredit [evidence] *selectively*, depending on whether the researcher has induced the study subjects to believe that the piece of evidence in question supports or challenges, affirms or threatens, a position congenial to their respective group commitments."[87] He further claims that, if motivated reasoning is mainly about identity protection, then priming subjects with self-affirming thoughts should result, across the board, in less defensiveness and greater impartiality in assessing otherwise threatening evidence. And, in fact, we know that "self-affirmation reduces the resistance of liberal Democrats as well as conservative Republicans to ideologically noncongruent information."[88] This effect "is evidence that the source of the motivated reasoning at work is identity-protective cognition; there's no reason to expect self-affirmation to have any effect in dispelling motivated reasoning that arises from a generalized disposition toward dogmatism."

Further, a couple of recent studies have cast some doubt on the Nyhan/Reifler "backfire effect," wherein conservative attitudes allegedly harden in response to new, dissonant information.[89] The original observed effect has not really shown up clearly in attempts to replicate it—particularly when the subject matter is not currently a particularly salient "hot-button" issue.[90] So, even if this reactive response can occur under certain specific and heated circumstances, it does not appear, as of now, to be the consistent or robust phenomenon it may have seemed to be at first.

Consider, again, the 76% of liberals who accept the science of AGW, according to the polling. Are liberals endorsing the science because they just generally take a more rational, accuracy-motivated approach to listening to experts, whatever the subject? Drawing from his own emphasis on personality differences between liberals and conservatives, Chris Mooney thinks that liberals are more trusting of science—though, admittedly, only by happy accident:

> And then there is still another factor, one that I ultimately decide ... is probably most important. And it is that liberals and scientists (and social scientists) share a deep psychological affinity—they are explorers, tolerant of uncertainty, always seeking out the different, and the new. They have similar personalities. This leads liberals to want to be scientists, and leads the ranks of scientists to be full of liberals—and thus builds a natural allegiance and affinity between the two groups. So when it then comes to determining what's true about reality, liberals are lucky enough to have the "right friends," as the psychologist Peter Ditto put it to me. And conservatives have the "wrong enemies." This—not an inherent asymmetry in motivated reasoning—is the most important underlying explanation here, in my mind.[91]

Everyone is equally subject to motivated reasoning in principle, according to Mooney, but liberals—especially in the post–Cold War era—generally identify with the scientists.[92] So cultural affinity and tribalism tend to work in liberals' favor when it comes to science.

At the same time, to endorse this explanation is just to uphold the asymmetry thesis for all practical purposes. Post-Scientific Revolution and development of the scientific method, "science" is just the term for the generation of knowledge via the best possible methods. There are scientific and unscientific approaches to describing reality in just about any area of human investigation and judgment, be it physical science, psychology, economics, or history. To say one's approach is "scientific" is, in essence, just to say one is executing a systematically scrupulous collection and analysis of evidence—and this, in turn, is to say one is using the best practices possible to avoid error and confirmation bias. That is the reason for modern scientific norms requiring control groups, blind studies, peer review, and transparency regarding methods, data, and potential conflicts of interest. Mooney agrees that liberals have the same general strategic and emotional incentives to motivated reasoning identified by Kahan, Suhay, and Haidt; but he also claims they are, typically, motivationally allied with science and scientists. This would still put them on the correct side of the policy argument most of the time.

But is it true that liberals are generally right on the science? Mooney's perspective (along with the asymmetry thesis) is belied to some extent by a number of areas where liberals do particularly badly with regard to the science, or where some form of chronic science denial shows no consistent correlation with any particular political ideology.

Political scientists Ted Jelen and Linda Lockett did an extensive analysis of the 2006 General Social Survey.[93] They looked at whether political partisan identification predicted attitudes toward science across three issues: Belief in evolution by natural selection, support for government funding of stem cell research, and belief that there is a scientific consensus regarding the existence and causes of climate change. Jelen and Lockett found that there was no consistent association between political partisan affiliation and responses to these science-related questions, with the exception of a slight boost for government spending on stem cell research among Democrats. The latter, they argue, could very well be explained by Democrats' stronger support for government spending in the public interest, rather than by a higher level of confidence in science generally. They conclude that "party identification is virtually irrelevant to skeptical attitudes toward science issues," and thus that "there is no evidence that there exists any constituency of science policy skeptics."

Erik Nisbet and R. Kelly Garrett compared responses by self-identified conservatives to statements challenging their views on climate change and evolution to the responses by self-identified liberals to statements challenging their views on nuclear power and natural gas mining through hydraulic fracturing (or "fracking").[94] They found that "conservatives who read statements about climate or evolution had a stronger negative emotional experience and reported greater motivated resistance to the information as compared to liberals who read the same statements and other conservatives who read statements about geology or astronomy."[95] However, they also found "a similar pattern amongst liberals who read statements about nuclear power or fracking. And, like conservatives who read statements about climate change or evolution, liberals expressed significantly lower levels of trust in the scientific community as compared to liberals who read the ideologically neutral statements." It is true that, in the same study, conservatives presented with "conservative-dissonant" science information had a negative reaction four times stronger than that of liberals presented with "liberal-dissonant" information;[96] however, this may have been due simply to a greater current political salience on the part of climate and evolution over nuclear power and fracking—in other words, liberal feelings about nuclear power might have run more strongly negative shortly after a nuclear accident like that at Three Mile Island or Chernobyl. The authors argue that these results support the **contextual thesis**—that is, the thesis that "ideological differences in the public's scientific denialism and distrust are a consequence of which science policy issues are most salient in political and public discourse"—over the intrinsic thesis. According to this view, any asymmetry in science denial is only incidental to the current scientific and political environment.

As observed in chapter 1, supporters of the cultural cognition thesis have found that ideological identifications predict perception of scientific consensus across a wide range of issues; this includes "egalitarian-communitarians," who were more likely to dispute both the scientific consensus that nuclear waste can safely be stored underground and the consensus that laws permitting concealed carry of handguns are not associated with an increase in violent crime.[97]

Rather surprisingly, the World Health Organization, along with the U.S. National Academy of Sciences and the Centers for Disease Control, agrees that nuclear power is the safest source of power in the world (including solar and wind), in terms of mortality per kilowatt hour produced.[98] Among the largest-scale forms of energy production, it is the only one that produces no greenhouse gases as an effect of power generation.[99] It's not a consensus, but it is notable that, while 65% of members of the American Association for the Advancement of Science (AAAS) favor building more nuclear power plants, only 45% of Americans agree.[100] Those opposing new nuclear power generation include 25% of "conservative Republicans" and 61% of "liberal Democrats."[101]

According to a 2015 survey by Pew Research, "a majority of the general public (57%) says that genetically modified (GM) foods are generally *unsafe* to eat, while 37% says such foods are safe; by contrast, 88% of AAAS scientists say GM foods are generally *safe*."[102] Journalist William Saletan reports that hundreds of organizations have "demanded mandatory labeling of genetically engineered foods," including the left-leaning Consumers Union, Friends of the Earth, Physicians for Social Responsibility, the Center for Food Safety, the Ecumenical Ecojustice Network, and Global Awareness Local Action.[103] He also notes that the World Health Association, the American Medical Association, and the American Association for the Advancement of Science "have all declared there's no good evidence GMOs are unsafe." (The most sweeping report yet, from the National Academy of Sciences in May 2016, looked at almost 900 studies and publications on the effects of GM agriculture, and found no evidence of adverse effects on human health, agriculture, or the environment.) Anti-GMO activists, Saletan explains, ignore both the paucity of evidence against GM food safety and the cost–benefit analysis in looking at, say, the reductions in pesticide use made possible by GM crops. He documents a list of public misconceptions about various GM crops and foods; he also found a number of instances of environmental activist disinformation tactics—no doubt, in most cases, fueled by a sincere concern about safety and the environment.

The efficacy of GMO disinformation tactics is likely enhanced by an information environment in which, according to a 2015 Oklahoma

State University study, 80% of respondents favored warning labels on foods containing DNA.[104] In the case of fears about GMOs, it may be that information deficit, rather than outright denial, is responsible for some anti-GMO public opinion: While many of the objections raised are not based on evidence, it is not clear that most people have been exposed to good reasons to reject those concerns, either. Officers of nonprofit advocacy organizations lobbying against GM foods have less of an excuse, however: They are unlikely to be wholly ignorant of the state of the evidence on consuming GM foods.

It seems at least plausible that some people feel opposition to, say, nuclear power and/or genetically modified foods is just part of what it means to be an anti-corporate, pro-environment progressive. Actual evidence, or even authoritative consensus, pertaining to the safety of these technologies is discounted or ignored. Anecdotally at least, there seems to be some further overlap between this group and devotees of some of the more fishy products for sale in Whole Foods—or what journalist Michael Schulson calls "America's temple of pseudoscience."[105] Some consumers may choose to shop at certain stores in order, say, to support local farmers. But many would cite health reasons as well. Like other stores catering to a certain demographic, Whole Foods sells herbal supplements, probiotics, and organic foods, the benefits of which have little or no evidentiary support.[106] It also sells expensive vials of water called "homeopathic medicine." Presumably, at least some of the purchasers of homeopathic medicine have some sense of what these remedies contain (in most cases, a substance with no proven therapeutic value is diluted in water until no trace of the substance remains). Most of these same individuals have at least a high school science background and enough other rudimentary background knowledge about chemistry and medicine to at least question the concept behind these products.

Anti-fluoridation activists in progressive Portland, Oregon, recently celebrated their victory in the latest referendum on city water fluoridation. The evidence against fluoridation cited by these activists concerns the health effects of naturally occurring fluoride contamination, at levels much higher than would be permitted in municipal drinking water.[107] In fact, as *Scientific American* points out, "decades of studies in different cities in different states, involving millions of people, have concluded that there is a safe level of fluoride—one part-per-million—that can be added to water for enormous benefit to our teeth and oral health with little to no adverse effects."[108] Anti-fluoridation efforts, where active, have achieved broad ideological support: The 2013 Portland referendum secured 61% of the vote, despite a heavy pro-fluoridation public health education campaign. Some activists seem to be energized by concerns about "unnatural" chemical contamination and others by a concern about freedom from government mandates. Fluoridation is widespread and totally uncontroversial in most parts of the country. Yet, in areas where the issue has taken on cultural-political significance, denialism follows.

This brings us to the anti-vaccination movement. According to a 2015 Gallup poll, "Six percent of American adults say they believe certain vaccines cause autism in children. Forty-one percent expressly disagree with this claim, while slightly over half of Americans are unsure."[109] Another 2015 Pew survey found that almost one in ten Americans today consider common vaccines to be "unsafe," including 5% of Republicans and 9% of Democrats.[110] Much has been made of a sharp drop in vaccination rates for children in certain elite, progressive enclaves such as Boulder, Colorado, and Southern California's Malibu and Santa Monica.[111] Anti-vaccination sentiment has deeper historical roots than some might realize. Pamphlets appeared opposing the smallpox vaccine in the early twentieth century, even though the value of that inoculation had been overwhelmingly endorsed by medical science for decades. An extraordinarily insightful 1927 editorial in the medical journal *The Lancet* took on smallpox vaccine denialism:

> We still meet the belief . . . that vaccination is a gigantic fraud deliberately perpetuated for the sake of gain. . . . The opposition to vaccination . . . still retains the "all or none" quality of primitive behaviour and, like many emotional reactions, is supported by a wealth of argument which the person reacting honestly believes to be the logical foundation of his behavior. An antivaccinator is generally an antivivisector, often a vegetarian, but he is ready to base his objection on arguments, statistical or individual, that have no relation to his other negativisms, and are therefore not the true foundation upon which his objection rests. In this common tendency to produce reasons for beliefs already

formed upon an emotional basis we find the explanation for the failure to settle some controversies by appeal to facts.[112]

Note the ideological clustering identified by this unnamed *Lancet* editorialist: Apparently, even in 1927, anti-vaccination activism was associated with progressive identifiers like vegetarianism and animal-rights concerns. It is difficult not to speculate on some connection between contemporary progressive concerns about vaccines and fears raised by other "unnaturals" like genetically modified crops, nonorganic foods, nuclear power, and fluoridated water. Psychologist Stephan Lewandowsky and colleagues also found an association between free-market, anti-government ideology and anti-vaccination feelings; they speculate this has to do with associating vaccines with government mandates.[113] (This may explain why the heavily conservative and libertarian state of Idaho actually leads the nation in unvaccinated children.[114])

Here are some examples of responses of the question, 'Why do you think vaccines are unsafe?'

- "Because you are injecting a virus into a healthy kid, and I don't understand why." —Woman, age 39
- "Because they are injecting you with a disease to prevent a disease." —Woman, age 35
- "They make them sicker, it weakens the immune system, instead of allowing the body to use its own natural antibodies to fight them off." —Woman, age 22
- "Some children cannot take the vaccine. They cause autism and other problems, muscular problems occasionally, but not very often." —Man, age 66.

Much of the disinformation about vaccines originates in a single, tiny study from the 1990s, now thoroughly discredited and retracted. The medical consensus is that vaccines are highly effective, do not cause autism, and that any other slight risks are vastly outweighed by the benefits.[115] Yet concerned parents, including well-educated parents from wealthy, progressive communities, seize on pronouncements of danger by misinformed celebrities as confirmation of their fears about the injection of disease-related substances into their children. (A mistrust of pharmaceutical companies is often mentioned as well, but that doesn't explain the exclusive focus on vaccines over all other drugs and medical interventions.) The anti-vaccination websites and celebrity interviews feed a highly biased and selective search for confirmation of vaccination fears. Reassuring sources of confirmation, however wildly unqualified, are given special attention (prominent anti-vaccination celebrity Jenny McCarthy was featured on the *Oprah Winfrey Show*, where she unironically professed a degree in medicine from "the University of Google").

Denial is about finding comfort in beliefs contradicted by evidence. There is nothing inherently comforting about overestimating the risk presented by vaccines (or fluoridation, or GM foods, etc.). Denialism about vaccine science follows from the need to feel reassured in rejecting vaccines. Anti-vaccination sentiments may originate in progressive "back to nature" ideologies or in libertarian anti-government ideologies. Vaccination feels unnatural and invasive, and parents subsequently want to feel justified in avoiding it; medical information contradicting this desire is dissonant and therefore subject to motivated avoidance and dismissal.[116] It is only in this context that public trust in the medical advice of minor celebrities and known charlatans can exceed public trust in pediatricians backed by overwhelming medical science.

Attempts to correct anti-vaccination positions produce patterns similar to what is seen in attempts to correct ideologically charged misinformation. In two different studies, Brendan Nyhan found a paradoxical, behavioral backfire effect among vaccination "skeptics":

Refuting claims of an MMR/autism link successfully reduced misperceptions that vaccines cause autism but nonetheless decreased intent to vaccinate among parents who had the least favorable vaccine attitudes.[117]

And, in the second study,

Corrective information adapted from the Centers for Disease Control and Prevention (CDC) website significantly reduced belief in the myth that the flu vaccine can give you the flu as well as concerns about its safety. However, the correction also significantly *reduced* intent to vaccinate among respondents with high levels of concern about vaccine side effects—a response that was not observed among those with low levels of concern.[118]

There could not be a clearer illustration of the fact that a deficit of information is not exclusively responsible for the failure to listen to medical advice on vaccination.

One should look at a person's total circumstances before blaming him or her for maintaining a silly belief; but someone living in a modern, industrialized, media-saturated society should not be compared to a child raised in a cult, who has been utterly isolated from different worldviews. Most of the sincere science deniers we are talking about spent at least twelve years in school, get 200 TV channels, have internet access, and are not helplessly dependent on some particular source for information. The question is, why are they selectively deferring to a minority or discredited opinion—the one denier in the room full of experts? To a considerable extent, people learn what is "known" to be true from authority figures and sources they trust. As Kahan likes to point out, most people don't know much about science. Consequently, they need to know whom to defer to— such as their physician—in assessing risk.[119] The (often implicit) decision about whom to trust is informed by their background and their affinities. Kahan characterizes certain scientific claims as having taken on "antagonistic cultural meanings"; he identifies a particular emotional need as decisive in such cases: the desire to be loyal to and maintain standing in an affinity group.[120] This emotion, he claims, is what is driving the highly selective perception of who is trustworthy and what is "known." Under the right conditions, suspicion of vaccines spurred by protective parents with some ecological purity issues and/or anti-government concerns can become dominant in certain subcommunities. Cultural deviants within these peer communities can expect to be judged and excluded, so they conform their reasoning about the science to the group's mores. Identity informs the perception of expertise.

2.4 Science and Societal Change

So it seems leftists and progressives are perfectly capable of believing false and dubious claims, and even behaving contrary to their own interests, in the face of decisive scientific consensus to the contrary. Does this mean that the asymmetry thesis is wrong? The correct answer is yes and no.

As noted earlier, sociologist Gordon Gauchat has documented a decline in trust in science specifically among U.S. conservatives between 1974 and 2010.[121] What happened over this period? Sociologist Aaron McCright's distinction between **production science** and **impact science** may help answer this question. As they had anticipated, McCright and colleagues found that "conservatives will report significantly less trust in, and support for, science that identifies environmental and public health impacts of economic production (i.e., impact science) than liberals."[122] They also found that, conversely, "conservatives will report a similar or greater level of trust in, and support for, science that provides new inventions or innovations for economic production (i.e., production science) than liberals." Fifty years ago, for much of the public, the thought of science gave rise to representations of a world where new developments in technology, energy, and industrial production efficiency, and transcendence of nature through pesticides and herbicides, interstate highways, and jet-powered flight, foretold a lasting era of universal prosperity and leisure. (Think the GE/Disney exhibit "Progressland" at the 1964 New York World's Fair.) The decades since have brought greater evidence of the negative impacts of industrial production, development, and consumption. "Conservative audiences," as Nisbet et al observe, "have faced a steady stream of dissonance-inducing science messages—a process augmented by the emergence of partisan news outlets that vary greatly in their treatment of issues such as climate change, and lead to greater polarization about the issue among viewers."[123] The ascendancy of impact science has coincided with an explosion of news and opinion media options, including media outlets providing messages tailored to particular ideological audiences.

In a separate study, McCright and collaborator Riley Dunlap also found that climate science skepticism is strongly correlated not simply with ideological conservatism but in particular with white males.[124] In other words, conservatives who are not white males are much less likely to be AGW deniers. McCright and Dunlap hypothesize that this phenomenon is tied up with white male identity politics, which in turn is tied up with conservative status quo bias and system justification. White males have benefited disproportionately from the status quo social and economic order; this could make them particularly sensitive to impact science, simply from a self-serving perspective. Our climate problem represents an existential threat to the established system of capitalist production and consumption with which, McCright and Dunlap propose, white males in particular have reason to feel an attachment. White male "identity as an in-group" is thus challenged by this scientific bad news for the production science status quo.[125] Any adequate response to climate change will certainly include greatly increased government regulation of energy production and consumption. "None of this is about the science," as Naomi Oreskes puts it. "All of this is a political debate about the role of government."[126]

This perspective unifies the system-protective cognition explanation of AGW denial and the identity-protective cognition explanation.[127] If conservative white male identity is bound up with the established socioeconomic system, then to defend one is to defend the other. There is no reason to think people cannot be influenced by a combination of different emotional needs. A need for stability and security is not inconsistent with a need for affinity and belonging; indeed, these needs are quite compatible under a variety of conditions. System-protective reactivity and identity-protective cognition mutually reinforce and energize AGW denial because of what AGW represents in this historical context.

Compare the continuing development of the consensus within the biological sciences regarding facts that are dissonant with some traditional religious claims. In addition to conservatism, the other factor Gauchat found associated with the decline in public confidence in science was high church attendance. Analysis of the data from Pew's Religious Landscape Survey by biologist Josh Rosenau shows a striking correlation between denial of evolution and opposition to environmental regulations.[128] Evolution by natural selection, in combination with population genetics, is settled science. Further, even if they were taught as children not to believe in this theory, most members of modernized societies today have had significant exposure to the fact of the relevant scientific consensus. And yet, according to a 2014 Gallup survey, 42% of Americans believe that human beings were created by God in their present form; another 31% concede that humans evolved, but only under God's guidance, rather than by natural selection.[129] The 2014 Pew Religious Landscape Study yielded almost identical results, with 71% either denying that evolution operates by natural selection or denying evolution altogether.[130] This means that over 70% of Americans deny the central explanatory principle of the biological sciences.[131] Other information that might trigger a threat response in social conservatives may include growing evidence that homosexuality is a naturally occurring, innate tendency.[132] Or evidence from the social sciences that abstinence-based sex education is ineffective at reducing either teen sexual activity or pregnancy rates.[133] What social conservatism and economic conservatism have in common is an attachment to established lifestyles, established ways of organizing society, and established ways of understanding reality. To the extent that social conservative identity is tied up with traditional religious conceptions of nature and its origins, and to the extent that (in the current political environment) social conservative identity is tied up with economic conservative identity, then the respect to which modern science as an institution feels threatening to conservative identity may be thereby magnified. This might contribute to the AGW denialism of some social conservatives, wherein we sometimes see them drawing on religious texts in rationalizing their position, as in the Shimkus quote earlier in this chapter. Indeed, a coalition of major evangelical groups, including Focus on the Family and the Family Research Council, has launched a movement opposing "The Green Dragon"—that is, "the false world-view and theology of secular and pagan religious environmentalism," which "is striving to put America, and the world, under its destructive control."[134]

Christians in the United States, especially evangelical Christians, identify as environmentalists at very low (and declining) rates compared to the general U.S. population.[135] Evangelicals tend to stress that the world was given to humans, and that humans stand separate from nature in a fundamental way. Professor of religion Lucas

Johnston argues that "Christianity has been competing for market share against nature-venerating pagan groups from its inception, and that continues today. The Christians who rejected the environmental consciousness in the 1960s and '70s perceived a dangerous, nature-venerating, pagan-esque religious sentiment."[136]

Social scientist and professor of law Donald Braman insists that science denial is entirely context dependent: "If it's conservative white males on global warming, pick a different issue and you'll find another group that has trouble thinking in a way that agrees with experts."[137] Indeed, as we have seen, there are whole swaths of progressive populations in whom motivated cognition is triggered by production science—for example, nuclear power and GMOs. Imagine the reaction by the left if (in an alternate reality) an actual, well-founded scientific consensus were to emerge saying that white-skinned people are inherently intellectually superior to persons of other races. Braman is correct that there exists ample evidence for some universal human tendency to motivated cognition under dissonance-triggering circumstances—a kind of self-protective, doxastic "fight-or-flight" response. Consider, however, that perhaps the single essential aspect of science per se is that it has no respect for conventional wisdom, established thinking, or tradition. When cut loose from political and religious constraints, science has no inherent bias in favor of what is familiar or system preserving. As Thomas Kuhn famously observed in his classic text *The Structure of Scientific Revolutions*, the history of science is characterized by periodic, often societally disruptive "paradigm shifts." (Think of Galileo's findings on the motion of the Earth, or Darwin on evolution by natural selection.) Individual scientists are, of course, not immune to implicit bias or motivated reasoning. But when they follow their own norms about bias avoidance, scientists go where the evidence leads, heedless of how disruptive the conclusions might be. (And these norms are policed by their skeptical peers: Prepublication peer review and post-publication peer criticism are critical to the success of modern science.) In accounting for an increasing, broad opposition to science on the part of conservatives, Chris Mooney cites "the dynamism of scientific inquiry—its constant onslaught on old orthodoxies, its rapid generation of new technological possibilities."[138]

One emotional need that system justification theorists have consistently found to be strongly associated with conservatism is the need for **cognitive closure**. The "Need For Closure Scale" (NFCS) is a tool developed by psychologists Donna Webster and Arie Kruglanski to test individual differences with respect to the general emotional need for resolution and the broad dislike for ambiguity, uncertainty, and change.[139] The NFCS asks respondents to indicate their level of agreement with statements like:

- Even after I've made up my mind about something, I am always eager to consider a different opinion.
- When dining out, I like to go to places where I have been before so that I know what to expect.
- I usually make important decisions quickly and confidently.
- In most social conflicts, I can easily see which side is right and which is wrong.

In a meta-analysis of twenty different studies performed in six different countries, Jost et al. found "stable and reasonably strong support for the notion that these specific epistemic motives [i.e., representing a need for closure] are associated with a wide variety of politically conservative attitudes and orientations."[140] Gauchat's analysis of the General Social Survey (covering 2006–2010, after questions about the meaning of science were added) reveals that "conservatives were far more likely to define science as knowledge that should conform to common sense and religious tradition."[141]

Scientific practice requires that no situation is entirely resolved: If disconfirming evidence appears, you have to revisit the theory. Thus science as a practice—independent of context, independent of the production versus impact factor—is fundamentally inconsistent with any felt need for closure, certainty, or resolution. Some discoveries may confirm the efficacy of the technological and developmental path we are on, but the only way to guarantee that the status quo is safe from disruptive discovery is to restrict or quash the pursuit of knowledge altogether—as when the government of the state of North Carolina—a state whose coast is characterized by heavily developed, low-lying barrier islands—prohibits the use of climate-related sea-rise projections in its coastal development policy;[142] when the Wyoming state legislature blocks the implementation of new national science standards for schools that include material on AGW;[143] or when the U.S. Congress prohibits government-funded research into the health effects of gun ownership.[144] Officials with the incoming Trump administration scrubbed the websites for the Environmental Protection Agency and the Departments of Interior and Energy of all references to "climate change" and "clean energy."[145] Texas Republican and former chair of the House Science, Space, and Technology Committee Lamar Smith launched an investigation into the National Oceanic and Atmospheric Administration in response to its conclusion (echoing many other scientific organizations) that the data do not support any recent slowdown in global warming.[146] Such moves don't rise to the level of burning Giordano Bruno at the stake, but they share the characteristic of fulfilling a need for cognitive closure by protecting policy positions from inconvenient facts.

Kahan characterizes conservatives as ideological hierarchicalists; Jonathan Haidt thinks conservatives place special moral emphasis on authority and group loyalty. Science as a practice is nonhierarchical: Authority (under ideal scientific practices) belongs only to the data, not to any experimenter, scientific organization, or theory.* Conformity to established results in the face of recalcitrant data is not a value in science; dissent is encouraged, and success in overturning theories is rewarded. Scientists keep raising questions, even after consensus is reached; many of the most significant discoveries in the history of science have come about by unexpected results that defy the expectations of the theory being tested. This is what makes scientific consensus so authoritative when it is sustained. Modern science as a practice is inherently pro-uncertainty, pro-dissent, and anti-closure. In this way, a proponent of the intrinsic thesis might argue that some tension exists between conservative dispositions and attachments and the very nature (or culture) of science *in general*, regardless of context.

---

* Evolution denialists like to call the theory of evolution "Darwinism," as though evolutionary biologists are mere ideological followers of some charismatic figure.

None of this requires that the asymmetry thesis be true in the strong sense that political conservatives are fundamentally more prone to denial than liberals because they are somehow cognitively or emotionally deficient. Different issues trigger different biases; sometimes the context "favors" one set of biases over another. Setting aside one's biases is always technically possible, but obviously can be extremely challenging when the circumstances are particularly threatening to one's personality and worldview. The climate change issue is a perfect storm for conservative personality and conservative ideology. It is a form of impact science that represents a massive threat to the existing social and economic order, and in so doing, incidentally threatens demographic identity groups invested in the status quo. Solutions will require massive government intervention, the prospect of which is particularly threatening to the especially individualistic, small-government aspects of American conservative ideology. (Academic scientists themselves are overwhelmingly left-leaning,[147] so the information being delivered may be received as an out-group message, implicitly viewed with suspicion as alien and potentially hostile.) Add to this a large number of powerful actors, with vested interests in preserving the status quo, using political messaging, hired obfuscators with science degrees, and allied media outlets to question the scientific consensus—but more important, to whip up the (self-, system-, and identity-) protective emotional responses that power the motivated rejection of that consensus. This is the situation that explains the following 2010 message in reference to AGW science from Rush Limbaugh, host of what has been the most popular radio show in the United States since 1991:[148]

> We really live, folks, in two worlds. There are two worlds. We live in two universes. One universe is a lie. One universe is an entire lie. Everything run, dominated, and controlled by the left here and around the world is a lie. The other universe is where we are, and that's where reality reigns supreme and we deal with it. And seldom do these two universes ever overlap. . . . The Four Corners of Deceit: Government, academia, science, and media. Those institutions are now corrupt and exist by virtue of deceit. That's how they promulgate themselves; it is how they prosper.[149]

Production science has had the greatest historical effect on humanity. It was responsible for the Industrial Revolution and great improvements in food production, medicine, transportation, and overall quality of life (for those societies with access to it), as well as the technological leaps of computing and the internet. However, the secondary science examining the impacts of these developments, such as contemporary climate science, represents the most consequential science of our time. (Note how conservative politicians, when asked how best to address environmental concerns, characteristically stress the promise of new technologies—new forms of production—over conservation.) The failure to come to a broad societal and political consensus on addressing AGW, pollution, and general overuse of resources could not have greater significance for the future of the human species. The famous **tragedy of the commons**, popularized by biologist Garrett Hardin in his classic 1968 essay on overpopulation, refers to the problem in shared-resource situations wherein individuals, each acting out of "rational" self-interest, will, almost invariably, collectively produce a result very much against the interests of the group as a whole.[150] One standard illustration of this phenomenon involves a group of individual sheep herders sharing a common pastureland for grazing their sheep. A herd of twenty undernourished sheep is more profitable than a herd of ten well-fed sheep. It is in the individual self-interest of each sheep herder to add to his or her herd, regardless of what the others are doing. Yet the seemingly inevitable, "tragic" consequence of these individual rational decisions will be overgrazing and destruction of the commons. This fundamental dynamic, Hardin argues, extends to many social and environmental situations; one really important example, of course, is the collective effect of many individual decisions to produce and use energy in ways that increase the levels of greenhouse gasses in the atmosphere. Solving commons problems requires, in each case, a solution to a **collective action problem**. Self-interested actors (individuals, communities, or nations) must somehow be convinced to forgo immediate self-interest for the collective good. This can be difficult, but especially so when large swaths of the population deny the problem in the first place.

In a clever application of the "tragedy of the commons" concept, Kahan explains how denial can be individually rational, yet collectively harmful. Again, according to his cultural cognition thesis, motivated cognition is primarily a symptom of identity-protective thinking. Recall Elizabeth Anderson's concept of "expressive rationality": A member of a cultural-ideological community has very good, self-interested reasons to conform not just his or her behavior but also his or her very *beliefs* to that of the community. Failure to think like your community can have negative personal consequences in the form of personal, social, and financial penalties. Unfortunately, as Kahan puts it,

> As reliably as it promotes expressive rationality at the individual level, cultural cognition will often be collectively irrational. . . . What makes it expressively rational for individuals to adopt particular beliefs about risk is not the truth of those beliefs but rather the congruence between those beliefs and individuals' cultural commitments. As a result, if beliefs about a societal risk such as climate change come to bear meanings congenial to some cultural outlooks but hostile to others, expressively rational individuals will fail to converge on the best available scientific information (or at least fail to converge as rapidly as they otherwise would). . . . Thus, while it is, for all intents and purposes, costless for any individual to form a perception of risk that is wrong but culturally congenial, it is not costless for society—indeed, it is very harmful to its collective welfare—for individuals in aggregate to form beliefs this way.[151]

This dynamic is catastrophic. As journalist Ezra Klein puts it, "The ice caps don't care if it's rational for us to worry about our friendships. If the world keeps warming, they're going to melt regardless of how good our individual reasons for doing nothing are."[152] How, then, to move forward, and solve this critical collective action problem?

Proponents of the contextual thesis maintain that even mentioning the intrinsic thesis is a bad move from a science communication perspective. Both Dan Kahan and Erik Nisbet have argued not only that the intrinsic thesis fails to capture the universality and context dependency of motivated cognition and denial but also that it is massively counterproductive as a science communication message. Nisbet explains:

> [A]dvocates of the intrinsic thesis have done science communicators a disservice. By promoting the idea that there are inherent

psychological differences between conservatives and liberals when forming attitudes and making judgments about science, they are effectively—and ironically—contributing to the very political polarization of science they decry and thereby inhibiting more effective science communication. . . . [B]y targeting conservatives specifically as somehow uniquely deficient when it comes to science, the overall framework of the intrinsic thesis lends itself to focusing on ideological countermobilization and/or a conversion of worldviews ("If only everyone were liberal!"), rather than to bridging ideological gaps (because the intrinsic thesis holds that they cannot be bridged). Demonizing a third of the population in a science policy debate by claiming they have an insurmountable psychological deficit does nothing to promote a solution to the challenges of effective science communication.[153]

An atmosphere of ideological polarization and divisive rhetoric is not a good atmosphere for achieving good public policy outcomes. Regardless of whether conservatives have a unique psychological and/or ideological resistance to science, or at least a particular resistance to the most salient and critical science of our era, the message that conservatives are from Mars and liberals are from Venus renders each group as fundamentally alien to the other. This is a message that extremists are all too happy to embrace (as evidenced by the Limbaugh quote): Extremists of every stripe like to employ "us against them" framing, as it helps consolidate in-group political support for their inflexible ideology.

The research on cultural cognition suggests messages delivered by in-group spokespeople might seem less threatening. Yet the example of former congressman Bob Inglis is not encouraging: Loss of effective in-group status can happen quickly.*

Everyone is susceptible to motivated reasoning to some extent; it is just triggered by different inputs in different contexts, depending on the particular emotional needs of the individual. Regardless of the debate

* I'll have more on positive proposals about science communication in the afterword.

over the asymmetry thesis, we know that identifiable dispositional factors linked to ideology have a lot to do with how members of different identity groups respond to certain scientific messages. Some of these messages are urgent.

Notes

1. "Scientific Consensus: Earth's Climate Is Warming," *Global Climate Change*, July 21, 2016, http://climate.nasa.gov/scientific-consensus/.

2. See Brian O'Neill and Vanessa Schweizer, "Projection and Prediction: Mapping the Road Ahead," *Nature Climate Change* 1 (2011), pp. 352–353; see also David Roberts, The Uncertainty Loop Haunting Our Climate Models," *Vox*, October 23, 2015, http://www.vox.com/2015/10/23/9604120/climate-models-uncertainty.

3. See Stuart D. Jordan, "Global Climate Change Triggered by Global Warming," in *Science Under Siege: Defending Science, Exposing Pseudoscience*, ed. Kendrick Frazier (Amherst, NY: Prometheus Books, 2009).

4. Americans as Concerned as Ever About Global Warming by Lydia Saad, Gallup. https://news.gallup.com/poll/248027/americans-concerned-ever-global-warming.aspx

5. Jocelyn Kiley, "Ideological Divide over Global Warming as Wide as Ever," Pew Research Center, June 16, 2015, http://www.pewresearch.org/fact-tank/2015/06/16/ideological-divide-over-global-warming-as-wide-as-ever/.

6. Cary Funk and Lee Rainie, "Public and Scientists' Views on Science and Society," Pew Research Center, January 15, 2015, http://www.pewinternet.org/2015/01/29/public-and-scientists-views-on-science-and-society/.

7. "Information Deficit Model," Wikipedia, n.d., https://en.wikipedia.org/wiki/Information_deficit_model.

8. Chelsey Harvey, "Science Confirms It: Denial of Climate Change Is All About the Politics," *Washington Post*, February 22, 2016, https://www.washingtonpost.com/news/energy-environment/wp/2016/02/22/science-confirms-it-denial-of-climate-change-is-all-about-the-politics/.

9. Matthew J. Hornsey, Emily Harris, Paul Bain and Kelly Fielding, "Meta-Analyses of the Determinants and Outcomes of Belief in Climate Change," *Nature Climate Change*, February 22, 2016, pp. 622–626.

10. Dan Kahan, "How 'Cognitive' Adaptation Relates to Mitigating a Polluted Science Communication Environment," Cultural Cognition Project at Yale Law School, November 4, 2014, http://www.culturalcognition.net/blog/2014/11/4/how-cognitive-adaptation-relates-to-mitigating-a-polluted-sc.html. See also P. Sol Hart and Erik Nisbet, "Boomerang Effects in Science Communication: How Motivated Reasoning and Identity Cues Amplify Opinion Polarization About Climate Mitigation Policies," Communication Research 39 (2012), pp. 701–723; and Ariel Malka, Jon A. Krosnick, and Gary Langer, "The Association of Knowledge with Concern About Global Warming: Trusted Information Sources Shape Public Thinking," Risk Analysis 29 (2009), pp. 633–647.

11. Gordon Gauchat, "Politicization of Science in the Public Sphere: A Study of Public Trust in the United States, 1974 to 2010," American Sociological Review 77 (2012), pp. 167–187.

12. Meteor Blades, "Open Thread: Climate-Change Skeptics," Daily Kos, March 6, 2010, http://www.dailykos.com/story/2010/03/06/843473/-Open-Thread-Climate-Change-Skeptics.

13. Jay Newton-Small and Katy Steinmetz, "Eight More Deep Thoughts from Rep. Joe Barton," Time, June 18, 2010, http://content.time.com/time/politics/article/0,8599,1997963,00.html.

14. Eli Watkins, "GOP Congressman Asks if Rocks Are Causing Sea Levels to Rise," CNN, May 18, 2018, https://www.cnn.com/2018/05/17/politics/mo-brooks-nasa-climate-change/index.html.

15. Adam Doster, "Shimkus: Capping CO_2 Emissions Will 'Take Away Plant Food,'" Progress Illinois, March 27, 2009, http://www.progressillinois.com/2009/3/27/shimkus-carbon-emissions-plant-food.

16. Cathal Kelly, "God Will Save Us from Climate Change: U.S. Representative," The Economist, November 10, 2010, http://www.thestar.com/news/world/2010/11/10/god_will_save_us_from_climate_change_us_representative.html.

17. John Cook, "Climate Misinformer: James Inhofe," Skeptical Science, n.d.,https://www.skepticalscience.com/skeptic_James_Inhofe.htm.

18. Mitch Jones, "Top 10 Misguided Climate Deniers' Quotes of 2014," Common Dreams, December 31, 2014, http://www.commondreams.org/views/2014/12/31/top-10-misguided-climate-deniers-quotes-2014.

19. Scott Pruitt and Luther Strange, "The Climate-Change Gang," National Review, May 17, 2016, http://www.nationalreview.com/article/435470/climate-change-attorneys-general.

20. Kate Sheppard, "Perry: Climate Change a Hoax to 'Keep the Money Rolling In,'" *Mother Jones*, August 17, 2011, http://www.motherjones.com/blue-marble/2011/08/perry-climate-change-hoax-keep-money-rolling.

21. Charles Johnson, "Lewis, Zinke Debate Federal Budget, Health Care, Global Warming," *Billings Gazette*, October 4, 2014, http://billingsgazette.com/news/local/government-and-politics/lewis-zinke-debate-federal-budget-health-care-global-warming/article_d062bc3c-c8e9-5909-854f-5e78efc52868.html.

22. Dan Kahan, "What's to Explain? Kulkarni on 'Knowing Disbelief,'" Cultural Cognition Project at Yale Law School, August 27, 2014, http://www.culturalcognition.net/blog/2014/8/27/whats-to-explain-kulkarni-on-knowing-disbelief.html.

23. Robert Paul Wolff, "Trump the Man-Child," *RobertPaulWolff* blog, January 27, 2017, http://robertpaulwolff.blogspot.com/2017/01/trump-man-child.html.

24. Newton-Small and Steinmetz, "Eight More Deep Thoughts from Rep. Joe Barton."

25. Phillip Bump, "Jim Inhofe's Snowball Has Disproven Climate Change Once and for All," *Washington Post*, February 26, 2015, https://www.washingtonpost.com/news/the-fix/wp/2015/02/26/jim-inhofes-snowball-has-disproven-climate-change-once-and-for-all/.

26. Bump, "Jim Inhofe's Snowball Has Disproven Climate Change Once and for All."

27. "Burn Noticed," *The Daily Show*, September 22, 2014, http://www.cc.com/video-clips/8q3nmm/the-daily-show-with-jon-stewart-burn-noticed.

28. Charles Jaco, "Jaco Report: Full Interview with Todd Akin," *Fox 2 Now*, August19,2012,https://fox2now.com/2012/08/19/the-jaco-report-august-19-2012/

29. George Will, interviewed by Jamie Weinstein, in "George Will: 'Global Warming Is Socialism by the Back Door,'" *Real Clear Politics*, April 28, 2014, http://www.realclearpolitics.com/video/2014/04/28/george_will_global_warming_is_socialism_by_the_back_door.html.

30. Formerly found at http://inhofe.senate.gov/pressreleases/climate.htm. (Link appears to have since been taken down.)

31. Laura Barron-Lopez, "Paul Ryan Says Climate Rule Is Illegal," *The Hill*, July 30, 2014, http://thehill.com/policy/energy-environment/213814-paul-ryan-says-climate-rule-is-illegal#ixzz38zElA5ai.

32. Michael Oakeshott, *Rationalism in Politics and Other Essays* (London: Methuen, 1962), pp. 168–196; qtd. in Corey Robin, "The

Conservative Reaction," *Chronicle of Higher Education*, January 8, 2012, http://chronicle.com/article/The-Conservative-Mind/130199/.

33. Jerry Z. Muller, "Conservatism: Historical Aspects," in *International Encyclopedia of the Social and Behavioral Sciences*, Vol. 4, ed. Neil J. Smelser and Paul B. Baltes (Amsterdam: Elsevier, 2001), p. 2625; qtd. in Jost et al., "Political Conservatism as Motivated Social Cognition," p. 342n3.

34. A discussion with Elizabeth Suhay helped me think through this point.

35. Scott Edelman and Christian S. Crandall, "A Psychological Advantage for the Status Quo," in *Social and Psychological Bases of Ideology and System Justification*, ed. by John Jost, Aaron Kay, and Hulda Thorisdottir (Oxford: Oxford University Press, 2009), p. 93.

36. Edelman and Crandall, "A Psychological Advantage for the Status Quo," p. 100.

37. Edelman and Crandall, "A Psychological Advantage for the Status Quo," p. 85.

38. E.g., Daniel Kahneman and Amos Tversky, "Prospect Theory: An Analysis of Decision under Risk," *Econometrica* 47 (1979), pp. 263–291; also see Edelman and Crandall, "A Psychological Advantage for the Status Quo," p. 94.

39. Edelman and Crandall, "A Psychological Advantage for the Status Quo," p. 88.

40. Alan Gerber, Gregory Huber, Shang Ha, Conor Dowling, and David Doherty, "Personality Traits and the Dimensions of Political Ideology," March 31, 2009. http://ssrn.com/abstract=1412863 or http://dx.doi.org/10.2139/ssrn.1412863. See also Alan Gerber, Gregory Huber, Shang Ha, and Conor Raso, "Personality and Political Behavior," February 11, 2009, http://ssrn.com/abstract=1412829; and Hibbing et al., *Predisposed*.

41. Cindy D. Kam and Elizabeth N. Simas, "Risk Orientations and Policy Frames," *Journal of Politics* 72 (2010), pp. 381–396.

42. Douglas Oxley, Kevin Smith, John Alford, Matthew Hibbing, Jennifer Miller, Mario Scalora, Peter Hatemi, and John Hibbing, "Political Attitudes Vary with Physiological Traits," *Science* 321 (2008), pp. 1667–1670.

43. Hibbing et al., *Predisposed*.

44. University of Exeter, "The Party in Your Brain," *EurekAlert!*, February 14, 2013, http://www.eurekalert.org/pub_releases/2013-02/uoe-tpi021113.php; citing Darren Schreiber et al., "Red Brain, Blue Brain: Evaluative Processes Differ in Democrats and Republicans," *PLoS ONE* 8 (2013), p. e52970.

45. Ryota Kanai, Tom Feilden, Colin Firth, and Geraint Rees, "Political Orientations Are Correlated with Brain Structure in Young Adults," *Current*

Biology 21 (2011), pp. 677–680. See also University of South Carolina, "This is Your Brain on Politics: Neuroscience Reveals Brain Differences between Republicans and Democrats," *ScienceDaily*, November 1, 2012, www.sciencedaily.com/releases/2012/11/121101105003.htm. The results here are quite striking and need to be replicated to see if the relation is really this robust.

46. As stressed by Elizabeth Suhay (private correspondence).

47. See John Ehrenreich, "Why Are Conservatives So Obsessed with Gun Rights Anyway?," *Slate.com*, February 26, 2018, https://slate.com/technology/2018/02/why-conservatives-are-so-obsessed-with-guns.html

48. Jost et al., "Political Conservatism as Motivated Social Cognition."

49. Aaron Kay and Justin Friesen, "On Social Stability and Social Change: Understanding When System Justification Does and Does Not Occur," *Current Directions in Psychological Science* 20 (2011), pp. 360–364.

50. Erin Hennes, H. Hannah Nam, Chadly Stern, and John Jost, "Not All Ideologies Are Created Equal: Epistemic, Existential, and Relational Needs Predict System-Justifying Attitudes," *Social Cognition* 30 (2012), pp. 669–688.

51. Glenn D. Wilson, "Development and Evaluation of the C-Scale," in *The Psychology of Conservatism*, ed. Glenn D. Wilson (London: Academic Press, 1973). See Jost et al., "Political Conservatism as Motivated Social Cognition," p. 344.

52. Jost et al., "Political Conservatism as Motivated Social Cognition," p. 364.

53. Jost et al., "Political Conservatism as Motivated Social Cognition," p. 365.

54. Jost et al., "Political Conservatism as Motivated Social Cognition," p. 366.

55. Jost and Amodio, "Political Ideology as Motivated Social Cognition," p. 57; see Jost et al., "Political Conservatism as Motivated Social Cognition."

56. "Christie on Climate Change," *Morning Joe*, December 1, 2015, http://www.msnbc.com/morning-joe/watch/christie-on-climate-change-577053763864.

57. "Weathering Fights—Science: What's It Up To?," *The Daily Show*, October 26, 2011, http://www.cc.com/video-clips/x1h7ku/the-daily-show-with-jon-stewart-weathering-fights---science--what-s-it-up-to-.

58. See Oreskes and Conway, *Merchants of Doubt*; Suzanne Goldenberg, "Secret Funding Helped Build a Vast Network of Climate Denial Thinktanks," *The Guardian*, February 14, 2013, https://www.theguardian.com/environment/2013/feb/14/funding-climate-change-denial-thinktanks-network; and Justin Gillis and John Schwartz, "Exxon Mobil Accused of Misleading Public on Climate Change Risks," *New York Times*, October 30, 2015, https://www.nytimes.com/2015/10/

31/science/exxon-mobil-accused-of-misleading-public-on-climate-change-risks.html.

59. Lauren Feldman, Edward Maibach, Connie Roser-Renouf, and Anthony Leiserowitz, "Climate on Cable: The Nature and Impact of Global Warming Coverage on Fox News, CNN, and MSNBC," *International Journal of Press/Politics* 17 (2012), pp. 3–31.

60. Alon Harish, "New Law in North Carolina Bans Latest Scientific Predictions of Sea-Level Rise," *ABC News*, August 2, 2012, http://abcnews.go.com/US/north-carolina-bans-latest-science-rising-sea-level/story?id=16913782.

61. Daniel Gilbert, *Stumbling on Happiness* (New York: Alfred A. Knopf, 2006); ctd. in Marshall, *Don't Even Think About It*, p. 47.

62. Anthony Giddens, *Modernity and Self-Identity: Self and Society in the Late Modern Age* (Stanford, CA: Stanford University Press, 1991); ctd. in Kari Marie Norgaard, "Cognitive and Behavioral Challenges in Responding to Climate Change," World Bank Policy Research Working Paper Series #4940 (2009).

63. Suhay, "Explaining Group Influence."

64. Dan Kahan, "Why We Are Poles Apart on Climate Change," *Nature*, August 15, 2012, http://www.nature.com/news/why-we-are-poles-apart-on-climate-change-1.11166.

65. Shanto Iyengar, Gaurav Sood, and Yphtach Lelkes, "Affect, Not Ideology: A Social Identity Perspective on Polarization," *Public Opinion Quarterly* 76 (2012), pp. 932–951; see Ezra Klein and Alvin Chang, "'Political Identity Is Fair Game for Hatred': How Republicans and Democrats Discriminate," *Vox*, December 7, 2015, http://www.vox.com/2015/12/7/9790764/partisan-discrimination.

66. Lynn Vavreck, "A Measure of Identity: Are You Wedded to Your Party?," *New York Times*, January 31, 2017, https://www.nytimes.com/2017/01/31/upshot/are-you-married-to-your-party.html.

67. Brendan Nyhan, and Jason Reifler, "When Corrections Fail: The Persistence of Political Misperceptions," *Political Behavior* 32 (2010), pp. 303–330; discussed in Mooney, "The Science of Why We Don't Believe Science."

68. Brendan Nyhan, Jason Reifler, and Peter A. Ubel, "The Hazards of Correcting Myths About Health Care Reform," *Medical Care* 51 (2013), pp. 127–132.

69. Brain Schaffner and Cameron Roche, "Misinformation and Motivated Reasoning: Responses to Economic News in a Politicized Environment," *Public Opinion Quarterly* 81 (2017), pp. 86–110.

70. P. Sol Hart and Erik Nisbet, "Boomerang Effects in Science Communication: How Motivated Reasoning and Identity Cues Amplify Opinion Polarization About Climate Mitigation Policies," *Communication Research* 39 (2012), pp. 701–723.

71. Zakary Tormala, "A New Framework for Resistance to Persuasion: The Resistance Appraisals Hypothesis," in *Attitudes and Attitude Change*, ed. William Crano and Radmila Prislin (New York: Taylor and Francis, 2008), p. 218.

72. Thomas Wood and Ethan Porter, "The Elusive Backfire Effect: Mass Attitudes' Steadfast Factual Adherence," *SSRN*, August 5, 2016, https://ssrn.com/abstract=2819073.

73. Alan Gerber, Gregory Huber, David Doherty, Conor Dowling, and Costas Panagopoulos, "Big Five Personality Traits and Responses to Persuasive Appeals: Results from Voter Turnout Experiments," *Political Behavior* 35 (2013), pp. 687–728.

74. Joshua M. Blank and Daron Shaw, "Does Partisanship Shape Attitudes Toward Science and Public Policy? The Case for Ideology and Religion," *Annals of the American Academy of Political and Social Science* 658 (2015), pp. 18–35. See Tom Jacobs, "Ideology Often Trumps Science, Especially Among Conservatives," *Pacific Standard*, February 10, 2015, http://www.psmag.com/politics-and-law/ideology-often-trumps-science-especially-among-conservatives.

75. Erik Nisbet, Kathryn Cooper, and R. Kelly Garrett, "The Partisan Brain: How Dissonant Science Messages Lead Conservatives and Liberals to (Dis)Trust Science," *Annals of the American Academy of Political and Social Science* 658 (2015), p. 37.

76. George Lakoff, *Don't Think of an Elephant!* (White River Junction, VT: Chelsea Green, 2004).

77. Paul Krugman, "Interests, Ideology, and Climate," *New York Times*, June 8, 2014, https://www.nytimes.com/2014/06/09/opinion/krugman-interests-ideology-and-climate.html.

78. Jonathan Chait, "Fact Finders," *The New Republic*, February 28, 2005, https://newrepublic.com/article/61829/fact-finders.

79. Amanda Marcotte, "Reason vs. The Right: Have Conservatives Abandoned Science and Rationality?," *Salon*, June 20, 2014, http://www.salon.com/2014/06/20/reason_vs_the_right_have_conservatives_abandoned_science_and_rationality_partner/.

80. Peter Ditto, Brittany Liu, Cory Clark, and Sean Wojcik, "At Least Bias Is Bipartisan: A Meta-Analytic Comparison of Partisan Bias in Liberals and Conservatives", *Perspectives on Psychological Science* 14 (2019), pp. 273–291.

81. Dan Kahan, "The Ideological Symmetry of Motivated Reasoning," Cultural Cognition Project at Yale Law School, December 13, 2011, http://www.culturalcognition.net/blog/2011/12/13/the-ideological-symmetry-of-motivated-reasoning.html.

82. Dan Kahan, "Mooney's Revenge?! Is there 'Asymmetry in Motivated Numeracy?,'" Cultural Cognition Project at Yale Law School, October 10, 2013, http://www.culturalcognition.net/blog/2013/10/10/mooneys-revenge-is-there-asymmetry-in-motivated-numeracy.html.

83. Julie Beck, "Americans Believe in Science, Just Not Its Findings," *The Atlantic*, January 29, 2015, https://www.theatlantic.com/health/archive/2015/01/americans-believe-in-science-just-not-its-findings/384937/. While educational attainment is positively correlated with acceptance of evolution, Kahan likely is referring here to acceptance of evolution by natural selection; the latter is much less clearly correlated with education in the United States. See Benjamin Heddy and Louis Nadelson, "The Variables Related to Public Acceptance of Evolution in the United States," *BMC*, January 8, 2013, https://evolution-outreach.biomedcentral.com/articles/10.1186/1936-6434-6-3.

84. Haidt, *The Righteous Mind*, pp. 128–154. For a critique of Haidt's methodology in arriving at this distinction between liberals and conservatives, see Lawrence Blum, "Political Identity and Moral Education: A Response to Jonathan Haidt's The Righteous Mind," *Journal of Moral Education* 42 (2013), pp. 298–315.

85. Kahan, "Ideology, Motivated Reasoning, and Cognitive Reflection," pp. 407–424.

86. Kahan et al., "The Polarizing Impact of Science Literacy and Numeracy on Perceived Climate Change Risks."

87. Dan Kahan, "Proof of Ideologically Motivated Reasoning—Strong vs. Weak," Cultural Cognition Project at Yale Law School, July 16, 2013, http://www.culturalcognition.net/blog/2013/7/16/proof-of-ideologically-motivated-reasoning-strong-vs-weak.html. See Dan Kahan et al., "'They Saw a Protest': Cognitive Illiberalism and the Speech-Conduct Distinction," *Stanford Law Review* 64 (2012), pp. 851–906.

88. Kahan, "The Ideological Symmetry of Motivated Reasoning." See, for example, Geoffrey Cohen, David Sherman, Anthony Bastardi, Lillian Hsu, Michelle McGoey, and Lee Ross, "Bridging the Partisan Divide: Self-Affirmation Reduces Ideological Closed-Mindedness and Inflexibility in Negotiation," *Journal of Personality and Social Psychology* 93 (2007), pp. 415–430.

89. Wood and Porter, "The Elusive Backfire Effect: Mass Attitudes' Steadfast Factual Adherence."

90. D. J. Flynn, Brendan Nyhan, and Jason Reifler, "The Nature and Origins of Misperceptions: Understanding False and Unsupported Beliefs About Politics," *Political Psychology* 38 (2017), pp. 127–150.

91. Chris Mooney, "Are Conservatives Inherently More Biased than Liberals? The Debate Rages On," *Desmog* blog, August 2, 2012, http://www.desmogblog.com/are-conservatives-inherently-more-biased-liberals-scientific-debate-rages.

92. See Jeffrey Mervis, "Politics, Science, and Public Attitudes: What We're Learning, and Why It Matters," *Science*, February 25, 2015, https://www.sciencemag.org/news/2015/02/politics-science-and-public-attitudes-what-we-re-learning-and-why-it-matters

93. Ted Jelen and Linda Lockett, "Religion, Partisanship, and Attitudes Toward Science Policy," *SAGE Open*, January 14, 2014, pp. 1–8; ctd. by Tom Jacobs, "Science Denialism Crosses Party Lines," *Pacific Standard*, January 17, 2014, http://www.psmag.com/books-and-culture/science-denialism-crosses-party-lines-73021.

94. Nisbet et al., "The Partisan Brain."

95. Erik Nisbet and R. Kelly Garrett, "Our Partisan Brains: Exploring the Psychology Behind Denying Science," *The Conversation*, March 12, 2015, http://theconversation.com/our-partisan-brains-exploring-the-psychology-behind-denying-science-38411.

96. See Tom Jacobs, "Ideology Often Trumps Science, Especially among Conservatives," *Pacific Standard*, February 10, 2015, http://www.psmag.com/politics-and-law/ideology-often-trumps-science-especially-among-conservatives.

97. Kahan et al., "Cultural Cognition of Scientific Consensus."

98. National Research Council, *Hidden Costs of Energy: Unpriced Consequences of Energy Production and Use* (New York: National Academies Press, 2010); and Phil McKenna, "Fossil Fuels Are Far Deadlier than Nuclear Power," *New Scientist*, March 23, 2011, https://www.newscientist.com/article/mg20928053.600-fossil-fuels-are-far-deadlier-than-nuclear-power.

99. Adam Galas, "Why the Safest Form of Power Is Also the Most Feared," *The Motley Fool*, September 14, 2014, https://www.fool.com/investing/general/2014/09/14/why-the-safest-form-of-power-is-also-the-most-fear.aspx.

100. From Funk and Rainie, "Public and Scientists' Views on Science and Society."

101. Cary Funk and Lee Rainie, "Americans, Politics, and Science Issues," Pew Research Center, July 1, 2015, http://www.pewinternet.org/2015/07/01/americans-politics-and-science-issues/.

102. From Funk and Rainie, "Public and Scientists' Views on Science and Society."

103. William Saletan, "Unhealthy Fixation," *Slate*, July 15, 2015, http://www.slate.com/articles/health_and_science/science/2015/07/are_gmos_safe_yes_the_case_against_them_is_full_of_fraud_lies_and_errors.html. (The full list of sponsors of the Just Label It! advocacy group includes hundreds of organic food purveyors who would likely benefit financially from mandatory GM food labeling laws.)

104. Jason Lusk and Susan Murray, *Food Demand Survey* 2 (2015), pp. 1–5.

105. Michael Schulson, "Whole Foods: America's Temple of Pseudoscience," *The Daily Beast*, February 23, 2014, http://www.thedailybeast.com/articles/2014/02/23/whole-foods-america-s-temple-of-pseudoscience.html.

106. Crystal Smith-Spangler, Margaret Brandeau, Grace E. Hunter, J. Clay Bavinger, Maren Pearson, Paul Eschbach, Vandana Sundaram, Hau Liu, Patricia Schirmer, Christopher Stave, Ingram Olkin, and Dena Bravata, "Are Organic Foods Safer or Healthier than Conventional Alternatives? A Systematic Review," *Annals of Internal Medicine* 157 (2012), pp. 348–366.

107. Fluoride Action Network, "Portland Uses Science & Integrity to Defeat Fluoridation," *FluorideAlert.org*, May 21, 2013, http://fluoridealert.org/articles/portland_victory/.

108. Kyle Hill, "Why Portland Is Wrong About Water Fluoridation," *Scientific American*, May 22, 2013, http://blogs.scientificamerican.com/but-not-simpler/why-portland-is-wrong-about-water-fluoridation/.

109. Frank Newport, "In U.S., Percentage Saying Vaccines Are Vital Dips Slightly," Gallup, March 6, 2015, http://www.gallup.com/poll/181844/percentage-saying-vaccines-vital-dips-slightly.aspx.

110. "83% Say Measles Vaccine Is Safe for Healthy Children," Pew Research Center, February 9, 2015, http://www.people-press.org/2015/02/09/83-percent-say-measles-vaccine-is-safe-for-healthy-children/.

111. Soumya Karlamangla, "California Lags in Vaccinating Children, CDC Says," *Los Angeles Times*, August 28, 2015. http://www.latimes.com/science/la-me-california-vaccinations-20150828-story.html.

112. "The Psychology of Antivaccination," *The Lancet* 210 (1927), pp. 1401–1402; ctd. by Clive Hamilton, "Climate and Vaccine Deniers Are the Same: Beyond Persuasion," *The Conversation*, January 27, 2014, http://theconversation.com/climate-and-vaccine-deniers-are-the-same-beyond-persuasion-22258.

113. Stephan Lewandowsky, Gilles E. Gignac, and Klaus Oberauer, "The Role of Conspiracist Ideation and Worldviews in Predicting Rejection of

Science," *PLoS ONE*, October 2, 2013, https://journals.plos.org/plosone/article?id=10.1371/journal.pone.0075637

114. "Vaccination Coverage Among Children in Kindergarten—United States, 2014-2015 School Year," Centers for Disease Control and Prevention, August 28, 2015, https://www.cdc.gov/mmwr/preview/mmwrhtml/mm6433a2.htm.

115. See Steven Novella, "The Anti-Vaccination Movement," in *Science Under Siege: Defending Science, Exposing Pseudoscience*, ed. Kendrick Frazier (Amherst, NY: Prometheus, 2009).

116. See Mark Navin's *Values and Vaccine Refusal* (New York: Routledge, 2016) for an excellent discussion of parents' moral rationalizations of vaccine refusal.

117. Brendan Nyhan, Jason Reifler, Sean Richey, and Gary Freed, "Effective Messages in Vaccine Promotion: A Randomized Trial," *Pediatrics* 133 (2014), pp. 835–842.

118. Brendan Nyhan and Jason Reifler, "Does Correcting Myths About the Flu Vaccine Work? An Experimental Evaluation of the Effects of Corrective Information," *Vaccine* 33 (2015), pp. 459–464.

119. Dan Kahan, "Five Theses on Science Communication: The Public and Decision-Relevant Science, Part 2," Cultural Cognition Project at Yale Law School, June 7, 2013, http://www.culturalcognition.net/blog/2013/6/7/five-theses-on-science-communication-the-public-and-decision.html.

120. Dan Kahan, "Science Literacy & Cultural Polarization: It Doesn't Happen Just with Global Warming, but It Also Doesn't Happen for All Risks. Why?," Cultural Cognition Project at Yale Law School, June 13, 2013, http://www.culturalcognition.net/blog/2013/6/13/science-literacy-cultural-polarization-it-doesnt-happen-just.html.

121. Gauchat, "Politicization of Science in the Public Sphere," pp. 167–187.

122. Aaron McCright, Katherine Dentzman, Meghan Carters, and Dietz, "The Influence of Political Ideology on Trust in Science," *Environmental Research Letters* 8 (2013), pp. 1–9.

123. Nisbet et al., "The Partisan Brain."

124. McCright and Dunlap, "Cool Dudes."

125. Qtd. in Julia Pyper, "Why Conservative White Males Are More Likely to Be Climate Skeptics," *Scientific American*, October 5, 2011, https://www.scientificamerican.com/article/why-conservative-white-maes-are-more-likely-climate-skeptics/.

126. From *The Merchants of Doubt* (film), directed by Robert Kenner (Mongrel Media and Sony Pictures Classics, August 30, 2014).

127. See McCright and Dunlap, "Cool Dudes," p. 1171.

128. Josh Rosenau, "Evolution, the Environment, and Religion," National Center for Science Education blog, May 15, 2015, http://ncse.com/blog/2015/05/evolution-environment-religion-0016359.

129. Frank Newport, "In U.S., 42% Believe Creationist View of Huma Origins," Gallup, June 2, 2014, https://news.gallup.com/poll/170822/believe-creationist-view-human-origins.aspx

130. "Religious Landscape Study: Christians by State," Pew Research Center, n.d., http://www.pewforum.org/religious-landscape-study/christians/christian/

131. A popular option among Enlightenment-era intellectuals—now virtually unknown—was (classical) Deism, according to which there is a creator god who established the laws of nature and then let them take their course, without further direction or intervention. The god of Deism could be thought to have allowed evolution to proceed via random mutation and natural selection. A reader suggests that this survey may not reflect the views of some respondents who accept both evolution by natural selection and the biblical Christian God. This, however, would require some stark compartmentalization, as the biblical God shares few characteristics with the god of Deism.

132. See Jeremiah Garretson and Elizabeth Suhay, "Scientific Communication about Biological Influences on Homosexuality and the Politics of Gay Rights," *Political Research Quarterly* 69 (2016), pp. 17–29.

133. Kathrin Stanger-Hall and David Hall, "Abstinence-Only Education and Teen Pregnancy Rates: Why We Need Comprehensive Sex Education in the U.S," *PLoS ONE*, October 14, 2011, https://journals.plos.org/plosone/article?id=10.1371/journal.pone.0024658.

134. John Rudolf, "An Evangelical Backlash Against Environmentalism," *New York Times*, December 30, 2010, http://green.blogs.nytimes.com/2010/12/30/an-evangelical-backlash-against-environmentalism/.

135. Brian Palmer, "God's EPA Administrator," *Slate*, June 8, 2018, https://slate.com/technology/2018/06/evangelicals-lack-of-environmentalism-explains-scott-pruitt.html.

136. Qtd. in Palmer, "God's EPA Administrator."

137. Qtd. in Pyper, "Why Conservative White Males Are More Likely to Be Climate Skeptics."

138. Chris Mooney, *The Republican War on Science* (New York: Basic Books, 2005), p. 5; qtd. in Gauchat, "Politicization of Science in the Public Sphere," p. 171.

139. Donna Webster and Arie Kruglanski, "Individual Differences in Need for Cognitive Closure," *Journal of Personality and Social Psychology* 67 (1994), pp. 1049–1062.

140. Jost et al., "Political Conservatism as Motivated Social Cognition," p. 360. As Jost notes (p. 343), the paired needs to preserve status quo institutions and to resolve situations (perhaps by eliminating possible sources of disagreement) are why we might call a hardline Soviet communist like Stalin the "conservative" as compared to the reformer Trotsky—Stalin wants to preserve what is the established order.

141. Gauchat, "Politicization of Science in the Public Sphere," p. 183.

142. Harish, "New Law in North Carolina Bans Latest Scientific Predictions of Sea-Level Rise."

143. Motoko Rich, "Science Standards Divide a State Built on Coal and Oil," *New York Times*, May 18, 2014, http://www.nytimes.com/2014/05/19/us/science-standards-divide-a-state-built-on-coal-and-oil.html.

144. Erin Schumaker, "Doctors Condemn the NRA-Fueled Ban on Gun Violence Research," *Huffington Post*, June 14, 2016, http://www.huffingtonpost.com/entry/dickey-amendment-gun-violence-research-ban_us_56606201e4b072e9d1c4eaaa.

145. Megan Jula and Rebecca Leber, "2017 Was a Big Year for Scrubbing Science from Government Websites. Here's the List," *Mother Jones*, December 29, 2017, http://www.motherjones.com/environment/2017/12/2017-was-a-big-year-for-scrubbing-science-from-government-websites-heres-the-list/.

146. Alan Neuhauser, "Lamar Smith Is Hot and Bothered About Climate Science," *U.S. News*, November 23, 2015, http://www.usnews.com/news/articles/2015/11/23/lamar-smith-is-hot-about-noaas-climate-science.

147. "Public Praises Science; Scientists Fault Public, Media," Pew Research Center, July 9, 2009, http://www.people-press.org/2009/07/09/public-praises-science-scientists-fault-public-media/.

148. *Talkers Magazine*, http://www.talkers.com/top-talk-radio-audiences/.

149. "ClimateGate Hoax: The Universe of Lies versus the Universe of Reality," *Rush Limbaugh Show*, November 24, 2009, http://www.rushlimbaugh.com/daily/2009/11/24/climategate_hoax_the_universe_of_lies_versus_the_universe_of_reality. Qtd. by David Roberts, "The Right's Climate Denialism Is Part of Something Much Larger," *Grist*, September 10, 2010, http://grist.org/article/2010-09-09-the-rights-climate-denialism-is-part-of-something-much-larger/.

150. Garrett Hardin, "The Tragedy of the Commons," *Science* 162 (1968), pp. 1243–1248.

151. Dan Kahan, Maggie Wittlin, Ellen Peters, Paul Slovic, Lisa Ouellette, Donald Braman, and Gregory Mandel, "The Tragedy of the Risk-Perception Commons: Culture Conflict, Rationality Conflict, and Climate Change," Temple University Legal Studies Research Paper No. 2011-26 (2011), http://ssrn.com/abstract=1871503 or http://dx.doi.org/10.2139/ssrn.1871503.

152. Ezra Klein, "How Politics Makes Us Stupid," *Vox*, April 6, 2014, http://www.vox.com/2014/4/6/5556462/brain-dead-how-politics-makes-us-stupid.

153. Nisbet et al., "The Partisan Brain: How Dissonant Science Messages Lead Conservatives and Liberals to (Dis)Trust Science," p. 53.

3

Pride, Prejudice, and Political Economy

3.1 Political Economics

In the natural sciences, the ideal procedure is for investigators to run controlled experiments, in which the effects of some manipulation are tested against a control group that is the same as the experimental group in relevant respects, except for the experimental condition being tested. The results of such experiments can then be confirmed though replication. This is not possible when studying the effects of economic policies: Economics is ostensibly a science that relies on evidence in making predictions about the effects of economic policies, yet in practice the phenomena studied in economics are chaotic in the technical sense of involving hugely complex, interrelated systems and innumerable individual decisions. Replication of economic "experiments" is impossible because conditions will always be uncontrollably (in both senses of the word) different from one application of a given policy to the next. Cause and effect is thus difficult to definitively establish. Consequently, there is a lot of room for ideologues to exercise selective interpretation of economic data in service to their own goals.

Political economics is the study of how government policies affect the economy; by extension, it also refers to ideological positions on how and to what extent the state should involve itself in economic matters. The beliefs one holds about such matters constitute a primary dimension of political ideology: An individual's feelings about the desirability of various forms of state interventions in the economy are, commonly, heavily determinative as to whether that individual aligns with the political left or political right. Liberals favor a variety of government interventions in economic life, via regulation (such as minimum-wage laws), taxation, social insurance, and redistributive social welfare programs, to produce an economy where the fruits of production are shared more broadly than in a free-market economy. Economic conservatives oppose regulation and social welfare spending, largely because they believe that a low taxation, pro-business regime is the most productive, and will in the long run produce the highest level of both individual satisfaction and well-being for the greatest number. In this respect, liberals and conservatives largely agree on the *value* of economic activity generally—namely, its contribution to overall well-being, as well as to the achievement of individual goals. They differ on the *factual* question as to whether the best way to achieve well-being is via a laissez-faire approach to economic policies (where overall well-being is thought to be best achieved by minimizing interference in individual pursuits), or through a heavier state investment in public goods and equality of opportunity (where individuals are thought to be best served by interventionist policies aimed at the greater good).

To what extent do emotional needs and motivated reasoning contribute to ideological positions on political economy? There are several respects in which the sorts of motives we have been discussing are brought into play by the central questions of political economy. Some of the policy positions we see commonly taken in political economy, when compared to the state of the evidence, could be sustained only by confirmation bias and denial.

System justification theory observes the pervasive influence of individual needs for order and stability on political ideology, which in turn can affect beliefs about scientific claims either amenable to or undermining the individual's ideological stance. The nature of the "system" in which individuals live is heavily determined by state policies regarding property rights, regulation of economic exchanges, employment, trade, and taxation. Thus system justification theory would predict extensive motivated cognition with regard to beliefs about the pros and cons of economic policies. And with plenty of room for confirmation bias in looking at economics, we should expect system-justifying ideologues to conveniently find just what they need to validate existing economic systems and status quo distributions.

The cultural cognition thesis notes that some persons, partly because of the cultural-ideological communities with which they identify, are highly individualistic and emotionally more comfortable with inegalitarian socioeconomic arrangements; others are more communitarian, and are dismayed by the prospect of very inegalitarian societies. This theory further notes the emotional pressures—and strategic motives—to conform to the beliefs of one's identity group(s). Economic policy has a huge effect on individual freedoms and social equality. Therefore, like the proponents of system justification theory, proponents of cultural cognition theory would also expect to see affect bias implicated in factual judgments about the economy.

Naturally, there is also tremendous room for self- and group-serving bias in forming views about how economic systems are affected by political decisions. It is not difficult to imagine how someone's judgments about the costs and benefits of economic policies might be swayed simply by the expected effects of those policies on him or herself, or on the community with which he or she identifies.

The self-serving, the system justifier, and the cultural cognizer among us should all be expected occasionally to succumb to distorted thinking about what the government should or should not do vis-à-vis the economy. Multiple motives to denial and rationalization are strongly instigated by issues in political economy; and because of the inherent complexity of economics, the kind of wiggle room needed to selectively interpret the economic lessons of history and to selectively assess the claims of economists and lawmakers is always there for the ideologue. Conditions are ripe for denial. If ideologues can confidently deny the overwhelming evidence behind anthropogenic global warming, evolution by natural selection, and vaccine safety, what chance does the science of economics have?

We saw in the last chapter that some left-leaning proponents of the asymmetry thesis believe there is a particular propensity to deny science and reality on the part of political conservatives. A set of leftist economists and pundits have recently been making the case that the *central* economic tenets of contemporary conservatism are the product of motivated reasoning—and even have gone so far as to draw an analogy between this phenomenon and climate science denialism. "Denial" is a strong word to use in explaining political disagreement, be it over economic policy or anything else. To justify employing this concept, we need to see two main elements: First, the dogmatic rejection of evidence that otherwise really should cause one to rethink one's position; and second, some good reasons to interpret this rejection of evidence as deriving from implicit bias consequent on underlying emotional needs.

In this chapter, I look at two familiar routes to an ideology of small-government conservatism with regard to the economy: supply-side economics and property-rights libertarianism. The first rests on a factual claim about the broad growth effects of low taxation (and minimal regulation) on corporations and the investor class. The second relies on a moral claim about the fundamentality of individual liberty and the right to private property. These seem like very different ways to arrive at roughly the same conclusions about political economy. As we shall see, however, they are quite similar in an essential respect: Informed true believers in each case are engaging in motivated reasoning that demonstrably stems from identical roots in attributional biases related to race and class.

One factual assertion about political economics has become a central orthodoxy in U.S. political conservatism over the last thirty-five years—namely, that cutting taxes on businesses and the wealthier investor class, reducing regulation on business and finance, and cutting spending on social welfare programs will lead to more investment, economic expansion, and job growth, thus growing the economy in ways that materially benefit everyone. That the economy is driven by the investment class is the fundamental belief underlying what is known as **supply-side** economics, or sometimes colloquially as "trickle-down" economics. The opposing school of thought is **demand-side**, or "Keynesian," economics, which holds that total economic product is most heavily influenced by demand, and so policies that put more resources in the hands of working people are best for overall growth and well-being: The demand-sider thinks that directly stimulating bottom-up demand will most efficiently spur investment and growth. During a downturn or recession, the demand-side theorist's recommendation for economic stimulus is more government spending, whereas the supply-side theorist recommends tax cuts and spending cuts.

U.S. economic policy has moved strongly toward the recommendations of supply-side economics since the 1970s. The Reagan administration cut the top marginal federal income tax rate from 70% to 28%; the top rate eventually rebounded somewhat into the thirties, and since then has been occasionally raised or lowered by a couple percentage points or so depending on the political party in power. Perhaps even more significant are changes to the long-term capital gains tax on investment income, because many of the wealthiest citizens make the bulk of their income from investments: This rate declined from a high of 39.5% in 1978 to 15% for most investors now.[1] Taxes on dividend income also declined sharply, and estate taxes have been heavily curtailed. Corporate taxes were slashed (just as they were considerably reduced again in 2018, for the same stated reasons). Over the same period of time, the U.S. government made several significant moves toward deregulation of the banking and investment sectors. The Reagan-era enactment of supply-side policies was accompanied by cuts in aid to the poor, including food aid, housing, health care, job training, unemployment, and community block grants.[2] The stated rationale was that this assistance was both wasteful and unnecessary, as the increased job opportunities for the poor deriving from the benefits of supply-side tax cuts and deregulation would more than make up for the losses in aid. (Total social spending has increased since that time, but that increase has been driven mainly by the costs of social insurance programs like Medicare and Social Security, not social welfare programs.)

According to the story of supply-side economics, these moves should have combined to increase overall economic growth, and, further, the effects of this growth should have been enjoyed to some extent by all (if not necessarily equally). And yet, over the period of time since the U.S. economy pivoted strongly toward supply-side economics, the income of the wealthiest 1% has increased by hundreds of percentage points while, according to a comprehensive 2017 analysis, "average pre-tax real national income per adult . . . has stagnated for the bottom 50% of the distribution at about $16,000 a year."[3] Indeed, income for most of the bottom 90% (depending on exactly how it is measured) has either declined, remained flat, or grown very modestly, at best.[4] And this statistic doesn't take into account the fact that, over the same period of time, the number of dual-income households increased from less than 50% to more than 60%, and the rise in the cost of housing, health care, and college tuition have outpaced inflation by wide margins[5]: Merely noting the stagnation of household income for the bottom 90% thus masks the much-increased financial burdens borne by middle- and lower-income families. Consequently, most middle- and lower-income U.S. families have experienced either no gain or negative gain in household wealth over the last few decades, with all the considerable gains from overall growth going to upper-income Americans (and almost all of that increase going to the very wealthiest).[6] Life for the middle class has improved in some ways—in the form of greater access to high-tech communication and entertainment devices, for example—but has regressed in terms of financial security and long-term debt burden. Supply-side policy has patently failed to live up to its promises.

Further, small corrections to the supply-side course have not resulted in the negative growth impacts predicted by supply-side theory. Modest federal tax increases for the wealthy under the two post-Reagan Democratic presidents in 1993, 2009, and 2013 were, in each case, met by conservative economists and pundits with predictions of economic downturns. They were instead each followed by extended periods of economic expansion.[7]

And yet, leading conservatives continue to find the key to overall prosperity in reducing the tax burden for the top earners, so as to spur investment and growth. According to former Speaker of the House John Boehner, in 2010: "We've seen over the last 30 years that lower marginal tax rates have led to a growing economy, more employment and more people paying taxes."[8] The conservative economic policy advocacy group The Club for Growth agrees: "Just as Keynesian stimulus has failed every time it has been tried, "supply side" tax cuts have worked every time they have been tried. . . . To stimulate GDP growth, a tax cut has to cut the marginal tax rates upon which the decision makers in the economy base their decisions to work and, above all, to invest."[9]

Is there evidence that tax cuts stimulate GDP growth? Let's look at the actual relationship between top marginal income tax rates and U.S. GDP growth since 1950 (see figure 3.1).[10] Overall, higher income tax

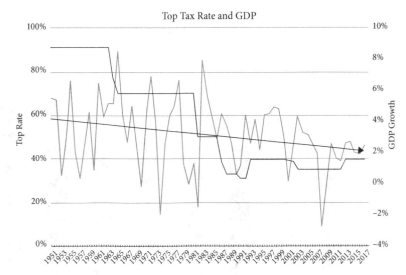

Figure 3.1 Top Marginal Income Tax Rates and U.S. GDP Growth Since 1950

Source: Based on GDP data from the Bureau of Economic Analysis (https://www.bea.gov/data/gdp/gross-domestic-product#gdp), and tax rate data from the Brookings Institution's Tax Policy Center (https://www.taxpolicycenter.org/statistics/historical-highest-marginal-income-tax-rates).

rates are correlated with higher average GDP growth, and lower rates are correlated with lower growth.

Figure 3.2 is another way of visualizing the association between top tax rates and overall growth, covering the period from 1950 through 2017.[11]

This is all mere correlation. It is entirely possible that factors unrelated to supply-side policy have been responsible for lower average growth in low-tax eras. Conservatives blame the recessions and slow growth we have seen over the last thirty-five years on government regulations, wasteful bureaucracy, expensive social programs, excessive demands by labor unions, illegal immigration, tariffs, and/or economic globalization. However, in light of the correlational data, it is utterly obtuse to maintain that cutting taxes on the wealthy has actually been *proven* to be the best way to spur growth.

Recent years have provided two examples of experiments on the effects of supply-side economics that are as close to controlled studies as one

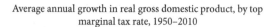

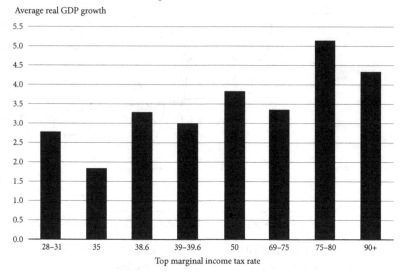

Figure 3.2 Top Tax Rates and Overall Growth, 1950–2017.

Source: Based on GDP data from the Bureau of Economic Analysis (https://www.bea.gov/data/gdp/gross-domestic-product#gdp), and tax rate data from the Brookings Institution's Tax Policy Center (https://www.taxpolicycenter.org/statistics/historical-highest-marginal-income-tax-rates).

could hope for: Kansas and Wisconsin. Each state saw the ascension of a conservative Republican governor and a Republican legislative majority in 2011. Each state immediately began a program of tax cuts for wealthy individuals and businesses, even as public spending benefiting the poor and middle class was cut. New Kansas governor Sam Brownback and the Republican-controlled legislature instituted a steep cut in personal income taxes on the wealthy and eliminated taxes for most Kansas businesses. Brownback himself described this as an "experiment" by which the basic principle of supply-side economics could be proven—namely, that tax cuts stimulate economic growth. He explained, "On taxes, you need to get your overall rates down . . . in my estimation to create growth. And we'll see how it works. We'll have a real-life experiment."[12] As he put it, "My focus is to create a red-state model that allows the Republican ticket to say, 'See we've got a different way, and it works.' "[13]

Subsequently, Kansas and Wisconsin have each lagged badly both regionally and nationally in economic recovery and job growth.[14] Each state has had to make very large spending cuts to balance their respective budgets, as revenues from the growth that was expected did not materialize. Over the same period, Minnesota and California went in the opposite direction: They raised taxes and increased spending, and proceeded to lead the nation in job growth. These sorts of comparisons make it difficult to rationalize the failure of supply-side policies entirely in terms of excessive spending, regulation, or economic globalization and foreign competition.

Tax policy organizations from across the political spectrum agree that the 2017 tax cut for corporations and the wealthy will fail to create enough growth to pay for itself; the most optimistic projections— including those by conservative economists, right-wing think tanks, and Congress' own nonpartisan Joint Committee on Taxation— foresee meager additional growth and an increase of between 1 and 1.5 trillion in new debt over ten years.[15] All these projections were denied by politicians pushing the measure. U.S. unemployment overall is low, but wages haven't budged and quality of life for labor and the middle class continues to degrade.

The high standard of living for the working classes in the highly progressive, socialist democracies of Western Europe and Scandinavia also presents problems for claims about the benefits of low taxes and deregulated financial and employment markets. As psychologist and *Evonomics* columnist Denise Cummings puts it,

> So let us ask the question: Has socialism ever worked? The Prosperity Index measures over 100 countries on 89 economic analysis variables. The top 10 countries on this index in 2015 were Norway, Switzerland, Denmark, New Zealand, Sweden, Canada, Australia, Netherlands, Finland and Ireland. (The United States ranked 11th). What do these countries have in common? They all incorporate generous social programs with capitalist democracies. They confer generous welfare benefits through the redistribution of wealth, yet civil liberties are abundant, and there are few restrictions on the flow of capital or of labor. So it seems that countries that incorporate social programs into their socioeconomic policies do in fact thrive.[16]

(Further, upward mobility in all of these countries is markedly better than in the United States.[17]) One fundamental presumption behind calls for supply-side tax cuts for the wealthy and for corporations seems to be that taxation is a burden rather than an investment. Economic policy expert Ha-Joon Chang recently wrote:

> If tax really were a pure burden, all rich individuals and companies would move to Paraguay or Bulgaria, where the top rate of income tax is 10%. Of course, this does not happen because, in those countries, in return for low tax you get poor public services. . . . Japanese and German companies don't move out of their countries in droves despite some of the highest corporate income tax rates in the world (31% and 30%, respectively) because they get good infrastructure, well-educated workers, strong public support for research and development, and well-functioning administrative and legal systems.[18]

Critics of socialism claim that high-tax and high-regulation economies stifle entrepreneurship and innovation. Writing for *The Atlantic*, Finnish-born journalist Anu Partenen pointed out:

> Sweden has Ikea, H&M, Spotify, and Volvo, to name a few. From Denmark have come Lego, Carlsberg, and one of the world's largest pharmaceutical companies, Novo Nordisk. A Swede and a Dane co-founded the video calling service Skype. The core programming code of Linux—the leading operating system running on the world's servers and supercomputers—was developed by a Finn. The Finnish company Nokia was the world's largest mobile phone maker for more than a decade. And newer players like Finland's Supercell and Rovio, creators of the ubiquitous video games *Clash of Clans* and *Angry Birds*, or Sweden's Mojang, the publisher of the equally popular video game *Minecraft*, are changing the face of online gaming. Nordic countries are well-ranked when it comes to helping facilitate starting a business. At the most basic level, what the Nordic approach does is reduce the risk of starting a company, since basic services such as education and health care are covered for regardless of the fledgling company's fate. In addition, companies themselves

are freed from the burdens of having to offer such services for their
employees at the scale American companies do.[19]

In Sweden, there are twenty new startup businesses per 1000
employees, as opposed to just five in the United States.[20] Swedish entrepreneurship benefited from some targeted tax cuts and deregulation in the 1990s, but entrepreneurs in Sweden have also benefited
greatly from universal access to health care, government-subsidized
child care, and free university.

In 2012, the Library of Congress' nonpartisan Congressional
Research Service produced a report concluding that various cuts to top
tax rates since 1945 have had no positive effect on growth:

> The reduction in the top tax rates appears to be uncorrelated with
> saving, investment and productivity growth. The top tax rates ap-
> pear to have little or no relation to the size of the economic pie.
> However, the top tax rate reductions appear to be associated with
> the increasing concentration of income at the top of the income
> distribution.[21]

In 2015, a report by several International Monetary Fund economists
similarly found that tax policies favoring the wealthy have been counterproductive for growth, and called for an overall focus on policies—
such as laws mandating higher minimum wages—that directly
increase the income share for the poor. The report's analysis of the
results of economic policy in over 150 countries showed that:

> If the income share of the top 20% increases, then GDP growth actu-
> ally declines over the medium term, suggesting that the benefits do
> not trickle down. In contrast, an increase in the income share of the
> bottom 20% is associated with higher GDP growth.[22]

The TV host and former Republican congressman Joe Scarborough
recently was called upon to explain the surprising wave of anti-
establishment populism among working-class Republican primary
voters in the run-up to the 2016 presidential election. Scarborough
described the disconnect between the theory of supply-side economics

and what has actually happened since that theory became politically predominant in the United States:

> The problem with the Republican Party over the past 30 years is they haven't—and I'll say, we haven't—developed a message that appeals to the working class Americans economically in a way that Donald Trump's does. We talk about cutting capital gains taxes that the 10,000 people that in the crowd cheering for Donald Trump, they are never going to get a capital gains cut because it doesn't apply. . . . We talk about getting rid of the death tax. The death tax is not going to impact the 10,000 people in the crowd for Donald Trump. We talk about how great free trade deals are. Those free trade deals never trickle down to those 10,000 people in Donald Trump's rallies. . . . But herein lies the problem with the Republican Party: It never trickles down! Those people in Trump's crowds, those are all the ones that lost the jobs when they get moved to Mexico and elsewhere. The Republican donor class are the ones that got rich off of it because their capital moved overseas and they made higher profits.[23]

Note that Scarborough was a founder of the ultra-conservative, small-government "New Federalist" group in Congress, and had a lifetime 95% rating from the American Conservative Union. He even received awards, while in Congress, from the pro–supply-side, anti-taxation groups Americans for Tax Reform and Citizens Against Government Waste. Bruce Bartlett, a key architect of the successful 1981 Reagan administration push for supply-side tax policy, now says that there is no evidence that tax cuts generally spur growth. Bartlett notes that aggregate real U.S. GDP growth was higher in the high-tax '70s than in the supply-side '80s.[24] Conservative policy expert Henry Olsen laments that "The G.O.P. remains intellectually wedded to dying dogma. The congressional party really wants to do nothing other than cut taxes for businesspeople and the top bracket based on what can only be called religious devotion to supply-side theory."[25]

Low corporate tax rates don't contribute to job growth, either. Profitable companies enjoying particularly low tax burdens in recent years have used their resources to pay dividends, to buy back stock, to increase executive salaries, and to automate production and/or move operations overseas.[26]

Yet none of this has led to any detectable change in view on the part of other conservative political leaders, economists, or pundits. The major Republican candidates for president in 2016 all called for very large tax cuts aimed primarily at the wealthy investor class, coupled with cuts to social welfare programs. Marco Rubio's plan, for example, called for large cuts to income tax rates and for the elimination of "all taxes on capital gains, dividends, interest, and inherited estates."[27] This plan would have reduced tax revenues by about $6.8 trillion dollars over ten years,[28] yet the conservative Tax Foundation claims that, by the end of that period, the positive effects on growth would be so great that the result would be a budget surplus.[29] Donald Trump's campaign initially promised $9.5 trillion in cuts over ten years while, as usual, promising that these cuts would pay for themselves in increased GDP growth.[30] After widespread ridicule of the original plan, his revised plan involved $6.2 trillion in cuts (applying almost entirely to the wealthy and to corporations) over the same period.[31] The 2017 Trump tax bill was more of the same: a massive reduction in taxes to corporations and the wealthy. This reduction is claimed to be "revenue neutral" at worst in the long-term because of the economic growth it will spur. No nonpartisan private or public analysts agree.[32] When it comes to Republican politicians, one possible explanation for this obstinacy is that these policies please their wealthy donors: Regardless of predictions about their effects on overall well-being, supply-side policies directly serve the immediate interests of the wealthy and conversely for demand-side policies. This by itself could provide sufficient motivation to bullshit about the benefits of supply-side economic policies. But this wouldn't explain the ongoing devotion of conservative economists, plus other sophisticated pundits and supporters, to this untenable economic theory.

Any genuine confusion that conservative elites seem to be experiencing over economic data and economic history is more plausibly attributed to motivated reasoning than to ignorance. The evidence distinctly fails to support any notion that conservatives know less about the economy than leftists: A 2011 Pew survey, for example, showed that self-identified Republicans were much more likely than self-identified Democrats to correctly estimate the unemployment rate and to be aware that the United States is running a trade deficit.[33] System justification theory would predict conservative opposition to redistributive economic policies that disrupt the status quo social-economic order by reducing inequality. As we have discussed, this theory detects in ideological conservatives emotional needs for order and structure, and heightened sensitivity to uncertainty and threat; psychologist John Jost and others argue that these traits are closely tied to conservatives finding comforting stability in inegalitarian socioeconomic arrangements:

> Fear, aggression, threat, and pessimism, we propose, may be reciprocally related to the endorsement of inequality. Insofar as inequality seems intrinsically linked to the struggle for dominance, its engagement may exact a price in the form of fear, anxiety, and suspiciousness. Fear, in turn, may be (temporarily) allayed by admitting the reality of threat and preparing to address it by single-mindedly confronting one's foes (real or imaginary) and hence embracing inequality as a social necessity. In summary, then, we argue that fear and uncertainty are centrally linked to the core convictions of political conservatives to resist change and justify inequality, especially to the extent that the status quo breeds inequality.[34]

The theory that conservatives are conservative, in part, *because* of their distinctive attraction to stability and tradition would explain motivated reasoning on the part of conservatives in favor of supply-side economic policies: Supply-side economics, by limiting or eliminating redistributive and regulatory burdens on existing economic elites and their business concerns, serves the status quo economic hierarchy. Political scientist Corey Robin broadly characterizes conservatism—in any social or national context—as an ideology of reactionary hierarchicalism that exists to preserve an existing, inegalitarian socioeconomic order:

> Since the modern era began, men and women in subordinate positions have marched against their superiors. They have gathered under different banners—the labor movement, feminism, abolition, socialism—and shouted different slogans: freedom, equality,

democracy, revolution. In virtually every instance, their superiors have resisted them. That march and démarche of democracy is one of the main stories of modern politics. And it is the second half of that story, the démarche, that drives the development of ideas we call conservative. For that is what conservatism is: a meditation on, and theoretical rendition of, the felt experience of having power, seeing it threatened, and trying to win it back.[35]

Where hierarchicalist conservatives are pro-government, it is mainly with regard to those functions of government that protect property—and social position—via enforcement of contracts, policing, and military defense; they are anti-government where government action counters inegalitarian social and economic arrangements. Economist Paul Krugman argues that the same reactionary essence of conservatism described by Robin lends itself to deep-seated anti-government sentiments, where government is viewed as the avenue for redress of complaints about systemic unfairness and structural inequality:

> Why the dogmatism? Why the rage? And why do these issues go together, with the set of people insisting that climate change is a hoax pretty much the same as the set of people insisting that any attempt at providing universal health insurance must lead to disaster and tyranny? Well, it strikes me that the immovable position in each of these cases is bound up with rejecting any role for government that serves the public interest. If you don't want the government to impose controls or fees on polluters, you want to deny that there is any reason to limit emissions. If you don't want the combination of regulation, mandates and subsidies that is needed to extend coverage to the uninsured, you want to deny that expanding coverage is even possible. And claims about the magical powers of tax cuts are often little more than a mask for the real agenda of crippling government by starving it of revenue.[36]

The system justification story is consistent with the aspect of cultural cognition theory that identifies a kind of cultural-identity group of hierarchical individualists who are attracted a do-it-yourself ethics, and who are dismayed (potentially, to the point of the "rage" Krugman perceives) by redistributive and egalitarian socioeconomic policies. But cultural cognition theorist Dan Kahan would dispute that hierarchical-individualists are different in their fundamental psychology from egalitarian-communitarians. Kahan is adamant that cultural cognition is equal opportunity: Egalitarian-communitarian liberals, he claims, are just as vulnerable to motivated reasoning as are conservatives. They should be expected to exhibit confirmation bias about the benefits of egalitarian demand-side policies. For example, liberals are often criticized by the political right for their knee-jerk opposition to any reductions in certain government programs and subsidies, and to the privatization of various public institutions, despite being unable to present evidence of the superior efficiency of the public sphere in enhancing self-reliance and providing public goods.

Responding to Kahan, pundit Ezra Klein makes a couple of plausible points in defense of an asymmetry between conservative Republicans and liberal Democrats on political economy. Klein agrees with Kahan that motivated cognition is something all individuals are subject to, but notes that decisions with regard to political economy are made not at the individual level but, rather, at the party level.

> A point Kahan makes in his research is that being wrong about policy is costless for most people. "Nothing any ordinary member of the public personally believes about the existence, causes, or likely consequences of global warming will affect the risk that climate changes poses to her, or to anyone or anything she cares about," he writes. But that's not true for political parties—particularly political parties that have to govern. . . . The debt ceiling is a perfect example. Raising the debt ceiling always polls terribly. But the governing party always does it anyway because they know the alternative is worse. Their incentives to get reelected trump their incentives to pander to their base. That's less true for minority parties. They have the luxury of being irresponsible. They can posture against the debt ceiling and complain about the deficit and swear they have a better way to reform health care that they're just not ready to reveal. For them, bad evidence can often lead to good electoral outcomes.[37]

Political party posturing, in turn, affects what identity means to the individual already ideologically allied to a political party. As Klein notes, the Republican Party is much more ideologically monolithic than the Democratic Party. (In 2014, 70% of Republicans identified themselves as "conservative," while only 44% of Democrats identified themselves as "liberal."[38]):

> Another argument here is that the Democratic Party has to face up to the fact that there are fewer liberals in America than conservatives. Surveys consistently show that there are about twice as many self-identified conservatives as self-identified liberals. That might mean that the Republican Party is pulled more towards the groupthink of conservatives than the Democratic Party is towards the groupthink of liberals.

We could certainly point out historical leftist denialism with respect to, say, the promise of communism long after massive inefficiencies in heavily managed economies became evident; liberals more recently are often accused of defending particular government institutions, programs, and/or regulatory schemes in the face of high costs and a lack of proven results. Some of these accusations have undoubtedly been true, and probably some still are. But the overall trend in the United States for over thirty-five years has been toward the tax-cutting, privatizing, deregulating supply-side economic program. There has been no major pushback over this period, even when the Democratic Party has been in power. Note that a major revision to welfare, the Personal Responsibility and Work Opportunity Reconciliation Act, which eliminated the Aid to Families with Dependent Children program and imposed stringent work requirements on welfare, was supported and signed by Democratic president Bill Clinton in 1996, despite bitter opposition by progressive elements in his party; Clinton also signed several major pieces of financial market deregulation into law, notably the Gramm-Leach-Bliley Act and the Commodity Futures Modernization Act. Obama's Affordable Care Act expanded access to medical care in large part by subsidizing private health insurance coverage—a considerable transfer of public funds to private companies, via a strategy originally devised by the conservative Heritage Foundation and promoted in the 1990s by conservatives in Congress. Neither of the two post-Reagan, Democratic presidential administrations has fundamentally challenged the supply-side consensus that superseded the Roosevelt New Deal consensus.

So the ascendancy of supply-side and pro-business thinking makes that approach more salient to the issue of denial in political economics. Further, as we saw with denialism in the face of impact science, a de facto asymmetry can arise when the most salient *economic* data works systematically against a particular ideology. A liberal economist like Krugman can claim—with justification—that the failure of supply-side policies to "raise all boats" over the last thirty-five years is evident. A relatively engaged conservative should have access to enough information at least to question the ongoing conservative supply-side, tax-cutting, financial-deregulation orthodoxy.

Are some conservatives in denial about their favored theory of economic growth? Given the state of the evidence, how else to explain the unshakeable belief on the part of many political and economic sophisticates that overall well-being is always best served by less taxation and less social spending?

3.2   Poverty and the Fundamental Attribution Error

Attraction to stability and hierarchy may play a part in conservative motivated cognition about political economics, as may cultural cognition within an ideologically monolithic political party and its network of supportive media and interest groups. But there are other significant biases that may be even more fundamental, in that they may themselves explain the visceral anti-egalitarian impulses that in turn fuel the rationalizations of economic conservatism.

Consider the famous 2012 remark from presidential candidate Mitt Romney, captured surreptitiously on video as he addressed a group of wealthy donors at a private dinner:

> There are 47 percent of the people who will vote for the president no matter what. All right, there are 47 percent who are with him, who are dependent upon government, who believe that they are victims, who believe that government has a responsibility to care for them,

who believe that they are entitled to health care, to food, to housing, to you name it. That that's an entitlement. And the government should give it to them. . . . These are people who pay no income tax. Forty-seven percent of Americans pay no income tax. So our message of low taxes doesn't connect. And he'll be out there talking about tax cuts for the rich. I mean that's what they sell every four years. And so my job is not to worry about those people—I'll never convince them that they should take personal responsibility and care for their lives.[39]

So individuals representing 47% of the country have issues with irresponsibility and an unwarranted sense of entitlement. This is the reason for their lack of economic success, and this is the reason they will not support the Republicans on their supply-side program of cutting taxes and benefits. Romney's running mate, Paul Ryan, subsequently House Speaker, agreed, and attributed the problem to a culture of dependency:

We have got this tailspin of culture, in our inner cities in particular, of men not working and just generations of men not even thinking about working or learning the value and the culture of work, and so there is a real culture problem here that has to be dealt with.[40]

Heritage Foundation associate Matthew Spalding explains:

Under a culture of dependency, poverty becomes a trap, and recipients get stuck. Long-term welfare recipients lose work habits and job skills and miss out on the marketplace contacts that lead to job opportunities. That's a key reason the government should require welfare recipients to work as much as they can.[41]

In an essay on "The Nature of Poverty" in the *New York Times*, well-known conservative pundit David Brooks explains that "the real barriers to mobility" for those in poverty are not a lack of resources but, rather, "are matters of social psychology, the quality of relationships in a home and a neighborhood that either encourage or discourage responsibility, future-oriented thinking, and practical ambition."[42] In the social sciences, this theory is sometimes referred to as the **deficit theory of poverty**, according to which "poor people are poor because of their own moral and intellectual deficiencies."[43]

Each of the above conservative thinkers is highly educated, in possession of his own research staff, and extremely engaged in the relevant issues. Each, one supposes, must be aware of the fact that most poor people in the United States are either employed or are a family dependent of a working person: The Census Bureau reports that, as of 2011, about two-thirds of the 33 million people living in families below the poverty line had at least one family member working.[44] As Romney noted, about 47% of Americans pay no federal income tax. This is not because they do not work and pay taxes, but because their income is too low for them to be subject to the federal income tax, and/ or they qualify for the Earned Income Tax Credit. Federal income tax (which many of the wealthy mostly avoid because much of their income is investment income) represents only about one-fifth of the total tax burden as a share of income. The working poor pay federal payroll taxes, state and local income taxes, property taxes, sales taxes, utility taxes, and excise taxes. A plurality of the 47% of Americans who pay no income taxes are elderly and on a fixed income.[45] Many of the others are unwillingly unemployed due to lack of opportunity or to disability. The notion that social welfare programs discourage work is not supported by the evidence. A recent study, by Harvard and MIT economists, of direct cash-transfer programs for the poor in seven countries found no evidence of a negative impact on number of people employed or hours worked.[46] The biggest U.S. subsidy for working-age poor adults is the Earned Income Tax Credit, which we know increases work participation substantially.[47] It strains credibility to suggest that these leading political figures, pundits, and members of economic think tanks have never even been exposed to these facts about the working poor, the unemployed, the elderly, and the disabled. Yet opponents of social safety-net policies persist in attributing poverty not to a lack of resources, opportunity, or ability but, rather, to failures of character stemming from membership in a subculture that does not value work.

Sociologists John Levi Martin and Matthew Desmond argue that, in ideological contexts, stereotypes function as a kind of cognitive shortcut.[48] For example, if you believe that "corporations are evil," or

"Black people have a culture of poverty," you know what policies to support without having to examine the details and use complex reasoning. Martin and Desmond cite research supporting the conclusion that the politically sophisticated are even more inclined to work off stereotypes in forming political opinions.[49] Consequently—and paradoxically—the most politically sophisticated are the ones best able to avoid complex reasoning about policy:

> [S]ophisticated ideologues have a world that corresponds to their position in contrast to those of their opponents. In other words, ideology carries with it a sense of the political landscape and the ways persons are situated in it. The politically knowledgeable are, not surprisingly, more likely to think they know the world—even when their knowledge is inaccurate. They are more confident that they know who the average welfare recipient is and are more likely to marshal this "knowledge" in support of their ideological predispositions. . . . This suggests that what political ideology does in terms of orienting citizens to forming policy opinions is not to give them a set of values or images of the good society that can then be used as major premises in syllogistic reasoning. For ideology, like other developed senses-of-place, allows for a switch to a simplistic, top-down form of cognition, and an avoidance of detailed logical reasoning.[50]

As Zaller noted in *The Nature and Origins of Mass Opinion*, political sophistication—far from guaranteeing critical engagement with the issues—can facilitate automatic partisanship, resulting in well-informed citizens "react[ing] mechanically to political ideas based on political cues about their partisan implications."[51] Martin and Desmond suggest that, while the politically sophisticated may be in possession of more information than the unsophisticated, "what sets politically astute ideologies apart from the less astute is not that they know how their values and beliefs should produce opinions, but that they know what to believe given what they value."[52] This conclusion is very much in line with what we see in the social psychology research on motivated reasoning, where greater sophistication is associated with greater confidence in those ideological positions arrived at by motivated cognition. Greater levels of education are very evidently

associated with greater political polarization, including greater negative assessments of adherents of opposing political views.[53]

The deficit theory understanding of why poor people are, or remain,
poor is not limited to elites, however; it is broadly reflected among
Republicans, according to a 2014 Pew survey. When asked which has
more to do with a person being wealthy, 57% of Republicans answered
"Because he or she worked harder than others," versus 32% who
answered "Because he or she had more advantages." When asked which
is more to blame if a person is poor, 51% chose "Lack of effort on his
or her part," versus 32% who chose "Circumstances beyond his or her
control." (Democrats came down even more strongly on the opposite
side for each of these.[54]) Might these results simply be a reflection of
conservatives valuing hard work and self-reliance more than liberals?
Martin and Desmond studied this very question. They found that a
group of people ranging across the political spectrum from "strong liberal" to "strong conservative" demonstrated uniform and enthusiastic
support for the value of "self-reliance." But when members of that same
group were asked why the poor are poor, the strong conservatives were
25 *times* more likely than the strong liberals to select "not working
hard enough" over "lack of education." As we discussed in chapter 1,
the difference between ideologues on this point, as on many others, *is
not a difference in values but a difference in factual beliefs.* Much of the
time, when liberals and conservatives differ on political economy and
the appropriateness of policies directed at helping the poor, they differ
not on how much they value self-reliance but, rather, on how "worthy"
the prospective recipients are. In turn, the assessment of how worthy
someone is depends on one's perception of how much an individual's
success depends on his or her circumstances.[55]

To understand this phenomenon, and how it plays out in politics, we
need to talk about self-serving and group-serving bias, and how these
biases feed on something called the **fundamental attribution error**.

It's easy to discern the potential for self-serving bias as it affects reasoning about political economy. Naturally, those individuals who, for
whatever reason, find themselves in a good (relative) material position
will be motivated to buy into factual claims that would tend to sustain
and justify their accustomed position. One central respect in which
such beliefs are rationalized is through a particular way of interpreting

different relative economic positions. Social psychologist José Duarte and colleagues complain that system justification theorists have uncritically interpreted "endorsement of the efficacy of hard work" as "rationalization of inequality."[56] Psychologists John Chambers and Barry Schlenker argue that endorsement of the efficacy of hard work should be interpreted in terms of a belief in "personal agency" rather than in "meritocracy."[57] Yet it remains the case that it would be difficult for most individuals to feel justified in their superior economic position if they attributed any substantial portion of that difference in position to circumstantial factors. Consider the potential dissonance in believing both that "The system under which I thrive and others do less well is justified" and "Most people who are financially well off under this system are lucky, and most others are victims of undeserved disadvantages." Rationalizing an inegalitarian economic system, while simultaneously maintaining the sense of an overall moral justification for the resulting unequal distribution of goods and resources, *requires* that one represent success and failure under this system as generally due to merit rather than luck. In fact, the language of "meritocracy" (as opposed to "personal agency") is well represented among conservative economic spokespersons: Prominent conservative economist and *New York Times* columnist Tyler Cowen, for example, has claimed that, thanks to technological developments and globalization, our economy has progressed from a meritocracy to a "hyper-meritocracy," where success in wealth creation tracks merit more closely than ever.[58] An economic system the justification of which is tied to overall well-being, and manifests some appropriate level of fairness, simply *must* be one in which success is mainly due to hard work and superior character, and in which failure is due to failure of the individual to exercise the right dispositions, work hard, and make the right choices. This is where the fundamental attribution error (FAE) is so useful in explaining the how and why of motivated reasoning in conservative political economics.

The FAE is the pervasive phenomenon wherein persons, in explaining the behavior of others, tend to *under*estimate the effects of situation or circumstance and *over*estimate the effects of inherent personality traits.[59] Interpreters of others' behavior often seem to act on the egocentric assumption that the situation as they see it is the same one faced by the actor whose behavior they are interpreting, even though there may be unknown situational factors at work.[60] This kind of error is neither surprising nor inexplicable: There are multiple informational, cognitive, and emotional factors weighing in favor of this very form of misattribution. Misattributions are often explained, in part, simply by the fact that one often has little information about the circumstances leading up to others' actions. When I don't return someone else's call, I am able to explain this failure in terms of my having been occupied with something else, or by the fact that my phone battery died. If someone doesn't return my call, I don't typically have any other information to go on, so it is easy to interpret his or her silence in terms of disinterest or hostility. If someone is staggering around, intoxicated in public, a stranger sees a useless bum with no self-control; but people who know him might be aware of his struggles with a recent family tragedy, schizophrenia, or post-traumatic stress. Such slanted attributions often take on a self-serving asymmetry: When the other guy runs a red light, it's because he's an asshole; but when I run a red light, it's because I was in a hurry or because my vision was obstructed. The old expression, "Don't judge a person until you have walked a mile in his or her shoes," is an admonition to take this sort of chronic, self-serving, implicit bias into account.

As we discussed in chapters 1 and 2, there is substantial evidence of broad, cross-situational personality dispositions (as measured, for example, by the OCEAN personality test). We noted that these (learned, cultured, or genetically programmed) dispositions are loosely correlated with political ideology, and as such have some predictive power with regard to accepting or denying certain ideologically charged factual claims. But it would be wildly overstating the case for personality-based explanations of behavior to maintain that internal character traits are the sole determinants of behavior. The results of nearly a century of scientific study have shown that human behavior is not totally determined by internal dispositions, but is also enormously influenced by the individual's situation.[61] Social psychologists Lee Ross and Richard Nisbett showed in their research that, to the extent that we are able successfully to predict others' choices, we often do so by unconsciously taking external circumstances into account—even as we may consciously account for those choices exclusively in terms of internal character traits.[62]

Instinctively attributing others' actions to fixed behavioral traits—like "lazy" or "industrious"—is just another example of the easy, unconscious cognitive shortcuts we so often take (as extensively documented by Daniel Kahneman), like jumping to conclusions from anecdotal evidence or loss-aversive decision-making.[63] Attributing others' behavior to simple, enduring, and cross-situational dispositions versus investigating the circumstances of every decision you are trying to understand saves time and energy.

Emotional needs are likely also a key factor. The expectation of consistency from others can be comforting: It makes your world feel more predictable, which in turn gives you more of a sense of control. Social psychologist Melvin Lerner proposed that the FAE is part of what he called the **just-world phenomenon**: A general desire to see the world as fair and just. When successes and failures are due to situational causes beyond our control, they seem arbitrary; successes and failures owing to disposition, on the other hand, seem deserved. Attributing others' actions to internal factors thus makes the world seem like a fairer—and less threatening—place, where we have control over our destinies so long as we live virtuously and make good decisions.[64] David Woodruff, professor of comparative politics at the London School of Economics, writes,

Early in July, Angela Merkel's party, the CDU, held its "Economy Day." The head of the party's economic council began with a pronouncement. "Economic success is no gift," he said, "rather, it must be earned every day through hard work." I have a name for this kind of thinking: The "theodicy of markets." In the study of religion, theodicy refers to the problem of reconciling the existence of evil with the presence of a god both omnipotent and benevolent. . . . But Max Weber used the term more generally, to refer to a doctrine that explains and justifies good and bad fortune. He wrote: "The fortunate is seldom satisfied with the fact of being fortunate. Beyond this, he needs to know that he has a *right* to his good fortune. He wants to be convinced that he 'deserves' it, and above all, that he deserves it in comparison with others." A theodicy, in Weber's sense, explains why people deserve what they get. A theodicy of markets argues that those who flourish in a market economy deserve to do so. The sentiment expressed above is an example: economic success is no gift—it's deserved, because it results from hard work. Weber's argument—made in the context of religion—is that intellectuals work hard on their theodicies trying to make them logically coherent. The intellectual difficulties they confront drive the development of doctrine and thereby influence action.[65]

As Lerner pointed out, one negative consequence of the just-world phenomenon is the tendency to blame victims for their suffering while overlooking circumstantial or structural factors in bad outcomes. And this brings us back to the self-serving impulse to rationalize the current unequal distribution of goods. This impulse provides a further motivation to uphold the view of the world as fair and just by misattributing poverty in general to bad habits and bad decisions. I tend to attribute my own successes to hard work and good character, and others' successes to good fortune. Conversely, others' failures are the result of bad decisions and failures of character, whereas my failures are due to unfair situations or incidental factors beyond my control. This is how you get former governor and 2016 Republican presidential candidate Jeb Bush, son and grandson of millionaires, arguing that the solution to recent slow economic growth is for working people to work harder. From a 2015 newspaper interview: "People need to work longer hours, and through their productivity gain more income for their families. That's the only way we are going to get out of this rut that we're in."[66] In fact, Americans work longer hours, take less vacation, and retire later than their counterparts anywhere else in the industrialized world.[67] American worker productivity has risen 80% since the 1970s,[68] and U.S. workers are the most productive in the world.[69]

Does Jeb Bush really, truly believe that the main reason for the continuing struggles of the extremely hard-working and uniquely productive American middle class—despite an extended period of overall economic growth—has to do with their not working hard enough? I cannot say. But if he does believe that, then this looks like a case of denial. Bush has many reasons not to believe this claim, while having many reasons to *want* to believe it. The same is true of many well-educated and engaged conservative politicians, economists, pundits, and voters. For the supply-side true believer, the problem *cannot* be conservative economic policy or structural unfairness but, rather, personal failures on the part of individual poor- and middle-class workers. The underlying, universal, self-serving human tendency to engage in the particular sort of confirmation bias represented by the FAE is the foundation for this explanatory strategy.

The parallel here to the climate change denier seems clear. For the person materially and emotionally invested in the fossil fuel industry, in small government, in the maintenance of the current socioeconomic system, and/or in a cultural worldview favoring individualism over collective action, AGW *cannot* be happening. There must be some other explanation for the data, such as the systematic big-government bias of liberal climate scientists. And, just as in the case of science denial, we see some of the most recalcitrant denial regarding the factual bases of political economy among those who are the most knowledgeable and engaged in the issues. We saw that the highest levels of education, science literacy scores, and so on were associated with the highest levels of AGW denial, thanks to an enhanced ability to argue oneself out of being convinced by the evidence. In practice, the effect of having more information seems to be to enable ever more sophisticated motivated reasoning in defense of desired conclusions about factual matters. As we now understand, in ideological contexts reasoning habitually functions as a tool (or weapon) wielded by emotion; the stronger the cognitive and informational resources are, the more effective the rationalizations become. No doubt there is some point where denial becomes untenable for the nondelusional person, as the evidence piles up and the amount of dissonance that has to be overcome in order to maintain a desired conclusion becomes overwhelming. But as we see in the cases of both climate change and the causes of poverty, the dissonance-resolving machinations of those motivated to deny can be impressive.

So does all this mean liberals are more rational than conservatives and pay more attention to evidence, as the liberal pundits claim? No—or, in any event, not entirely. Conservatives could have been right about the causes of and solutions to poverty. In a nearby possible world where human beings responded differently to incentives, or where structural inequalities had less impact on outcomes, supply-side economics might have been successful in producing great results for broad segments of society. Even in this world, the wealthy can be overtaxed and businesses overregulated, and the working classes can be overprotected. As economist Arthur Laffer pointed out, a theoretical top marginal tax rate of 100% would deprive wealthy investors of any economic incentive to earn more past a certain point; a tax cut in that situation would surely increase investment and growth. Large-scale communist societies are notoriously inefficient and require massive centralization of political power in order to administer the strict production controls inherent to the system. Some of Greece's recent problems arguably stemmed from overgenerous rules about benefits; French law limits opening hours for businesses, even in the face of high unemployment and willing prospective workers. Progressive, lefty liberals would probably have their doubts about supply-side economics even if the economic evidence were against them, just as some of them have their doubts about vaccines, fluoridation, nuclear power, and/or genetically engineered food crops in the face of good reasons to pursue those technologies. After all, wouldn't characterizing liberals as being more accuracy-oriented by nature be an example of the FAE? Any liberal advantages on political economy have as much to do with contingent economic facts as they do with some special epistemic virtuousness exhibited by those on the ideological left. You could argue that, like people born rich, liberals just got lucky.

3.3 Classism and Racial Stereotyping

Romney's 47% remark exemplifies not only a self-serving and system-justifying prejudice but also a group-serving classism that extends the denialist justification of economic inequality from the superior merits of the wealthy individual to the superior merits of the entire wealth-controlling economic upper class. As we discussed in chapter 1, one of the most significant emotional factors in ideological belief is the motive to believe that the group or community with which one identifies is inherently superior to others. Human history features innumerable examples of claims to the inherent superiority of some religious, national, geographical, family, caste, cultural/ethnic, racial, or gender identity. One way to satisfy an emotional need to justify one's own place in the existing economic order is to justify the existing economic order generally by reference to the inherent merit and superiority of the entire economic upper class.

Further, members of the upper class in the United States (as in many other countries) have historically shared narrow cultural and racial markers, so identity issues with regard to class have overlapped significantly with cultural and racial identity issues. A study published in 2016 found that, even though U.S. whites and African Americans receive welfare in roughly equal numbers (and many more whites receive food stamps), subjects asked to imagine a generic welfare recipient overwhelmingly imagined someone African American.[70] And, as part of the same study, other subjects were less likely to support welfare for the more African American–looking of a set of composite images, rating that person as less competent, hardworking, and responsible. Expressions of classism are characteristically intertwined with indications of other forms of prejudice and stereotyping; note how the Paul Ryan statement in the previous section—about the poor not valuing work—cites a work ethic deficit in "the inner cities in particular." "Inner city" has functioned as an unsubtle code for "black" since the 1960s, when it was becoming increasingly problematic for public figures to criticize groups under explicit racial designations.[71] (Note also the way Ryan's diagnosis ignored the issue of rural poverty, in addition to the fact that there are more whites in the United States receiving some form of government assistance than nonwhite "inner-city" residents.) Just as with Ronald Reagan's Cadillac-driving "welfare queens," Ryan's "inner city" culture problem and Romney's "47%" were widely interpreted as examples of "dog-whistle" politics, wherein the point is to trigger resentment by reminding the intended audience of shared, negative stereotypes.[72]

Evidence for the fundamental attribution error is paralleled by evidence for what social psychologist Thomas Pettigrew called the "**ultimate attribution error**" (UAE), which refers to a tendency to excuse negative behavior on the part of perceived in-group members by reference to situational factors, but not so for out-group members.[73] In a 2016 survey, American political scientist Michael Tesler found that 58% of whites agreed with the statement that, "over the last few years, average Americans have gotten less than they deserve"; by contrast, only 28%

of whites agreed with the statement that "over the last few years, blacks have gotten less than they deserve."[74] He notes this is part of a vast and easily identifiable pattern of whites viewing poor whites as more deserving than poor blacks. This, according to Tesler, is an example of the UAE: "When whites struggle, their troubles are generally attributed to situational forces (e.g., outsourcing); but when nonwhites struggle, their plight is more often attributed to dispositional traits (i.e., poor work ethic). Consequently, whites are considered 'more deserving' than blacks." Philosopher Sarah-Jane Leslie cites evidence for what she calls the "**supreme attribution error**" (SAE), which refers to the tendency to attribute negative out-group behavior to essential characteristics of groups or cultures, such as when terrorist attacks conducted by Muslims are attributed by some Westerners to a culture of violence (while no such attribution to white Christian culture is made by Americans as a result of mass shootings or acts of domestic terrorism conducted by white Americans like Timothy McVeigh).[75] Poverty in majority-black communities is an issue of innate disposition or culture, whereas poor whites work hard but have been victimized by external circumstances like affirmative action or unfair foreign competition.

As with the professional "merchants of doubt" who are hired to give cover to AGW denial by obfuscating scientific consensus, political and economic elites have their academic and mass-media surrogates whose job it is to create doubt about lower-class work ethic and the effects of economic inequality, and to reinforce the fear of loss of accustomed position on the part of socioeconomic—and racial—system justifiers. A century-long history of social science research has established that "attitudes are acquired through a pattern of complex and cumulative associations."[76] A famous series of infant-conditioning studies (the ethics of which would never pass review today) by early twentieth-century psychologist John Watson "showed that attitudes toward a previously neutral target (e.g., furry rabbit) can be conditioned by associating it with fear-arousing stimuli (e.g., loud noise)."[77] Certain media outlets and public commentators repeatedly stress negative, frightening news reports about people who are poor, nonwhite, and/or immigrants, thereby reinforcing a preexisting status quo bias by associating changes to the white supremacy status quo with threats to person, order, and stability.[78]

The rather glaring problem with blaming poverty primarily on the cultural and moral deficits of those in poverty is that it ignores obvious systemic barriers to achievement faced by the poor. Naturally—and it hardly seems necessary to point this out—children of poor families start out with financial and social network capital deficits that mean fewer opportunities of many different kinds. Existing social welfare programs do not come close to compensating for this starting-line inequality. Growing up in poor neighborhoods means decreased access to quality public schools and other developmental opportunities. Poor children are much more likely to suffer from asthma.[79] Children living in poverty are much more likely to suffer from lead poisoning; it is likely that more than half a million poor American children today have blood lead levels at or above the level known to cause lifelong neurological impairments.[80] Poverty also means worse nutrition and greatly reduced access to health care. These factors help explain how babies born a few miles apart in Chicago can have a sixteen-year gap in life expectancy, and how babies born in a wealthy suburb of Richmond, Virginia, have a life expectancy twenty years greater than babies born in a much poorer neighborhood just five miles away.[81] It is not unusual to find a twenty-year differential in life expectancy between the wealthiest and the poorest counties in the United States; further, the average such gap has been on the increase since 1980.[82]

Large shifts away from industrial manufacturing since the 1970s have been matched by the movement of both jobs and the middle- and upper-middle classes to economically segregated communities and suburbs, where the poor cannot afford to follow. The result has been a concentration of poor Americans in areas with greatly diminished employment opportunities.[83] Public transportation options are typically limited, and affordable child care for parents who want to work is scarce.

The situation is exacerbated for Paul Ryan's "inner-city" (= racial minority) kids. Four out of ten African American children live in poverty, as contrasted with one in ten white children.[84] A public school having a high minority population is strongly correlated with relatively low public investment: The Center for American Progress discovered that, on average, "a 10 percentage point increase in students of color at a school is associated with a decrease in per-pupil spending of $75."[85] Of course, the poor are much less likely to be able to respond to subpar public schools by sending their kids to elite private schools. People with fewer educational opportunities are not in a good position to adjust to labor markets increasingly favoring higher-educated workers.[86]

Policing and law enforcement are disproportionately tougher on African Americans. Unarmed black suspects are twice as likely as whites to be shot by police.[87] (Racial disparities in police shootings have been shown to be unrelated to local, race-specific crime rates.[88]) Although the rate of marijuana use is roughly the same between whites and African Americans, the latter are 3.7 times more likely to be arrested for marijuana possession.[89] Overall, as the NAACP reports, "5 times as many whites are using drugs as African Americans, yet African Americans are sent to prison for drug offenses at 10 times the rate of whites."[90] The infamous "stop-and-frisk" policy in New York City, where officers were empowered to detain and search people at will and without cause, was aimed almost exclusively at nonwhites. In 2011, the NYC police stopped and searched 685,724 people under this policy; of these, 87% were black or Latino, and 9% were white.[91] A report by the U.S. Department of Justice "found that blacks and Hispanics were approximately three times more likely to be searched during a traffic stop than white motorists. African Americans were twice as likely to be arrested and almost four times as likely to experience the use of force during encounters with the police."[92] Racial disparities in policing are matched by systemic racial disparities in sentencing: Prison sentences for black men are, on average, 20% longer than sentences for white men convicted of the same crimes.[93] Significant racial disparity in the application of the death penalty is well documented.[94] The combination of disparities in policing, arrest rates, and sentencing have contributed to the current situation, in which African Americans are incarcerated at nearly six times the rate of whites. The U.S. Bureau of Justice Statistics finds that, under current trends, one in three black men can expect to go to prison during his lifetime.[95]

This level of incarceration in turn contributes to the fact that 67% of African American children are raised in single-parent homes.[96] Children raised in single-parent homes—even after adjusting for factors like economic background and race—have been shown to suffer, on average, a wide range of social, financial, and physical and mental health disadvantages.[97]

Those young people living in poverty who manage to transcend the challenges of broken families, poor educational and economic opportunities, poor health, and a racially biased criminal justice system go on to face substantial challenges in the form of bias in hiring, housing, and credit. In a landmark 2003 study, researchers at the University of Chicago and M.I.T. sent out 5,000 resumes in response to job ads:

> The catch was that the authors manipulated the perception of race via the name of each applicant, with comparable credentials for each racial group. Each resume was randomly assigned either a very white-sounding name (Emily Walsh, Brendan Baker) or a very African-American-sounding name (Lakisha Washington, Jamal Jones). The authors find that applicants with white-sounding names are 50 percent more likely to get called for an initial interview than applicants with African-American-sounding names.[98]

A 2009 study of hiring for entry-level positions found that "black applicants were half as likely as equally qualified whites to receive a callback or job offer," and that "black and Latino applicants with clean backgrounds fared no better than white applicants just released from prison."[99] A 2014 audit of hiring for college graduates found that black applicants needed to have degrees from elite universities in order to receive as many employer responses as otherwise equivalent white candidates from less selective universities, and the positions offered to black candidates were of lower rank.[100]

A large 2013 study by the U.S. Department of Housing and Urban Development comparing the experiences of whites and nonwhites looking to buy a home found that "minority customers were shown fewer available units than whites with similar qualifications. . . . They were also asked more questions about their finances, according to the study, and given fewer offers of help financing a loan."[101] Many studies have shown that African American applicants for small business loans are more likely to have the loan denied,[102] and black-owned businesses are charged higher interest rates on the loans they receive.[103]

These facts help explain why, even equalizing for other factors, having a college degree means more for the wealthy than for the poor: The Brookings Institution found that "college graduates from families with incomes above 185% of the federal poverty level earn 162% more throughout their careers compared with those with just high school diplomas," whereas college graduates from poorer families earn only 91% more than their high school graduate counterparts.[104]

Economic inequality itself, regardless of absolute well-being, may have its own, indirect but significant impacts on opportunity. Inequality has increased greatly over the last few decades. The richest 1% of the U.S. population now controls about 40% of national wealth, while the bottom 80% controls about 7%.[105] This discrepancy results in significant differences in ability to influence the political process in favor of oneself and one's economic class.* Political scientists Martin Gilens and Benjamin Page analyzed the outcomes of 1,779 public policy debates from the last thirty-five years, looking for cases where the policy preferences of affluent Americans differed from those of average and lower-income Americans. They concluded that "economic elites and organized groups representing business interests have substantial independent impacts on U.S. government policy, while average citizens and mass-based interest groups have little or no independent influence."[106] Wealthy individuals and corporations can use lobbying, political contributions, and reciprocal arrangements with lawmakers and regulators to engage in what economists call **rent-seeking**: securing advantageous special treatment in the form of bailouts, targeted tax breaks, subsidies, special regulatory treatment, exemptions from environmental restrictions, protective tariffs on foreign goods, and so on.

It is extremely unlikely that the prominent politicians, pundits, and academics endorsing the deficit theory of poverty somehow have collectively missed these facts. If blaming poverty broadly on individuals

---

* Better voter turnout by the poor would probably be helpful. But the average working poor person, burdened with having two or three jobs, inadequate access to child care, limited transportation options, and a general sense of irrelevance and hopelessness may have a tough time finding either the opportunity or the motivation to vote. Many also lack credentials like a driver's license or the free time to acquire one, so recent voter ID laws disproportionately impact poor voters.

(or their "culture") rather than policy derived entirely from a lack of information, we wouldn't see conservative elites like Ryan, Bush, Brooks, and Cowen embrace the deficit theory. Self-interest, status quo bias, just-world bias, and self- and group-serving classism and racism all contribute to the motivated reasoning that sustains meritocratic claims about the causes of poverty and economic inequality. Use of anecdotal evidence in rationalizing inequality is standard practice: "I pulled myself up by my own bootstraps. The poor just make excuses for their own lack of motivation." This combines two errors. First is the methodological error of extrapolating from anecdotal evidence. Second, such anecdotes are likely to overlook individual and structural advantages that made success possible in a given instance. Confirmation bias in service of rationalizing desired policies is enabled by the nature of economics data, which always leave room for alternate interpretations of otherwise reliable correlations. The underlying human tendency to attribute negative out-group behavior to character (or culture) rather than circumstances—the FAE, the UAE, and the SAE—provides the well-oiled cognitive track to an explanation of outcomes that avoids implicating conservative economic policies in ongoing unequal outcomes for the poor and for racial minorities.

While 68% of Americans think the wealthy should pay more in federal income tax,[107] and 80% are at least somewhat bothered by the notion that the wealthy are not paying their fair share,[108] opposition to social welfare programs is by no means limited to economic elites. Opinion polls vary widely depending on how the issue is described, but by any measure, a large percentage of the lower middle class expresses either skepticism or strong opposition to many such programs.

Why would lower- and middle-class Americans, of all people, reject candidates advocating higher minimum wage laws and better worker protections? Why are they so commonly among the most fervent opponents of social welfare programs? This is the central question of Thomas Frank's book *What's the Matter with Kansas?*, in which he wonders why a state with a large working-class population—as well as a historical tradition of anti-slavery and racial equality attitudes—has become such a reliable "red state" supporter of highly conservative politicians who oppose more egalitarian economic policies. No one likes the prospect of his or her hard-earned tax dollars being spent on lazy, sniveling drug addicts who just want to live off social welfare handouts. But low-income workers are in the best position to see that economic hard times can befall families through no fault of their own. These folks are the ones—unlike the economic elites—who experience firsthand the struggles of the family next door whose breadwinner is bankrupted by medical bills or who loses a job to automation. If anyone should be able to resist the error of attributing all poverty to laziness, it is the low-paid, economically insecure blue-collar, service, or agricultural worker.

Frank's thesis was that political and economic elites have a strategy of targeted messages on, say, abortion or gay marriage, designed to trick socially conservative, low-income voters into supporting politicians whose real priorities center on pushing economic, rather than social, conservatism. Frank's thesis seems to be at least partly contradicted by data on working-class attitudes. In a thorough analysis of twenty years of National Election Survey results, political scientist Larry Bartels found that, "contrary to Frank's account, most of his white working-class voters see themselves as closer to the Democratic Party on social issues like abortion and gender roles but closer to the Republican Party on economic issues."[109] He found that less affluent voters' positions on economic issues generally, and on "government aid to blacks" specifically, has been much more predictive of voting behavior than positions on social issues. Surveys have very clearly indicated that the increasing economic hardships faced by the white working class are manifesting in stronger anti-welfare, anti-immigration, and anti-minority attitudes, thanks to the perception of economic competition between poor/lower-middle-class whites and nonwhites, and to the perception of unjust economic advantages being enjoyed by nonwhites due to government interventions. The recent Public Religion Research Institute's American Values Survey found that about 60% of working-class whites believe that "discrimination against whites is as big a problem today as discrimination against blacks and other minorities."[110] These results were echoed in separate studies from Harvard,[111] Tufts,[112] and the University of Maryland.[113]

This kind of data explains the school of thought that points to racial bias deriving from a kind of status anxiety as explaining low-income, white working-class opposition to a more egalitarian political economics. Low perceived relative social position means a sense of not being in control, and consequently a feeling of vulnerability. System justification theorists have found that individuals under stress exhibit system-justifying tendencies, and this includes greater endorsement of stereotypes.[114] Further, as studies testing **relative deprivation theory** have shown, individuals perceiving their group as relatively deprived—with respect to other groups or just with respect to their past situation—"display greater levels of intergroup antagonism and prejudice."[115] Some Princeton political scientists reviewed studies of the overlap between lower-class white opposition to social programs aimed at lower-class economic advancement and lower-class white racial attitudes. They found broad evidence that this phenomenon can be explained by "psychological responses of out-group aversion" triggered by low-status contexts:

> Low-status settings, defined by low rates of education and employment, expose residents to a daily dose of petty crime, concentrated physical decay and social disorder, such as abandoned buildings, verbal harassment, and public drug consumption. This exposure in turn leads to a constellation of negative psychological states which are experienced by residents: feelings of anxiety and fear, alienation from neighbors, lack of trust in others, and suspicion toward out-groups in general. In settings characterized by general anxiety and fear, anti-black affect may arise because African Americans are a salient target in a racially divided society. The stigma and stresses of living in a low-status environment also may propagate more racial animosity from feelings of relative deprivation. In other words, whites in low-status settings may seek to denigrate out-groups as a means of maintaining their own sense of well-being.[116]

This is just one possible example of the broader phenomenon known as **last-place aversion**, wherein individuals exhibit a distinct aversion to being in last place relative to peers or comparison groups—be it regarding their social position, economic position, or otherwise. Social science research has repeatedly confirmed that "a potential drop in rank creates the greatest disutility for those already near the bottom of the distribution."[117] This may explain why those "making just above the minimum wage are the most likely to oppose its increase," and, in general, why "low-income individuals often oppose redistributive policies that would seem to be in their economic interest."[118] Philosopher Robert Paul Wolff appears to have this sort of idea in mind with his status anxiety interpretation of out-group hostility among the white working class as the civil rights era progressed:

> Thus a new relationship emerged between free and bound, between White and Black, a relationship encapsulated in Jim Crow laws. Whereas previously, White women expected to be served in every way by Black women, now these same women, or their daughters, found it intolerable to be served in department stores by Black clerks, so that for a long time Black women could not find even low-paying service jobs that might bring them into direct contact with Whites. Residential segregation, which of course was impossible under slavery, when slaves had to live close to where they were required to serve Whites, produced a sorting out of the two populations and the creation of all-Black ghettoes. The segregation was officially enforced and written into Federal and State law by means of covenants restricting the sale of properties. During all of this time, it remained the case that poor Whites, exploited and oppressed by White capitalists, could tell themselves that they were free, White and twenty-one, that they were, at the very least, not black. The Civil Rights Movement, launched by African-Americans half a century ago, threatened, and eventually began to break down even these legal, customary, residential, and employment barriers. It was at this time that the old familiar political rhetoric about "working men and women" also began to change. The new rhetoric spoke of "middle-class Americans," which, although no one acknowledged it, was a thinly veiled code for "not Black." As economic pressures mounted on those in the lower half of the income pyramid, Whites wrapped themselves in the oft-reiterated reassurance that at least they did not live in the Inner City (which is to say, Black neighborhoods), that they were "Middle Class." All of the political discourse came to be about the needs, the concerns, the prospects of the Middle Class, which to millions of Americans, whether they could even articulate it, meant "not Black."[119]

This is a classic Marxist "false consciousness" take, according to which it is typical for the working class to be coopted into supporting status quo economic systems that favor the wealthy capitalist class—in this case, by appeals to status itself. Wolff is only the latest to claim that working-class whites often (consciously or unconsciously) choose racial inequality over greater economic opportunity for themselves because of a felt need for self-affirmation. Historically, the cheap and abundant labor supplied by African slaves (and, later, by Jim Crow–era impoverished blacks) had a detrimental effect on white workers' opportunities and salaries. Yet slavery and subsequent social arrangements keeping descendants of slaves in poverty had broad support among working-class whites in much of the country. Why would this be? According to W. E. B. DuBois, even though white lower-class workers "received a low wage they were compensated in part by a sort of public and psychological wage, they were given public deference . . . because they were white. They were admitted freely, with all classes of white people, to public functions. . . . The police were drawn from their ranks, and the courts dependent upon their votes treated them with leniency."[120] Historian David Roediger agrees that "the pleasures of whiteness could function as a 'wage' for white workers. . . . Status and privileges conferred by race could be used to make up for alienating and exploitative class relationships."[121] President Lyndon Johnson saw things just the same way: "If you can convince the lowest white man he's better than the best colored man, he won't notice you're picking his pocket. Hell, give him somebody to look down on, and he'll empty his pockets for you."[122] Jared Bernstein of the Center for Budget and Policy Priorities argues that precisely this manner of exploiting lower-class whites' racial and status anxiety has become key to contemporary conservative political strategy (and fueled the success of Donald Trump): "The core theme of Republican establishment lore has been to demonize not unregulated finance or trade or inequality, but 'the other'—e.g., the immigrant or minority taking your job and claiming unneeded government support."[123] The slogan "Make America Great Again" could be expected to trigger thoughts of loss of relative status (both economic and social) in distressed communities. Living in distressed, racially isolated white communities was highly predictive of support for Trump in 2016.[124] Columnist Jamelle Bouie noted that Trump won the presidential election after running on a supposedly "populist" message, yet his supporters seem unfazed by his having appointed Wall Street bankers and free-trade corporate tycoons to top positions in his administration. His explanation is that Trump's populism is "white populism," driven in part by racialized economic resentment, rather than economic populism itself:

> But Trump won't suffer, and here's why. When Trump railed against "elites," he wasn't decrying the rich and powerful. His appeal was built on the fact of his wealth and power, on his promise to bring that wealth and power to bear on Washington and deliver benefits to the deserving. For Trump, "elites" are defined by the people with whom they sympathize. And in his narrative, they sympathize with the racial adversaries of his supporters: Hispanic immigrants, Muslim Americans, and black protesters. . . . With echoes of George Wallace and Richard Nixon, Trump tied economic pain to a racialized picture of "elites." *Those elites, with their sympathy for the "other," are the reason you are hurting; they are the reason America isn't great.* To elect Trump was to reclaim the country from those elites.[125]

In fact, although Trump did a lot better than Clinton among poor, non–college-educated whites than he did among wealthy, college-educated whites, the negative effect of college education on support for Trump disappears after controlling for racial resentment, resentment of immigrants, and white ethnocentrism.[126] Among white millennials, after controlling for employment status, ideology, location, and other factors, high levels of racial resentment far and away predicted support for Trump.[127] This assessment has been confirmed repeatedly since the election: a large 2017 survey by the Public Religion Research Institute found that white fear of "cultural displacement" explained support for Trump far better than economic status or economic anxiety.[128] A 2018 study published in the *Proceedings of the National Academy of Sciences* indicated that white working class support for Trump was explained not primarily by economic concerns but, rather, by concern over "issues [such as immigration and race-based affirmative action] that threaten white Americans' sense of dominant group status."[129]

In a recent series of studies, social psychologists from the University of North Carolina and Duke University manipulated subjective perceptions of socioeconomic status (SES) in groups of test subjects.[130] What these researchers found, across multiple studies, was that ideological support for redistribution was highly sensitive to SES. Rather than their ideology determining their views about fairness and redistribution, test subjects will conform their ideological views about fairness and redistribution to the situation. What is very pertinent to our question is that perception of SES here is found to depend more on immediate, "local" contrast groups than on how one's situation stacks up, say, nationally or globally. A poor, working-class white person, in other words, may not be unconsciously comparing him- or herself to wealthy whites but, rather, to the poor, working-class black folks across the tracks. Given low perceived relative status, feelings of vulnerability are almost inevitable. Signs of system justification characteristic of threatened populations typically include greater endorsement of racial (and gender) stereotypes and existing de facto racial-economic hierarchies. The racial element was the real key to Trump's "populist" appeal, not any economic element like opposition to economic elites and free trade. Indeed, racist and sexist attitudes correlated with support for Trump far more strongly than economic dissatisfaction.[131]

In an analysis of polling data on public support for government assistance programs, Martin Gilens notes broad support for universal health care, public education, and child care support, and for social welfare programs providing aid to the elderly, but strong opposition to "welfare" per se.[132] He found a robust link between opposition to welfare as such and the perception that people on welfare were not making an effort to support themselves; this perception is prevalent among white Americans, whose implicit notion of a generic welfare recipient is that of an African American,[133] who tend to overestimate the number of blacks on welfare and who attribute poverty to a problem of motivation in "urban," or "black," culture. Philosopher Elizabeth Anderson argues that these attitudes are exacerbated by widespread de facto segregation between racial groups in the United States, which makes both out-group circumstances and individual differences within out-groups harder to appreciate (thereby enabling group-serving confirmation bias, via the UAE and SAE).[134]

A psychological link between racial attitudes and issues of social identity differentiation would not be surprising, given the human propensity to in-group favoritism and out-group hostility. There is a long record of psychological and evolutionary studies of systematic group-level bias against people perceived—for whatever reason— as *other*. According to **realistic group conflict theory**, the instinctive hostility to out-groups is due to the fact that humans evolved under conditions where different groups would compete for critical resources.[135] It is easy to see how humans would go on to develop a default suspicion of those who are perceived as outsiders to their community or coalition, as other groups would so typically present a greater threat—physical and otherwise—to the individual than those with whom one has family ties and/or standing reciprocal arrangements. Researchers have found that those with a measurably greater disposition to "social fear" (i.e., those disposed to react more negatively to unfamiliar persons and social situations) feel more threatened by members of perceived out-groups; this disposition is further associated with support for anti-immigration and pro-segregation political positions.[136] (Perceived) "race" is widely viewed by evolutionary psychologists as significant not in itself but, rather, as a cue to group membership that triggers the generalized threat response leading to in-group favoritism and out-group negativity.[137] **Social identity theory** adds that

> [P]eople are intrinsically motivated to perceive themselves as good, so if they are functioning on the level of the group, they are motivated to perceive their group positively as well. As a result, group members are motivated to differentiate their group from other groups and to maintain a positive image of themselves and their in-groups in comparison to out-groups.[138]

With these two impulses in play—a feeling of competitiveness instinctively directed at perceived out-groups and a self-affirming emotional need to distinguish one's perceived in-group from others as superior—a natural favoritism toward one's own group and a derogatory animosity toward others is to be expected. And this bias is characteristically expressed in terms of self- and group-serving attributional asymmetries precisely along the lines of the FAE, the UAE, and the SAE.

The **contact hypothesis** is the longstanding hypothesis that implicit (and explicit) prejudicial attitudes can change for the better when members of opposing groups come into extended contact with each other in nonthreatening contexts.[139] The idea is that, if out-group hostility and stereotyping go hand-in-hand, then extended, stereotype-undermining contact between groups should eventually ameliorate their in-group/out-group issues.[140] The flip side of this, of course, is the concern that de facto racial, cultural, and/or economic segregation will tend to prolong and/or exacerbate prejudices. Separation breeds perceived "grouping," and grouping breeds motivated cognition about inherent differences. Psychologist David Dunning describes a typical result of research on in-group/out-group attributions:

> Positive behaviors of in-group members are immediately categorized in a broad and abstract way; positive behaviors of out-group members remain concrete and compartmentalized in scope. For example, if shown a cartoon of a person who was helping another, participants characterize the group members as *helpful* but out-group members as *having helped*. The opposite occurs if the behavior is negative. When shown an in-group member hitting another person, respondents describe the in-group member as *hitting* but an out-group member as *being violent*.[141]

The result is negative stereotyping, such as derogatory racial and ethnic stereotyping, that can in turn be deployed as shortcuts in rationalizing policy positions about, say, political economics.

This would explain the strong overlap between class and status attitudes, on the one hand, and racial stereotyping, on the other. (In a well-known essay, philosopher Gilbert Harman expressed the hope that a better understanding of the FAE would mitigate intolerance and ethnic hatred.[142]) Race already is strongly associated with class and relative status. Given existing de facto racial and economic segregation, and natural human inclinations to status quo bias, to just-world bias, to misattributing individual behavior to character or culture, to out-group derogation, and to last-place aversion, it not the least bit surprising to find elites and nonelites alike stereotyping poor minorities and ignoring evidence of structural unfairness, in order to rationalize economic policies that maintain inegalitarian social conditions.

3.4 The Liberty Argument

We would be remiss in neglecting to examine the *other* main argument against egalitarian social welfare policies and in favor of laissez-faire economic policy—namely, the argument that any attempt to regulate the economy so as to better equalize opportunity or to redistribute wealth for the purpose of compensating for a lack of opportunity is an unjust violation of individual liberty. Supply-side economics is only one side of the coin with respect to conservative arguments about political economics. The other major line of reasoning associated with economic conservatives is founded on the premise that everyone has a basic right to individual "liberty," meaning, in this context, that the only legitimate restrictions on individual freedom of action are those that protect others from interference with their freedom of action. Of the 22% of Americans who identify as strong or moderate libertarians, most also identify as "very conservative" or "conservative" (and only 3% as "liberal"); about 45% identify as Republicans, and only 5% as Democrats.[143] The libertarian economic conservative position depends on the conception of the right to own property as a **natural right**, rather than as an artificial or civil right (i.e., the right to own property exists independently of any social agreement, and so confers a moral entitlement that supersedes any civil arrangement), and an **absolute right** (i.e., cannot be outweighed by some other claim, such as a claim to assistance). Consequently, the state cannot have the moral authority to seize property via taxation except for the purpose of protecting it (i.e., through policing and national defense, in addition to providing ways of adjudicating civil disputes over property). According to this view, the presumption should be that state taxation on income for the purposes of redistribution or equalization of opportunity is unjust taking of individual property. I will refer to this position as **property-rights libertarianism.**[*] The property-rights libertarian often also coincidentally agrees with the economic conservative that a free market capitalist economy is the most efficient at providing individuals with the best opportunity to achieve their goals. But this is not what makes such a system the most just: The fundamental problem with taxes, regulation, and social spending is not that it is inefficient as a way of promoting collective and individual goals, but rather that all state interventions involve morally illegitimate violations of individual rights to life, liberty, and property, unless themselves directed at protection of life, liberty, and property. It just so happens that the factual claims libertarian conservatives make about economics are almost exactly the same as the claims of supply-side economic conservatives. Consequently, each group exhibits heavily overlapping positions on political economy: minimal taxation, minimal regulation of business, and minimization of—or elimination of—state spending for social welfare.

My thesis here is that this similarity in results is no coincidence: Property-rights libertarianism, like supply-side economics, is fundamentally a vehicle for the rationalization of self-interest, racism, and status quo classism. Demonstrating this requires first an extended explanation of the poverty of the philosophical foundations of property-rights libertarianism.

Ronald Reagan described his own political philosophy along these lines: "The basis of conservatism is a desire for less government interference or less centralized authority or more individual freedom and this is a pretty general description also of what libertarianism is."[144] Libertarians cite, among others, editor and activist Frank

---

[*] I use the term "property-rights libertarian" for the libertarian conservative, instead of just "libertarian," to distinguish this ideological position from that of "left-libertarians"; left-libertarians share a presumption in favor of noninterference with individual pursuits, but also recognize the essentially shared status of naturally occurring resources. Left-libertarians overlap with property-rights libertarians on social issues like drug decriminalization, regulations on private sexual behavior, etc.; but for left-libertarians property rights are artificial civil conventions and do not supersede a right to opportunity and a fair share of social product. In practical terms, this puts them on the opposite side of the political economics spectrum. See, for example, Hillel Steiner, "Land, Liberty, and the Early Herbert Spencer," *History of Political Thought* 3 (1983), pp. 515–533; and Steiner's *An Essay on Rights* (New Jersey: Wiley-Blackwell, 1994).

Chodorov in explicating their ideology, and its implications for political economy:

> On this question of morality there are two positions, and never the twain will meet. Those who hold that political institutions stem from "the nature of man," thus enjoying vicarious divinity, or those who pronounce the state the keystone of social integrations, can find no quarrel with taxation per se; the state's taking of property is justified by its being or its beneficial office. On the other hand, those who hold to the primacy of the individual, whose very existence is his claim to inalienable rights, lean to the position that in the compulsory collection of dues and charges the state is merely exercising power, without regard to morals.[145]

Law professor and pundit Andrew Napolitano agrees:

> [J]ust as we don't have the power to take our neighbor's property and distribute it against his will, we lack the ability to give that power to the government. Stated differently, just as you lack the moral and legal ability to take my property, you cannot authorize the government to do so. Here's an example you've heard before. You're sitting at home at night, and there's a knock at the door. You open the door, and a guy with a gun pointed at you says: "Give me your money. I want to give it away to the less fortunate." You think he's dangerous and crazy, so you call the police. Then you find out he *is* the police, there to collect your taxes.[146]

The property-rights libertarian's position originates in philosopher John Locke's monumental *Second Treatise of Civil Government*. Private property rights, Locke argues, are natural, in that rightful moral claims to property in land and other resources can be established in the "State of Nature"—that is, in the absence of civil society or social conventions, and without the consent of others. The right to remove land and other resources from the commons—to deprive others of the opportunity to make use of those resources—derives from labor and from the value that labor can add to those resources. (The classic example is the productive value added to a piece of arable land when it is cleared, plowed, and cultivated for food crops.) Once appropriated, resources may be sold, traded, or bequeathed without restriction. These property rights are fundamental, and they derive from the individual right to life. As Austrian economist Ludwig von Mises puts it:

> If we assume that the individual has an indisputable right to life, we must concede that he has a similar right to the enjoyment of the products of his labor. This we call a property right. The absolute right to property follows from the original right to life because one without the other is meaningless; the means to life must be identified with life itself.[147]

For Locke and his philosophical followers, the origin and proper function of civil government is to mediate disputes between people about otherwise justly claimed property, and to create a legal system of mutual protection against each other (humans being naturally partial to their own cause). Any taxation on the part of the government for the purpose of social welfare, and any regulation of consensual economic transfers between individuals, is a prima facie violation of natural property rights. The economic conservative and the libertarian conservative are natural allies in the sphere of political economy—so much so that their stated rationales for small government often are combined and treated as complementary. The main text of the 2012 Republican Party platform begins with a passage that alludes both to supply-side economic theory and to the distinct goal of "independence from government" in accounting for the party's support for small government and its opposition to redistributive programs:

> We are the party of maximum economic freedom and the prosperity freedom makes possible. Prosperity is the product of self-discipline, work, savings, and investment by individual Americans, but it is not an end in itself. Prosperity provides the means by which individuals and families can maintain their independence from government, raise their children by their own values, practice their faith, and build communities of self-reliant neighbors.[148]

There are two glaring problems with the property-rights libertarian's argument in support of an economic order in which property rights are natural and absolute. The first has to do with freedom and libertarianism's own moral foundations; the second has to do with the provision of public goods.

First, in a world of limited resources, the notion of natural and absolute property rights is fundamentally and inescapably incompatible with the libertarian's acknowledged duty to respect others' equal right to liberty. Political philosopher Herbert Spencer's 1851 text *Social Statics* includes a potent argument for this point. Spencer agrees with the libertarian that individual liberty is basic, and a moral right. And he agrees that, from this premise, it follows that no one may act in such a way as to infringe upon others' freedom. Yet he draws a very different conclusion about property rights:

> Given a race of beings having like claims to pursue the objects of their desires—given a world adapted to the gratification of those desires— a world into which such beings are similarly born, and it unavoidably follows that they have equal rights to the use of this world. For if each of them "has freedom to do all that he wills provided he infringes not the equal freedom of any other," then each of them is free to use the earth for the satisfaction of his wants, provided he allows all others the same liberty. And conversely, it is manifest that no one, or part of them, may use the earth in such a way as to prevent the rest from similarly using it; seeing that to do this is to assume greater freedom than the rest, and consequently to break the law.[149]

From this principle, it follows that property rights of all but a limited and conditional sort are incompatible with respect for individual liberty:

> Equity, therefore, does not permit property in land. For if one portion of the earth's surface may justly become the possession of an individual, and may be held by him for his sole use and benefit, as a thing to which he has an exclusive right, then other portions of the earth's surface may be so held; and eventually the whole of the earth's surface may be so held; and our planet may thus lapse altogether into private hands. Observe now the dilemma to which this leads. Supposing the entire habitable globe to be so enclosed, it follows that

if the landowners have a valid right to its surface, all who are not landowners, have no right at all to its surface. Hence, such can exist on the earth by sufferance only. They are all trespassers. Save by the permission of the lords of the soil, they can have no room for the soles of their feet. Nay, should the others think fit to deny them a resting-place, these landless men might equitably be expelled from the earth altogether. If, then, the assumption that land can be held as property, involves that the whole globe may become the private domain of a part of its inhabitants; and if, by consequence, the rest of its inhabitants can then exercise their faculties—can then exist even—only by consent of the landowners; it is manifest, that an exclusive possession of the soil necessitates an infringement of the law of equal freedom. For, men who cannot "live and move and have their being" without the leave of others, cannot be equally free with those others.

Any claim to private property represents a taking that limits others' opportunities: Any removal of resources—land, trees, coal, lithium, and so on—from the commons means others have lost the opportunity to make use of those very materials. In a world of infinite bounty of all things, this would not infringe on individual liberty. But in a world of limited resources, the institution of unrestricted private property would allow, in principle, for the privatization of all natural resources, leaving the property-less—many just having had the bad fortune to not be the first on the scene—utterly at the mercy of their landlords.

The Lockean notion that "mixing one's labor" with natural resources (thereby increasing their value) gives one a title to ownership is incompatible with the principle of equal liberty as a moral right. In a riveting passage, Spencer imagines a dialogue with a hypothetical Lockean pioneer—someone who has come across unclaimed land and cleared and cultivated it, thereby (according to Lockean principles) gaining a permanent property right to the land without requiring any sort of consent from society:

> Now I want to understand how, by exterminating one set of plants, and making the soil bear another set in their place, you have constituted yourself lord of this soil for all succeeding time.

Oh, those natural products which I destroyed were of little or no use; whereas I caused the earth to bring forth things good for food—things that help to give life and happiness.

Still you have not shown why such a process makes the portion of earth you have so modified yours. What is it that you have done? You have turned over the soil to a few inches in depth with a spade or a plough; you have scattered over this prepared surface a few seeds; and you have gathered the fruits which the sun, rain, and air, helped the soil to produce. Just tell me, if you please, by what magic have these acts made you sole owner of that vast mass of matter, having for its base the surface of your estate, and for its apex the centre of the globe? All of which it appears you would monopolise to yourself and your descendants for ever.

Well, if it isn't mine, whose is it? I have dispossessed nobody. When I crossed the Mississippi yonder, I found nothing but the silent woods. If some one else had settled here, and made this clearing, he would have had as good a right to the location as I have. I have done nothing but what any other person was at liberty to do had he come before me. Whilst they were unreclaimed, these lands belonged to all men—as much to one as to another—and they are now mine simply because I was the first to discover and improve them.

You say truly, when you say that "whilst they were unreclaimed these lands belonged to all men." And it is my duty to tell you that they belong to all men still; and that your "improvements" as you call them, cannot vitiate the claim of all men. You may plough and harrow, and sow and reap; you may turn over the soil as often as you like; but all your maltipulations will fail to make that soil yours, which was not yours to begin with. Let me put a case. Suppose now that in the course of your wanderings you come upon an empty house, which in spite of its dilapidated state takes your fancy; suppose that with the intention of making it your abode you expend much time and trouble in repairing it—that you paint and paper, and whitewash, and at considerable cost bring it into a habitable state. Suppose further, that on some fatal day a stranger is announced, who turns out to be the heir to whom this house has been bequeathed; and that this professed heir is prepared with all the necessary proofs of his identity: what becomes of your improvements? Do they give you a valid title to the house? Do they quash the title of the original claimant?

No.

Neither then do your pioneering operations give you a valid title to this land. Neither do they quash the title of its original claimants—the human race.

Whether the Earth was created by God or by accident, no human person is responsible for the existence of the basic materials necessary to generate wealth. Any appropriation of, say, a parcel of land, immediately constitutes a restriction on the freedom and opportunity of others, in that all others are now unable to make use of that parcel of land. And, by extension, any *system* of private property rights restricts the opportunities of others. Once the commons has been mostly or fully privatized, regardless of other side benefits they may enjoy from production and economic activity, the majority of humankind will not have the opportunities the owners have had: In the absence of any state intervention, they will work for the owners, or borrow from the owners, on the owners' terms or else die.

Elizabeth Anderson argues that the most important libertarian rationale for a more egalitarian approach is not so much equalizing for all kinds of bad fortune (and, potentially, bad choices) as it is the need to guarantee to "all law-abiding citizens effective access to the social conditions of their freedom at all times."[150] The point is not to compensate for all undeserved inequalities but, rather, for individuals and institutions to recognize the right of all in a democratic society to function as equals—not in terms of results, but in terms of *access* to the means necessary to function as a human being and as an equal member of political society.[151] Either way, however, the concept of unrestricted natural property rights as the fundamental expression of liberty is inconsistent with respect for individual liberty.

One way of understanding this problem for the property-rights libertarian is that his or her ideology focuses exclusively on **negative rights**. A negative right is a right to not be interfered with, such as one's right not to be murdered. For the libertarian conservative, the very nature of a right to property, however that property was (allegedly) justly acquired (say, by Lockean appropriation through labor or by inheritance), is that of a right to noninterference—namely, a right that one's property not be unjustly confiscated or trespassed upon—and nothing more. Libertarian conservatives do not—and cannot—recognize positive rights to resources; otherwise, so long as some individual or group can show that he or she or the group has suffered some inequality of opportunity, any state-mandated redistributive scheme is on the table.

The imposition of a system of negative (and exclusively negative) property rights entails continual and massive inference with the freedom of the majority of the people to make use of the world around them. The property-less, would-be entrepreneur will not be able to mine for coal or plant an apple orchard without becoming indebted to some owner of capital under terms set by that owner. A person standing on a patch of land, surrounded by private property, cannot even walk in any direction without being justly arrested for trespassing. When all the forests have been privatized, a child born into the world to a poor family cannot even go for a walk in the woods, nor can she ever see the ocean, after all the property near the coast has been claimed. How does a philosophy that places personal liberty above all else reconcile the dissonance between valuing personal freedom of action and endorsing a system that places the public sphere entirely at service to the private? Individuals under a property-rights libertarian, free-market scheme are guaranteed a kind of formal freedom *not to be interfered with*, but many—even most—will lack *substantive self-determination*; that is, they will lack the resources actually to pursue their goals without living at the service of others.[152] The freedom to choose between starvation and indebtedness, or low-wage employment at the pleasure of the owners of the means of production, is not a substitute for the kind of liberty that is enjoyed by the wealthy property owner in a free-market society.

What is the property-rights libertarian's answer to this conundrum? The libertarian's standard answer rests heavily on the assumptions of supply-side economics. Implicitly—and often explicitly—in the rationalization of property-rights libertarianism one finds the claim that a free-market society upholding natural, negative, and absolute property rights will be so productive that jobs will be plentiful, and wages accordingly so high, that any industrious, entrepreneurial individual will have the capacity to accumulate capital and achieve substantive independence. This is the message of the Republican Party platform, quoted earlier.

The acceptability of this answer depends entirely on the real-world evidence for the trickle-down effect claimed by supply-side economics. As we have seen, the evidence is not good at all. Even if the evidence were better, that theory doesn't account for discrimination, disability, or plain bad luck. The prioritizing of property rights over all else removes any guarantee of access to a minimum of goods to ensure equal participation in democratic life. Things are actually even worse here for the property-rights libertarian conservative than for the supply-side economic conservative. Unless the trickle down of wealth and opportunity is not only likely but also *guaranteed*, libertarian conservatism still allows, in principle, the otherwise-deserving individual to have no substantive self-determination whatsoever. And the possibility of this scenario under a libertarian conservative regime vitiates the entire rationale for libertarianism—that is, the maximization of individual freedom.

One possible response from the hardline property-rights conservative is that a laissez-faire economic system will have winners and losers, and that life just isn't fair sometimes. Libertarian conservative economist Milton Friedman notably spoke of the "lottery of life" in his book *Capitalism and Freedom*. He describes the case of a "Robinson Crusoe" who happens to land on a rich and fertile island, as compared to some other castaways who land on poor, infertile ones. The fortunate Robinson Crusoe, he argues, is under no obligation to share with the less fortunate. He just got lucky, and that's just too bad for the others. Comparing outcomes of a free-market capitalist system to the results of a lottery is to abandon the claim that capitalism necessarily or characteristically rewards merit or that it is justified by productivity and the trickle-down effect. Friedman here is essentially conceding that, under free-market capitalism, mere circumstance can be the difference between belonging to the haves or to the have-nots—between having or not having substantive self-determination. Even so, he argues, the negative right to noninterference trumps others' claims to equal opportunity. (As a supply-sider, he also opposes compensating for bad luck in the lottery of life because of the harm higher taxes and social welfare do to the economy.)

Friedman's answer is oddly mercenary, and self-undermining from a moral standpoint. Why shouldn't the property-less masses respond to the "life isn't fair" argument by revolting against their landlords and seizing what they want? The former property holders can hardly turn around and complain about how "unfair" this seizure is. But more to the point, the great political philosopher John Rawls finds Friedman's argument about life's inherent unfairness quite irrelevant:

> We may reject the contention that the ordering of institutions is always defective because the distribution of natural talents and the contingencies of social circumstance are unjust, and this injustice must inevitably carry over to human arrangements. Occasionally this reflection is offered as an excuse for ignoring injustice, as if the refusal to acquiesce in injustice is on a par with being unable to accept death. The natural distribution is neither just nor unjust; nor is it unjust that persons are born into society at some particular position. These are simply natural facts. What is just and unjust is the way that institutions deal with these facts.[153]

No one is claiming that life itself is, or can be, fair: Fairness and justice are concepts that govern human institutions (like the institution of private property), not life itself.

Spencer agrees that no one should be expelled from his or her holdings without being compensated for the product he or she has created through labor and entrepreneurship.[154] It is consistent with the principle of equal liberty for persons to be able to "lease" property from "society" and profit from their labor, but such tenants would justly owe society for the use of humanity's common property and owe a portion of their product as compensation for the fact that others' opportunities to pursue their own goals are curtailed under a system of legal, exclusive resource exploitation. (The effect of present resource exploitation on future generations is a whole other question, and likely requires some pretty massive restrictions on such exploitation in order to not violate the rights of our descendants. The conviction that we will somehow "solve" environmental degradation and resource shortages with technological advances, like geoengineering or fusion power, is probably a good example of self-serving denial, or at least wishful thinking.)

This issue should be of obvious concern to those who value freedom over all else. How can the property-rights libertarian reconcile his or her commitment to freedom with his or her commitment to a system of ownership and inequality that by its very nature restricts the freedom of others? The only way to ignore the injustice of a strict property-rights regime is to pretend one's own control of limited resources, and the consequent decrease in opportunities for others, is a product *purely* of hard work and character—and vice versa for those who have less property and less freedom. But there is no way to get luck out of the equation. Suppose we start with a clean slate, and we eliminate all current holdings (the full history of the current distribution of property, no doubt, includes innumerable cases of improper acquisition by force or fraud[155]); now everyone goes to the starting line and is cut loose to go out and appropriate resources by labor, like a giant Oklahoma Land Rush. Suppose, further, that we ignore the inherent unfairness of how this process would be affected by inequality in natural abilities and disabilities. Even if the distribution that results is just, what happens to the next generation? As a result of this prior appropriation, future generations will be divided into powerful heirs and powerless peons. Spencer asks, even if we figure out a fair and equal way to allocate hitherto unclaimed resources:

> [L]et us inquire who are to be the allottees. Shall adult males, and all who have reached twenty-one on a specified day, be the fortunate individuals? If so, what is to be done with those who come of age on the morrow? Is it proposed that each man, woman, and child, shall have a section? If so, what becomes of all who are to be born next year? And what will be the fate of those whose fathers sell their estates and squander the proceeds? These portionless ones must constitute a class already described as having no right to a resting-place on earth—as living by the sufferance of their fellow men—as being practically serfs. And the existence of such a class is wholly at variance with the law of equal freedom.

If freedom is the arbiter of justice, the overall productivity of a free-market system (which even Marx wouldn't deny[156]) can't absolve capitalism of this inequality of opportunity. Even in the wildly hypothetical case of a "fair" initial apportionment, there is no way to eliminate unfair circumstance from a system where property rights are basic rights, rather than conditional civil rights. The only way to sustain a liber-tarian commitment to a laissez-faire economic system, and the conse-quent unequal socioeconomic order, is by denying this fact and blindly (and self-servingly) insisting that whatever results you see from a free-market system are ultimately (i.e., at the point of initial appropriation) the product of individual merit—of "human capital"—rather than circumstance. You must further deny the implications of any system of natural property rights on the liberty of future generations, the un-lucky, the disabled, and the victims of discrimination.

If you are committed to prioritizing freedom of action, your only choices are to deny any rightful claims to property whatsoever, or to allow that any system of property rights must be accompanied by a system wherein taxation on income from property is used to compen-sate the less fortunate for the impoverishment of their opportunities actuated by society's recognition of private property claims. John Rawls proposes that society be guided by two principles of justice: first, equality with regard to all basic rights and duties; and second—recognizing that the right to property can only be understood as an ar-tificial social convention, not as a natural right—all inequalities in the distribution of wealth should benefit everyone, especially the least for-tunate.[157] Many inequalities are beneficial: Special access to resources can result in innovation, greater efficiency in productivity, and the de-velopment of useful specialists like teachers and doctors.

This point leads us to the second glaring problem with the property-rights libertarian's argument: It ignores the problem of **public goods**, and the importance of the collective provision of public goods to eco-nomic production and individual success.

Laissez-faire capitalism is great at incentivizing the production of **private goods**, like toasters, melons, and automobiles. Such goods are "private" because their use can be restricted, and the use of a pri-vate good by one person limits use of the same good by others. But a thriving entrepreneurial, capitalist economy requires solutions to a large number of huge problems known in the economic and social sci-ences as "public goods problems."[158] Public goods are goods that are relatively "non-excludable" (persons cannot easily be excluded from enjoying them) and "non-rivalrous" (use by one does not preclude use by others). For example, a lighthouse's signal cannot be restricted just to ships belonging to the lighthouse builder, and use of the lighthouse signal by some does not reduce its utility to others. A shipping magnate might have the incentive to unilaterally pay for building a lighthouse despite these facts. But most public goods either cannot be produced by individuals working alone or are such that (because of their non-excludability) no individuals working alone would ordinarily have the incentive to provide them unilaterally. Thus, we have the corollary concept of **market failure**, which is the failure of market incentives alone to produce public goods. Examples of public goods, the provision of which is either unlikely or impossible without some sort of collective, coordinated action, include national defense, policing, and a judicial system; breathable air and a stable climate; sewage systems and a potable water distribution system; transportation and communication infrastructure; and a system of public education. "Information goods" like scientific discoveries and technological developments—exploited in the production of private goods—often require expensive basic research programs with no immediate practical application; research in the context of publicly funded facilities and academic institutions have contributed greatly to technological innovation and economic prosperity. Modern capitalism—and individual entrepreneurs—can thrive only in a context where these and other public goods have been provided. In fact, in many respects, wealthy and successful owners of the means of production are more dependent on these goods than are the working classes: They have more property to protect; their use of infrastructure and information goods is greater; and their businesses rely on educated, healthy workers. The collectivist argument for a political ideology that balances property rights against the social contribution to individual success rests on the public goods issue. The productivity of a market economy with regard to private goods, cited by property-rights libertarians and supply-siders alike in defending property rights, is impossible without massive social cooperation in the provision of public goods. As Elizabeth Anderson puts it, we are not "a system of self-sufficient Robinson Crusoes, producing everything all by themselves until the point of trade."[159] Because individuals have neither the ability nor the incentive to solve public goods issues themselves, modern states collect taxes and mobilize the population to provide and maintain these goods. To the extent that the ideology of libertarian conservatism either ignores or massively discounts this essential public role in modern capitalism, that worldview is simply indefensible. U.S. Senator Elizabeth Warren was recorded making just this argument during a campaign event:

> There is nobody in this country who got rich on their own. Nobody. You built a factory out there—good for you. But I want to be clear. You moved your goods to market on roads the rest of us paid for. You hired workers the rest of us paid to educate. You were safe in your factory because of police forces and fire forces that the rest of us paid for. You didn't have to worry that marauding bands would come and seize everything at your factory.... Now look. You built a factory and it turned into something terrific or a great idea—God bless! Keep a hunk of it. But part of the underlying social contract is you take a hunk of that and pay forward for the next kid who comes along.[160]

Outside of this example, it is difficult to find major public figures in the United States making this rather obvious point about the link between production and public goods. The relative avoidance of this argument on the part of the American political left is likely due to the disastrous twentieth-century experiments in large-scale communist regimes and their lingering effects on collectivism's reputation—communism being a way of taking the collectivist point about prosperity as a social product to radical and disruptive extremes.

No doubt the American heritage as a nation largely under the control of the descendants of entrepreneurial immigrants has also contributed to a certain emphasis on individualism as a fundamental value and on individual effort as the predominant explanation for success. In modern times, collectivism only achieved a temporary ascendancy in the United States in the context of an economic catastrophe (the Great Depression), followed by a need for collective mobilization in the face of external threat (World War II).

Note how, in the Republican Party platform cited earlier, the party states that "prosperity is the product of self-discipline, work, savings, and investment by individual Americans." In accounting for prosperity, it does not mention the collective provision of public goods; neither does it mention the effects of inherited poverty versus inherited access to capital; ability versus disability; or race, gender, and sexual-orientation discrimination. There is lots of room to have legitimate differences of opinion as to just *how much* of one's success is due to social product, how much is due to luck or unfair treatment, and how much is due to individual hard work and risk-taking. But the fact that both access to capital and collective social cooperation are necessary to individual success is indisputable. To sincerely deny such facts altogether requires either a grave misunderstanding of how the economy works or motivated reasoning about how the economy works. Some sophisticated and well-informed property-rights libertarians do indeed appear to deny these facts; it is difficult to interpret such denials as deriving from ignorance, and therefore devoid of some motivated self-deception.

Spencer was correct in pointing out how odd is the notion that some expenditure of effort should give one—and one's descendants—an eternal, exclusive claim to some part of the Earth. However, it is an extreme step to go from that to his recommendation that all property claims in anything but the direct fruits of one's labor should be abolished. There are many incentives that derive from granting conditional ownership rights to resources. There is a strong incentive to benefit one's family and children by investing and building for the future; this process depends importantly on the sense of security and permanence that property ownership engenders. The liberal (or democratic socialist) just adds that the role of circumstance, and the right to equal access to political institutions, needs also to be taken into account, as does the collective contribution to the provision of those public goods necessary to growth. A progressive scheme that provides economic regulation, social insurance, and opportunity to all, while still allowing for property rights, investment, and risk-taking for personal gain, acknowledges the obligations of fairness and the social contribution to prosperity, while also recognizing the benefits of market incentives.

The *Annals of Congress* describes James Madison as having stated, in a 1794 speech to Congress, "that he could not undertake to lay his finger on that article in the Federal Constitution which granted a right of Congress of expending, on objects of benevolence, the money of their constituents."[161] Madison was correct on this point, but this observation is of no relevance to the issue of taxation or regulation for the purpose of social welfare and opportunity. As we have seen, the

repudiation of property-rights libertarianism requires neither the existence of a general duty of benevolence nor the authority on the part
of the state to engage in charitable activities.

A standard answer on the part of the libertarian conservative is
to refer to the reasoning of economist and libertarian hero Friedrich
Hayek in his *Road to Serfdom*.[162] There he argued that any concession
to the notion of a right to well-being, or fair shares to resources, places
society on a slippery slope to a coercive, centrally planned economy.
The ability to manipulate economic life in order to guarantee equitable
outcomes, he argued, requires absolute political power over the lives
of all citizens. The ineluctable result of socialism, in other words, is
totalitarianism. Hayek's warning—issued in 1944 in the face of both
National Socialism and Stalinism—has been decisively refuted by
history. The post-World War II social democracies of Western and
Northern Europe, Japan, and Canada have remained obstinately free
and democratic, despite their generous social welfare and social insurance programs, their extensive regulations on business, and their relatively high effective taxation rates for the wealthy. The contemporary
libertarian obsession with communism denies this history, just as bla-
tantly as the Turkish government denies the Armenian genocide.

Progressive state redistribution is not benevolence, but as Elizabeth
Warren puts it, part of the "social contract" that makes legal protection
of a (limited) right to private property permissible. The following four
facts are indisputable: (a) The Earth and its limited resources are not the
creation of any person or persons, and any removal of resources from
this commons impinges to some degree on the free pursuit of happiness
on the part of others; (b) mere circumstance plays some substantial role
in unequal opportunity in a laissez-faire economic system; (c) the alleged trickle-down effect of supply-side economic policy does not, in
actual practice, make up for this inequality of opportunity; and (d) the
economic prosperity achievable via capitalism is dependent on the provision of public goods requiring collective action to achieve. Together,
these four facts mean that, in a capitalist system, those with fewer
opportunities are *owed compensation* by the more fortunate. That some
of the beneficiaries of free-market capitalism would sincerely dispute
these facts is no more surprising than that some oil company executives
sincerely dispute the existence and causes of global warming.

A democratic political process can and should include data-driven negotiations on *the degree to which* privatization of natural resources negatively impacts others in terms of self-determination, on *the degree to which* it positively impacts others in terms of self-determination, on *the degree to which* prosperity depends on collective action, on *the degree to which* success is due to hard work vs. circumstance, on *the degree to which* economic inequality undermines effective political participation, and on *the degree to which* individuals are affected by systemic discrimination. Ongoing adversarial variance on these questions is healthy because each side will work to expose the other's motives to exaggerate one way or the other. But many mainstream, contemporary libertarian conservatives, along with their supply-side conservative allies, do not appear to take these factors into account in rationalizing their policy positions.

In the face of the disqualifying misapprehensions and internal inconsistencies of property-rights libertarianism, should we conclude that proponents of property-rights libertarianism are in denial? Mere information deficit seems like an unlikely interpretation, as prominent libertarian conservatives seem pretty clearly to be neither less educated nor less intelligent than the average person: Libertarian conservatives include Nobel committee-cited economists (Hayek and Friedman); highly credentialed members of advocacy groups like The Cato Institute, The Heartland Institute, and The Federalist Society; and many other prominent officials, businesspeople, and politicians. I suggest we turn to motivated reasoning deriving from implicit bias to explain the way so many conservatives manage to resolve the massive dissonance between a commitment to freedom and a commitment to inviolable natural, exclusively negative property rights. The striking consilience between the claims of the supply-sider and the property-rights libertarian regarding basic facts about how the economy works is not a coincidence: The incentives to adopt the ideology of libertarian conservatism are exactly the same as those of the supply-side conservative. Thomas Frank expresses a rather cynical attitude as to the true, underlying motives behind the ideology of libertarian conservatism:

> Libertarianism is good [for the conservative] because it helps conservatives pass off a patently probusiness political agenda as

a noble bid for human freedom. Whatever we may think of libertarianism as a set of ideas, practically speaking, it is a doctrine that owes its visibility to the obvious charms it holds for the wealthy and the powerful. The reason we have so many well-funded libertarians in America these days is not because libertarianism suddenly acquired an enormous grassroots following, but because it appeals to those who are able to fund ideas. Like Social Darwinism and Christian Science before it, libertarianism flatters the successful and rationalizes their core beliefs about the world. They warm to the libertarian idea that taxation is theft because they themselves don't like to pay taxes. They fancy the libertarian notion that regulation is communist because they themselves find regulation intrusive and annoying. Libertarianism is a politics born to be subsidized. In the "free market of ideas," it is a sure winner.[163]

In a 2014 study, the Pew Research Center found that a strong plurality of self-identified libertarians reported a yearly income greater than $75,000; most of the rest are middle- to upper-middle income.[164] This means that libertarians are much more likely to occupy the upper economic strata than the average American. All the forms of self-serving and group-serving bias explaining elite support for supply-side conservatism are applicable here as well, and this fact is reflected in libertarian factual beliefs about the social welfare state. For example, self-identified libertarians are more likely than other Americans to say that government aid to the poor, along with government regulation, does more harm than good.[165] One prominent exemplar of the elite-class libertarian is David Koch, the industrialist, prolific donor to conservative causes, and former Libertarian Party vice-presidential candidate. His ideological commitments suggest a conviction that government interference with business is both inefficient and unjust. He and his brother Charles (co-founder of the libertarian Cato Institute) have supported dozens of political advocacy groups that oppose minimum wage laws, regulations on business and financial markets, and social welfare and social insurance programs.[166] With his siblings, David Koch inherited a lucrative oil pipeline business from his father; he was educated at elite private academies, and had enormous amounts of capital at his disposal when it was time for him to go into business for himself. The Koch brothers have every reason to engage in motivated reasoning about the economic and moral appropriateness of the status quo economic hierarchy. Their politics utterly discount the impacts of inheritance, circumstance, and the many social contributions to an individual's opportunity to reap the benefits of access to capital. They and the organizations they support also ignore the overwhelming historical evidence against supply-side economic theory. Selectively ignoring these facts is essential to creating the libertarian's self- and group-serving image of a just-world meritocracy.

As with supply-side economic conservatism, there are currents of racial supremacy in libertarian politics. The August 3, 1980, kickoff to the libertarianism-infused Reagan presidential campaign was held outside the town of Philadelphia, Mississippi, an infamous segregation-era Ku Klux Klan stronghold and locus for black church bombings and murders of civil-rights workers. There, Reagan's speech focused on restoring "states' rights," a phrase that for decades had been a dog whistle for the nullification of federal civil rights oversight. According to the 2013 Public Religion Research Institute's American Values Survey, self-identified libertarians in the United States skew heavily white (94%) and male (68%).[167] Though most libertarians are wealthy or upper-middle income, some nonelite, white landowners and some working-class allies have expressed support for stringent property-rights libertarianism. Think of recent standoffs in the American West over federal land use and grazing rights, wherein protesters have articulated a fundamental objection to any federal oversight of land that private citizens find useful. The protesters (100% white and mostly male) included a number who had previously opposed federal water-use regulations and other environmental and cultural heritage protections on public lands.[168] Obviously, self-interest among, say, ranchers who would benefit from unrestricted access to public lands would provide a motive to dismiss the artificial and conditional nature of individual claims to natural resources. In addition, as with working-class white voters who identify as economic conservatives, there are plenty of indications that prejudicial racial attitudes are a factor. Some of the same land-use protesters had also been active in radical anti-immigration movements and anti-Muslim protests. Working-class libertarians (again, almost entirely white) overlap heavily in attitudes and voting behavior with political conservatives who blame immigration for economic problems and oppose aid to poor minorities.[169] Nevada rancher Cliven Bundy was at the center of a recent flare-up over federal land management versus his private appropriation of public resources. The following is an excerpt from a *New York Times* article, quoting from a speech Bundy gave to a group of supporters:

> "I want to tell you one more thing I know about the Negro," he said. Mr. Bundy recalled driving past a public-housing project in North Las Vegas, "and in front of that government house the door was usually open and the older people and the kids—and there is always at least a half a dozen people sitting on the porch—they didn't have nothing to do. They didn't have nothing for their kids to do. They didn't have nothing for their young girls to do." "And because they were basically on government subsidy, so now what do they do?" he asked. "They abort their young children, they put their young men in jail, because they never learned how to pick cotton. And I've often wondered, are they better off as slaves, picking cotton and having a family life and doing things, or are they better off under government subsidy? They didn't get no more freedom. They got less freedom."[170]

It's that "culture of poverty" again, rather than inequality of opportunity and other structural disadvantages, that is responsible for the problems experienced by impoverished "Negroes"; state interventions in poverty are invariably counterproductive. Unless Bundy grossly misread the views of his audience (and the *Times* correspondent does not mention any overt disapproval having been expressed at the event), the fact that he felt comfortable declaiming such views, in such terms, before his supporters says a great deal about the particular libertarian subculture in which he operates.

The biopolitics and system justification theorists each stress the evidence that political conservatism is associated with higher sensitivity to threat, both physical and social. One thing that jumps out when looking at a strong property-rights ideology stressing noninterference, accompanied by a small-government ideology stressing protection of life and property, is the way this narrative creates a sort of inviolable, protective force field around the individual. Wherever fear of external threat is at the forefront of emotional need, system justification theory would predict a factual belief system organized around security and control. A belief in the natural, moral inviolability of property is perfectly suited to an ideology in which security is paramount—that is, for those who already happen to own property. The correlation we see between economic conservatism, on the one hand, and conservative anti-immigration and strong tough-on-crime political positions, on the other, is also to be expected on this interpretation.

In addition to demographics, certain personal traits set libertarians apart. They are, on average, less empathetic, more individualistic than others in their value commitments, and they rate moral concerns as less important than most others do.[171] The Lockean property-rights story is highly congenial to a worldview based on a self-conception as an individual who owes nothing to others (either legally or morally): Under this conception, ownership claims ultimately are founded on individual labor and risk-taking, and then passed down via individual decisions to bequeath. These claims are inviolable, with no provision for the public interest, as long as the use of resources does not violate others' negative rights to noninterference (limiting others' opportunities via acts of appropriation, of course, does not count for the property-rights libertarian as violations of their right to liberty). To the extent the defender of this view acknowledges any concern with the effects of an absolutist property-rights regime, we can expect confirmation bias in dealing with (a) alleged evidence for the positive trickle-down effects of the unregulated exploitation of privatized resources, and (b) the personal or cultural failings of those left out of the ownership class.

3.5 Asymmetry Again

How does this approach to understanding opposition to egalitarian social welfare policies account for the difference between liberal and conservative attitudes? We have already seen that conservative opposition to a more egalitarian political economics cuts across class lines. Elites have self-serving motives to hold beliefs about economics—and about the poor—that would favor a free-market system;

working-class white conservatives have self- and group-protective motives relating to relative status and status quo social hierarchy. But liberal elites and white liberal working-class persons have, in principle, the same incentives to maintain the inegalitarian economic status quo as do their conservative counterparts. So what is different about conservatives in general? Are liberals by nature fair and objective in their approach to political economics, while conservatives are slaves to implicit bias?

Denial is the fundamental—and very *human*—expression of the attachment to emotionally compelling beliefs in the face of contrary evidence. It is unlikely that political liberals belong to some superior, more evolved species, the members of which superficially resemble politically conservative human beings but are more rational than them. Consider the much discussed Implicit Association Test for automatic racial bias, which has been completed online by over 17 million visitors.[172] As Chris Mooney explains, "Bias in the test occurs when people are faster at categorizing negative words when they are paired with African American faces, or faster at sorting positive words when they're paired with white faces—suggesting an uncontrolled mental association between negative things or concepts and African Americans."[173] Results show that measurable unconscious bias of this sort is evident in the vast majority of test-takers, including most "strong liberal" egalitarians. (Implicit racial bias has not been shown reliably to predict racist *behavior*, wherein unconscious bias translates into explicit bias and actual discrimination.[174] No one has said that all measurable implicit attitudes are straightforwardly linked to behavioral dispositions; supporters of the idea that implicit attitudes are nevertheless relevant to racism argue that the point of research into implicit attitudes is to examine which attitudes might influence behavior under which circumstances.[175])

No one is above bias and motivated reasoning. However, the evidence shows that different people experience somewhat different emotional needs, depending on environment, experience, personality type, and cultural-group affiliation. Something, after all, must explain why one is attracted to a particular ideology over another. In the context of political economy, the habitual biases of those traits characteristically exhibited more strongly in conservatives—and the conservative ideology they motivate—help explain certain patterns of motivated reasoning we see on economics and property rights:

I. We know, for example, that conservatives have a stronger tendency to status quo bias and a greater comfort with existing, hierarchical social and economic relationships. These preferences are satisfied by an ideology of laissez-faire capitalism, be it rationalized in terms of economic efficiency, natural rights to property, the attribution of inferior characteristics to other individuals and/or ethnic groups, or to some combination of these.

II. As we have seen, ideological conservatism is associated with greater sensitivity to instability and uncertainty. We also know that a greater tendency to experience *social* fear is associated with hostility to out-groups, along with the political attitudes—such as anti-immigration and pro-segregation attitudes—that characteristically accompany such hostility. Open borders and changes to accustomed economic and racial hierarchies are destabilizing. The language of meritocracy, efficiency, and property rights, and the implicit conviction of class and racial superiority, all restore a sense of order, control, and safety by reducing uncertainty and validating accustomed position in the economic and/or social hierarchy.

III. While the magnitude of effect sizes remains controversial, we have seen across many studies that liberals tend to score higher on empathy and acceptance of differences. Empathy is a natural antidote to out-group bias and the fundamental attribution error, which underlies much of the motivated cognition behind inegalitarian denials of reality. Business law professor Lynn Stout agrees that the "*Homo economicus*" typically held up in business and economics as a model of rational choice "is a sociopath."[176] She disputes this as a characterization of actual business people, despite, for example, psychological studies confirming a high incidence of sociopathy and narcissism among financiers and corporate chief executive officers.[177] Economics and finance students are measurably less altruistic and less cooperative than their peers, and they demonstrate a greater willingness to deceive for profit; but perhaps more significantly, they are more likely to see *others* as primarily motivated by selfishness.[178] Viewing others as more self-interested suggests viewing others more as one's competition. This sort of individualism, as Dan Kahan has argued, is associated with political conservatism.[179]

Greater sensitivity to threat means a greater sensitivity to signs of in-group/out-group membership. Humans by instinct fear the "other." Again, one really consistent finding in personality research is a higher threat sensitivity among ideological conservatives. Enhanced threat sensitivity amplifies tribalistic attitudes toward other classes, races, and so on. The more threat sensitive one is, the more one will respond to other groups negatively, which in turn primes attributions that neglect the universality of susceptibility to circumstance.

IV. In raising children, some parents will stress conscientiousness, responsibility, and obedience as key values; other parents will stress openness and empathy. Cognitive scientist George Lakoff puts an imaginative spin on the roots of the individualist-hierarchicalist-authoritarian conservative worldview, as he investigates why certain ideological positions on seemingly unrelated economic and social issues tend to go together. Lakoff argues for the formative importance of family dynamics on the individual's understanding of governance. He speculates that conservatives are informed in their understanding of merit and success by their experience of (and/or, perhaps, personal disposition to) an authoritarian family model he calls the **strict father family**.

> In the strict father family, father knows best. He knows right from wrong and has the ultimate authority to make sure his children and his spouse do what he says, which is taken to be what is right. Many conservative spouses accept this worldview, uphold the father's authority, and are strict in those realms of family life that they are in charge of. When his children disobey, it is his moral duty to punish them painfully enough so that, to avoid punishment, they will obey him (do what is right) and not just do what feels good. Through physical discipline they are supposed to become disciplined, internally strong, and able to prosper in the external world. What if they don't prosper? That means they are not disciplined, and therefore cannot be moral, and so deserve their poverty. This reasoning shows up in conservative politics in which the poor are seen as lazy and undeserving, and the rich as deserving their wealth. Responsibility is thus taken to be *personal responsibility* not social responsibility. What you become is only up to you; society has nothing to do with it.

You are responsible for yourself, not for others—who are responsible for themselves.[180]

He argues that the family is our implicit model for governance generally, and so our attitudes toward a wide range of economic and social issues are impacted by what we anecdotally understand to be the normal and proper family type: "We are first governed in our families, and so we grow up understanding governing institutions in terms of the governing systems of families." (This may be most evident in more strongly individualist societies like the United States, whereas in traditional societies the child may experience, say, the village community as the basic social unit.) By contrast, the progressive understands governance more according to a **nurturant parent model**, wherein one looks for systemic or environmental causes of behavior, and where governing structures are more oriented toward empowerment.

This speculative analysis would also predict that religious political conservatives would be more likely to belong to sects describing a relatively authoritarian deity, and liberals to sects representing a more loving and forgiving one. Large surveys designed by the Baylor University Institute for Studies of Religion have supported just this sort of link, for U.S. Christians, between political ideology and one's views about God's personality and God's priorities.[181]

Neither is it a coincidence, for Lakoff, that the language of moral authority and personal responsibility is also the language of the political conservative's typically punishment-oriented approach to criminal justice, whereas the language of empathy and circumstantial/environmental determinants of behavior is the language of a politically liberal, rehabilitation-oriented approach.

As we have discussed, cultural-cognition and group-polarization effects kick in whenever, for any reason, groups of motivationally similar persons come to identify with each other as a cultural/ideological community. The feeling of being part of a community is a positive feeling, and the fear of being ostracized from one's community is very real. Liberals and conservatives each have their identifying worldviews that bring them into groups, motivationally and ideologically—and even geographically, as people self-sort into more homogenous neighborhoods. These effects reinforce ideology and profoundly affect one's perception of reality and risk (as Kahan and others have demonstrated). Virtual self-sorting online on social media platforms enhances this effect.

High-status conservatives may be for low taxes and small government because they are accustomed to their privileged position, whereas low-status conservatives may feel particularly threatened by a redistributive political economics thanks to their tenuous position on the status hierarchy. Conservatives generally are more likely to exhibit high conscientiousness and a moral hierarchicalism that inclines them to stress personal responsibility more and circumstance less. They tend to be more comfortable upholding the inegalitarian status quo. Identity-protective cultural cognition works side by side with these causes. Once the community with which you identify decides it's for property rights and small government, and against "handouts," for that reason alone you now have compelling motives to conform your beliefs to the factual worldview necessary to sustaining this ideology. The tenets that poverty is the result of bad decisions and a toxic culture, that property rights take moral precedence over the right to a share of resources, and that economic growth is best achieved by a laissez-faire regime, all function as building blocks that support the desired political result. The outcome is the dogmatic, fact-resistant "market fundamentalism" Richard Hofstadter identified in 1970 as coming to dominate political conservativism.[182]

Identity-protective cultural cognition happens across the ideological spectrum. It affects interpretation and assimilation of information, judgments of expertise, perception of risk, and the ultimate explanations one accepts for ideologically charged phenomena. Liberal empathy and egalitarianism no doubt biases liberal thinking toward the thesis that circumstance is the primary determinant of individual outcomes, and thus toward collectivism (or vice versa); the result is a downplaying of the efficiency of markets, of the benefits of privatization, and of personal responsibility and perseverance. But conservative political economy is currently the more salient topic of discussion. Just as a focus on left-wing science denial in the United States may have been more pertinent in the '60s, a discussion focusing on left-wing denial in the area of political economy may have been more pertinent in an era—say, the 1930s through the 1960s—when socialism was ascendant.

Notes

1. Twenty percent for those in the highest income tax bracket.
2. Robert Benenson, "Social Welfare Under Reagan," *CQ Researcher*, March 9, 1984, http://library.cqpress.com/cqresearcher/document.php?id=cqresrre 1984030900.
3. Thomas Piketty, Emmanuel Saez, and Gabriel Zucman, "Distributional National Accounts: Methods and Estimates for the United States," *The Quarterly Journal of Economics* 133 (2018), pp. 553–609.
4. "Nine Charts About Wealth Inequality in America," Urban Institute, February 2015, http://apps.urban.org/features/wealth-inequality-charts/.
5. "Here Is the Full Inequality Speech and Slideshow that Was Too Hot for TED," *The Atlantic*, May 17, 2012, http://www.theatlantic.com/business/ archive/2012/05/here-is-the-full-inequality-speech-and-slideshow-that-was-too-hot-for-ted/257323/.
6. Richard Fry and Rakesh Kochhar, "America's Wealth Gap Between Middle-Income and Upper-Income Families Is Widest on Record," Pew Research Center, December 17, 2014, http://www.pewresearch.org/fact-tank/2014/ 12/17/wealth-gap-upper-middle-income/.
7. Sam Ro, "This Is the 6th Longest US Economic Expansion We've Had Since the 1850s," *Business Insider*, April 10, 2015, http://www.businessinsider.com/ duration-of-us-economic-expansions-since-the-1850s-2015-4.
8. Jay Heflin, "Boehner: Bush Tax Cuts Didn't Lead to the Deficit," *The Hill*, June 10, 2010, http://thehill.com/policy/finance/102443-boehner-bush-tax-cuts-didnt-lead-to-the-deficit; ctd. by Ezra Klein, "Tax Rates and Economic Growth in One Graph," *Washington Post*, June 21, 2011, https://www.washingtonpost.com/blogs/ezra-klein/post/tax-rates-and-economic-growth-in-one-graph/2011/05/19/AGLaxJeH_blog.html.
9. Louis Woodhill, "Another Nail in the Keynesian Coffin," *Real Clear Markets*, May 9, 2011, http://www.realclearmarkets.com/articles/2011/05/ 09/another_nail_in_the_keynesian_coffin_99010.html; ctd. by Michael Linden, "The Myth of the Lower Marginal Tax Rates: Conservatives' Go-To Growth Solution Doesn't Hold Up," *Center for American Progress*, June 20, 2011, https://www.americanprogress.org/issues/tax-reform/news/2011/ 06/20/9841/the-myth-of-the-lower-marginal-tax-rates/.

10. The design of this chart is based on an older one provided by Linden, "The Myth of the Lower Marginal Tax Rates."

11. The design of this chart is based on an earlier effort from Dave Johnson, "So Do Tax Cuts Create Jobs?," *Huffington Post*, October 5, 2012, http://www.huffingtonpost.com/dave-johnson/so-do-tax-cuts-create-job_b_1943500.html.

12. Season 6, Episode 119, *Morning Joe*, June 18, 2012; ctd. by Sarah Burris, "Seth Meyers: GOP Wrecked Kansas Economy So Bad They Had to Auction off Dildos for Cash," *Raw Story*, March 22, 2016, http://www.rawstory.com/2016/03/seth-meyers-gop-wrecked-kansas-economy-so-bad-they-had-to-auction-off-dildos-for-cash/.

13. Neil King Jr. and Mark Peters, "Party Eyes 'Red-State Model' to Drive Republican Revival," *Wall Street Journal*, February 4, 2013, http://www.wsj.com/articles/SB10001424127887324761004578281932072421560; ctd. by Burris, "Seth Meyers."

14. Menzie Chin, "Kansas Macro and Fiscal Crash," *Econbrowser*, May 30, 2015, http://econbrowser.com/archives/2015/05/kansas-macro-and-fiscal-crash.

15. Ezra Klein, "The Republican Party's Reality Problems—and Ours," *Vox*, December 12, 2017, https://www.vox.com/policy-and-politics/2017/12/12/16762032/trump-moore-republicans-taxes-lies.

16. Denise Cummins, "Science Proves Ayn Rand Wrong About Altruism and Laissez-Faire Economics," *Evonomics*, March 17, 2016, http://evonomics.com/what-ayn-rand-got-wrong-human-nature-and-free-markets/.

17. See Katie Sanders, "It Is Easier to Obtain the American Dream in Europe?," *Politifact*, December 19, 2013, http://www.politifact.com/punditfact/statements/2013/dec/19/steven-rattner/it-easier-obtain-american-dream-europe/.

18. Ha-Joon Chang, "The Myths About Money that British Voters Should Reject," *The Guardian*, June 1, 2017, https://www.theguardian.com/commentisfree/2017/jun/01/myths-money-british-voters-economy-britain-welfare.

19. Anu Partanen, "What Americans Don't Get About Nordic Countries," *The Atlantic*, March 16, 2016, http://www.theatlantic.com/politics/archive/2016/03/bernie-sanders-nordic-countries/473385/.

20. Alana Semuels, "Why Does Sweden Have So Many Start Ups?" *The Atlantic*, September 28, 2017, https://www.theatlantic.com/business/archive/2017/09/sweden-startups/541413/

21. Thomas Hungerford, "Taxes and the Economy: An Economic Analysis of the Top Tax Rates Since 1945," CRS Report for Congress, September 14, 2012; ctd. by Rick Ungar, "Non-Partisan Congressional Tax Report Debunks Core Conservative Economic Theory—GOP Suppresses Study," *Forbes*, November 2, 2012, http://www.forbes.com/sites/rickungar/2012/11/02/non-partisan-congressional-tax-report-debunks-core-conservative-economic-theory-gop-suppresses-study/#32c2e2e1431b.

22. Era Dabla-Norris, Kalpana Kochar, Nujin Suphaphiptat, Frantisek Ricka, and Evridiki Tsounta, *Causes and Consequences of Global Economic Inequality: A Global Perspective* (Washington, DC: International Monetary Fund, 2015); ctd. by Larry Elliott, "Pay Low-Income Families More to Boost Economic Growth, Says IMF," *The Guardian*, June 15, 2015, http://www.theguardian.com/business/2015/jun/15/focus-on-low-income-families-to-boost-economic-growth-says-imf-study.

23. David Edwards, "Joe Scarborough Gives Up the Game: After 30 Years, the GOP Base Realized 'It Never Trickles Down,'" *Raw Story*, March 8, 2016, https://www.rawstory.com/2016/03/joe-scarborough-gives-up-the-game-after-30-years-the-gop-base-realized-it-never-trickles-down/.

24. Bruce Bartlett, "I Helped Create the GOP Tax Myth. Trump Is Wrong: Tax Cuts Don't Equal Growth," *Washington Post*, September 38, 2017, https://www.washingtonpost.com/news/posteverything/wp/2017/09/28/i-helped-create-the-gop-tax-myth-trump-is-wrong-tax-cuts-dont-equal-growth.

25. Ross Douthat, Daniel McCarthy, and Henry Olsen, "Can Trumpism Survive Trump?," *New York Times*, November 14, 2017, https://www.nytimes.com/2017/11/14/opinion/trump-republicans-douthat.html.

26. Sarah Anderson, "It's a Myth that Corporate Tax Cuts Mean More Jobs," *New York Times*, August 30, 2017, https://www.nytimes.com/2017/08/30/opinion/corporate-tax-cuts-jobs.html.

27. Jonathan Chait, "Has Marco Rubio Finally Created a Tax Cut So Huge Republicans Don't Like It?," *New York* magazine, April 20, 2015, http://nymag.com/daily/intelligencer/2015/04/rubio-tax-cut-so-huge-republicans-dont-like-it.html.

28. Elaine Maag, Roberton Williams, Jeff Rohaly, Jim Nunns, "An Analysis of Marco Rubio's Tax Plan," Tax Policy Center, February 11, 2016. http://www.taxpolicycenter.org/publications/url.cfm?ID=2000606.   Because Rubio also promised a balanced budget, he would also have had to find an additional $9.5 trillion in budget cuts over the same period. And pay for his promised $1 trillion in increased spending on the military.

29. Michael Schuyler and William McBride, "The Economic Effects of the Rubio-Lee Tax Reform Plan," Tax Foundation blog, March 9, 2015, http://taxfoundation.org/article/economic-effects-rubio-lee-tax-reform-plan.

30. Ezra Klein and Jeff Stein, "We've Lost Sight of How Wildly Irresponsible the Republican Tax Plans Are," *Vox*, February 25, 2016, http://www.vox.com/2016/2/25/11110526/gop-tax-plans.

31. James Nunns, Leonard Burman, Jeffery Rohaly, Joseph Rosenburg, "An Analysis of Trump's Revised Tax Plan," Tax Policy Center website, October 16, 2018, http://www.taxpolicycenter.org/publications/analysis-donald-trumps-revised-tax-plan/full.

32. Bob Ryan, "Republicans Are Still Making a Huge Claim About the Tax Bill that Every Independent Analysis Rejects," *Business Insider*, December 4, 2017, http://www.businessinsider.com/trump-republican-tax-reform-bill-deficit-debt-claims-2017-12.

33. "Public Knows Basic Facts About Politics, Economics, but Struggles with Specifics," Pew Research Center, November 18, 2010, http://www.pewresearch.org/2010/11/18/public-knows-basic-facts-about-politics-economics-but-struggles-with-specifics/.

34. Jost et al., "Political Conservatism as Motivated Social Cognition," p. 351.

35. Robin, "The Conservative Reaction."

36. Paul Krugman, "Hating Good Government," *New York Times*, January 18, 2015, http://www.nytimes.com/2015/01/19/opinion/paul-krugman-hating-good-government.html.

37. Ezra Klein, "What's the Liberal Equivalent of Climate Denial?," *Vox*, April 23, 2014, http://www.vox.com/2014/4/23/5642116/liberal-climate-denial.

38. Lydia Saad, "U.S. Liberals at Record 24% but Still Trail Conservatives," Gallup, January 9, 2015, http://www.gallup.com/poll/180452/liberals-record-trail-conservatives.aspx.

39. "Full Transcript of the Mitt Romney Secret Video," transcribed by Sydney Brownstone, Maya Dusenbury, Ryan Jacobs, Deanna Pan, and Sarah Zhang, *Mother Jones*, September 19, 2012, http://www.motherjones.com/politics/2012/09/full-transcript-mitt-romney-secret-video.

40. Matt Bruenig, "Why Paul Ryan Is Wrong to Blame Black Culture for Poverty," *Demos*, March 12, 2014, http://www.demos.org/blog/3/12/14/why-paul-ryan-wrong-blame-black-culture-poverty.

41. Matthew Spalding, "Why the U.S. Has a Culture of Dependency," *CNN*, September 21, 2012, http://www.cnn.com/2012/09/21/opinion/spalding-welfare-state-dependency/.

42. David Brooks, "The Nature of Poverty," *New York Times*, May 1, 2015, http://www.nytimes.com/2015/05/01/opinion/david-brooks-the-nature-of-poverty.html.
43. Paul Gorski, "The Myth of the Culture of Poverty," *Educational Leadership* 65 (2008), pp. 32–36.
44. Tami Luhby, "The Poor Do Have Jobs," *CNN Money*, September 21, 2012, http://money.cnn.com/2012/09/21/news/economy/poor-jobs/index.html?hpt=hp_t2.
45. Adam Sorensen, "Romney's 47% Video: Five Charts to Fact-Check the Remarks," *Time*, September 18, 2012, http://swampland.time.com/2012/09/18/five-charts-illustrating-the-problem-with-romneys-47-remarks/.
46. Abhijit Banerjee, Rema Hanna, Gabriel Kreindler, and Benjamin Olken, "Debunking the Stereotype of the Lazy Welfare Recipient: Evidence from Cash Transfer Programs Worldwide," Harvard Kennedy School Working Paper No. 076 (2015), http://ssrn.com/abstract=2703447 or http://dx.doi.org/10.2139/ssrn.2703447; ctd. by Dylan Matthews, "Economists Tested 7 Welfare Programs to See If They Made People Lazy. They Didn't," *Vox*, November 20, 2015, http://www.vox.com/policy-and-politics/2015/11/20/9764324/welfare-cash-transfer-work.
47. Hilary Hoynes and Ankur Patel, "Effective Policy for Reducing Inequality? The Earned Income Tax Credit and the Distribution of Income," NBER Working Paper No. 21340 (2015); ctd. by Matthews, "Economists Tested 7 Welfare Programs."
48. John Martin and Matthew Desmond, "Political Position and Social Knowledge," *Sociological Forum* 25 (2010), p. 9.
49. Paul Goren, "Race, Sophistication, and White Opinion in Government Spending," *Political Behavior* 25 (2003), pp. 201–220; ctd. in Martin and Desmond, "Political Position and Social Knowledge," p. 9.
50. Martin and Desmond, "Political Position and Social Knowledge," p. 21.
51. Zaller, *The Nature and Origins of Mass Opinion*, p. 45.
52. Martin and Desmond, "Political Position and Social Knowledge," p. 10.
53. P. J. Henry and Jaime Napier, "Education Is Related to Greater Ideological Prejudice," *Public Opinion Quarterly* 81 (2017), pp. 930–942.
54. "Most Republicans Say the Rich Work Harder than Others, Most Democrats Say They Had More Advantages," Pew Research Center, January 22, 2014, http://www.people-press.org/2014/01/23/most-see-inequality-growing-but-partisans-differ-over-solutions/poverty-3/
55. Martin, "What Is Ideology?," p. 15.

56. José Duarte, Jarret Crawford, Charlotta Stern, Jonathan Haidt, Lee Jussim, and Philip Tetlock, "Political Diversity Will Improve Social Psychological Science," *Behavioral and Brain Sciences* 38 (2015), p. 5.

57. John Chambers and Barry Schlenker, "Political Homogeneity Can Nurture Threats to Research Validity," *Behavioral and Brain Sciences* 38 (2015), p. 21.

58. Tyler Cowen, *Average Is Over: Powering America Beyond the Age of the Great Stagnation* (New York: Penguin, 2013). See William Black, "The Faux Hyper-Meritocracy that Threatens to Destroy Us," *New Economic Perspectives*, October 8, 2013, http://neweconomicperspectives.org/2013/10/faux-hyper-meritocracy-threatens-destroy-us.html.

59. Lee Ross, "The Intuitive Psychologist and His Shortcomings: Distortions in the Attribution Process," in *Advances in Experimental Social Psychology* by Leonard Berkowitz, 10th ed. (New York: Academic Press, 1977).

60. Daniel Gilbert and Patrick Malone, "The Correspondence Bias," *Psychological Bulletin* 117 (1995), p. 26.

61. Indeed, a prevailing view in both psychology and philosophy is that the so-called moral character traits, such as honesty or courage, are only weakly cross-situational, and, to the extent they exist at all, they require much narrower descriptions than usually employed. See John Doris, *Lack of Character: Personality and Moral Behavior* (New York: Cambridge University Press, 2002); and Miller, *Moral Character*.

62. See Lee Ross and Richard Nisbett, *The Person and the Situation* (New York: McGraw-Hill, 1991).

63. See David McRaney, *You Are Not So Smart* (New York: Gotham Books, 2011), p. 268.

64. Melvin Lerner, *The Belief in a Just World: A Fundamental Delusion* (New York: Springer, 1980).

65. David Woodruff, "Export Orientation, Supply-Side Thinking, and the Theodicy of Markets," *Political Economy in Public* blog, September 11, 2014, http://politicaleconomyinpublic.blogspot.co.nz/2014/09/theodicyofmarkets.html?spref=fb.

66. Dan Tuohy, "Jeb Bush: 'We've Got to Start Solving Problems,'" *Union Leader*, July 8, 2015, http://politicaleconomyinpublic.blogspot.co.nz/2014/09/theodicyofmarkets.html.

67. Dean Schabner, "Americans Work More than Anyone," *ABC News*, May 1, 2016, http://www.unionleader.com/apps/pbcs.dll/article?AID=/20150709/NEWS0605/150709206; ctd. by Matthew Pulver, "Jeb Bush's Plutocratic Fantasy Land: Why His Comments About American Workers Are Completely Divorced from Reality," *Salon*, July

9, 2015, http://www.salon.com/2015/07/09/jeb_bushs_plutocratic_fantasy_land_why_his_comments_about_american_workers_are_completely_divorced_from_reality/.

68. Steven Greenhouse, "Our Economic Pickle," *New York Times*, January 12, 2013, http://www.nytimes.com/2013/01/13/sunday-review/americas-productivity-climbs-but-wages-stagnate.html. See Pulver, "Jeb Bush's Plutocratic Fantasy Land."

69. "U.S. Workers World's Most Productive," *CBS News*, September 3, 2007, http://www.cbsnews.com/news/us-workers-worlds-most-productive/. See Pulver, "Jeb Bush's Plutocratic Fantasy Land."

70. Jazmin L. Brown-Iannuzzi, Ron Dotsch, Erin Cooley, and Brian Keith Payne, "The Relationship Between Mental Representations of Welfare Recipients and Attitudes Toward Welfare," *Psychological Science* 28 (2017), pp. 92–103.

71. David Sirota, "What Does Paul Ryan Really Mean by the Phrase 'Inner City'? Google Ngram Offers a Clue," *Moyers & Company*, March 13, 2014, https://billmoyers.com/2014/03/13/what-does-paul-ryan-really-mean-by-the-phrase-"inner-city"-google-ngram-offers-a-clue/.

72. See Ian Haney López, *Dog Whistle Politics: How Coded Racial Appeals Have Reinvented Racism and Wrecked the Middle Class* (New York: Oxford University Press, 2014), pp. 162–163.

73. Thomas Pettigrew, "The Ultimate Attribution Error: Extending Allport's Cognitive Analysis of Prejudice," *Personality and Social Psychology Bulletin* 5 (1979), pp. 461–476. See Miles Hewstone, "The 'Ultimate Attribution Error'? A Review of the Literature on Intergroup Causal Attribution," *European Journal of Social Psychology* 20 (1990), pp. 311–335.

74. Michael Tesler, "Trump Voters Think African Americans Are Much Less Deserving than 'Average Americans,'" *Huffington Post*, December 20, 2017, https://www.huffingtonpost.com/michael-tesler/trump-voters-think-africa_b_13732500.html.

75. Sarah-Jane Leslie, "The Original Sin of Cognition: Fear, Prejudice, and Generalization," *Journal of Philosophy* 114 (2017), pp. 393–421. (My thanks to Alex Madva for the pointer.)

76. Joseph Forgas, "The Role of Affect in Attitudes and Attitude Change," in *Attitudes and Attitude Change*, ed. William Crano and Radmila Prislin (New York: Psychology Press, 2008), pp. 132–133.

77. Forgas, "The Role of Affect in Attitudes and Attitude Change," p. 133.

78. Mackenzie Weinger, "Fox News Obsessed with Lone Black Panther," *Politico*, November 6, 2012. http://www.politico.com/blogs/media/2012/11/fox-news-obsessed-with-lone-black-panther-148638.

79. Institute for Patient Access, "Poor & Black Children Bear the Brunt of Asthma, Research Confirms," March 14, 2017, https://allianceforpatientaccess.org/poor-black-children-bear-the-brunt-of-asthma-research-confirms/.

80. Centers for Disease Control and Prevention, October 10, 2018, https://www.cdc.gov/nceh/lead/default.htm.

81. Sarah Kliff, "Babies Born 3 Miles Apart in New York Have a 9-Year Life Expectancy Gap," *Vox*, April 30, 2015, http://www.vox.com/2015/4/30/8517375/babies-born-3-miles-apart-in-new-york-have-a-9-year-life.

82. Laura Dwyer-Lindgren, Amelia Bertozzi-Villa, Rebecca Stubbs, Chole Morozoff, Johan Mackenbach, Frank van Lenthe, Ali Mokdad, and Christopher Murray, "Inequalities in Life Expectancy Among US Counties, 1980 to 2014: Temporal Trends and Key Drivers," *JAMA Internal Medicine* 177 (2017), pp. 1003–1011.

83. Michael Teitz and Karen Chapple, "The Causes of Inner City Poverty: Eight Hypotheses in Search of Reality," *Cityscape: A Journal of Policy Development and Research* 3 (1998), pp. 33–70.

84. Tanzina Vega, "2 Out of 5 Black Children Are Living in Poverty," *CNN Money*, July 15, 2015, http://money.cnn.com/2015/07/14/news/economy/black-children-poverty/.

85. "Students of Color Still Receiving Unequal Education," Center for American Progress website, August 22, 2012, https://www.americanprogress.org/issues/education/news/2012/08/22/32862/students-of-color-still-receiving-unequal-education/.

86. Teitz and Chapple, "The Causes of Inner City Poverty," p. 40.

87. Jon Swaine, Oliver Laughland, and Jamiles Lartley, "Black Americans Killed by Police Twice as Likely to Be Unarmed as White People," *The Guardian*, June 1, 2015, https://www.theguardian.com/us-news/2015/jun/01/black-americans-killed-by-police-analysis.

88. Cody Ross, "A Multi-Level Bayesian Analysis of Racial Bias in Police Shootings at the County-Level in the United States, 2011–2014," *PLoS ONE* 10 (2015), https://journals.plos.org/plosone/article?id=10.1371/journal.pone.0141854.

89. American Civil Liberties Union, "The War on Marijuana in Black and White," ACLU Foundation website, June 2013, https://www.aclu.org/report/war-marijuana-black-and-white.

90. "Criminal Justice Fact Sheet," NAACP website, n.d., http://www.naacp.org/pages/criminal-justice-fact-sheet.

91. "Stop-and-Frisk Data," New York Civil Liberties Union website, n.d., http://www.nyclu.org/content/stop-and-frisk-data.

92. Sophia Kerby, "The Top 10 Most Startling Facts About People of Color and Criminal Justice in the United States," Center for American Progress website, March 13, 2012, https://www.americanprogress.org/issues/race/news/2012/03/13/11351/the-top-10-most-startling-facts-about-people-of-color-and-criminal-justice-in-the-united-states/.

93. Joe Palazzolo, "Racial Gap in Men's Sentencing," *Wall Street Journal*, February 14, 2013, http://www.wsj.com/articles/SB10001424127887324432004578304463789858002.

94. Justin Levinson, Robert Smith, and Danielle Young, "Devaluing Death: An Empirical Study of Implicit Racial Bias on Jury-Eligible Citizens in Six Death Penalty States," *NYU Law Review* 89 (2014), pp. 513–581.

95. See Christopher Lyons and Becky Pettit, "Compounded Disadvantage: Race, Incarceration, and Wage Growth," *Social Problems* 58 (2011), pp. 257–280.

96. Louis Jacobson, "CNN's Don Lemon Says More than 72 Percent of African-American Births Are out of Wedlock," *PolitiFact*, July 29, 2013, http://www.politifact.com/truth-o-meter/statements/2013/jul/29/don-lemon/cnns-don-lemon-says-more-72-percent-african-americ/.

97. See, for example, Matthew Bramlett and Stephen Blumberg, "Family Structure and Children's Physical and Mental Health," *Health Affairs* 26 (2007), pp. 549–558.

98. See Marianne Bertrand, "Racial Bias in Hiring," *Capital Ideas* 4 (2003), http://www.chicagobooth.edu/capideas/spring03/racialbias.html. Race (and gender) bias in evaluating resumes may have diminished since then: Rajeev Darolia, Cory Koedel, Paco Martorell, Katie Wilson, and Franisco Perez-Arce, "Race and Gender Effects on Employer Interest in Job Applicants: New Evidence from a Resume Field Experiment," *Applied Economic Letters* 23 (2016), pp. 853–856.

99. Devah Pager, Bruce Western, and Bart Bonikowski, "Discrimination in a Low-Wage Labor Market: A Field Experiment," *American Sociological Review* 74 (2009), pp. 777–799.

100. Steven Michael Gaddis, "Discrimination in the Credential Society: An Audit Study of Race and College Selectivity in the Labor Market," *Social Forces* 93 (2015), pp. 1451–1479.

101. Shaila Dewan, "Discrimination in Housing Against Nonwhites Persists Quietly, U.S. Study Finds," *New York Times*, June 11, 2013, http://www.nytimes.com/2013/06/12/business/economy/discrimination-in-housing-against-nonwhites-persists-quietly-us-study-finds.html.

102. See, for example, Robert Fairlie and Alicia Robb, "Disparities in Capital Access Between Minority and Non-Minority-Owned Businesses:

The Troubling Reality of Capital Limitations Faced by MBEs," U.S. Department of Commerce Minority Business Development Agency, January 2010, https://www.researchgate.net/publication/292936391_ Disparities_in_capital_access_between_minority_and_non-minority-owned_businesses_The_troubling_reality_of_capital_limitations_ faced_by_MBEs; and David Blanchflower, Phillip Levine, and David Zimmerman, "Discrimination in the Small Business Credit Market," *Review of Economics and Statistics* 85 (2003), pp. 930–943; and "Access to Capital Is Still a Challenge for Minority Business Enterprises," Minority Business Development Agency, March/April 2010, https://www. mbda.gov/news/blog/2010/07/access-capital-still-challenge-minority-business-enterprises.

103. See, for example, Blanchflower, Levine, and Zimmerman, "Discrimination in the Small Business Credit Market," *National Bureau of Economic Research*, December 1998, https://www.nber.org/papers/w6840.

104. Tara Golshan, "Why a College Degree Means Less for the Poor, Explained in One Paragraph," *Vox*, March 8, 2016, http://www.vox. com/2016/3/8/11178802/college-degree-income-discrimination; citing Brad Hershbein, "A College Degree Is Worth Less If You Are Raised Poor," Brookings Institution blog, February 19, 2016, http://www. brookings.edu/blogs/social-mobility-memos/posts/2016/02/ 19-college-degree-worth-less-raised-poor-hershbein.

105. Michael Kelley, "Wealth Inequality Is MUCH Worse than You Realize," *Business Insider*, March 5, 2013, http://www.businessinsider. com/inequality-is-worse-than-you-think-2013-3.

106. Martin Gilens and Benjamin Page, "Testing Theories of American Politics: Elites, Interest Groups, and Average Citizens," *Perspectives on Politics* 12 (2014), pp. 564–581. This strong conclusion has been questioned by a number of critics. (For an overview, see Dylan Matthews, "Remember that Study Saying America Is an Oligarchy? 3 Rebuttals Say It's Wrong," *Vox*, May 9, 2016, http://www.vox.com/2016/ 5/9/11502464/gilens-page-oligarchy-study). However you interpret the data, it would be difficult to dispute that there is some influence on policy on the part of the very wealthy that is disproportionate to their numbers.

107. Stephen Ohlemacher and Emily Swanson, "AP-GfK Poll: Most Back Obama Plan to Raise Investment Taxes," *AP News*, February 22, 2015, http://bigstory.ap.org/article/a4c12478a5bb480e9b6d773c08e96271/ ap-gfk-poll-most-back-obama-plan-raise-investment-taxes.

108. Seth Motel, "5 Facts on How Americans View Taxes," Pew Research Center, April 10, 2015, http://www.pewresearch.org/fact-tank/2015/04/10/5-facts-on-how-americans-view-taxes/.

109. Larry Bartels, "What's the Matter with What's the Matter with Kansas?," *Quarterly Journal of Political Science* 1 (2006), pp. 201–226.

110. Betsy Cooper, Daniel Cox, Rachel Lienesch, and Robert Jones, "Anxiety, Nostalgia, and Mistrust: Findings from the 2015 American Values Survey," PPRI website, n.d., http://www.prri.org/research/survey-anxiety-nostalgia-and-mistrust-findings-from-the-2015-american-values-survey/.

111. Michael Norton and Samuel Sommers, "Whites See Racism as a Zero-Sum Game that They Are Now Losing," *Perspectives on Psychological Science* 6 (2011), pp. 215–218.

112. Kim Thurler, "Whites Believe They Are Victims of Racism More Often than Blacks," *Tufts Now*, May 23, 2011, http://now.tufts.edu/news-releases/whites-believe-they-are-victims-racism-more-o.

113. Brian McKenzie, "Political Perceptions in the Obama Era Diverse Opinions of the Great Recession and Its Aftermath Among Whites, Latinos, and Blacks," *Political Research Quarterly* 67 (2014), pp. 823–836. (Thanks to Alex Madva for the pointer.)

114. Aaron C. Kay, Danielle Gaucher, Jennifer M. Peach, Kristin Laurin, Justin Friesen, Mark P. Zanna, and Steven J. Spencer, "Inequality, Discrimination, and the Power of the Status Quo: Direct Evidence for a Motivation to See the Way Things Are as the Way They Should Be," *Journal of Personality and Social Psychology* 97 (2009), pp. 421–434.

115. Vincent Yzerbyt and Stéphanie Demoulin, "Intergroup Relations," *Handbook of Social Psychology*, 2, 5th edition, ed. Susan Fiske and Daniel Gilbert (Hoboken, NJ: Wiley, 2010), p. 1040.

116. J. Eric Oliver and Tali Mendelberg, "Reconsidering the Environmental Determinants of White Racial Attitudes," *American Journal of Political Science* 44 (2000), pp. 574–589.

117. Ilyana Kuziemko, Ryan Buell, Taly Reich, and Michael Norton, "'Last-Place Aversion': Evidence and Redistributive Implications," *Quarterly Journal of Economics* 129 (2014), pp. 105–149.

118. Kuziemko et al., "'Last-Pace Aversion,'" pp. 105–106.

119. See http://robertpaulwolff.blogspot.com/2013/09/why-does-right-hate-obamacare.html.

120. W. E. B. DuBois, *Black Reconstruction in America, 1860–1880* (New York: Free Press, 1998), p. 700; ctd. by Tim Wise, *Under the Affluence: Shaming*

the Poor, Praising the Rich and Jeopardizing the Future of America (San Francisco: City Lights, 2015).

121. David R. Roediger, The Wages of Whiteness: Race and the Making of the American Working Class (London: Verso, 1991), pp. 12–13; ctd. by Wise, Under the Affluence.

122. 1960, remark to Bill Moyers, "What a Real President Was Like," Washington Post, November 13, 1988, https://www.washingtonpost. com/archive/opinions/1988/11/13/what-a-real-president-was-like/ d483c1be-d0da-43b7-bde6-04e10106ff6c.

123. Thomas Edsall, "Why Trump Now?," New York Times, March 1, 2016, http://www.nytimes.com/2016/03/02/opinion/campaign-stops/why-trump-now.html.

124. Jonathan T. Rothwell and Pablo Diego-Rosell, "Explaining Nationalist Political Views: The Case of Donald Trump," SSRN, November 2, 2016,https://ssrn.com/abstract=2822059 or http://dx.doi.org/10.2139/ ssrn.2822059.

125. Jamelle Bouie, "Trump's Ungovernment," Slate, December 4, 2016, http:// www.slate.com/articles/news_and_politics/politics/2016/12/trump_is_ building_an_ungovernment_and_his_supporters_won_t_care.html.

126. Michael Tesler, "A Newly Released Poll Shows the Populist Power of Donald Trump," Washington Post, January 27, 2016, https:// www.washingtonpost.com/news/monkey-cage/wp/2016/01/27/a-newly-released-poll-shows-the-populist-power-of-donald-trump/. See also Brenda Major, Alison Blodorn, and Gregory Major Blascovich, "The Threat of Increasing Diversity: Why Many White Americans Support Trump in the 2016 Presidential Election," Group Processes & Intergroup Relations 21 (2018), pp. 931–940.

127. Matthew Fowler, Vladimir E. Medenica, and Cathy J. Cohen, "Why 41 Percent of White Millennials Voted for Trump," Washington Post, December 15, 2017, https://www.washingtonpost.com/news/monkey-cage/wp/2017/12/15/racial-resentment-is-why-41-percent-of-white-millennials-voted-for-trump-in-2016.

128. Daniel Cox, Rachel Lienesch, and Robert P. Jones, "Beyond Economics: Fears of Cultural Displacement Pushed the White Working Class to Trump," PRRI website, May 9, 2017, https://www.prri.org/ research/white-working-class-attitudes-economy-trade-immigration-election-donald-trump/.

129. Diana Mutz, "Status Threat, Not Economic Hardship, Explains the 2016 Presidential Vote," Proceedings of the National Academy of Sciences 115 (2018), pp. 4330–4339.

130. Jazmin Brown-Iannuzzi et al., "Subjective Status Shapes Political Preferences," *Psychological Science* 26 (2015), pp. 15–26.
131. German Lopez, "Study: Racism and Sexism Predict Support for Trump Much More than Economic Dissatisfaction," *Vox*, January 4, 2017, http://www.vox.com/identities/2017/1/4/14160956/trump-racism-sexism-economy-study.
132. Martin Gilens, *Why Americans Hate Welfare* (Chicago: University of Chicago Press, 1999).
133. Again, see Brown-Iannuzzi et al., "The Relationship Between Mental Representations of Welfare Recipients and Attitudes Toward Welfare."
134. Elizabeth Anderson, *The Imperative of Integration* (Princeton, NJ: Princeton University Press, 2010). (My thanks to Alex Madva for the pointer.)
135. Susan Fiske and Courtney Tablante, "Stereotyping: Processes and Content," In *APA Handbook of Personality and Social Psychology*, Vol. 1, ed. Mario Mikulincer et al. (Hoboken, NJ: Wiley, 2015), pp. 457–507.
136. Peter Hatemi et al., "Fear as a Disposition and an Emotional State: A Genetic and Environmental Approach to Out-Group Political Preferences," *American Journal of Political Science* 57 (2013), pp. 279–293.
137. Steven Neuberg and Mark Schaller, "Evolutionary Social Cognition," in *APA Handbook of Personality and Social Psychology*, ed. Mario Mikulincer et al. (Hoboken, NJ: Wiley, 2015), pp. 1:3–45.
138. Fiske and Tablante, "Stereotyping: Processes and Content," p. 460. See also Joanne Smith and Michael Hogg, "Social Identity and Attitudes," in *Attitudes and Attitude Change*, ed. William Crano and R. Prislin (New York: Psychology Press, 2008), pp. 337–360.
139. Gordon Allport, *The Nature of Prejudice* (Reading, MA: Addison-Wesley, 1954).
140. See Thomas Pettigrew and Linda Tropp, "A Meta-Analytic Test of Intergroup Contact Theory," *Journal of Personality and Social Psychology* 90 (2006), pp. 751–783; R. Brown and M. Hewstone, "An Integrative Theory of Intergroup Contact," in *Advances in Experimental Social Psychology*, ed. M. P. Zanna (San Diego, CA: Elsevier Academic Press, 2005), pp. 37:255–343; and S. C. Wright, "Cross-Group Contact Effects," in *Intergroup Relations: The Role of Emotion and Motivation*, ed. S. Otten, T. Kessler, and K. Sassenberg (New York: Psychology Press, 2009), pp. 262–283.
141. David Dunning, "Motivated Cognition in Self and Social Thought," in *APA Handbook of Personality and Social Psychology*, ed. Mario Mikulincer et al. (Hoboken, NJ: Wiley, 2015), p. 1:781; emphasis added.

142. Gilbert Harman, "Moral Philosophy Meets Social Psychology: Virtue Ethics and the Fundamental Attribution Error," *Proceedings of the Aristotelian Society* 99 (1999), pp. 328–329.

143. Cooper et al., "Anxiety, Nostalgia, and Mistrust."

144. Manuel Klausner, "Inside Ronald Reagan," *Reason.com*, July 1975, https://reason.com/archives/1975/07/01/inside-ronald-reagan

145. Frank Chodorov, *From Out of Step: The Autobiography of an Individualist* (New York: The Devin-Adair Company, 1962), pp. 216–217.

146. Andrew Napolitano, "Taxation Is Theft," *Reason.com*, April 18, 2013, http://reason.com/archives/2013/04/18/taxation-is-theft.

147. Frank Chodorov, "Taxation Is Robbery," Mises Institute website, November 8, 2007, https://mises.org/library/taxation-robbery.

148. "Restoring the American Dream: Economy & Jobs," GOP platform, n.d., https://www.gop.com/platform/restoring-the-american-dream/.

149. This passage and all the following from Spencer's *Social Statics* are from the chapter entitled "The Right to the Use of the Earth" (Herbert Spencer, *Social Statics* [London: John Chapman, 1851], pp. 122–133).

150. Elizabeth Anderson, "What Is the Point of Equality?," *Ethics* 109 (1999), p. 289. (My thanks to Alex Madva for the suggestion.)

151. Anderson, "What Is the Point of Equality?," pp. 318–319.

152. See Will Kymlicka, *Contemporary Political Philosophy: An Introduction*, 2nd ed. (Oxford: Oxford University Press, 2002), pp. 148–152.

153. John Rawls, *A Theory of Justice* (Cambridge, MA: Harvard University Press, 1971), p. 87.

154. Spencer, *Social Statics*.

155. As libertarian philosopher Robert Nozick admitted in *Anarchy, State, and Utopia* (New York: Basic Books, 1974); see, for example, pp. 152–153.

156. Karl Marx and Friedrich Engels, *The Communist Manifesto* (London: Verso, 1998), pp. 40–41.

157. See Rawls, *A Theory of Justice*, ch. 1.

158. See Peter Ordeshook, *Game Theory and Political Theory: An Introduction* (Cambridge: Cambridge University Press, 1986), pp. 210–213.

159. Anderson, "What Is the Point of Equality?," p. 321.

160. Lucy Madison, "Elizabeth Warren: 'There Is Nobody in this Country Who Got Rich on His Own,'" *CBS News*, September 22, 2011, http://www.cbsnews.com/news/elizabeth-warren-there-is-nobody-in-this-country-who-got-rich-on-his-own/.

161. "A Century of Lawmaking for a New Nation: U.S. Congressional Documents and Debates, 1774-1875," Annals of Congress, n.d., p. 169,

http://memory.loc.gov/cgi-bin/ampage?collId=llac&fileName=004/
llac004.db&recNum=82

162. Friedrich Hayek, *Road to Serfdom* (Chicago: University of Chicago Press, 1944).

163. Thomas Frank, *The Wrecking Crew: How Conservatives Rule* (New York: Metropolitan Books, 2008), p. 117.

164. Jocelyn Kiley, "In Search of Libertarians," Pew Research Center, August 25, 2014, http://www.pewresearch.org/fact-tank/2014/08/25/in-search-of-libertarians/.

165. Kiley, "In Search of Libertarians."

166. Brian Duignan, "Charles G. and David H. Koch: American Businessmen," *Encyclopædia Britannica*, n.d., http://www.britannica.com/biography/Koch-Charles-G-and-David-H.

167. Daniel Cox, Juhem Navarro-Rivera, and Robert Jones, "In Search of Libertarians in America," PRRI website, October 29, 2013, http://publicreligion.org/research/2013/10/2013-american-values-survey.

168. "41 Days: An OPB Documentary on the Oregon Occupation," *OPB*, February 15, 2016, http://www.opb.org/news/series/burns-oregon-standoff-bundy-militia-news-updates/oregon-standoff-occupation-malheur-41-days-opb-documentary/.

169. Cooper, et al., "Anxiety, Nostalgia, and Mistrust."

170. Adam Nagourney, "A Defiant Rancher Savors the Audience That Rallied to His Side," *New York Times*, April 23, 2014, http://www.nytimes.com/2014/04/24/us/politics/rancher-proudly-breaks-the-law-becoming-a-hero-in-the-west.html.

171. Ravi Iyer, Spassena Kloeva, Jesse Graham, Peter Ditto, and Jonathan Haidt, "Understanding Libertarian Morality: The Psychological Dispositions of Self-Identified Libertarians," *PLoS ONE* 7 (2012), p. e42366.

172. Saul Kassin and Steven Fein, *Social Psychology*, 10th ed. (Boston: Wadsworth, 2016), p. 163; see "Project Implicit," Project Implicit website, n.d., https://implicit.harvard.edu/implicit/aboutus.html.

173. Chris Mooney, "Across America, Whites Are Biased and They Don't Even Know It," *Washington Post*, December 8, 2014, https://www.washingtonpost.com/news/wonk/wp/2014/12/08/across-america-whites-are-biased-and-they-dont-even-know-it/.

174. See, for example, Frederick Oswald, Gregory Mitchell, Hart Blanton, James Jaccard, and Philip Tetlock, "Predicting Ethnic and Racial Discrimination: A Meta-Analysis of IAT Criterion Studies," *Journal of Personality and Social Psychology* 105 (2013), pp. 171–192.

175. See Alex Madva's comment on John Schwenkler, "What We Can Learn from Implicit Association Test, a Brains Blog Roundtable," *Brains blog*, January 17, 2017, http://philosophyofbrains.com/2017/01/17/how-can-we-measure-implicit-bias-a-brains-blog-roundtable.aspx.

176. Lynn Stout, "Taking Conscience Seriously," in *Moral Markets: The Critical Role of Values in the Economy*, ed. Paul Zak (Princeton, NJ: Princeton University Press, 2007), pp. 158–159; ctd. by Black, "The Faux Hyper-Meritocracy that Threatens to Destroy Us."

177. See Belinda Board and Katarina Fritzon, "Disordered Personalities at Work," *Psychology, Crime & Law* 11 (2005), pp. 17–32; and Paul Babiak and Robert Hare, *Snakes in Suits: When Psychopaths Go to Work* (New York: HarperCollins, 2006).

178. Adam Grant, "Does Studying Economics Breed Greed?," *Psychology Today*, October 22, 2013, https://www.psychologytoday.com/blog/give-and-take/201310/does-studying-economics-breed-greed; see also Robert Frank, *Passions Within Reason: The Strategic Role of the Emotions* (New York: W. W. Norton, 1988).

179. Kahan and Braman, "Cultural Cognition and Public Policy."

180. George Lakoff, "Why Trump?," George Lakoff blog, March 2, 2016, http://georgelakoff.com/2016/03/02/why-trump/.

181. "Surveys of Religion," Baylor Institute for Studies of Religion, n.d., http://www.baylorisr.org/programs-research/global-studies-of-religion/surveys-of-religion/.

182. Richard Hofstadter, *Anti-Intellectualism in American Life* (New York: Random House, 1970); ctd. by Gauchat, "Politicization of Science in the Public Sphere," p. 170n3.

4

Religion

4.1 Reasons to Believe

In a text on denial and ideological denialism, it is impossible to avoid a discussion of religious belief. Within any widely practiced religious worldview there are innumerable variations in how revelatory texts may be interpreted. One important variation pertains to the extent to which factual claims within a foundational text are taken to be literally true. "Believers" fall on a spectrum somewhere between understanding a religious text as predominantly allegorical and understanding a text as factual and inerrant.[1] Of particular interest in the study of the phenomenon of denial is monotheistic religious literalism, according to which the supreme deity worshiped is taken to exist as an actual entity with his or her own independent existence and intentions, and who has actually performed miracles corresponding to those described in that religion's texts or teachings.

The term "fundamentalism" appears to originate in an early twentieth-century Protestant movement stressing biblical infallibility and the historical reality of the miracles of Jesus, along with the literal facts of Jesus's virgin birth, the opportunity for atonement presented by his death, and his resurrection. This term has come to be applied more broadly to sects of other religious traditions similarly emphasizing the literal fact of central real-world assertions made by their respective foundational texts. It is a more recent development for "fundamentalist" to sometimes take on the pejorative sense of "fanatic," and—like the term "ideologue"—to be associated automatically with inflexibility and intolerance. Because of this pejorative connotation, I shall instead employ the term **literalist** to describe anyone who upholds a given set of religious teachings as factually true in all or most details.

How common is religious literalism? Fifty percent of U.S.-born Muslims hold that the Quran is the "literal word of God."[2] In a Pew survey of fifteen Sub-Saharan African nations, majorities of up to 93% maintained that the Quran "should be read literally, word for word."[3] Majorities of Muslims in thirty-two of thirty-nine predominantly Muslim countries and territories agree that there is "only one correct way to understand the teachings of Islam."[4] Very large majorities of Muslims polled in these thirty-nine countries expressed a belief in predestination and in the literal existence of angels, heaven, and hell. About two-thirds of Americans have made a "personal commitment to Jesus Christ," and in turn, "nearly two-thirds of those who have made a personal commitment to Jesus say they believe that after they die they will go to heaven because they have confessed their sins and accepted Jesus Christ as their savior."[5] An ABC News poll released in 2004 found that 61% of Americans take the creation story in the Bible's Genesis to be "literally true," with 60% agreeing that the story of Noah's Ark and the Great Flood happened as described, "word for word."[6] Sixty-four percent believed that Moses parted the Red Sea as described in the Bible. Pew's 2014 Religious Landscape Study found that 39% of Christians view their holy scriptures as the "word of God" and that they "should be taken literally"; 59% of U.S. evangelical Protestants agree that the Bible is the "literal word of God."[7] Another survey commissioned by the BBC in 2017 found that 57% of active (church-attending) Christians believed in the resurrection of Jesus "word-for-word as described in the Bible."[8] According to a 2018 Pew Research Center survey, 56% of Americans, including 80% of self-described Christians, "believe in God as described in the Bible" (other self-described Christians say they believe in a "spiritual or higher power," but not God as described in the Bible).[9]

"I even believe in the Devil," announced former U.S. Supreme Court justice Antonin Scalia in a 2013 magazine interview.[10] He did not appear to have been articulating some sort of merely figurative or allegorical understanding of the biblical Satan: Scalia went on to discuss the Devil's particular "desires"; and to account for an absence of direct evidence for his existence by the fact that the Devil has learned to be "wilier." When the interviewer expressed surprise at such assertions, Scalia was offended:

You're looking at me as though I'm weird. My God! Are you so out
of touch with most of America, most of which believes in the Devil?
I mean, Jesus Christ believed in the Devil! It's in the Gospels! You
travel in circles that are so, so removed from mainstream America
that you are appalled that anybody would believe in the Devil! Most
of mankind has believed in the Devil, for all of history. Many more
intelligent people than you or me have believed in the Devil.

This highly educated judge was quite clear in this interview that, for
him, the biblical Satan is a real entity with conscious intentions and
tactics. And it was, furthermore, his considered view that this is typical
for Christians.

Such professions regarding the literal truth of religious doctrines are
backed up by practices like church attendance and prayer. More than two-
thirds of Americans (mostly Christians) attend worship services of some
kind at least a few times a month.[11] Sixty-nine percent of Muslims worldwide pray daily. Presuming that we are to take people seriously when they
profess to believe something, we should consider religious literalism to
be widespread—indeed, a majority view among Christians and Muslims
generally—unless we discover good reasons to the contrary.

A literalist religious worldview is paradigmatically ideological in
that it involves a set of factual claims that systematically inform one's
evaluative attitudes toward all kinds of personal, social, cultural, and
political issues. Despite their enormous consequence, few factual
claims exhibit *less* evidentiary support and are subject to *less* critical
scrutiny than the central assertions of (literalist) religious ideologies.
At the same time, those professing belief in divine supernatural entities,
and in their powers, activities, and intentions, often express a level of
certainty with regard to these alleged facts that far surpasses their confidence in many more mundane assertions of fact. (Seventy-six percent
of U.S. Christians describe their belief in God as "absolutely certain."[12])

Any claim that a denier is *in denial* is a judgment call, based on one's
notion of, among other things, the subject's access to evidence and
his or her motivations.* Climate, human biology, and economics all

* And yes, accusations of denialism themselves must always be read in the context of
the accuser's motives and treatment of evidence!

involve complex systems with lots of moving parts and uncertainties. No one fully understands every detail of each of these systems. There is always room, in principle, for evidence-based denial of some consensus scientific, medical, or historical analysis regarding AGW, vaccine safety, the relation between tax cuts and economic growth, and so on. The universe itself is the ultimate complex system, and our understanding of the fundamental forces governing it is incomplete. We have certainly made some progress, but there are vast mysteries about the nature of reality itself that may yet prove utterly beyond even our most sophisticated current and future physical sciences. But this incompleteness in our understanding makes the level of certainty expressed by the devout about the most profound, hidden truths of the cosmos all the more puzzling. As in the last chapter, I need to explain the key problems for the leading philosophical justifications for religious belief in order to make the case that much religious belief rests on motivated reasoning.

Billions of human beings today profess a firm belief in a real and actual invisible, all-powerful, all-knowing, and benevolent Creator of all things—a Creator who, further, occasionally miraculously intervenes in worldly events. And they assert this *as incontrovertible fact* despite many or most of them having some access to or awareness of a number of concerns that should at least cast some doubt on such an assertion:

- The reasons for the existence of a Creator of absolutely everything would itself be a mystery, so the entire religious program just replaces one mystery (i.e., the existence and nature of the universe) with another (i.e., the existence and nature of a vaguely anthropomorphic Creator, who further would seem to have to somehow subsist outside of [?] space and time in order to be responsible for the creation of all spatiotemporal reality itself).

- The mostly textual basis for belief in a supernatural Creator violates rules of evidence believers implicitly accept in most other contexts. As Pierre-Simon Laplace put it, "The weight of evidence for an extraordinary claim must be proportioned to its strangeness."[13] Most people, most of the time, live by the rule that extraordinary claims require extraordinary evidence. The second-hand testimony of a casual acquaintance is perfectly sufficient for ordinary claims like that the vending machine down the hall is out of Pepsi. But if the very same co-worker reports that there is a ghost in the break room or that he has recently captured an extraterrestrial invader, it is unlikely these claims would be accepted by anyone without further confirmation.

- According to one recent survey, "56% of Americans agree or mostly agree that God is in control of all Earthly events."[14] But they do not call a priest to fix their refrigerator, nor do they (with some exceptions) address a broken ankle with prayer alone. Lacking explanations for amazing natural phenomena like changing seasons, lightning, or biological life, primitive societies turned to supernatural explanations involving intention and purpose to account for such wonders. The history of supernatural belief has followed a trend according to which the number of phenomena explained by supernatural forces or interventions has decreased, as scientific explanations of the hitherto inexplicable have become available. Should this not suggest that, historically, supernatural explanations for events have derived in part from scientific ignorance? And should this fact not raise some doubt about the truth of the supernatural worldview itself?

- Typical of many major religious origin stories is the notion that the entire universe was created specifically for human beings or with human beings playing a central role. Yet we now know that our solar system belongs to a galaxy of between 100 and 400 billion stars, and recent observations have raised the official estimate of the number of galaxies in the local, observable universe from hundreds of billions to between 1 and 2 trillion.[15] The idea that all that stuff is pretty much incidental to the whole point of the universe—namely, the well-being of a small tribe in the Middle East on this particular planet—seems a bit provincial.

- I won't rehash the extensive history of discussions of the "problem of evil" (dating back at least as far as the ancient Greek philosopher Epicurus), except to briefly reiterate that the widespread existence of pointless suffering caused by natural and moral evils seems inconsistent with the existence of an all-powerful, benevolent, and interventionist deity. It is possible that God has some hidden reasons to allow earthquakes, malaria, birth defects, and the sexual slavery of children (say, to inspire greater acts of kindness or a closer relationship to God), and so each of these horrors is necessary somehow to a better world. But, in the absence of conclusive evidence for the existence of God, one should also consider the hypothesis that these things happen just because of plate tectonics, parasites, and people being cruel to each other. Our evidence for these phenomena is much stronger than our evidence for a loving deity who has a secret reason to instigate tsunamis and permit child molestation.

- At this point in history, most believers are aware that there are billions of others who hold incompatible religious beliefs with equal fervor and on similar grounds (i.e., some set of texts conveying ancient testimonies and the cultural traditions that have developed around these testimonies). It would be difficult for an educated person to be wholly oblivious to the fact that the particular religious beliefs people hold are highly correlated with the particular views of their childhood caregivers. Most believers, in other words, should be able easily to infer that, had they been born into a different family and culture, they would almost certainly worship—with equal confidence—a different god or gods. As a believer, you have to simultaneously consider yourself lucky to have been born into the one true faith, while being aware that most other people in the world (who worship a false god) feel just as lucky, for the same reasons. Every devout Muslim has exactly the same reasons for being a Muslim as Christians do for being Christians.[16] Muslims also have holy writings and testimony of miracles, and are just as convinced as Christians are of their beliefs. But Christians reject that evidence as totally inadequate and reject Islam as a false religion. Same for all the other religions, except their own. For exactly the same reasons, and with exactly the same conviction, Muslims reject Christianity as a false religion, along with all the other ones.

Despite all this, billions of human beings even today profess the literal truth of the teachings of the Abrahamic religions—Christianity, Islam, Judaism—and so identify with a monotheistic tradition that maintains the existence of a benevolent supreme being, who in turn has views about what behaviors and social structures are appropriate;

a large majority of human beings subscribe to *some* set of facts about a supernatural realm that in some way informs their opinions about how one ought to live, what cultural traditions ought to be followed, and how society ought to be structured. And again, these beliefs are quite often characterized by a degree of certainty that far outstrips the believer's confidence in many more mundane facts that do not suffer from anything like these dissonant concerns. As John Locke observed, for someone in the grips of religious fervor, neither contrary evidence nor inherent absurdity in the doctrine can shake this certainty:

> This opinion of his principles (let them be what they will) being once established in any one's mind, it is easy to be imagined what reception any proposition shall find, how clearly soever proved, that shall invalidate their authority, or at all thwart these internal oracles; whereas the grossest absurdities and improbabilities, being but agreeable to such principles, go down glibly, and are easily digested. The great obstinacy that is to be found in men firmly believing quite contrary opinions, though many times equally absurd, in the various religions of mankind, are as evident a proof as they are an unavoidable consequence of this way of reasoning from received traditional principles. So that men will disbelieve their own eyes, renounce the evidence of their senses, and give their own experience the lie, rather than admit of anything disagreeing with these sacred tenets.[17]

Locke also argued that, for many, there is little salience in the issue of conflicts between faith and reason. Most of the time, the religious worldview has little or no practical effect on how the masses live their lives. When called upon, people go along with it because they don't really have occasion to question it—and indeed, have every reason *not* to critically reflect on what religious authorities and cultural elites profess:

> *There are not so many men in errors and wrong opinions as is commonly supposed.* Not that I think they embrace the truth; but indeed, because concerning those doctrines they keep such a stir about, they have no thought, no opinion at all. For if any one should a little catechise the greatest part of the partizans of most of the sects

in the world, he would not find, concerning those matters they are so zealous for, that they have any opinions of their own: much less would he have reason to think that they took them upon the examination of arguments and appearance of probability. They are resolved to stick to a party that education or interest has engaged them in; and there, like the common soldiers of an army, show their courage and warmth as their leaders direct, without ever examining, or so much as knowing, the cause they contend for. If a man's life shows that he has no serious regard for religion; for what reason should we think that he beats his head about the opinions of his church, and troubles himself to examine the grounds of this or that doctrine? It is enough for him to obey his leaders, to have his hand and his tongue ready for the support of the common cause, and thereby approve himself to those who can give him credit, preferment, or protection in that society. Thus men become professors of, and combatants for, those opinions they were never convinced of nor proselytes to; no, nor ever had so much as floating in their heads: and though one cannot say there are fewer improbable or erroneous opinions in the world than there are, yet this is certain; there are fewer that actually assent to them, and mistake them for truths, than is imagined.[18]

We have talked a lot about how ideological beliefs can be tightly intertwined with social and cultural identity. For some, professed religiosity may function primarily as a signal of group membership, so it may say less about the individual's factual beliefs than about his or her cultural identifications. Others may be said to really hold literalist beliefs about the supernatural, but they successfully avoid dissonance through compartmentalization: They really think about their religious beliefs only in ritual contexts, and they set them aside almost entirely in daily life. There is no need for dissonance-resolving rationalization of belief if the religious worldview of ritual and the naturalistic worldview of everyday life never occupy the same cognitive space at the same time.

It's a different story when it comes to theologians and philosophers who explicitly defend the rationality of religious literalism. Elite intellectuals who have devoted a career to defending the factual truth of religious teachings represent the clearest cases of individuals who have reflected on their beliefs and the reasons therefor. In most cases—among elites and otherwise—religious belief originates with familial and cultural indoctrination. But how is such belief *sustained* by well-informed and reflective persons, given the massive cognitive dissonance involved? Rationalization strategies employed by the defenders of the faith have fallen roughly into three main categories: (1) testimony regarding supernatural events; (2) direct, revelatory knowledge of the divine based on a special faculty of perception; and (3) philosophical arguments purporting to show the necessity of a Creator in order to explain the existence and/or nature of the universe.

4.1.1 Evidence of Miracles

Philosopher William Lane Craig has spent over twenty-five years engaging in illuminating public debates with nonbelievers over the state of the evidence for the existence of the Christian god. He maintains that the evidence for key Christian miracles—such as the resurrection of Jesus—is sound, and so belief in the Christian god is straightforwardly justified by the evidence at hand.

The following is Craig's own summary of his reasons for accepting the claim that "On different occasions and under various circumstances different individuals and groups of people experienced appearances of Jesus alive from the dead," which is in turn the key piece of evidence for the all-important resurrection miracle:

This is a fact which is virtually universally acknowledged by scholars, for the following reasons:
1. *Paul's list of eyewitnesses to Jesus's resurrection appearances guarantees that such appearances occurred.* Paul tells us that Jesus appeared to his chief disciple Peter, then to the inner circle of disciples known as the Twelve; then he appeared to a group of 500 disciples at once, then to his younger brother James, who up to that time was apparently not a believer, then to all the apostles. Finally, Paul adds, "he appeared also to me," at the time when Paul was still a persecutor of the early Jesus movement (1

Cor. 15.5–8). Given the early date of Paul's information, as well as his personal acquaintance with the people involved, these appearances cannot be dismissed as mere legends.

2. *The appearance narratives in the Gospels provide multiple, independent attestation of the appearances.* For example, the appearance to Peter is attested by Luke and Paul; the appearance to the Twelve is attested by Luke, John, and Paul; and the appearance to the women is attested by Matthew and John. The appearance narratives span such a breadth of independent sources that it cannot be reasonably denied that the earliest disciples did have such experiences.[19]

Similarly, Craig defends his belief in the historical fact of various other miracles specific to the Christian tradition by citing documents that describe witnesses of the event or secondhand accounts of the event. He frequently adds considerations such as that some of the alleged witnesses were described as skeptics or as people who otherwise had little motivation to invent their stories. He concludes that the best explanation for these accounts is the truth of the Christian miracles. This "historical" approach to confirming the events in the Christian Bible is not unusual: It is reflected in, conservatively, hundreds of English-language books (and websites) providing sympathetic historical and textual examinations of the accuracy of biblical claims about Jesus.

Let's suppose everything Craig says is true. Let us suppose these were actual eyewitness accounts, rather than anonymous second- or third-hand accounts written decades later.[20] Let us suppose these various accounts were mutually consistent on the details, and let us ignore the fact that these accounts also include a variety of other incredible events for which little or no corroborating testimony is available. David Hume's famous essay "On Miracles" explains the essential problem with testimony as to the occurrence of miracles (such as the Resurrection).[21] The laws of nature are based on experience—that is, we find in experience certain regular associations that we take to represent underlying rules that determine what is or is not possible. (The point of the scientific method is to describe the best and only reliable way to form and test these hypotheses, and to incorporate them into larger theories about how the universe works.) By definition, a miracle is an event that violates a law of nature. So any alleged experience of a miracle by definition stands in opposition to the whole of human experience, and the probability of the alleged miracle must be judged in that context.

Hume lists a number of reasons why we should be suspicious of testimony of supernatural events. He notes the human propensity to enjoy both hearing and delivering accounts of miracles, motivated by the pleasurable passions of surprise and wonder. He notes the motive to religion itself, wherein humans can derive comfort, satisfaction, and individual self-affirmation from religious belief (and we might add the self-satisfaction to be gleaned from being a member of the Chosen People). He reminds us of the potential benefits of being considered a prophet or a member of religious leadership. He also observes that miracle reports always seem to pertain to events distant from us in space and time (and always seem to occur in the absence of reliable recording devices). Biblical times seem to have abounded in obvious and unambiguous miracles, but we are less fortunate now. Hume proposes that, when presented with a claim about an extraordinary event irreconcilable with the bulk of human experience, and taking into account the quality, quantity, and provenance of testimony, we should consider which is the "greater miracle": That the miracle happened as reported, or that the witnesses are lying, exaggerating, deceived, self-deceived, or delusional. He proposes that we should reject the greater miracle— that is, the less likely option. Which is the more likely option? The phenomena of human gullibility, error, misinterpretation, and hallucination are familiar and not at all uncommon. That a miracle report is an artifact of error or motivated self-deception is always more likely than a supernatural explanation, which by definition violates our understanding as to how things normally work.

We must always be open to surprising, hitherto-thought-impossible discoveries. The history of science is full of these, and these discoveries expand our scientific understanding of the world. But discoveries that can be incorporated into larger, fully naturalistic theories about the world are not evidence for the supernatural. The defender of supernaturalism needs the notion of a well-established law of nature in order to identify the truly miraculous: An event is only evidence for the supernatural if it cannot be reconciled with a naturalistic worldview.[22]

Hume's reasoning need not be taken to rule out the possibility of a miracle a priori; rather, the takeaway should be that the bar for establishing the occurrence of a miracle should be set very high.

Plus, there is the issue of equally well-supported miracle stories representing views of the world incompatible with other religions. The Quran reports that, when Muhammad was challenged by the pagan Meccans to prove the existence of Allah, the moon split in two. This event was witnessed by multitudes, and led to many conversions on the part of the hitherto skeptical.[23] The Hadith report many miracles performed by Muhammad (or perhaps one should say Allah, in support of Muhammad), such as the production of food and water for thousands of troops both before and after the Battle of Tabouk in the year 630.[24] Accounts of these events are based on eyewitness reports, which have been passed down by named scholars. According to eyewitness reports in Buddhist holy texts, Gautama Buddha had superhuman powers. Many contemporary miracles related to Buddhism have been reported, including, for example, the spontaneous emission of light from statues of the Buddha in a temple in Sri Lanka in 2006—a fact attested to by thousands of witnesses.[25] Christians citing a text and testimony of miracles as proof of their unseen God must simultaneously reject evidence of exactly the same kind and quality when it is cited in support of other deities. As Hume put it,

> To make this the better understood, let us consider, that, in matters of religion, whatever is different is contrary; and that it is impossible the religions of ancient Rome, of Turkey, of Siam, and of China should, all of them, be established on any solid foundation. Every miracle, therefore, pretended to have been wrought in any of these religions (and all of them abound in miracles), as its direct scope is to establish the particular system to which it is attributed; so has it the same force, though more indirectly, to overthrow every other system. In destroying a rival system, it likewise destroys the credit of those miracles, on which that system was established; so that all the prodigies of different religions are to be regarded as contrary facts, and the evidences of these prodigies, whether weak or strong, as opposite to each other.[26]

We have living eyewitnesses who can attest to the existence of the Loch Ness Monster, a sort of aquatic dinosaur holdover allegedly living in a large lake in Scotland. There is even photographic and video evidence of the Monster, plus some intriguing sonar contacts.[27] There is no comparable evidence for Jesus and the Resurrection. Our evidence for the existence of the Loch Ness Monster is vastly, vastly stronger than our evidence for the divinity of Jesus. (Further, the Monster is not even alleged to be a supernatural being, and so the Monster hypothesis is not burdened with the inherent improbability of a miraculous violation of a law of nature.) Even so, few people take evidence for the Monster seriously, mainly because the prior probability of these reports being true is very low. One suspects that things might have been different had people been raised from infancy according to a worldview that included the Monster, wherein their cultural identity, values, sense of self, and feelings of stability, inclusion, and purpose rested on the factual existence of the Monster. Under such circumstances, contemporary social psychology would give us every reason to expect strong and enduring belief in the Monster. From our experience of many other cases of motivated credulity, we would also expect believers to engage in the selective gathering, recall, and interpretation of evidence in rationalizing their commitment to the existence of the Monster.

Even if you ignore all the texts and testimonies lending support to competing religious traditions, the level of credulity involved in accepting at face value the assertions of a text like the Bible is highly suspect. Neuroscientist and anti-religionist author Sam Harris describes the problem concisely:

> Tell a devout Christian that his wife is cheating on him, or that frozen yogurt can make a man invisible, and he is likely to require as much evidence as anyone else, and to be persuaded only to the extent that you give it. Tell him that the book he keeps by his bed was written by an invisible deity who will punish him with fire for eternity if he fails to accept its every incredible claim about the universe, and he seems to require no evidence whatsoever.[28]

Belief in the factual truth—the *unassailable* factual truth—of some particular religion on the basis of some set of ancient testimonies can only be sustained by confirmation bias of an unparalleled class and magnitude. From what we know about motivated reasoning and denial, it should not be surprising that brilliant scholars can be subject to this sort of self-deception. We know that well-educated, capable elites are as prone to motivated reasoning as anyone else, and more immovably confident in their conclusions than most. In a bizarre display of unintentional self-parody, respected Oxford philosopher Richard Swinburne cited Bayesian probability theory in assigning a probability of 97% to Jesus' resurrection, based on (a) an extremely selective canvassing of the evidence, and (b) a set of confident assumptions about the quality of the selected evidence.[29] Note that it takes a scholar familiar with Bayesian probability theory to generate this spurious line of reasoning, just as it takes some knowledge of solar flares or Milankovitch cycles to come up with spurious technical arguments denying AGW. The well-educated just have more information to select from when looking for supporting evidence, and they have a wider range of techniques available to help rationalize their evidentiary choices. They consequently can exhibit all the more confidence in their selective interpretation of the evidence.

The most commonly claimed variety of miracle is a divine intervention in human life following intercessory prayer. Many religious sects, Christian and non-Christian, formally claim that their god or gods, and/or allied entities like saints, sometimes intervene in human life in response to prayer.[30] Over 90% of Christians, Jews, and Muslims report praying at least once a week.[31] Surveys show several reported reasons for prayer, including intimacy with God and the expression of gratitude. But other primary reasons include helping oneself and others by asking for an intervention of some sort. Over 90% of each group (Christians, Jews, and Muslims) report their prayers are at least sometimes "answered." When asked to account for why a given prayer might not "come true," most respondents rationalize such failures as "not being God's plan"; only a tiny fraction—4.8% of Christians and 2.4% of Muslims—think the most important reason must be because "God does not answer specific prayers." A stated belief that one's prayers have been answered, or that some event would not or could not have happened without prayer, is extremely common, including among those with a scientific background. Thirty-nine percent of

U.S. physicians believe that "the Bible's miracle stories are literally true"; a majority of physicians report praying for God to help their patients, and 55% report having seen treatment results in their patients that they consider "miraculous."[32] Among the general population as well, perhaps the most common reason to call for divine intervention is to help someone recover from illness or injury. There is a selectivity about the use of intercessory prayer in cases of illness or injury that is very revealing. People pray to God all the time to cure their relative's cancer or to help someone recover from a stroke, but they never pray for the restoration of lost or amputated limbs.[33] While sincerely believing in the healing power of prayer, they somehow just know not to bother with it in cases that are non-ambiguous. People pray for their house to be spared from a tornado, but never for it to be magically restored the day after it was destroyed. Prayer never brings about events that would otherwise be impossible. This is a terrific example of building confirmation bias into the practice itself: The practice of intercessory prayer is only deployed in cases where there is some chance of being able to claim success.*

It is not uncommon for believers to say that evidence is irrelevant and that the nature of religious belief is different from other sorts of belief. The appropriate attitude is one of "faith," or a sort of trust despite a lack of evidence. Faith is an odd notion because it abandons the usual prescriptive characteristic of knowledge claims/claims of fact—namely that, given the same evidence, others should rationally accept the same claim. There are no other areas of human knowledge such that it would be considered acceptable to say "I believe this (and with unshakeable certainty!), but I have no evidence for my belief."[34] Why should propositions about an invisible realm of the most fantastic entities imaginable get a pass on evidence? Most poignantly, those who eschew the notion of reasoned religious belief have thereby ruled out the possibility of explaining why one should have faith in any one particular deity rather than another. Harris asks us to consider a hypothetical scenario:

---

* The fact that some theologians reject intercessory prayer is irrelevant here. The vast majority of followers of multiple major sects—such as Roman Catholicism—accept it and practice it regularly.

What if all our knowledge of the world were suddenly to disappear? Imagine that all six billion of us were to wake up tomorrow morning in a state of utter ignorance and despair. Our books and computers are here, but we can't make heads or tails of their contents. What knowledge would we want to reclaim first?[35]

He suggests we would prioritize knowledge about finding shelter and growing food, learning a common language, and learning how to use machines. Eventually we would doubtless turn our attention to existential matters. But Harris asks,

When in the process of reclaiming our humanity will it be important to know that Jesus was born of a virgin? Or that he was resurrected? And how would we relearn these truths, if they are indeed true? By reading the Bible? Our tour of the shelves will deliver similar pearls from antiquity—like the "fact" that Isis, the goddess of fertility, sports an impressive pair of cow horns. Reading further, we will learn that Thor carries a hammer and that Marduk's sacred animals are horses, dogs, and a dragon with a forked tongue. Whom shall we give top billing in our resurrected world? Yahweh or Shiva? . . . And what will we think of those curious people who begin proclaiming that one of our books is distinct from all others in that it was actually written by the creator of the universe?[36]

By contrast, because scientific observations and experiments are replicable, we could expect eventually to be able to re-identify our science textbooks as factually accurate. Harris's point is that "most of what we currently hold sacred is not sacred for any reason other than that it was thought sacred *yesterday*."

The fallback is that the Christian god, say, is the right one to have faith in because the evidence supports his existence over the others. But faith was supposed to be the answer to the inadequacy of the evidence.

Nicholas Rescher is another leading Christian philosopher (with no fewer than 176 books to his name so far). He recognizes the problem of accounting for one's choice of faith. In a recent book, *Reason and Religion*, he answers by discounting the importance of "historically factual correctness":

But if adopting a religion involves commitment taken "on faith" that goes beyond what rational inquiry (in its standard "scientific" form) can manage to validate, how can a rational person ever appropriately join in? How can there be a cogent rationale for a faith whose doctrines encompass reason-transcending commitments? The answer lies in the consideration that factual claims are not the crux here. For religious commitment is not a matter of historically factual correctness so much as one of life-orienting efficacy, since the sort of "belief" at issue in religion is at bottom a matter of life orientation rather than historical information. . . . What is at issue looks not to historical factuality but to parabolic cogency—the ability to provide appropriate life-orientation for us—putting people on the right track. It is a matter of achieving appropriate life-goals, realizing rational contentment (Aristotelian eudemonia), getting guidance in shaping a life one can look back on with rational contentment.[37]

As a reviewer dryly notes in reference to this passage, "Some might, perhaps, balk at the minimizing of historical correctness."[38] Rescher's rationalization downgrades religion to the status of a moralizing fairy tale, which is not what the defender of the literal truth of his or her supernatural worldview is looking for.

4.1.2 Sensing God

The language of "feeling the presence of God" or of "entering into communion with the Lord" is familiar. John Calvin introduced the term *sensus divinitatis* to describe a direct *sense* of the presence of God, deriving from an occult faculty of human perception analogous to our powers of visual or auditory perception. He claimed "That there exists in the human mind and indeed by natural instinct, some sense of Deity, we hold to be beyond dispute, since God himself, to prevent any man from pretending ignorance, has endued all men with some idea of his Godhead."[39] The notion of a belief in God based on some direct, inimitable experience recalls the visions, auditory experiences, and ecstasies of mystics like Joan of Arc, Teresa of Ávila, or Bernadette of Lourdes. But rather than some images, sounds, or bodily feelings to be interpreted, proponents of the *sensus divinitatis* believe in a faculty of perception distinct from—but on an epistemic par with—our other sensory faculties. We know (or can know) that God is present, using this faculty, just as we can know that a bad smell is there because we smell it or that we are sad because we feel sad. Philosopher and Christian apologist Alvin Plantinga has termed beliefs arising from this sense "properly basic."[40] A **properly basic** belief is one that is either self-evident or founded on the direct evidence of the senses. I can't really corroborate the evidence of my senses except by reference to other deliverances of my (or others') sense experience. I can't really justify my belief in 2 + 2 = 4 except by relying on other, similarly founded claims in mathematics. These facts do not stop us from thinking of belief based on sense experience or self-evidence as rational. If believing that I have two hands because I feel and see them is rational, or if believing that 2 + 2 = 4 just because it is self-evidently true is rational, then believing in God just because I sense his divine presence is rational. After all, if we assume that God exists, and that he wants us to know him, then we can reasonably infer that he would give us reliable "intuitions" as to his existence.[41] (The failure of many to detect their own *sensus divinitatis* is explained by inattention or by signal interference caused by sin.[42]) A number of leading scholars, including major recent and contemporary philosophers like Plantinga, William Alston, Nicholas Wolterstorff, and Michael Rea,[43] have endorsed some version of this position. (I want to stress to the reader not familiar with academic philosophy that these persons have all been justly acclaimed as ranking among the most intelligent and accomplished scholars of philosophy of religion—each of them highly educated, scientifically literate, and fully informed about other religious traditions, as well as about the history of religious skepticism.) The phenomenology varies from distinctive feelings of joy and completion to an indescribable sense of infinite goodness. Essayist Romain Rolland describes an "oceanic feeling" of oneness with eternity that he identifies as the basis for religious belief.[44]

One problem with the claim that belief in God can be based on a special, private feeling is that it renders such belief beyond appraisal or criticism, and so makes it impossible to distinguish between the rationality of a belief in Jesus and the rationality of a belief in Poseidon or in any other otherwise-invisible forces.[45] Linda Zagzebski, another philosopher of religion and Christian apologist, finds the notion of a private *sensus divinitatis* problematic, for this reason: "It does not permit a rational observer outside the community of believers in the model to distinguish between Plantinga's model and the beliefs of any group, no matter how irrational and bizarre—sun-worshippers, cult followers, devotées of the Greek gods."[46] (As far as I can tell, Zagzebski is here using the terms "irrational" and "bizarre" unironically.) Some claims will be defeasible by their failure in testable situations, such as the failure of an apocalypse cult to produce the apocalypse upon the prophesied date, or the failure of Helios worshipers to explain away modern evidence inconsistent with a low-orbit chariot dragging the sun across the sky each day. However, neither of these options applies to any religious tradition (like most of those that have survived the Scientific Revolution) that avoids really specific predictions or other defeasible claims, choosing instead an intangible deity who remains mostly invisible and who works in mysterious ways.

Defenders of the rationality of their own religious belief based on a sense of the divine must, at the same time, utterly reject as confused the exact same sort of claim on the part of others who assert they have intimate knowledge of some other god. This is some serious cognitive dissonance. Their only option is to say that all divine experiences are not equal, in that only some have corroborating testimonies and historical evidence. Yet many do. Miracles witnessed by Muslims in predominantly Muslim territories tend to be Islamic miracles, and Buddhists in Buddhist-dominant cultures almost invariably experience miracles confirming the truth of Buddhism. Ecstatic religious visions experienced by Hindus are rarely visions of Jesus, as opposed to some more culturally apt divinity.[47] Each culture has its historical texts and testimonies. Suppose one were to do a comprehensive international study, not about miracle reports or visions, but on what different people report directly sensing about divinity. Would anyone really expect these reports to fail to be closely correlated with the particular religious tradition of each individual? To the extent people report directly sensing a god, Christians will "sense" only their god (and know him to be Jesus), Muslims will sense theirs (and know him to be Allah), and so on. The notion of a divine sense can be used to justify an irrefutable belief in any of an infinite variety of gods. So, in order to resolve a *sensus divinitatis* disagreement of this kind, one would have to advert to testimony or other evidence. But then it's really just about the publicly available evidence again, and such testimonials suffer from the inherent unlikelihood of the events they describe, plus the problem of conflicting miracle reports from other cultural traditions.

We must ask ourselves again which is the "lesser miracle" (i.e., the more likely explanation for this conviction): that the feeling of a special communion with God comes from an infinite supernatural being, or that the claimant is caught up in an ecstatic enthusiasm of his or her own making? If I may quote myself for a moment, here is something I concluded in chapter 1, after examining the psychological literature on denial:

> We are now in a better position to understand motivated cognition and denial. Motivated cognition is the sincere confounding of an emotional need—usually of a self-serving, self-protective, and/or social identity-defining sort—to hold a certain view of things with having good reasons to hold that view; to be in denial, then, is to engage in a kind of psychological projection—that is, *to unconsciously mistake the emotional value of denying something for actually having good reasons to deny it.*

Proponents of the *sensus divinitatis* take this variety of psychological projection one step further: They mistake the emotional value of believing in something for an actual sensation of that thing!

This phenomenon would not tell us much about the relation between ideology and human psychology if it were limited to fools or madmen. What is so interesting about this kind of claim is that it has been proclaimed and defended by such extremely thoughtful and capable people, from Calvin himself to elite present-day scholars who, unlike Calvin, do not suffer from any deficit of basic information about science and nature. Intellectuals like Plantinga have spent decades constructing elaborate rationalizations for taking this culturally relative—and obviously motivated—internal state as justification for a belief in God.[48] One thing philosophers do better than anyone else is demolish bad reasoning. That is why this embrace of really terrible reasoning on the part of Plantinga and other leading intellectuals, along with millions of well-informed, scientifically literate believers, is so strongly indicative of denial.

4.1.3 Cosmology and Teleology

One other important category of alleged proofs of God's existence has to do not with proofs based on human experience but, rather, on the fact of the universe's very existence (a.k.a. **cosmological arguments**), or on some apparent purposiveness in the way nature is constituted (a.k.a. **teleological arguments**).

The very existence of the universe is a wonder. Why is there something rather than nothing? In our experience, there seems to always be a cause for any event, and a process of some kind explains the existence of any thing. So the fact of the existence of reality itself must have an explanation. Surely, as so many have asserted over the ages, something or someone is responsible for bringing it all about. The only thing that could be responsible for reality itself would have to be some transcendent, omnipotent agent. Therefore a supernatural creator exists.

We might first note that, to be the creator of everything, God must have created the spacetime environment itself. The creator of space itself would have to start out literally nowhere in space. Can we make sense of some real entity existing, but not existing in space? The creator of time itself would not have a time in which to create. There could be no moment before a first moment, so at what time would the creation have taken place, and why then? (Saying that God created everything at some time while existing outside of time is just to string some words together in a sequence that doesn't really mean anything.) Modern cosmology offers a number of suggestions to account for the existence of the universe, without adverting to an unnatural cause. Phenomena at the quantum level do not conform to our familiar notion of a world where all events are fully determined by causal laws. There we see the seemingly spontaneous generation of elementary particles and the uncaused determination of characteristics of those particles. This has led physicist Frank Wilczek to suggest that " 'nothing' is unstable," in that the laws of physics allow for the spontaneous and unpredictable generation of matter.[49] Proponents of **cosmic inflation theory** (a largely successful theory about the rapid expansion of the early universe) add that, as the universe expands, spacetime is in fact constantly being generated from nothing.

These are rather esoteric notions. A failure to consider quantum physics or inflation theory (or even to know about them) is not why I would suggest that many elite proponents of the cosmological argument for the existence of God are in denial. The more basic problems with the cosmological argument are (a) its explanatory poverty and (b) its internal inconsistency regarding causation. Bringing in a supernatural creator as the answer to everything really explains nothing. Where does the creator come from? What explains the characteristics of the creator that leads him or her to have both the desire and the ability to create the universe as we know it?[50] It seems to me any believer is capable of asking him- or herself these questions—but perhaps doesn't want to.

Then there are the issues with the notion of God (or anything) as a cause of all events. Immanuel Kant observed that it is perfectly natural to ask for the cause of a particular event, such as the movement of a billiard ball.[51] We expect there is a cause (even if we don't happen to know the cause) because we experience the world as fundamentally organized according to causal regularities. It is an easy transition, Kant continues, to asking about the cause of everything altogether. In terms of its form, this question does not seem any different from the question of why some particular thing happens. But this question implies the meaningfulness of the notion of a cause of all events that could themselves be causes of other events. There is a problem with the notion of a cause of all causes: The cause of all things either follows the rule "All events have a cause" or it doesn't. If the cause of all things follows the rule, then God must have a cause—but then God is not the cause of all things. (Going back to early Christian scholars like Augustine and Anselm, this sort of concern has often been answered with some sort of ill-defined statements about God being "eternal," "necessary," and/or "self-caused.") If the cause of all things doesn't follow the rule that all events are caused, then the rule is not a rule and we don't need an ultimate cause.[52] The notion of a cause only has meaning in the context of a chain of events. The question, "Why is there something rather than nothing?" therefore rests on a confusion.*

Either everything has a cause or it doesn't. If everything has a cause, then so must a god. If not everything has a cause, then why not stop at the universe itself (or the Big Bang)? A story of the universe just starting with a huge expansion in its earliest moments, leading to what we see today, has the advantage of being consistent with what we observe, and it doesn't require us to posit something both invisible and inexplicable—a supernatural creator. It is a much more parsimonious story that doesn't require the supernatural.

Is it cheating to suggest that the existence of the universe is just a "brute fact," with no ultimate explanation? Again, it isn't a cheat any more than positing a god whose existence is a brute fact, with no ultimate explanation. The supernatural creator answer, not the physicist's tentative speculations, is the ad hoc, hand-waving, deus ex machina answer. (And of course, the theist's *certainty* is spectacularly unearned.) There is every reason to expect scientific progress on our naturalistic understanding of the early universe. The god who is deployed to explain those things science has not explained is known as the "god of the gaps" (a term introduced by dismayed Christian apologists[53]). Science has a good track record of getting to the bottom of things. Our ancestors once cowered before the lightning that was an expression of the wrath of the gods. Diseases were the result of curses or of demonic meddling. Such accounts have ineluctably given way to evidence-based explanations. It is unlikely that the sophisticated defender of religion does not understand this fact about human intellectual history. Why should we not presume an ultimate naturalistic explanation for the universe itself, if naturalism has supplanted supernaturalism so many times before?

Today's sophisticated, first-world churchgoer would laugh off the notion of magic spells as an explanation for the workings of his or her computer. Neither would he or she take seriously a demonic possession

---

* Philosopher Robert Nozick points out that there are infinitely many logically possible variations of universes containing something, but only one way for there to be nothing. Hence, nothingness would be the state of affairs demanding an explanation, not somethingness. See Robert Nozick, *Philosophical Explanations* (Cambridge, MA: Harvard University Press, 1983), p. 127.

account of the stomach flu. The contemporary, educated person who trusts scientific expertise—and the deterministic, law-governed understanding of nature that underlies it—when it comes to medicines, cell phones, and air travel, can do better than uncritically accept that an uncaused, invisible, supernatural being is the answer to questions about the early universe. This inconsistency requires at some point a willful disregard for logic, in conjunction with a wild abandonment of one's usual standards of evidence. The lack of critical self-awareness when it comes to this issue is unsurprising, however, because of the profound emotional significance of the religious worldview to the believer. The cosmological question provides an opening to the believer, and the believer takes what he or she can get, no questions asked.

What philosophers call the "teleological argument," or the "argument from design," focuses not on the existence of the world itself but on alleged evidence of purposive design in nature. The best-known version of this reasoning is found in William Paley's 1805 book *Natural Theology*, in which he argues that biological function requires a designer. The human body has intricate parts—heart, lungs, and so on— that appear to serve a function both individually and jointly as they maintain the larger organism. If we found a watch on the ground, and examined its parts and how they function together to tell time, we would surely infer the existence of a conscious designer of that watch. Similarly, Paley argues, we must infer a designer of human beings.

This version of the design argument was, of course, exploded by the theory of biological evolution by natural selection. The explanation of the "function" of organs like the heart is etiological rather than teleological—that is to say, the heart works the way it does because of advantages conferred in the past by similar mechanisms in the environment of the animal species' development, rather than because of the purpose a designer intended it to serve.[54] The fact of the scientific consensus on evolution is well known. Yet denial of the theory is widespread. As I mentioned in chapter 2, 73% of Americans reject evolution by natural selection. Maintaining this state of denial requires dismissing the key concept underlying the biological sciences, along with much of genetics, anatomy, geology, archaeology, and the like. The same people denying evolutionary biology have no problem with, say, the science of chemistry that ensures them effective laundry detergent, or the science of physics that explains the workings of their automobile. The reasons for this inconsistency are not difficult to figure out. There are major threats to status quo culture, identity, and individual feelings of self-worth posed by the implications that (a) human beings were not created ex nihilo in their current form by a loving deity; that (b) human beings are not fundamentally distinct in nature from the lesser animals, and indeed share ancestors with them; and that (c) supernatural belief systems are variable artifacts of ancient, local cultures.

Some apologists have come up with the term "creation science" in an attempt to confuse the issue of the settled consensus on evolution. Organizations promoting creation science include the Institute for Creation Research and the Discovery Institute. The Discovery Institute's more prominent fellows include biologists Michael Behe and Douglas Axe, plus William Dembski, who holds doctoral degrees in both mathematics and philosophy.[55] The term "science" in "creation science" is a misnomer. Creation science offers **intelligent design** as an alleged alternate scientific theory. But intelligent design lacks key defining characteristics of a scientific theory. It is not testable because it makes no predictions about what characteristics we should expect to find in organisms under given conditions. Relatedly, it cannot offer differential explanations of biological characteristics—that is, it cannot explain why an animal has some particular characteristic rather than another.[56] It is not falsifiable, because any possible observation will be consistent with the will of an omnipotent creator who works in mysterious ways. Even obvious human vestigial characteristics, such as wisdom teeth and the coccyx, can be explained away in this fashion.

As usual, the educational background or relative sophistication of the individual in denial in no way mitigates these bias effects. Many books have been written by authors with advanced degrees purporting to refute the notion of evolution by natural selection, such as *The Genesis Flood*, *Darwin's Black Box*, and *Creation as Science*. Multiple websites today laud contemporary creationists with doctoral degrees in science, such as biologist Gary Parker, who has said:

> All of us can recognize objects that man has created, whether paintings, sculptures or just a Coke bottle. Because the pattern of relationships in those objects is contrary to relationships that time,

chance and natural physical processes can produce, we know an outside creative agent was involved. I began to see the same thing in a study of living things, especially in the area of my major interest, molecular biology. All living things depend upon a working relationship between inheritable DNA/RNA and proteins, the chief structural and functional molecules. Just as phosphorus, glass and copper will work together in a television set only if properly arranged by human engineers, so DNA and protein will only work in productive harmony if properly ordered by an outside creative agent.[57]

Accomplished hydraulic engineer Henry Morris founded the Institute for Creation Research. He wrote:

The lack of a case for evolution is clear from the fact that no one has ever seen it happen. If it were a real process, evolution should still be occurring, and there should be many "transitional" forms that we could observe. What we see instead, of course, is an array of distinct "kinds" of plants and animals with many varieties within each kind, but with very clear and—apparently—unbridgeable gaps between the kinds.[58]

This is all easily refutable, but identifying all the factual inaccuracies would be pointless. Statements like these are possible only in the context of a willful disregard for the evidence.

Creation-science organizations and their allies have pushed to include intelligent design as part of the public school biology curriculum. They do so in the name of scientific openness, but the transparent intention is to push an ideological agenda. This intention was a key issue in a successful 2005 legal challenge to a Pennsylvania district school board's mandate directing schools to push intelligent design as an alternate theory.[59] Part of the mandate was that a creation-science textbook called Of Pandas and People be used as a reference work. It came out during the trial that, in the latest edition of the book, the term "creationist" had simply been replaced with the term "design proponent" so as to make the book seem more like a science text than a religious tract. Ph.D. geologist Kurt Wise is unusually self-aware about the decision to reject the science when it conflicts with his religious commitments. Wise has explained:

> I had to make a decision between evolution and scripture. Either the scripture was true and evolution was wrong or evolution was true and I must toss out the Bible. . . . It was there that night that I accepted the word of God and rejected all that would ever counter it, including evolution. With that, in great sorrow, I tossed into the fire all my dreams and hopes in science. . . . If all the evidence in the universe turns against creationism, I would be the first to admit it, but I would still be a creationist because that is what the Word of God seems to indicate.[60]

Among the more sophisticated academic Christian apologists, the design argument has evolved (no pun intended) into the question of how the universe should be constituted, in terms of its fundamental laws, so as to allow life. This is based on a claim that various fundamental physical constants of our universe fall within a narrow range that allows stars and galaxies to form, as well as the carbon and oxygen necessary for the chemistry of life as we know it.[61] This set of conditions is so unlikely, the claim continues, that it must be the result of design. This is the **fine-tuning argument** (Craig and Plantinga are both fans[62]).

As with the cosmological argument, there are some esoteric proposals from theoretical physics that could come into play here. Physicists Alan Guth, Andrei Linde, and others have proposed a chaotic inflation model of the universe, according to which local fluctuations in the context of a massive spacetime expansion has left many (perhaps infinitely many) causally isolated subuniverses with their own sets of physical laws.[63] In this multiverse scenario, the existence of a subuniverse like ours—and conscious beings questioning the likelihood of a universe like ours—is unsurprising, because we should expect any number of scenarios (including ours) to be playing out among a vast number of subuniverses. This scenario is suggested by what we know about quantum physics, and it is consistent with observations of our universe's ancient background radiation.

But physicists themselves are not at all sure about this possibility, and even if they were more confident, one wouldn't expect most people to know about or understand the chaotic inflation model of the early universe. Rather, the fundamental problem with the fine-tuning argument is that it is an **argument from ignorance**. As many physicists have said in response to fine-tuning, we don't know enough to establish the probability of any particular set of fundamental physical constraints. It may be that there are some underlying physical laws that require the fundamental properties of the universe to fall within the bounds that they do. To jump from our not being able to explain the laws of nature to the necessity of a benevolent designer is exactly the same move our ancestors made when they concluded that angry gods exist just because they couldn't think of any other explanation for storms or sickness. It is the same move William Paley made when he concluded that there must be an intelligent designer of the human form just because he couldn't think of any other explanation for biological complexity in living organisms. It is the same move proponents of the cosmological argument make when they say there must be a god behind the existence of the universe because they cannot otherwise explain its origin. Uncritical acceptance of miracles rests either on ignorance of other possible explanations for an event or on willful blindness to alternative explanations for miracle testimony. In light of nonmagical explanations for all the phenomena now under the domain of science, in light of the nonmagical natural laws we depend on most of the time, and in light of our normal skepticism toward incredible claims that don't fit with our ordinary understanding of natural phenomena, isn't it strange to jump to the conclusion that only a supernatural explanation will do in this case?

The proponent of the fine-tuning argument claims to know that the current set of fundamental physical values would be extremely unlikely if it were the product of chance. God must be the explanation. But what is the explanation for God's existing or of wanting to create exactly this universe? (Who tuned the tuner?) Fine-tuning again just replaces one mystery with another one that is infinitely harder to dissolve.[64]

Most proponents of the fine-tuning argument are sufficiently knowledgeable to be aware that we live in an unimaginably vast universe, almost all of which is vacuum or otherwise uninhabitable. Even the Earth could be a lot better as a habitat for humanity: The Earth is mostly covered with salt water, and a lot of the rest is desert, or ice, or pestilent jungle, or excessively mountainous. If the universe were created for the sake of life, much less human life, then the creator did a terrible job. Not to mention that a life-loving, all-powerful creator god would likely have done a better job of preventing or alleviating the many terrible moral and natural evils we see in our world, such as genocide, earthquakes, and childhood cancer.

Even if you get past all these problems with the cosmological and teleological arguments, there is still the issue that neither argument gives you the god of religion. Neither gives you an anthropomorphic, divinely perfect being with a special interest in humanity. It's certainly no Jesus of the Bible, nor any other particular creator god. To arrive at any particular literalist theology, you have to go back to the miracle testimonies of some particular religious text. And to fix upon the testimonies of *that* text, and to accept its claims to the exclusion of all others, you once again need to suspend all normal rules of evidence— while also ignoring all the competing, equally (un)supported reports of miracles and divine appearances. Either that, or you maintain that you know Jesus to be real because you "feel him in your heart," or some such—while utterly discounting the credibility of the exact same sort of claim from literalist believers of other faith traditions.

But problems with testimony of miracles, the sense of the divine, the cosmological argument, creation science, and the fine-tuning argument are all moot for the true believer. Some will report that they started out as nonbelievers and came to believe in a god because an encounter with miracle testimony, a sudden experience of immediate revelation, or as a result of reflecting upon the best possible explanation for the existence and/or nature or the universe. But most of the defenders of these proofs would have to admit they were not convinced of God's existence by these means; rather, they came to accept these "proofs" long *after* developing an unshakeable conviction in childhood via familial and cultural indoctrination. I think it is uncontroversial to say that people are seldom reasoned into religion. The vast majority of believers were indoctrinated into their faith from an early age, and they usually retain that specific belief system into adulthood. Adult individuals raised in a Hindu family in a Hindu region know that Hinduism is true; adult individuals raised in a Christian family in a Christian region know that Christianity is true; and so on. Atheists are not special here, either. Atheists are not atheists because their world-view, unlike that of theists, is uniquely based on Pure Reason. Just like being raised religious, being raised atheist or agnostic strongly predicts how one will turn out in terms of belief in a creator god.

Where we do see adult conversions from nonbelief to belief, we are likely to see intense emotional need, arising from loneliness, a family breakup, hitting bottom as an alcoholic, diagnosis of terminal illness, wartime experience, or being sent to prison (the incidence of self-identified atheists is ten times higher in the general population than it is in the prison population[65]). Indeed, where we see *loss* of religious be-lief, we likely also see an emotional trigger, such as the death of a child or the discovery of some incompatibility between one's needs and one's religious ideology. The following account, from philosopher Elizabeth Barnes, is recognizable:

> It's hard to point to one particular thing, really. My alienation from conservative Christianity happened gradually, and it wasn't until I moved away from the South that I was fully able to process it all. By the time I was a teenager I started to question things, and to see aspects of the practice that didn't feel right to me. I'd become in-terested in environmental activism, and I remember getting very annoyed with the typical stance of the religious right on the envi-ronment. I think that was when I started to notice how people would conveniently pick and choose bits of the Bible to support what they wanted to believe. I also became increasingly uncomfortable with the attitudes towards women that were often expressed. I couldn't accept that it was my God-given lot in life to submit to a man, and it didn't make sense to me that I was intrinsically unsuited for leadership roles because of my gender. But what really sticks out in my mind as the moment I crossed the Rubicon, as it were, is when I realized that a family member of mine—someone I'd always been very close with—was gay. And then I thought about what people in my community would say to him if they knew. That was the point at which I basically decided "Yeah, no thanks."[66]

Note that the loss of faith here—even on the part of a professional philosopher—had nothing to do with discounting the historical evidence of miracles, considering conflicting faith systems, or deciding that proofs of God's existence fall short. Belief in God just became ideologically and emotionally *inconvenient*—just as when we do see belief in God, we typically see emotional *convenience*. That's why problems with the "reasons" given either to believe or disbelieve in some god are moot from a persuasion standpoint: These function not as genuine reasons but, rather, as tools for rationalizing an ideology to which the believer is already committed.

4.2 Is It Even a Belief?

Considering the all-encompassing implications of literalist religious belief—a belief that entails a supernatural explanation of the entire natural world, of every event in the world, and of the purpose of every event in the world—one would think more would be demanded by the believer in order to adopt this worldview, not to mention any particular theology associated with it. Yet, in practice, critical faculties are deployed less in this domain than in any other, even among the most erudite apologist scholars. The gap between, on the one hand, the nature and scope of the claim and, on the other, the quality of the reasoning employed in defending it is unparalleled in any other area of human affairs. Religion overall represents easily the most impressive disconnect between professed worldview and any sort of honest assessment of the likelihood of its being true. Partly for this reason, some thinkers have suggested that religious belief is not what it appears to be.

John Stuart Mill, from *On Liberty*, muses upon the frequent inconsistencies between the professed religious commitments of the typical "believer" and his or her actual behavior:

> By Christianity I here mean what is accounted such by all churches and sects—the maxims and precepts contained in the New Testament. These are considered sacred, and accepted as laws, by all professing Christians. Yet it is scarcely too much to say that not one Christian in a thousand guides or tests his individual conduct by reference to those laws. . . . All Christians believe that the blessed are the poor and humble, and those who are ill-used by the world; that

244 THE TRUTH ABOUT DENIAL

it is easier for a camel to pass through the eye of a needle than for a
rich man to enter the kingdom of heaven; that they should judge not,
lest they be judged; that they should swear not at all; that they should
love their neighbour as themselves; that if one take their cloak, they
should give him their coat also; that they should take no thought for
the morrow; that if they would be perfect, they should sell all that
they have and give it to the poor. They are not insincere when they say
that they believe these things. They do believe them, as people believe
what they have always heard lauded and never discussed. But in the
sense of that living belief which regulates conduct, they believe these
doctrines just up to the point to which it is usual to act upon them.[67]

Philosopher Georges Rey notes how incongruous it is to see believers
mourn their dead with such intensity while, supposedly, truly believing
that they will soon be reunited with their loved ones in heaven.[68]
The faithful pray to be cured of cancer, to be spared from oncoming
tornadoes, or for victory in war. They never pray for amputated limbs
to be restored or for collapsed buildings to be repaired overnight. In
other words, they never pray for divine intervention in situations
where such intervention would be unambiguous. This sort of disconnect between avowal and practice is a bad sign for a sincere believer
seeking to avoid the charge of self-deception. Lately we have seen a rise
of organized terrorism in the name of Islam, but this is only one recent example of atrocities under the banner of religion. Christians have
been responsible for innumerable colonizations, crusades, genocidal
ethnic cleansings, wars, and witch hunts, all committed specifically in
the name of their religion. Tens of thousands of Indian Muslims have
been killed in thousands of separate attacks by Hindus since the 1940s.
Gangs of Buddhist monks have recently been involved in murderous
attacks on the minority Muslim population in Myanmar.

This sort of inconsistency has given rise to a school of thought that
questions whether religious belief is what it seems—that is, a factual
belief about the world. Rather than conclude that religious believers
are self-deceived about the quality of the evidence for their claims,
Rey argues that some "who sincerely claim to believe in God" (in particular "members of [their] culture exposed to standard science") are
self-deceived about what it is they believe, and "at some level they

believe the claim is false."[69] He just can't make any other sense of the incongruity between the stated belief, on the one hand, and the reasons given (and the behavior exhibited), on the other.

As we noted earlier, Locke thought that professions of belief are often really just unreflective signals of solidarity or obedience. Philosopher Daniel Dennett says something similar when he characterizes many of the avowals of belief in God not as indicating genuine belief in God but as indicating "belief in belief"; that is, they uncritically accept the teachings of their culture or religious authorities for reasons other than actually believing that these teachings are true. What educated persons in developed nations really believe, according to Dennett, is that belief in God is advantageous and/or obligatory. As Locke alleged, the average follower professes devotion simply to "thereby approve himself to those who can give him credit, preferment, or protection in [his] society." Believers compartmentalize their avowal, isolating it from their usual standards of knowledge. (Recall Kahan's rural South Carolina barber, who would pay a social and economic penalty for taking climate change seriously.) Doubts are suppressed, allowing the person to maintain a state of denial and sincerely claim he or she is a true believer.

In a recent essay from the journal *Cognition*, Neil van Leeuwen elaborates on the idea that religious avowals often express an attitude not properly categorized as a factual belief. Van Leeuwen notes that genuine factual beliefs exhibit two defining characteristics. One is **evidentiary vulnerability**, meaning that they are "involuntarily prone to being extinguished" by contrary evidence or by evidence of self-contradiction or incoherence.[70] The other is **cognitive governance**—that is, genuine factual beliefs license inferences to other factual beliefs that in turn influence behavior. I infer that there is mail in my mailbox because I believe the mail carrier has come and delivered mail. This inference would be the basis for my actually getting up and going out to my mailbox to get the mail. By contrast, if I merely imagine what it would be like for the mail carrier to come, I do not thereby come to believe I have mail and go open my mailbox. Avowed religious belief as a cognitive state often lacks evidentiary vulnerability, cognitive governance, or both. First, the actual evidence, as we have noted, appears to be irrelevant either to the formation or to the maintenance of religiosity. Second, to observe that the behavior of the devout is frequently inconsistent with their religious avowals is to observe that their beliefs appear to lack cognitive governance. Van Leeuven concludes that what we call religious belief is often, or even characteristically, more like the product of imagining or hypothesizing (or hoping). Avowals and ritual behaviors associated with religiosity are more like playacting than acting. This would explain why religious "belief" is so resistant to refutation and why the behavior of the avowed devotee so often does not line up with his or her avowals. Van Leeuven calls the cognitive states associated with religious avowal "credences" rather than beliefs. Credences are sometimes loosely categorized as beliefs, but they exhibit characteristics that differentiate them from ordinary factual beliefs. Unlike most factual beliefs, religious credences are both seemingly unfalsifiable and "practical setting-dependent, becoming deactivated outside the religious-ritual setting."[71] He therefore agrees with Dennett and Rey that the devout are self-deceived, not about the evidence for their beliefs but, rather, about the beliefs themselves. However, where Dennett and Rey say they are self-deceived about the *content* of their beliefs, van Leeuven says that are self-deceived about the very nature of the attitudes they *call* beliefs. He explicitly compares credence to ideological denialism:

> For example, does a "belief" *that Mao's policies did not cause famine* count as factual belief? We don't know without more information. A mistaken history student in Cleveland may factually believe this, if he misread the history text and has the attitude of factual belief toward those contents. But an ideological Maoist may have a religious credence toward the same content. One cannot decide whether an attitude is a factual belief or religious credence just by looking at the contents. In fact, many ideological distortions, I suspect, involve religious credences toward what might be thought of as contents that concern facts (e.g., *global warming does not exist*, etc.).[72]

Psychologist Paul Bloom agrees, and he compares such credulous professions to other sorts of ideological positioning:

> Many religious narratives are believed without even being understood. People will often assert religious claims with confidence—there

exists a God, he listens to my prayers, I will go to Heaven when I die—but with little understanding, or even interest, in the details. The sociologist Alan Wolfe observes that "evangelical believers are sometimes hard pressed to explain exactly what, doctrinally speaking, their faith is," and goes on to note that "These are people who believe, often passionately, in God, even if they cannot tell others all that much about the God in which they believe." People defer to authorities not just to the truth of the religious beliefs, but their meaning as well. . . . None of this is special to religion. Researchers have studied those who have strong opinions about political issues and found that they often literally don't know what they are talking about. Many people who take positions on cap and trade, for instance, have no idea what cap and trade is. Similarly, many of those who will insist that America spends too much, or too little, on foreign aid, often don't know how much actually is spent, as either an absolute amount or proportion of GDP. These political positions are also *credences*, and one who holds them is just like someone who insists that the Ten Commandments should be the bedrock of morality, but can't list more than three or four of them.[73]

Bloom adds that many atheists will also profess agreement with, say, the theory of evolution by natural selection, without really being able to explain what it is or how it works. But, he continues, this form of deference to authority is different, because science has earned its epistemological authority by the nature of its evidence-based, self-critical practice (as well as its track record of success).

Usually, we take sincere factual claims more or less at face value. If someone claims there are eggs in her refrigerator, then (assuming we don't think she is lying) we take her to have a factual representation of the world that includes eggs in her refrigerator. She may be mistaken or even self-deceived about the reasons for her belief in some way, but we would not doubt that she has a belief to that effect. Locke, Mill, Rey, Dennett, van Leeuwen, and Bloom are correct in pointing out the behavioral inconsistencies and lack of critical self-reflection—or even full comprehension—commonly present in the religious believer. And yet, for all the hypocrisies on display, even among the common people religious belief does have some downstream effects on behavior. Many,

many self-sacrificing charitable acts (and acts of terror) are committed explicitly in the name of religion. Those who fail to live up to their charitable ideals can chalk up that failure to weakness of will, rather than insincerity or self-deception. Christian proponents of "original sin" can even present their failure to live up to their avowed ideals as confirmation of their belief system, which includes the essential sinful and hypocritical nature of human beings. (People in denial are terrific at turning apparent evidentiary inconsistencies into features of their view.)

Clearly, religious tenets, like many ideological positions, suffer, in practice, from an acute lack of evidential vulnerability. No doubt there are many cases in which expressions of religious devotion are less like attempts at factual descriptions of the world than expressions of an attitude of cultural solidarity. Like Donald Trump's infantile tweets, such expressions are more like bullshit than denial. Even so, to deny religious belief in general even its status as *belief* is a little uncharitable to billions of earnest adherents. Neither fundamentalist terrorists nor self-sacrificing aid workers seem to be merely playacting. Elite believers like William Lane Craig cite historical evidence for their claims, however selective and inadequate it might be. Other sophisticated apologists give reasons for their devotion—and many unsophisticated ones can and will do so when pressed. Philosopher Neil Levy notes that many factual, scientific beliefs appear to exhibit some practical setting dependence:

> For instance, adults with college level education in evolution often invoke a competing essentialist theory of species transformation and adults with college level education in mechanics invoke folk physics to explain and predict motion. This exhibits the practical setting dependence of factual beliefs: beliefs that guide behaviour (including verbal behaviour) in one setting fail to guide it in another, despite the relevance of the content of the beliefs to the second setting. These instances of practical setting dependence presumably arise because the agents fail to notice the conflict between the intuitive response and the one that is justified by the theory they accept.[74]

Depending on the circumstances, atheists can be as subject to superstition and magical thinking as the devout. Levy also cites familiar instances of motivated reasoning or confabulation in response to dissonance. There is nothing special about religious belief and its practical setting dependence, he argues: Any belief is context dependent if, in a given context, holding on to that belief is confusing or threatening. This is just how someone with a strong educational background and good scientific literacy skills can deny AGW. What the science of denial teaches us is that any belief can be ignored or discarded, given sufficient motivation.

Van Leeuwen is right in noting some similarities between religious ritual and imaginative play, and between stubborn credulity and ideology. However, given our usual, well-founded practice of taking factual claims at face value, the burden of proof is on those who want to claim that so many people, so much of the time, are wrong about either the content or the very nature of many of their own beliefs. At the very least, it's difficult to look at intellectual and cultural elite apologists like Craig, Plantinga, Alston, Swinburne, or Rea and describe them as confused about what they believe or as merely playacting.

What we do know is that individuals (including highly sophisticated scholars) frequently are terrible judges about the *quality of evidence* for their beliefs. Invulnerability to contrary evidence is hardly unique to religion; rather, as we have seen, such invulnerability is a distinguishing characteristic of those factual beliefs marshaled in support of an ideological position. We see it every time there is a strong emotional commitment to a belief being true. What distinguishes ideological belief from ordinary belief is not that it is not a belief but, instead, that there is an emotional attachment to its truth—and thus a motive to treat evidence for the belief in a biased way.

I do agree that many are in denial with regard to their religious beliefs. However, I think the overall explanation should center on motivated reasoning about the factual claims that form the basis for their literalist religious ideology. In other words, I think the correct approach to understanding religious belief is fundamentally the same as the correct approach to understanding climate change deniers (and their anti–big government ideology), or for understanding economic history deniers (and their anti-egalitarian ideology). Rey and Dennett are correct that, in a modern context, the factual claims of religion are massively underdetermined by the evidence cited in favor of them. These supernatural claims conflict with many things the same claimants themselves believe about the world and the predictable natural laws that govern it. And believers' behavior is frequently inconsistent with their religious worldview and its prescriptions. But it's easier to explain how you can be self-deceived about the quality of the evidence for your beliefs than it is to understand how you can be self-deceived about having a belief in the first place. It would be an advantage to a theory of religious belief if we can explain it parsimoniously in terms of the familiar mechanism of confirmation bias, rather than by speculatively adverting to a distinct mechanism of self-deception about the nature of one's own cognitive states. We now understand how the mechanisms of motivated cognition and rationalization allow people to form and maintain sincere and perfectly well-intentioned beliefs in the face of disqualifying evidential inadequacies. Through a similar process of selective attention, avowed religious ideology can be unconsciously compartmentalized off from decisions made in contexts where the ideology is inconvenient. The process of confirmation bias and motivated reasoning is well understood. This is a known phenomenon that is exemplified in many, many contexts. Denial of the reasons to reject the literal truth of supernatural miracles shares many of the same characteristics as denial of inconvenient facts in many other contexts.

4.3 The Origins of Religiosity

For those interested in understanding religious belief, there are two main issues: Understanding its *origins*, and understanding its *tenacity* in the face of scientific enlightenment and cosmopolitan awareness of religious diversity. The tenacity issue is more pertinent to a discussion of denial, but first examining the natural origins of religiosity may help us understand why denial is so automatically—and forcefully— engaged when challenges to religious belief crop up.

A recent book from medical researcher Ajit Varki and geneticist Danny Brower, *Denial: Self-Deception, False Beliefs, and the Origins of the Human Mind*, explains religiosity as a vehicle for cognitively advanced beings to satisfy a fundamental need to deny their mortality.

They wonder why more animals haven't developed the full self-awareness and "theory of mind" (i.e., an understanding of others as agents with perceptions and intentions) that we humans have, given its advantages in predicting behavior and in facilitating social cooperation. They suggest that self-awareness comes at a cost: a potentially paralyzing awareness of our own mortality. With mortality constantly at the forefront of our minds, we would never take the risks necessary for reproductive success—the critical condition for evolutionary success.[75] Their provocative hypothesis is that, for this reason, the gradual development of self-awareness would require the co-development of a particular talent for suppressing unwanted thoughts—in other words, a talent for denial. And this is where religion comes in: "Holding a full ToM [theory of mind] requires a large dose of mortality denial in order to compensate for the selective disadvantages that accompany the 'personal survival first' mentality. Religion supplies a formal device that can satisfy this requirement."[76] Religions promising life after death are ideological aids for the mortality denial that, in turn, permits reproductive success.

Other recent work on the origins of religiosity from cognitive science, neuroscience, anthropology, and evolutionary psychology points to built-in cognitive biases. These include biases in favor of attributing agency and intention to the sources of otherwise unexplained events. This bias is extensively examined in, for example, Pascal Boyer's *The Naturalness of Religious Ideas: A Cognitive Theory of Religion*, and Robert McCauley's *Why Religion Is Natural and Science Is Not*. With all the kaleidoscopic differences among religious traditions, there is one commonality—namely a hidden agent or agents underlying some or all observed phenomena. We know that human beings are (a) very quick to perceive patterns in sensory inputs both meaningful and meaningless, and (b) very quick to identify agency and intention as explaining those perceived patterns.[77] Our innate tendency to be overactive pattern-detectors starts with the higher costs of false negatives in pattern detection than false positives. If I hear a rustling in the bushes, I am better off jumping to the conclusion that it is a predator: The cost of my being wrong about being oversensitive to possible dangers is less than the potential cost of my being undersensitive. An instinctive overattribution of agency (Michael Shermer calls this characteristic agenticity[78]) has survival advantages for the same reason: I am better off being too quick to attribute malicious intent to things that go bump in the night than I am being not quick enough. The cost of the former is some excessive fearfulness (and superstition!), but the cost of the latter is the end of my life—and thus my ability to pass on my genes. An instinctive agenticity would explain a bias on the part of primitive humans in favor of supernatural explanations underlying the many otherwise mysterious events and patterns they found in nature.

In addition to its historical value in survival, agenticity may derive from the projection of self-awareness. We are aware of ourselves as thinking beings, and so may have a natural tendency to offer the same explanations for the patterns we detect around us that we do for the patterns in our own behavior.[79] This would explain a certain cognitive bias in favor of finding thought and intention in unexplained phenomena, as part of the process of making sense of the world around us. (Strikingly, atheism is more prevalent in persons with autism and other disorders that impair the capacity to represent other minds, and to reason about others' intentions.[80])

An additional adaptive value of this very sort of agent projection is the ease it confers to the process of socialization. Like other primates, human beings are highly social. A predominant view among evolutionary biologists (along with other scholars of human nature) is that the biggest adaptive advantage we have as competitors in the natural arena is our ability to form cooperative social groups. In fact, this advantage is a leading explanation for our large brains and the various advanced cognitive abilities that come with them; it is increasingly theorized (with support from primate studies[81]) that large increases in brain size and cognitive ability derived from the advantages our ancestors gleaned from an increased ability to navigate complex social interactions; to exchange ideas and build relationships; and to exercise various talents of integration, planning, persuasion, and collaboration. If social skills are advantageous, then so is being hardwired to grasp the mechanics of agency and thus to easily attribute intentions to others.

This brings us to another—not unrelated—major contender in the search for an explanation for a built-in bias in favor of religiosity. In his excellent book *The Evolution of Morality*, philosopher Richard Joyce summarizes the case for the evolutionary benefits of cooperation.[82]

Human beings prosper in social groups with shared belief systems that include norms of reciprocity, trust, and solidarity. Individual cheaters and defectors from those norms often fail to prosper because they are likely to be found out over time and are punished via shunning or worse.[83] The advantages of selective cooperation contribute to the very human tendency to in-group favoritism: to identify with certain groups and to favor members of those groups over others. As Jonathan Haidt argues, religious ideology, and the emotionally charged sense of "sacredness" it attaches to certain ideals, rules, and rituals, can function as the binding agent for mutually beneficial social cooperation within the group.[84] (The development of *religious* ideology insisting specifically on a supernatural source of binding norms is helped along by our aforementioned agent-detection bias.) In-group identification, religious ideology, and moralizing go hand in hand. As we have discussed, "cultural cognition" refers to the tendency of members of a community to respond to information in ways influenced by their cultural identifications. In certain peer communities, it is an article of faith that natural foods are more healthful than genetically modified foods, and that anyone who disagrees is morally suspect. In others, it is beyond question that one is safer owning a gun, and anyone who disagrees is trying to take away your freedom. Cultural influence has profound effects on the emotional salience of factual claims accepted by the community as foundational. Familial and cultural indoctrination, peer influence, and the incentive to conform all play a role in internalizing community beliefs, including religious belief. Eventually, this identification leads to genuine emotional connections with members of one's in-group, as well as emotional reactions to violations of norms set by the ideology—regardless of whether the ideologue can defend (or even explain) the reasons for holding that particular set of religious beliefs. As Haidt explains, "binding requires blinding."[85] For these advantageous norms—which require resistance to temptation and individual sacrifices—to be robust enough over the long term, they must derive from an ideology that incorporates its own immunity to criticism. Thus those ideologies that have been most effective in advantageously binding our ancestors together have also been the most dogmatic.

The benefits of religion as a vehicle for binding norms may also help explain the evolution of religion itself though human history.

In his recent book *Big Gods*, social/evolutionary psychologist Ara Norenzayan examines the overall historical trend from animist spirits and pagan demi-gods to moralizing, omnipotent, and omniscient superdeities like Ahura Mazda, YHWH, Jehovah/Jesus/Holy Spirit, Allah, Ramachandra, and Waheguru.[86] He accounts for this development by reference to the challenge of unifying large, post-agrarian nation-states. The stability of large societies would be enhanced by ideologies incorporating norms that regulate behavior among diverse populations. We know from social behavior studies that people who feel they are being watched will behave more in accordance with prevailing norms.[87] An omniscient parent-god who rewards for good behavior and punishes bad (and who is less selective about the specific ethnic background of the faithful) provides a universal regulative ideal allowing successful interaction between relative strangers. According to this theory, growing societies with "big gods" would be more successful over time than those without. Thus the rise of the omni-gods. We might also add that the cynical, top-down promotion of such a god could be of great benefit to political leaders who are looking to consolidate an empire or to rationalize their own right to rule.

4.4 Tenacity

It is possible to explain the origin and proliferation of religion(s) just by looking at natural cognitive dispositions, social dynamics, and evolution. Superstition arises out of innate cognitive biases. Religious ideology builds on these biases and has propagated because of the organizing and binding advantages it confers on societies.[88] But the naturalness and helpfulness of cooperation-reinforcing rituals revolving around supernatural agents only go part of the way in accounting for the *tenacity* of religion. The peculiar abidingness of religion despite exposure to the multiplicity of religious traditions, and despite the ongoing victory of naturalistic explanations of hitherto mysterious phenomena, is likely due to the many ways in which religiosity serves profound emotional needs. As we know, there is a baseline cognitive bias—status quo bias—favoring one's existing beliefs. We presume that what we know from a lifetime of experience is true and that inconsistent data are likely to be false. If we went around changing our views every time something unexpected pops up, we would have trouble building a picture of the world stable enough to be useful as a heuristic for making decisions. So we automatically resist new information undermining long-held beliefs. This is what we called "plain vanilla" dissonance reduction. This effect is usually rather mild: Despite a general tendency to look for confirmation for our existing beliefs, and to disregard disconfirming evidence, most of our non-ideological beliefs are pretty easily defeasible by new information. I may have thought for a long time that tomatoes are vegetables, and I may react incredulously when informed otherwise. My family has always referred to tomatoes as vegetables; my local grocer puts them in the vegetable section. Of course they are vegetables. But I have no emotional stake in the status of a tomato as a vegetable. When my plant biology instructor tells me that fruits are standardly defined as developments from the fertilized ovary of a flower, and shows me that tomatoes meet this definition, I might still express doubt. But then she corroborates this information using multiple sources; even my classmates concur, and they cite their own formal and informal sources. I may also discover that tomatoes are often referred to as fruit in other cultures. I eventually concede the point. I don't go into denial mode. I don't accuse the plant bio professor of lacking expertise or of being part of a conspiracy; I don't hunt for some obscure website debunking the myth that tomatoes are fruits. I don't quit the class and associate only with people who agree with me about tomatoes. I certainly don't have my classmates accused of heresy and tortured until they confess their error. But it can be quite a different story when you point out to someone that humans and apes share a common ancestor or that his or her god is a culturally relative superstition. Even today there are many societies around the world where the consequences for such declarations can be dire.

Plain-vanilla confirmation bias is enough all by itself to account for some of the broad resistance to change among those who have been indoctrinated into religion from day one. The worldview of religious ideology is utterly pervasive, informing one's interpretation of the meaning of all events, everywhere. Further, the lives of theists are typically organized around religious community activities; their religious community is the biggest peer influence on how information is gathered, attended to, and interpreted. Informational threats to religion represent more than enough disruption to the theist's web of beliefs for his or her natural cognitive defenses to kick in.

But only a strong emotional component can explain the unparalleled denialism exhibited by defenders of religion. A dogma abides in the face of overwhelming reason and evidence only because it serves emotional needs—needs that in turn trigger the dissonance-dissolving mechanisms of motivated reasoning. We would not be the first to look at emotional needs in explaining religious dogmatism. The three most notorious modern, Western critics of religion have been Karl Marx, Friedrich Nietzsche, and Sigmund Freud. Each had his own account of the emotional appeal of religion; though their accounts were speculative, each, in his own way, anticipated a different aspect of contemporary psychological research on motivated reasoning.

We have seen the familiar denialist patterns of motivated reasoning and confirmation bias in defenses of religious belief. The thesis here would be that the tenacity of religion in the face of science, reason, and cosmopolitanism (including and especially among high-information, high-education believers) derives from denial, which in turn derives from the way religious ideology satisfies emotional needs. The needs religious ideology can satisfy may include reassurance, purpose, certainty, stability, inclusion, superiority, and/or protection of (cultural) identity.

4.4.1 Marx and System Justification

As I mentioned in chapter 1, Marx was an early proponent of system justification as an explanation of the support of inegalitarian economic hierarchies by the downtrodden. His take on religion (specifically Christianity) incorporated the idea of religion as a system-justifying device into his analysis of the exploitation of the working classes:

> This state and this society produce religion, which is an inverted consciousness of the world, because they are an inverted world. Religion

is the general theory of this world, its encyclopedic compendium, its logic in popular form, its spiritual point d'honneur, its enthusiasm, its moral sanction, its solemn complement, and its universal basis of consolation and justification. . . . Religious suffering is, at one and the same time, the expression of real suffering and a protest against real suffering. Religion is the sigh of the oppressed creature, the heart of a heartless world, and the soul of soulless conditions. It is the opium of the people. The abolition of religion as the illusory happiness of the people is the demand for their real happiness. To call on them to give up their illusions about their condition is to call on them to give up a condition that requires illusions. The criticism of religion is, there-fore, in embryo, the criticism of that vale of tears of which religion is the halo.[89]

Marx and Engels thought the poor deceive themselves into accepting the exploitative class system as the natural way of things by way of consolation for the difficult life they lead. The afterlife is their re-ward for peaceful compliance. The consoling belief is a belief in the essential justice of the way things are; the result is system-justifying attitudes protecting the status quo. Describing the place of religion in ancient Rome, Edward Gibbon said, "The various modes of worship which prevailed in the Roman world were all considered by the people as equally true; by the philosopher as equally false; and by the mag-istrate as equally useful."[90] Napoleon Bonaparte puts the matter even more bluntly: "I do not see in religion the mystery of the incarnation so much as the mystery of the social order. It introduces into the thought of heaven an idea of equalization, which saves the rich from being massacred by the poor."[91]

John Jost and six other social scientists recently embarked on a major project to examine a thesis that expands upon Marx's view of religion as system justifying for the oppressed. Their view of religion is of an ideology that is system justifying generally, in that it would ap-peal not just to one economic class but also to anyone else looking for reassuring stability and a sense that the status quo is right and good. According to Jost et al., "religion provides an ideological justifica-tion for the existing social order, so that prevailing institutions and arrangements are perceived as legitimate and just, and therefore worth obeying and preserving." They set out in their research to summarize the evidence that:

> (a) religiosity is associated with the same set of epistemic, existential, and relational needs that motivate system justification; (b) religiosity is associated with the endorsement of the belief in a just world, Protestant work ethic, fair market ideology, opposition to equality, right-wing authoritarianism, political conservatism, and other system-justifying belief systems; and (c) religious ideology appears to serve the palliative function of making people happier or more satisfied with the way things are.[92]

Recall Melvin Lerner's just-world hypothesis, which explains much human ideology in terms of the motive to believe that this is essentially a world with a moral structure, in which persons eventually get what they deserve. Lerner argued that religion (particularly within the Judeo-Christian tradition) can supply a mythology—and a moralizing ideology—as a vehicle for just-world bias. Inspired by both Marx and Lerner, Jost et al. set out to test several related hypotheses that would follow from the idea that "religious ideology [is] a system-justifying belief system":

> First, religious ideologies, like other system-justifying ideologies, should be linked to underlying epistemic, existential, and relational motives to attain certainty, security, and solidarity. Second, religiosity should be positively associated with the endorsement of system-justifying beliefs, including the belief in a just world, the Protestant work ethic, rationalization of inequality, authoritarianism, political conservatism, and fair market ideology. Third, religion should serve the palliative function of making people happier and more satisfied with the way things are—and therefore less likely to challenge the status quo.[93]

Regarding the first hypothesis, Jost and colleagues cite a large meta-study by Vassilis Saroglou showing that, across "a variety of cultural contexts . . . the correlation between religiosity and constructs pertaining to uncertainty avoidance and motivated closed-mindedness are almost always positive (and statistically significant)."[94] Other studies find a consistent correlation between religiosity and a need for cognitive closure.[95]

Different personality types will be attracted to different conceptions of God: Liberals to a god of love and empathy; conservatives to a god of Lakoffian fatherly discipline and order. Religious texts tend to allow for vastly different interpretations of their doctrines, so there is a lot of room for different churches catering to different audiences (especially in the United States, with its diversity and a historical lack of a state religion, and thus a wide variety of churches competing for followers).

To investigate the hypothesis that "religiosity would be positively associated with the endorsement of . . . system-justifying belief systems," Jost and his collaborators analyzed data from 302,037 participants using the Project Implicit online laboratory. They found that self-reported religiosity is positively correlated with a "stronger endorsement of just-world beliefs."[96] Religiosity is also correlated with anti-egalitarian attitudes, authoritarianism, and political conservatism (both economic and social).[97]

The connection between conservatism and system-justifying religious ideology is to be expected, given the conservative by definition feels more comfortable with order and a fixed hierarchy of being. The Christian worldview is that of a universe resting on an eternal order and unchanging rules. Diversity of opinion and threats to religious belief unseat that comfortable sense of stability. Corey Rubin connects growing challenges to religious traditions over the course of modern history to the rise of conservatism as a political movement:

> The conservative faces an additional hurdle: how to defend a principle of rule in a world where nothing is solid, all is in flux. From the moment conservatism came onto the scene as an intellectual movement, it has had to contend with the decline of ancient and medieval ideas of an orderly universe, in which permanent hierarchies of power reflected the eternal structure of the cosmos. The overthrow of the old regime reveals not only the weakness and incompetence of its leaders but also a larger truth about the lack of design in the world. Reconstructing the old regime in the face of a declining faith in permanent hierarchies has proven to be a difficult feat.[98]

The universal cognitive bias in favor of confirmation of existing beliefs undergirds the conservative, system-justifying aspects of religious ideology. The worldview of your childhood and community is your baseline for dealing with all new information. Religious ideology, when inculcated since childhood, permeates how one views every event one experiences, every relationship one has, and every choice one makes. Disruption to that couldn't be more undermining in terms of doxastic stability and sense of self. This sort of dissonance would be especially impactful on those with preexisting inclinations toward cognitive closure, certainty, and status quo.

As for the hypothesized "palliative function" of religion, Jost and his colleagues point to a broad array of studies showing that both religiosity and the holding of system-justifying beliefs (such as that the existing economic and social inequalities are just and fair) reduce negative affect and increase positive affect, resulting in "increased life satisfaction" and "subjective well-being."[99] The faithful consistently self-report being happier with their lives, as Marx would have predicted.

4.4.2 Nietzsche and Group-Serving Bias

We have seen how group identification and in-group favoritism are adaptive, in that they serve strategic and material needs by facilitating cooperation. Clearly, group identification also carries with it a important emotional component. Feelings of in-group superiority and antipathy toward outsiders (be they identified by nationality, ethnicity, religion, etc.) are endemic to human societies. Nietzsche saw group identity, and correlative resentment of out-groups, as a major factor in the rise of Christianity. Further—and quite unlike Marx—Nietzsche saw in religion a potential use as a weapon of subversion. In *Beyond Good and Evil* and *On the Genealogy of Morals*, Nietzsche makes the case that the particular ideology represented in the Judeo-Christian tradition represents a sort of revolt on the part of the poor and downtrodden.[100] This ideology (he calls it "slave morality") maintains that all people are essentially the same, elevates the poor and meek as the most worthy, and offers rewards for humility and peacefulness. This ideology serves two needs, one strategic and one emotional. The strategy is one of sneaky assimilation. To the extent that members of the ruling class are converted to this way of thinking, it coopts them into a value system that forces them to see everyone as equally valuable in the eyes of the Lord. The religious skeptic Voltaire had long since noted—with some sympathy—this potential application for religious ideology, which he described in a famous passage from his "Epistle to the Author of the Book *The Three Impostors*":

> If God did not exist, it would be necessary to invent him.
> Let the wise man announce him and kings fear him. Kings,
>   if you oppress me, if your eminencies disdain
> The tears of the innocent that you cause to flow,
> My avenger is in the heavens: learn to tremble.
> Such, at least, is the fruit of a useful creed.[101]

A socially inferior caste can derive a lot of utility from the fear of a wrathful god who loves the poor. This was the strategic value of Judeo-Christian "slave morality," for Nietzsche.

The emotional value of Judeo-Christian religious morality seems to have a lot to do with self-esteem. Regardless of what one thinks of Nietzsche's theory about an occult political strategy behind the rise of Christianity, any religion remains an excellent vehicle for representing the needs and prejudices of one's own group as objectively important—and the superiority of the group and its ideology as beyond question. Religious ideology facilitates in-group "binding" and at the same time supplies a perfect vehicle for feeding the emotional need for self-affirmation through a sense of affiliation with a (presumptively) culturally and morally superior community. The peculiar ethos of the Abrahamic tradition permits the weak and oppressed proponent to feel better about his or her situation, thanks to the stipulated divine love and attention, plus an eternal reward in the afterlife. However miserable in terms of material goods or political position, the devout receive a tremendous boost to their sense of their own importance, because they follow the one true religion. And their specific group, in several historical strains of the tradition, is further elevated by being the one and only people to whom God has chosen to reveal the truth via revelations, prophets, and/or messiahs—the "Chosen People." Being the chosen followers of the one true religion elevates the community's self-image (even in the face of negative external conditions, such as foreign occupation). This enhances in-group solidarity while enhancing self-esteem for individuals identifying with the tradition.

It has long been recognized in studies from political science, psychology, and sociology that individuals base much of their self-image on the various groups (cultural, racial, political, religious, etc.) with which they identify. Social identity theory, as we saw in chapter 3, is a highly regarded theory about the emotional motives behind group identification, discrimination, and group-serving bias.[102] It is easy to see that people have a tendency to emotionally attach themselves to various groups (nations, political parties, cultural communities, sports teams, etc.), and to base a lot of their behavior on their fealty to that group—as well as a conviction about its inherent superiority. Victories achieved by the group are vicariously felt as personal victories, and losses can be experienced quite viscerally (multiple studies have shown that testosterone levels of male political partisans drop significantly after their party experiences a defeat at the polls[103]). Social and cultural group membership is an important part of self-image and identity, and can be a significant source of self-esteem. The emotional rewards of group identity depend on discriminating one's group from others by comparing it favorably to its competitors. When one's group is distinguished by its shared religious tradition (as social groups often are), the dependence of self-image on tribal identity creates a strong emotional motivation to defend the factual picture underlying one's religious ideology. (Correlatively, self-affirmations relating to individual identity have been shown to temporarily reduce both ideological closed-mindedness and group-serving bias in study participants.[104])

This understanding of motivation would explain why Nietzsche's resentful Jewish community—victims of occupation and under heavy self-esteem threat both individually and collectively—might be especially likely to develop an ideology that nevertheless allowed them to compare themselves favorably vis-à-vis their oppressors. As Nietzsche implies, downtrodden groups like these are especially likely to turn to otherworldly validation as they experience humiliating conditions in this world.

The result of the drive to group validation through religious ideology is implicit bias in favor of the factual basis of tribal traditions. This leads to familiar sorts of confirmation bias, such as the highly selective collection and interpretation of facts by those seeking to deny biological evolution. As we have seen, the same goes for rationalization of the belief in God itself, in the face of threats such as competing religious traditions and the encroachment of scientific naturalism. This percolates up to the most elite thinkers produced by a given cultural tradition. Nietzsche describes a familiar process of motivated self-justification on the part of the "philosophers" coming up with abstract systems of thought that conveniently validate traditional religious belief (and the in-group superiority that goes with it):

> They all pose as if they had discovered and reached their real opinions through the self-development of a cold, pure, divinely unconcerned dialectic . . . while at bottom it is an assumption, a hunch, indeed a kind of "inspiration," most often a desire of the heart that has been filtered and made abstract that they defend with reasons they have sought after the fact:—they are all advocates who resent that name, and for the most part even wily spokesmen for their prejudices which they baptize "truths"—and *very* far from having the courage of the conscience that admits this, precisely this, to itself.[105]

Ultimately the spokespeople for the belief systems that originate in tribal, group-serving instincts often are the most educated and, indeed, brilliant of their time. It takes a Thomas Aquinas to invent a metaphysical system that could lay a veneer of rationality over nonsensical notions like a "triune" god who is literally one person and three persons at the same time, or a cracker that literally turns into flesh yet still tastes like a cracker.

Unfortunately, the negative effects of group-serving bias are not trivial. It was the European Christians who eventually colonized most of the world; they plundered the conquered territories and enslaved native populations, all the while telling themselves they were doing their victims a favor by bringing them the one true religion. The notion of their own inherent superiority as practitioners of the one true faith legitimized the "civilizing mission" of colonialism.

The self-esteem–boosting, social identity motives behind implicit in-group favoritism are almost inseparable from out-group derogation and intergroup prejudice. Tribalism has both positive and negative effects: in-group solidarity, but also intergroup divisions. People are very sensitive to their social position relative to other individuals, and insofar as they identify with some social-cultural group, they are equally sensitive to the way their group is situated or perceived relative to other groups. In-group favoritism does not absolutely *require* derogation of other groups; regarding self-esteem, researchers have found that an elevated opinion of one's own group is more significant than a lower opinion of out-groups.[106] Yet, under low self-esteem conditions, or conditions under which individuals feel a momentary threat to their self-esteem, prejudiced, derogatory representations of others can enhance self-esteem.[107] Thus, under social identity theory—where individual self-image is tied up with one's image of the relative value of one's group—the motive to self-enhancement can be expected to lead to implicit negative attitudes toward other groups. One notorious example is the explosion of virulent anti-Semitism in interwar Germany, where the majority population was in the process of suffering multiple threats to its sense of identity and well-being. (Compare also chapter 3's discussion of U.S. white working-class resentment of racial out-groups.)

Results are decidedly mixed on the net contemporary impact of religiosity (and the groupings it creates) on peace and understanding among peoples. Political scientists Robert Putnam and David Campbell explored a number of ways to gauge differences between religious and nonreligious Americans. Their conclusion was that "By many different measures religiously observant Americans are better neighbors and better citizens than secular Americans—they are more generous with their time and money, especially in helping the needy, and they are more active in community life."[108] Yet it is unquestionable that religious ideology has historically led the way among reasons for discrimination, oppression, and war. Social psychologists C. Daniel Batson, Patricia Schoenrade, and W. Larry Ventis distinguished between three typical motives underlying religiosity: the "extrinsic" motive, where religion primarily serves as a means to the end of community and belonging; the "intrinsic" motive, where faith is experienced as an end in itself (a motive in turn associated with orthodoxy);

and the "quest" motive, where religion is part of a larger search for answers to existential questions.[109] (The last of these is typically associated with the least orthodoxy and the most flexibility.) After looking at fifty years of studies of the impact of religion on personal conduct, they concluded that, in both the extrinsic (means) and intrinsic (ends) manifestations of religiosity, there is no association between religion and greater love and compassion for others,[110] and that religion is associated with greater prejudice toward others.[111] Putnam and Campbell also found that the key factor in improved "neighborliness" was not actual belief in religious doctrines but, rather, "religious belongingness"—that is, participation in group activities with co-religionists.[112] Given those types of religiosity that Batson, Schoenrade, and Ventis found most common, religion is more predictive of prejudice toward, and exclusion of, others than it is of love and fellow-feeling for others. This would be consistent with the notion that group-serving motives are a primary element in religiosity. Unfortunately, group-serving motives inspire in-group favoritism more than egalitarianism and universal love, because the self-esteem we derive from our cultural identity is often facilitated by the derogation of others.

4.4.3 Freud and Terror Management

We have noted the evolutionary advantage deriving from a cognitive bias in favor of an overactive agency detector and how this may have contributed to the development of religious ideologies. Further, religion can be a particularly effective kind of cement for in-group solidarity and cooperation, which advantages both the group and the individual—and which also reciprocally advantages whatever cultural traditions are exhibited by successful groups! These factors help explain religion's origin, but they can't fully account for its perseverance in the face of increasing scientific sophistication and cosmopolitan awareness of other cultures. To explain religion's tenacity—and the heroic levels of motivated reasoning necessary to maintain belief in the actual existence of supernatural agents and invisible worlds—we have to look to emotional need. As we have seen, one plausible candidate is system justification, which can serve anyone seeking a comforting reassurance in the face of threats to social stability. Next, we saw how ideologies deployable under our natural propensity to in-group favoritism can be useful to self-esteem; and how religion is well-suited to serve this function alongside (and often in partnership with) ideologies of cultural or racial superiority.

Perhaps the most potent emotional need religion serves, however, is that of managing existential anxiety: the dreadful, very personal anxiety deriving from an awareness of our own mortality and a sense of powerlessness in the face of uncaring nature. What later became known as **terror management theory** was introduced by cultural anthropologist Ernest Becker in his 1973 book *The Denial of Death*. As John Jost and David Amodio put it, according to this theory, "The purpose of ideology . . . is to cope with anxiety concerning one's own mortality through denial, rationalization, and other defense mechanisms."[113] Terror management theory notes that humans are unique in their awareness of their own mortality; this awareness can cause profound feelings of insecurity. Becker's suggestion is that the characteristic response is to identify ever more closely with one's culture and ideology in trying to bolster self-esteem, as a way of managing anxiety about mortality, impermanence, and uncertainty. And such cultural and ideological wagon-circling is associated with motivated reasoning and denial in defense of these comforting worldviews. Terror management theory has been put to the test for decades, and it has been validated under a variety of test conditions.[114] Significantly, "mortality salience" studies have shown again and again that reminders of death trigger stronger cultural, racial, and ideological identification and differentiation.[115] When reminded of their own mortality, people seem to retreat to the comfort of distinguishing ideological identifiers and to a sense of belonging to something greater than themselves.

It is no coincidence that Dan Kahan focuses on risk perception in his study of the way cultural values inform factual conclusions.[116] Fear is the motivator most directly pertinent to survival, and it is therefore not surprising if it is found to play a large role in cultural and ideological identification—even as cultural and ideological identification is found, by Kahan and others, to play a large role in what one perceives to be threatening. Sam Harris calls death "the fount of illusions":

We live in a world where all things, good and bad, are finally destroyed by change. The world sustains us, it would seem, only to devour us at its leisure. Parents lose their children and children lose their parents. Husbands and wives are separated in an instant, never to meet again. Friends part company in haste, without knowing that it will be for the last time. This life, when surveyed with a broad glance, presents little more than a vast spectacle of loss. But it seems that there is a cure for all this. If we live rightly—not necessarily ethically, but within the framework of certain ancient beliefs and stereotyped behaviors—we will get everything we want after we die. When our bodies finally fail us, we just shed our corporeal ballast and travel to a land where we are reunited with everyone we loved while alive. . . . If one didn't know better, one would think that man in his fear of losing all that he loves, had created heaven, along with its gate keeper God, in his own image. . . . What one believes happens after death dictates much of what one believes about life, and this is why faith-based religion, in presuming to fill in the blanks in our knowledge of the hereafter, does such heavy lifting for those who fall under its power.[117]

Under test conditions, we see that subjects reminded of mortality express stronger religiosity and belief in supernatural agents—even with regard to culturally alien religious traditions: Christian subjects primed with thoughts of mortality expressed greater confidence in the existence of Buddha in one study and shamanic spirits in another.[118] (Any port in a storm, as the expression goes.)

But what about the evident willingness of individuals throughout history to sacrifice themselves in the name of their religion? How can religious identification simultaneously be strongly motivated by a fear of death and also inspire self-sacrifice? The answer on behalf of theories attributing religious belief to fear of death and/or existential anxiety would join the concept of cultural identity with **in-group entitativity**. As we have seen, cultural identity refers to the ways in which individuals identify on an emotional level with larger social and cultural groups. In-group entitativity refers to the extent to which a member of the group perceives the group as a real entity, with its own existence distinct from that of its individual members. Researchers have found that reminders of mortality increase not only in-group identification but also in-group entitativity.[119] The psychologists studying this phenomenon propose that in-group identification is an "anxiety buffer mechanism," wherein one's cultural identity, being noncorporeal,

> can be perceived as transcending the individual mortal fate. . . . [I]f the fear of death is essentially the fear of the total loss of one's identity, the fear of one's annihilation, self-immolation for the ingroup is quite a reasonable choice: Through the social extension of the self implemented by group belonging, individuals may have the feeling that they are offered transcendence.[120]

This identification with the group *qua* entity could positively affect choices to self-sacrifice even in the absence of a specific religious ideology promising a desirable afterlife for those who give their lives for their god. (Compare also the willingness of parents to sacrifice for their children, who, among other things, may represent a kind of continuation of the parent's identity after the latter's death.)

Recently, Aaron Kay of Duke University, along with various collaborators, has proposed an explanation of some forms of superstition and religious belief in terms of a mechanism he calls **compensatory control**. Compensatory control is a variation on terror management theory that focuses more on the discomfort of an inadequate sense of personal control over events. Kay and his coresearchers suggest that "people protect their belief in a controlled, nonrandom world by imbuing their social, physical, and metaphysical environments with order and structure when their sense of personal control is threatened," and that belief in an "interventionist God" helps people "cope with the anxiety and discomfort that lacking personal control fuels."[121] Where terror management theory predicts a retreat to any familiar ideology in the face of uncertainty and threat, the compensatory control model predicts a retreat specifically to variations on ideology that reassure by promising a greater sense of control. A belief in supernatural agents that can be influenced or appeased would satisfy this need to feel less helpless in the face of mortality and uncaring nature. Such feelings of vulnerability can be alleviated by a belief system that includes a directing agent with a plan for the universe. As Kay et al. note, most human cultures have featured a supernatural belief system revolving around some such agent or agents.[122] Many modern religions, including the major Abrahamic ones, promise (a) an orderly, directed universe created with human beings in mind; with (b) a beneficent agent behind it; and (c) some ability of humans to influence events in their favor (including their post-death existences).

Kay et al. hypothesized that, if subjects were asked to recall times when they felt a lack of personal control over events, they would subsequently express a greater confidence specifically in the existence of a "controlling God"—that is, a god who has a plan for the universe and who actively intervenes in events. Indeed, they discovered this very effect in multiple studies.[123] They also found that persons under conditions of external uncertainty—such as government instability— are more likely to express belief in a controlling god.[124] Kay et al. conclude that "some of the enduring psychological power of religious conviction may derive from its capacity to promote both external and personal control, which together provide a powerful shield from the anxiety aroused from randomness, confusion, or uncertainty."[125]

Freud anticipated the compensatory control model perfectly in his *The Future of an Illusion*, as he speculates upon the psychological origins of the superstitious belief in demons and spirits exemplified by animism and shamanism:

> There are the elements, which seem to mock at all human control: the earth, which quakes and is torn apart and buries all human life and its works; water, which deluges and drowns everything in a turmoil; storms, which blow everything before them; there are diseases, which we have only recently recognized as attacks by other organisms; and finally there is the painful riddle of death, against which no medicine has yet been found, nor probably will be. With these forces nature rises up against us, majestic, cruel and inexorable; she brings to our mind once more our weakness and helplessness, which we thought to escape through the work of civilization. . . . Impersonal forces and destinies cannot be approached; they remain eternally remote. But if the elements have passions that rage as they do in our own souls, if death itself is not something spontaneous but the violent act of an evil

Will, if everywhere in nature there are Beings around us of a kind that we know in our own society, then we can breathe freely, can feel at home in the uncanny and can deal by psychical means with our senseless anxiety. We are still defenceless, perhaps, but we are no longer helplessly paralysed; we can at least react. Perhaps, indeed, we are not even defenceless. We can apply the same methods against these violent supermen outside that we employ in our own society; we can try to adjure them, to appease them, to bribe them, and, by so influencing them, we may rob them of a part of their power.... And thus a store of ideas is created, born from man's need to make his helplessness tolerable and built up from the material of memories of the helplessness of his own childhood and the childhood of the human race.[126]

The beneficent, Abrahamic omni-god is, for Freud, only a development of the primitive response to feelings of helplessness in the face of the natural world. In the later, omni-god traditions,

Everything that takes place in this world is an expression of the intentions of an intelligence superior to us, which in the end, though its ways and byways are difficult to follow, orders everything for the best—that is, to make it enjoyable for us. Over each one of us there watches a benevolent Providence which is only seemingly stern and which will not suffer us to become a plaything of the stark and pitiless forces of nature. Death itself is not annihilation, is not a return to inorganic lifelessness, but the beginning of a new kind of existence which lies on the road of development to something higher.[127]

Why do we cling to superstition despite advances in natural science? Freud gives us a compensatory control explanation. The world is a scary place; supernatural agents may be controllable via sacrifice and prayer, whereas nature is not. In accounting for religious superstition in terms of emotional need, he cites compensation for the feeling of a lack of personal control in the face of nature and death—and society as well: "The gods retain the threefold task: they must exorcise the terrors of nature, they must reconcile men to the cruelty of Fate, particularly as it is shown in death, and they must compensate them for the sufferings and privations which a civilized life in common has imposed on them."[128] We used to be superstitious because we were terrified and we didn't know any better. Even though we know better now, we still face uncertainty and death. Human civilization may even exacerbate the problem by adding concerns about inequality, government instability, war, and environmental destruction.

Science writer Debora MacKenzie views science denial generally as a compensatory control issue:

> The first thing to note is that denial finds its most fertile ground in areas where the science must be taken on trust. There is no denial of antibiotics, which visibly work. But there is denial of vaccines, which we are merely told will prevent diseases—diseases, moreover, which most of us have never seen, ironically because the vaccines work. Similarly, global warming, evolution and the link between tobacco and cancer must be taken on trust, usually on the word of scientists, doctors and other technical experts who many non-scientists see as arrogant and alien. Many people see this as a threat to important aspects of their lives. In Texas last year, a member of a state committee who was trying to get creationism added to school science standards almost said as much when he proclaimed "somebody's got to stand up to experts." It is this sense of loss of control that really matters. In such situations, many people prefer to reject expert evidence in favor of alternative explanations that promise to hand control back to them, even if those explanations are not supported by evidence. All denialisms appear to be attempts like this to regain a sense of agency over uncaring nature: blaming autism on vaccines rather than an unknown natural cause, insisting that humans were made by divine plan, rejecting the idea that actions we thought were okay, such as smoking and burning coal, have turned out to be dangerous.[129]

Ideologies that promise protection against feelings of uncertainty, insecurity, and anxiety meet universal emotional needs. Terror management theory and the compensatory control model are variations on a theme—namely the essential notion that feelings of helplessness drive people toward comforting beliefs and identifications. These feelings are universal, as is some tendency to system justification and group-serving bias. Consequently religion, like pseudoscience, knows no political boundaries. (Though it is interesting to note that the safest and most comfortable societies today—meaning the Nordic and Western European states—are also the least religious.[130]) We should also remember the many positive emotions religiosity brings, such as the emotion of wonder cited by Hume, feelings of completeness and belonging, and the fellow-feeling experienced by those contemplating their ideological connection with like-minded worshipers. Belongingness and fellow-feeling are themselves emotions that enhance feelings of security, as well as self-esteem, as the authors of the self-help book *The Healthy Christian Life* explain:

> These "personal" needs are intimacy with God, fellowship with other people, and self-worth. . . . We must have unconditional love and acceptance, a feeling of being cared for, and a lifestyle that makes an impact on others with good and lasting effects. Our self-worth is enhanced to the extent that those emotions and qualities define our lives. Yet another way of describing these basic needs is that we need a sense of belongingness, an assurance that we are considered worthy by someone important to us, and a feeling that we are useful and competent. When I believe that someone important to me wants me and accepts me, I can regard myself as "good," approved, capable, and adequate to deal with daily life, partly to satisfy that person. . . . Security includes being able to regard ourselves as loved, accepted, and cared-for as individuals. Significance involves being able to regard ourselves as important and valuable to others in impacting their lives for good.[131]

In light of all that religion can do for us in the areas of group solidarity, stability, self-esteem, and reassurance (and in light of all we know about the deficits of the information deficit model of denial), it should come as no surprise that religion has easily survived cultural globalization and modern scientific progress.

4.5 The Problem(s) with Religion

Every ideology by definition incorporates the reflexive notion that it itself is both right and good, and that people should believe it. But this has special implications when it comes to religious literalism. When religious ideology involves an exclusive access to God's favor and an afterlife, the very existence of other belief systems—religious or atheist—represents a threat. Exposure to other ideas may turn one's children to the wrong path, putting their immortal souls at risk. All by itself, this particular threat is an ineluctable recipe for division. Conflict with practitioners of competing religious traditions is baked into the cake.

Religion also gives cover for all sorts of prejudices. Any discriminatory notions can be part of a given religious story, codified by revelation. Religion has enabled the immeasurably pervasive oppression of women throughout human history;[132] the same can be said for discrimination against other groups, such as ethnic minorities and homosexuals, and the suppression of political dissidents.

Now, most of this oppression would likely have happened anyway: Ideology is a tool of oppression, not the cause. When people really want to do something, they will come up with an ideology that supports it. (They will also, of course, conveniently find the evidence necessary to confirm the factual claims underlying these useful aspects of the ideology.) The Christian Bible has been cited in support of sexism, racism, and slavery,[133] free-market capitalism,[134] and as we saw in chapter 2, climate change denial. It has also been used to endorse social and economic egalitarianism, pacifism, and environmentalism. However, as Sam Harris has emphasized, the most inflexible and intolerant religious teachings derive from the most straightforward, nonselective readings of holy texts like the Bible and the Quran. Getting pacifism, tolerance, and inclusivity out of these texts requires that one flat-out ignore passages like those from the Bible's Deuteronomy 13:6, calling for proselytizing infidels to be killed, or from the Quran's 8:12, calling for the beheading of nonbelievers.

Religious ideology also can be cynically employed by elites as a tool for maintaining the status quo hierarchy, as Bonaparte, Marx, and Gibbon all observed. The multiple ways in which religiosity serves deep emotional needs makes it uniquely useful for purposes of exploitation and control.

Religious literalism may be both directly and indirectly implicated in obstructive anti-science bias. The notion that climate change will, if unchecked, bring about an end to human civilization goes against the

Christian apocalypse story, according to which the "end times" will be God-instigated rather than human-instigated (recall Representative Shimkus' assurance that AGW can't be real because God promised not to reflood the Earth). Echoing Zerubavel and Norgaard, climate activist George Marshall compares the public's response to climate change to its response to death: as embodying a "collective social norm" of silence and avoidance.[135] Dealing with climate change and resource depletion requires a willingness to face hard facts about the future; religion is all about avoiding hard facts about the future (i.e., mortality). The big-picture concern derives from the fact that, in the modern era, the denial of death that religion represents is only tenable when conjoined with some contempt for reason and evidence. Social psychologist Jesse Preston and behavioral scientist Nicholas Epley found that those primed to think about things God could explain subsequently showed a relatively lower automatic evaluation of science.[136] The authors propose that, as competing "ultimate explanations," religion and science are natural cognitive antagonists. The religious worldview is typically authority based. (Founder of the Jesuit order St. Ignatius of Loyola declared that "We should always be disposed to believe that that which appears to us to be white is really black, if the hierarchy of the church so decides."[137]) Any belief based on authority and traditional doctrine is at essential odds with modern science, which by contrast always allows for the overthrow of established theories by new evidence. Then there is the emotional component: Information about, say, evolution by natural selection represents a threat to an emotionally satisfying ideology that includes creationism as a central element. In the words of U.S. congressman Paul Broun in 2012, "God's word is true. I've come to understand that. All that stuff I was taught about evolution, embryology, Big Bang theory, all that is lies straight from the pit of hell. It's lies to try to keep me and all the folks who are taught that from understanding that they need a savior."[138] In a modern information environment, antiscience attitudes can be an expression of religious identity. This may help explain the significant correlation between biblical literalism and climate change denial, even after controlling for education and political ideology.[139] This may also explain why the Roman Catholics, under ideological threat from the Reformation, decided to go after Galileo and his evidence for the heliocentric model of the solar system.

The whole notion of scientific expertise is increasingly rejected by politically powerful, literalist Christian interest groups. As Dover, Pennsylvania, pastor Ray Mummert warned during the Intelligent Design trial, "We've been attacked by the educated, intelligent segment of the culture."[140] Christian writer Rachel Held Evans discusses her evangelical upbringing: "The deep distrust of the media, of scientific consensus—those were prevalent narratives growing up."[141] At the evangelical Bryan College, she was taught the "biblical worldview," which "was presented as cohesive worldview that you could maintain if you studied the bible. . . . Part of that was that climate change isn't real, that evolution is a myth made up by scientists who hate God, and capitalism is God's ideal for society."

There is debate over the degree to which anti-science attitudes are influenced by religiosity, as opposed to political partisanship or other cultural identification. In their 2014 study, "Religion, Partisanship, and Attitudes Toward Science Policy," political scientists Ted Jelen and Linda Lockett presented findings they interpreted as indicating a religiosity factor in science denial.[142] Dan Kahan disagrees; he asserts that religiosity only incidentally tracks science denial because some particularly salient scientific findings have become "culturally antagonistic" to some particular identity groups, which in turn happen to be partly defined by religious denomination.[143] More study of this important question would be desirable.

We discussed in chapter 1 how research by Daniel Kahneman and others has demonstrated the coexistence of distinct cognitive processes for solving problems: a conscious, analytic reasoning process, and a system of implicit cognition. We know from this research that some people are more analytic in their thinking and some are more habitually intuitive. We can also see directly that those who tend to go with their "gut" in solving problems are more likely to believe in God and the supernatural.[144] As Ara Norenzayan and Will Gervais note,[145] a whole slew of investigative programs have shown that "belief in gods and spirits is supported by core intuitive biases" (such as our aforementioned, innate bias in favor of explaining phenomena of unknown origin in terms of agents and their intentions[146]), and that "religious beliefs make good intuitive fits for human brains."[147] So a disinclination to analytic thinking in favor of intuition is associated with religiosity. Further, Norenzayan and Gervais have found that "experimental inductions that activate analytical processing . . . promote religious disbelief."[148] They observe that scientists are much less religious than the general public.[149] (This is the notable exception to the rule that education and sophistication does not immunize people from motivated reasoning and denial.) They speculate that "scientific training . . . cultivates habitual use of analytic thinking, possibly rendering it less cognitively effortful with practice."[150] The question is, could the causal arrow also go the other way? That is, could immersion in religious thinking prime the believer to think less analytically—and, in so doing, cause an even greater disregard for evidence at the cognitive level? Cognitive psychologists Marjaana Lindeman and Annika Svedholm-Häkkinen found that "Religious beliefs were linked with a weaker ability to understand physical and biological phenomena such as volcanoes, flowers, rocks and wind without giving them human qualities." They observed that their subjects' agent-centric explanations of religious mythology were reflected in their understanding of nature itself:

> The more the participants believed in religious or other paranormal phenomena, the lower their intuitive physics skills, mechanical and mental rotation abilities, school grades in mathematics and physics, and knowledge about physical and biological phenomena were . . . and the more they regarded inanimate targets as mental phenomena.[151]

In another study, they found that religious and supernatural beliefs were strongly associated with a willingness to assent to "bullshit statements" about physical reality like "Earth wants water" and "Force knows its direction."[152] One possible explanation of all this is that intuitive thinkers with a poor understanding of science are drawn to religious and other supernatural schemata for understanding the world. But my worry is that the true believer in the modern, cosmopolitan context is forced into constant rationalization and denial in order to reduce dissonance. As a consequence, the very concepts of "evidence" and "reasoning" could take on antagonistic associations for the faithful (which could in turn help explain the antagonism Preston and Epley found between religion and science as "ultimate" explanations). The ubiquity of religious ideology (and the various sorts of motivated reasoning and confirmation bias needed to sustain it) may increasingly be inimical to the public good of a citizenry that is *receptive to scientific expertise regarding issues of public importance.* "There is no societal issue in which social and natural sciences do not have an important role to play," as Peter Gluckman, chair of the International Network for Government Science Advice, recently observed.[153] A public accustomed to denial—one might even say addicted—is all the more resistant to expert opinion on public policy issues. Jeet Heer at *The New Republic* has something along these lines in mind as he tries to explain the Trump phenomenon:

> The anti-intellectualism that has been a mainstay of the conservative movement for decades also makes its members easy marks. After all, if you are taught to believe that the reigning scientific consensuses on evolution and climate change are lies, then you will lack the elementary logical skills that will set your alarm bells ringing when you hear a flim-flam artist like Trump. The Republican "war on science" is also a war on the intellectual habits needed to detect lies.[154]

This was William Clifford's concern about religious belief—and the active self-deception needed to sustain it—in his nineteenth-century essay "The Ethics of Belief":

> Every time we let ourselves believe for unworthy reasons, we weaken our powers of self-control, of doubting, of judicially and fairly weighing evidence. . . . The danger to society is not merely that it should believe wrong things, though that is great enough; but that it should become credulous, and lose the habit of testing things and inquiring into them; for then it must sink back into savagery.[155]

4.6 The Retreat into Abstraction

Ideologies that serve emotional needs have a way of adapting to dissonant information. Even as they have evolved to be even more comforting, religions have also evolved to be harder to directly disprove: The beneficent omni-god lives not on Mount Olympus but, rather, in an invisible, abstract realm or lacks even any sort of straightforward individual existence. According to **religious pluralism**, textual accounts of anthropomorphic deities performing specific miracles in support of particular cultural groups are to be understood as allegorical devices in understanding a more abstract and universally applicable divine concept. By way of explanation, theologian David Bentley Hart offers the following:

> [A]bstracting from the universal conditions of contingency, one very well may (and perhaps must) conclude that all things are sustained in being by an *absolute* plenitude of actuality, whose very essence is being as such: not a "supreme being," not another *thing* within or alongside the universe, but the infinite act of being itself, the one eternal and transcendent source of all existence and knowledge, in which all finite being participates.[156]

The sympathetic description of God as *existence* rather than as *existent* is an attempt to evade concerns like those earlier calling literalist readings of particular faith traditions into question. This approach goes hand in hand with theologian John Hick's (nonliteralist) religious pluralism, according to which all revelatory religious traditions pertain to a shared spiritual engagement with "the Real":

> The great world faiths embody different perceptions and conceptions of, and correspondingly different responses to, the Real from within the major variant ways of being human; and that within each of them the transformation of human existence from self-centeredness to Reality-centeredness is taking place.[157]

Hick writes that the Real "cannot be said to be one thing or many, person or thing, substance or process, good or bad, purposive or nonpurposive. None of the concrete descriptions that apply within the realm of human experience can apply literally to the unexperienceable ground of that realm. . . . We cannot even speak of this as a thing or an entity."[158] The Real is just this ineffable, transcendent basis for salvation, and each religious tradition represents a sort of perception or interpretation of it. Thus conflicts between particular factual claims made by competing traditions are irrelevant to the issue of justification in religious practice.

In reference to Richard Dawkins's book *The God Delusion*, in which Dawkins generally addresses the traditional (literal) anthropomorphic Christian deity, Terry Eagleton (like Hart and Hick) denies that God is "some kind of *chap*." Eagleton questions Dawkins' credentials:

> What, one wonders, are Dawkins's views on the epistemological differences between Aquinas and Duns Scotus? Has he read Eriugena on subjectivity, Rahner on grace or Moltmann on hope? Has he even heard of them? Or does he imagine like a bumptious young barrister that you can defeat the opposition while being complacently ignorant of its toughest case?[159]

This is one example of the latest move on the part of religious apologists, which is to accuse skeptics of a lack of theological sophistication—while backing off religious literalism and the factual truth of particular miracle stories. Biologist and religious skeptic P. Z. Myers calls this move "the courtier's reply," in reference to the fable of the Emperor's New Clothes; Myers imagines that, after the boy points out the emperor's nakedness, the emperor's courtiers reply that it is the boy's lack of appreciation for the subtleties of garment theory that explain his inability to see the emperor's new clothes. The problem is the boy's failure to study the most sophisticated work on fabrics and clothing design.[160] Philosopher A. C. Grayling replies directly to Eagleton:

> Terry Eagleton charges Richard Dawkins with failing to read theology in formulating his objection to religious belief, and thereby misses the point that when one rejects the premises of a set of views, it is a waste of one's time to address what is built on those premises. For example, if one concludes on the basis of rational investigation that one's character and fate are not determined by the arrangement of the planets, stars and galaxies that can be seen from Earth, then one does not waste time comparing classic tropical astrology with sidereal astrology, or either with the Sarjatak system, or any of the three

with any other construction placed on the ancient ignorances of our forefathers about the real nature of the heavenly bodies. Religion is exactly the same thing: it is the pre-scientific, rudimentary meta-physics of our forefathers, which (mainly through the natural gulli-bility of proselytised children, and tragically for the world) survives into the age in which I can send this letter by electronic means.[161]

Further, one wonders how many actual practitioners of particular traditions like Christianity or Islam would embrace the abstract plu-ralism of Hart, Hick, and Eagleton, given the survey data listed earlier. Few Christians would accept some fundamental equivalence between their beliefs and some belief system that explicitly denies the divinity of the historical Jesus. How many Muslims would agree that, on some fundamental level, a god lacking an actual and literal special relation-ship to the actual sixth- to seventh-century person Muhammad is the same god they worship? The plain fact is that most practitioners of the major world religions profess a literal belief in a specific entity-god, and express a literal belief in some or all of the particular miracle-reports that constitute the factual basis for their religious worldview.

In *Civilization and Its Discontents*, Freud remarks, "One would like to mix among the ranks of the believers in order to meet these philosophers, who think they can rescue the God of religion by replacing him by an impersonal, shadowy and abstract principle."[162] Freud offers a scathing assessment of the situation, in which he directly attributes the tenacity of religion to denial:

The whole thing is so patently infantile, so foreign to reality, that to anyone with a friendly attitude to humanity it is painful to think that the great majority of mortals will never be able to rise above this view of life. It is still more humiliating to discover how a large number of people living today, who cannot but see that this religion is not ten-able, nevertheless try to defend it piece by piece in a series of pitiful rearguard actions. . . . A special importance attaches to the case in which this attempt to procure a certainty of happiness and a protec-tion against suffering through a delusional remoulding of reality is made by a considerable number of people in common. The religions of mankind must be classed among the mass-delusions of this kind.

No one, needless to say, who shares a delusion ever recognizes it as such.[163]

The various philosophers and theologians mentioned in this chapter are not in denial because they are unintelligent or uninformed; we have seen that, in many contexts, greater education and sophistication is associated with a greater confidence in motivated conclusions. It took some education for David Bentley Hart to come up with the phrase "absolute plenitude of actuality" so he could use it to cobble together a sophisticated-sounding rationalization of his beliefs. Eagleton had to have read "Eriugena on subjectivity, Rahner on grace [and] Moltmann on hope" in order to feel so confident in dismissing Dawkins' questions. Consider again the way eminent scholars like Alston, Rea, Craig, Plantinga, Wolterstorff, and Swinburne exercise extravagant varieties of motivated reasoning in support of their favored religious traditions. The efforts of top contemporary academics like these to maintain their belief in fantastic ancient myths may represent some of history's most spectacular examples of motivated reasoning. If anyone should be able to overcome culturally inculcated myths, it should be highly sophisticated, scientifically literate, cosmopolitan academics deeply versed not just in philosophy and theology but also in the whole history of religious skepticism. Or so one would have thought on the information deficit model of denial.

The diversity of the phenomenon of religiosity itself suggests a complex array of causes. The amazing breadth of expressions of religious devotion across different cultures—as well as the depth of religious feeling—demonstrates the many needs served by religion. For the same reason, the asymmetry thesis is not a big factor here. Political conservatives tend toward threat sensitivity, system justification, and hierarchicalism; religion can address all these, but there is so much more religion can offer that is equally appealing to others. Everyone deals with self-esteem and social identity issues, and concerns about mortality; most everyone enjoys community and the positive emotion of wonder. Those with a more empathetic or egalitarian bent can find what they want to find in religious teachings. The reasons behind religious belief are too multifaceted to put it into a particular cultural or political box.

To question the religious worldview is to go up against the most emotionally helpful ideology imaginable. With such potent forces in play, we shouldn't be surprised to have seen a cultural evolution of religion that makes it more resistant to change—and all the more helpful to the individual. Given its essential malleability, there are many ways religion can be (and has been) adapted to better satisfy emotional needs associated with hierarchy, stability, in-group self-esteem issues, uncertainty, and fear of death. It burrows in even deeper as it becomes definitive of cultural communities, so that criticism of religion comes to represent an attack on identity itself. Community life, especially in small towns and villages, often revolves almost entirely around the local churches; to question religion can mean divorcing oneself from one's community, as well as alienating oneself from one's own deep-rooted self-conception.[164] The highly evolved, emotionally satisfying nature of modern religion explains its tenacity in the face of cosmopolitanism and scientific advances. We can add to this the ability to block off some sources of dissonant information through homeschooling, selective interaction with like-minded people, and now the social-media information bubble. Dissonance reduction is more urgent for the religious ideologue than for any other sort of ideologue, which explains why even elite, modern intellectuals are willing to manufacture such convoluted, strained rationalizations for theism.

Education and other modernizing factors are not irrelevant to overcoming religious superstition. Religiosity is actually very unusual among elite scientists and philosophers: Recent polling suggests that only about 14% of English-speaking philosophers are theists,[165] along with only 7% of members of the National Academy of Sciences.[166] Two separate studies showed declines in religiosity that seemed to be directly related to compulsory schooling laws when they were implemented, in Canada and in eleven European countries, respectively.[167] Norenzayan and Gervais argue that, as the scientific worldview becomes mainstream in a society, the academic-scientific community naturally favors a more "materialistic" approach to explanation—and consequently cultural cognition within that subculture may promote disbelief. It just becomes more culturally acceptable—and comfortable—to be secular.[168] They also note that religiosity is weakest (and science is strongest) in nations with strong and stable democratic institutions and low levels of existential insecurity—a correlation easily accounted for by the compensatory control model.[169] Finally, because the best predictor of religiosity is one's upbringing, as families (and communities) become more secular, so do their children.[170]

These factors are all accidents of birth and environment. Religious people are not particularly credulous by nature. It would be an injustice to conclude that the religious are weak and foolish, while atheists are strong and smart and feel no need for illusory comfort in their lives. Everybody is resistant to change in worldview, and everyone is tempted by comforting stories. Exactly which illusions are personally comforting, and how durable is their grip, is a contingent matter. Even the atheist social scientist must say, "There but for the grace of God go I."[171]

Notes

1. For an example of religion as allegory, here is rabbi and scholar Mordecai Kaplan, *Judaism without Supernaturalism* (New York: Reconstructionist Press, 1958), p. 10:

   > Transnaturalism is that extension of naturalism which takes into account much that mechanistic or materialistic or positivistic science is incapable of dealing with. Transnaturalism reaches out into the domain where mind, personality, purpose, ideals, values and meanings dwell. It treats of the good and the true. Whether or not it has a distinct logic of its own is problematic. But it certainly has a language of its own, the language of simile, metaphor and poetry. That is the language of symbol, myth and drama. In that universe of discourse, belief in God spells trust in life and man, as capable of transcending the potentialities of evil that inhere in his animal heredity, in his social heritage, and in the conditions of his environment. Transnaturalist religion beholds God in the fulfillment of human nature and not in the suspension of the natural order. Its function is not to help man overcome the hazards of nature, but to enable him to bring under control his inhumanity to his fellow man.

2. Rachel Gillum, "There Is No Difference in Religious Fundamentalism Between American Muslims and Christians," *Washington Post*, December 16, 2013, https://www.washingtonpost.com/news/monkey-cage/wp/2013/12/16/no-difference-in-religious-fundamentalism-between-american-muslims-and-christians.

3. "The World's Muslims: Unity and Diversity," Pew Research Center, August 9, 2012, http://www.pewforum.org/2012/08/09/the-worlds-muslims-unity-and-diversity-executive-summary/.

4. Pew Research Center, "The World's Muslims: Unity and Diversity."

5. "What Do Americans Believe About God? 5 Popular Beliefs," *Barna*, April 1, 2015, https://www.barna.com/research/what-do-americans-believe-about-jesus-5-popular-beliefs/.

6. http://a.abcnews.com/sections/us/PollVault/PollVault.html.

7. Pew Research Center, "Religious Landscape Study: Christians by State."

8. "Resurrection Did Not Happen, Say Quarter of Christians," *BCC News*, April 9, 2017, https://www.bbc.com/news/uk-england-39153121.

9. "When Americans Say They Believe in God, What Do They Mean?" Pew Research Center, April 25, 2018, http://www.pewforum.org/2018/04/25/when-americans-say-they-believe-in-god-what-do-they-mean/.

10. Antonin Scalia, "In Conversation: Antonin Scalia," *New York* magazine, n.d., http://nymag.com/news/features/antonin-scalia-2013-10/index3.html.

11. "Religious Landscape Study: Attendance at Religious Services," Pew Research Center, n.d., http://www.pewforum.org/religious-landscape-study/attendance-at-religious-services/.

12. Pew Research Center, "Religious Landscape Study: Christians by State."

13. Pierre-Simon Laplace, *Théorie analytique des probabilités* (Paris: Mme Ve Courcier, 1820), p. 1812.

14. Stephanie Pappas, "God's Hand? 44% of Americans See Natural Disasters as Sign of End Times," *Live Science*, March 25, 2011, http://www.livescience.com/13422-americans-natural-disasters-god.html.

15. Karl Hille, "Hubble Reveals Observable Universe Contains 10 Times More Galaxies than Previously Thought," NASA website, October 13, 2016, https://www.nasa.gov/feature/goddard/2016/hubble-reveals-observable-universe-contains-10-times-more-galaxies-than-previously-thought. The "observable universe" goes back over 13 billion years, so this number includes some galaxies that have since merged into larger ones.

16. See Sam Harris, *Letter to a Christian Nation* (New York: Vintage Books, 2006), pp. 6–7.

17. Locke, *Essay Concerning Human Understanding*, Bk. IV, Ch. 20, Sect. 10.

18. Locke, *Essay Concerning Human Understanding*, Bk. IV, Ch. 20, Sect. 18.

19. William Lane Craig and Bart D. Ehrman, "Is There Historical Evidence for the Resurrection of Jesus?," *Reasonable Faith*, March 2006, http://www.reasonablefaith.org/is-there-historical-evidence-for-the-resurrection-of-jesus-the-craig-ehrman.

20. Michael D. Coogan, ed., *The New Oxford Annotated Bible* (New York: Oxford University Press, 2010), p. 1744.
21. David Hume, *An Enquiry Concerning Human Understanding* (Indianapolis, IN: Hackett, 1977).
22. See John L. Mackie, *The Miracle of Theism: Arguments for and Against the Existence of God* (Oxford: Oxford University Press, 1982), p. 25.
23. Leaman, Oliver, ed., *The Qur'an: An Encyclopedia* (New York: Taylor & Francis, 2006).
24. Kenneth L. Woodward, *The Book of Miracles: The Meaning of the Miracle Stories in Christianity, Judaism, Buddhism, Hinduism and Islam* (New York: Simon & Schuster, 2001).
25. www.lankanewspapers.com, *The Island*, Sri Lanka; Agence France-Presse. Uncredited article, Share International Magazine October 2006. Article cites Siri Lankan publication The Island. http://w-ww.share-international.org/magazine/old_issues/2006/oct_06.htm#signs.
26. Hume, *An Enquiry Concerning Human Understanding*, p. 81.
27. Tony Harmsworth, "Welcome to the Loch Ness and Loch Ness Information Website," Loch Ness Information website, 2015, http://www.loch-ness.org/.
28. Sam Harris, *The End of Faith* (New York: W. W. Norton, 2005), p. 19.
29. Emily Eakin, "So God's Really in the Details?," *New York Times*, May 11, 2002, http://www.nytimes.com/2002/05/11/arts/so-god-s-really-in-the-details.html. See Craig–Ehrman debate for discussion (Craig and Ehrman, "Is There Historical Evidence for the Resurrection of Jesus?").
30. See, for example, "Praying to the Saints," *Catholic Answers: To Explain & Defend the Faith*, n.d., http://www.catholic.com/tract/praying-to-the-saints.
31. "U.S. News & Beliefnet Prayer Survey Results," *Beliefnet*, n.d., http://www.beliefnet.com/faiths/faith-tools/meditation/2004/12/u-s-news-beliefnet-prayer-survey-results.aspx.
32. "Poll: Doctors Believe in Miracles," *WND*, December 23, 2004, https://www.wnd.com/2004/12/28152/.
33. As extensively discussed by Marshall Brain, in "Why Won't God Heal Amputees?," *Why God Won't Heal Amputees*, n.d., (http://whywontgodhealamputees.com/god5.htm).
34. See Georges Rey, "Meta-atheism: Religious Avowal as Self-Deception," in *Philosophers Without God* (Oxford: Oxford University Press, 2005), p. 22. There are cases where we may put our *trust* in someone without much direct evidence that he or she will come through as promised, but even in

such cases, we would usually have some background experience with the person that tells us he or she is trustworthy. We would also usually have independent reasons to think that the person actually exists.

35. Harris, *The End of Faith*, pp. 23–24.
36. Harris, *The End of Faith*, p. 24.
37. Jacques Waardenburg, *Reason and Religion: Theory in the Study of Religion* (Berlin/Boston: De Gruyter, 2013), pp. 94–95.
38. Nicholas Rescher, "Reason and Religion," *Notre Dame Philosophical Reviews*, 2013, http://ndpr.nd.edu/news/40454-reason-and-religion/.
39. John Calvin, *Institutes of the Christian Religion*, trans. Henry Beveridge, ed. Anthony Uyl (Ontario: Devoted Publishing, 2016), p. 22.
40. Alvin Plantinga and Nicholas Wolterstorff, *Faith and Rationality: Reason and Belief in God* (London: University of Notre Dame Press, 1983).
41. See Helen de Cruz and Johan de Smedt, *A Natural History of Natural Theology* (Cambridge, MA: MIT Press, 2015), pp. 195–196 and 199.
42. Paul Helm, "John Calvin, 'The Sensus Divinitatis,' and the Noetic Effects of Sin," *International Journal for Philosophy of Religion* 43 (1998), pp. 87–107. Also, Alvin Plantinga, *Warranted Christian Belief* (Oxford: Oxford University Press, 2000), p. 214; qtd. by Rey, "Meta-atheism," p. 20.
43. Anthony Bolos and Kyle Scott, "Reformed Epistemology," *Internet Encyclopedia of Philosophy*, n.d., http://www.iep.utm.edu/ref-epis/.
44. In his letter to Sigmund Freud of December 5, 1927.
45. Bolos and Scott, "Reformed Epistemology."
46. Linda Zagzebski, "Plantinga's Warranted Christian Belief and the Aquinas/Calvin Model," *Philosophical Books* 43 (2002), pp. 117–123.
47. See also psychologist Michael Persinger's "ghost helmet" experiments, in which he (claims to have) instigated ecstatic experiences via external, electromagnetic stimulation of the brain. His Christian subjects report feeling the presence of Jesus; his Muslim subjects report the presence of Mohammed, etc. Discussed in Burton, *On Being Certain*, pp. 24–25.
48. See an interview with Plantinga in the *New York Times* on this subject (Gary Gutting, "Is Atheism Irrational?," *New York Times*, February 9, 2014, https://opinionator.blogs.nytimes.com/2014/02/09/is-atheism-irrational/?_r=1); and a helpful point-by-point reply by Massimo Pigliucci ("Is Alvin Plantinga for Real? Alas, It Appears So," *Rationally Speaking*, February 13, 2014, http://rationallyspeaking.blogspot.com/2014/02/is-alving-plantinga-for-real-alas-it.html).
49. Qtd. in Victor Stenger, "Why Is There Something Rather than Nothing?," *Skeptical Briefs* 16 (2006), https://skepticalinquirer.org/newsletter/why_

is_there_something_rather_than_nothing/?/sb/show/why_is_there_
something_rather_than_nothing.

50. For a recent criticism of the cosmological argument along these lines, see Richard Dawkins, *The God Delusion* (Boston: Mariner Books, 2006).

51. "Third Antinomy," in Kant's *Critique of Pure Reason*, 2nd ed. (1787).

52. As Kant argued, a cause of all causes would be a cause that lies "outside" of time and subsists independently of the causal order of the world. This is both nonsensical and a misapplication of the concept of a cause.

53. Charles Coulson, *Science and Christian Belief* (Chapel Hill: University of North Carolina Press, 1955).

54. Physicist Victor Stenger discusses instances of spontaneous self-organization in nature—for example, the symmetrical patterns of snowflakes. Snowflakes would be obvious examples of miracles of design, if we did not know about thermodynamics and crystal formation. Stenger further points out that not only does this crystallization happen spontaneously but it takes energy to disrupt the resulting organization: Orderliness in nature is not only explicable without design but also can be a default. (Stenger, "Why Is There Something Rather than Nothing?").

55. Discovery Institute, "Fellows," *Discovery Institute*, n.d., http://www.discovery.org/about/fellows.

56. See Mackie, *The Miracle of Theism*.

57. Gary Parker, "From Evolution to Creation," *The Evolution Crisis*, n.d., http://theevolutioncrisis.org.uk/testimony5.php.

58. Henry Morris, "The Scientific Case Against Evolution," Institute for Creation Research website, n.d., http://www.icr.org/home/resources/resources_tracts_scientificcaseagainstevolution/.

59. Edward Humes, *Monkey Girl: Evolution, Education, Religion, and the Battle for America's Soul* (New York: HarperCollins, 2009).

60. From John Ashton, ed., *In Six Days: Why 50 Scientists Choose to Believe in Creation* (Fitzroy Falls, Australia: New Holland Publishers, 1999); qtd. in Burton, *On Being Certain*, pp. 13–14.

61. John Gribbin and Martin Rees, *Cosmic Coincidences* (New York: Bantam Books, 1989).

62. See William Craig, "The Teleological Argument and the Anthropic Principle," in *The Logic of Rational Theism: Exploratory Essays*, ed. William Craig and Mark McLeod (Lewiston, NY: Edwin Mellen, 1990), pp. 127–153; and Alvin Plantinga, "The Dawkins Confusion: Naturalism ad absurdum," *Christianity Today*, March/April 2007, http://www.booksandculture.com/articles/2007/marapr/1.21.html.

63. Alan Guth, "Inflationary Universe: A Possible Solution to the Horizon and Flatness Problems," *Physical Review D* 23 (1981), pp. 347–356. See also Paul Davies, *Superforce* (New York: Simon & Schuster, 1983).

64. And fine-tuning makes puzzling assumptions about probabilities. As philosopher Robin Le Poidevin has pointed out, to assign a probability to an event, you have to know its propensity to happen given prior conditions. We can't talk about the inherent probability or improbability of the laws of nature without some process producing them—to talk about their likelihood, we need to talk about their likelihood under that process. If there is no such process, we can't assign a probability. The design argument introduces an extra-universal god with the intention to create life as the prior condition. But there is no way to determine the propensity of God existing, or of a life-giving universe with God (or, for that matter, of a life-giving universe without God). See Robin Le Poidevin, *Arguing for Atheism: An Introduction to the Philosophy of Religion* (New York: Routledge, 1996), pp. 53–54.

65. Mona Chalabi, "Are Prisoners Less Likely to Be Atheists?," *FiveThirtyEight*, March 12, 2015, http://fivethirtyeight.com/features/are-prisoners-less-likely-to-be-atheists/.

66. Clifford Sosis, "What Is It Like to Be a Philosopher?: Elizabeth Barnes," What Is It Like to Be a Philosopher website, n.d., http://www.whatisitliketo beaphilosopher.com/#/elizabeth-barnes/.

67. John Stuart Mill, *On Liberty* (London: J.W. Parker, 1859), pp. 13–45; qtd. in Rey, "Meta-atheism."

68. Rey, "Meta-atheism," p. 23.

69. Rey, "Meta-atheism," pp. 2–3.

70. Neil van Leeuwen, "Religious Credence Is Not Factual Belief," *Cognition* 133 (2014), p. 704.

71. Van Leeuwen, "Religious Credence Is Not Factual Belief," p. 706.

72. Van Leeuwen, "Religious Credence Is Not Factual Belief," p. 701.

73. Paul Bloom, "Scientific Faith Is Different from Religious Faith," *The Atlantic*, November 24, 2015, https://www.theatlantic.com/science/archive/2015/11/why-scientific-faith-isnt-the-same-as-religious-faith/417357/

74. Neil Levy, "Religious Beliefs Are Factual Beliefs: Content Does Not Correlate with Context Sensitivity," *Cognition* 161 (2017), p. 111.

75. Varki and Brower, *Denial*, pp. 128–129.

76. Varki and Brower, *Denial*, p. 150.

77. See Shermer, *The Believing Brain*, chs. 4 and 5, for an overview of research in these areas.

78. Shermer, *The Believing Brain*, p. 87.

79. See Daniel Dennett, *The Intentional Stance* (Cambridge, MA: MIT Press, 1987).

80. Ara Norenzayan, Will Gervais, and Kali Trzesniewski, "Mentalizing Deficits Constrain Belief in a Personal God," *PloS one* May 30, 2012, https://journals.plos.org/plosone/article?id=10.1371/journal.pone.0036880.

81. See, for example, Esther Herrmann et al., "Humans Have Evolved Specialized Skills of Social Cognition: The Cultural Intelligence Hypothesis," *Science* 317 (2007), pp. 1360–1366.

82. See especially ch. 1 in Joyce, *The Evolution of Morality*; also see Dennett, *Breaking the Spell*.

83. See Robert Frank, *Passions within Reason* (New York: W. W. Norton, 1988) for a discussion of this point.

84. Haidt, *The Righteous Mind*; see also Paul Bloom, "Is God an Accident?," *The Atlantic*, December 2005, https://www.theatlantic.com/magazine/archive/2005/12/is-god-an-accident/304425/.

85. Haidt, *The Righteous Mind*, p. 272.

86. Ara Norenzayan, *Big Gods: How Religion Transformed Cooperation and Conflict* (Princeton, NJ: Princeton University Press, 2015).

87. See, for example, Max Ernest-Jones, Daniel Nettle, and Melissa Bateson, "Effects of Eye Images on Everyday Cooperative Behavior: A Field Experiment," *Evolution and Human Behavior* 32 (2011), pp. 172–178.

88. See Ilkka Pyysiäinen and Marc Hauser, "The Origins of Religion: Evolved Adaptation or By-Product?," *Trends in Cognitive Science* 14 (2010), pp. 104–109; ctd. in Hibbing et al., *Predisposed*, p. 216.

89. From Karl Marx and Friedrich Engels, "A Contribution to the Critique of Hegel's Philosophy of Right, Introduction," in *On Religion*, trans. Reinhold Niebuhr (New York: Schocken Books, 1964 [1844]) , pp. 41–42.

90. Edward Gibbon, *The History of the Decline and Fall of the Roman Empire*, vol. 1, ch. 2 (New York: Random House, 2013).

91. Napoleon Bonaparte and Jules Bertaut, *Napoleon: In His Own Words (1916)* (Whitefish, MT: Kessinger, 2010).

92. John Jost, Carlee Hawkins, Brian Nosek, Erin Hennes, Chadly Stern, Samuel Gosling, and Jesse Graham, "Belief in a Just God (and a Just Society): A System Justification Perspective on Religious Ideology," *Journal of Theoretical and Philosophical Psychology* 34 (2013), pp. 56–81.

93. Jost et al., "Belief in a Just God," p. 4.

94. Jost et al., "Belief in a Just God," p. 4; citing Vassilis Saroglou, "Religion and the Five Factors of Personality: A Meta-Analytic Review," *Personality and Individual Differences* 32 (2002), pp. 15–25.

95. Jost et al., "Belief in a Just God," pp. 4–5.

96. Jost et al., "Belief in a Just God," p. 7.

97. Jost et al., "Belief in a Just God," pp. 8–17.

98. Robin, "The Conservative Reaction."

99. Jost et al., "Belief in a Just God," p. 20.

100. See esp. the first section of Friedrich Nietzsche, *On the Genealogy of Morals*, trans. Douglas Smith (Oxford: Clarendon Press, 1996).

101. From Voltaire's "Epistle to the Author of the Book *The Three Impostors*" (1768); qtd. in Jost et al., "Belief in a Just World," p. 21.

102. Susan Fiske, Daniel Gilbert, and Gardner Lindzey, *Handbook of Social Psychology* (Hoboken, NJ: John Wiley, 2010), p. 2:1029. See also Jost et al., " 'Hot' Political Cognition."

103. Charles Choi, "Jock the Vote: Election Outcomes Affect Testosterone Levels in Men," *Scientific American*, October 23, 2009, http://www.scientificamerican.com/article/vote-election-testosterone/.

104. Cohen, et al., "Bridging the Partisan Divide," pp. 415–430; also see Gaven Ehrlich and Richard Gramzow, "The Politics of Affirmation Theory: When Group-Affirmation Leads to Greater In-group Bias," *Personality and Social Psychology Bulletin* 41 (2015), pp. 1110–1122.

105. Nietzsche, *Beyond Good and Evil*, Sect. 5.

106. Gordon Allport, *The Nature of Prejudice* (Cambridge, MA: Addison-Wesley, 1954); Marilynn Brewer, "The Psychology of Prejudice: In-group Love or Out-group Hate?," *Journal of Social Issues* 55 (1999), pp. 429–444.

107. Steven Fein and Steven Spencer, "Prejudice as Self-Image Maintenance: Affirming the Self Through Derogating Others," *Journal of Personality and Social Psychology* 73 (1997), pp. 31–44; cited in Fiske et al., *Handbook of Social Psychology*, p. 1042.

108. Robert Putnam and David Campbell, *American Grace: How Religion Divides and Unites Us* (New York: Simon & Schuster, 2010), p. 461; qtd. in Haidt, *The Righteous Mind*, p. 267.

109. C. Daniel Batson, Patricia Schoenrade, and W. Larry Ventis, *Religion and the Individual: A Social-Psychological Perspective* (Oxford: Oxford University Press, 1993).

110. Batson et al., *Religion and the Individual*, p. 363.

111. Batson et al., *Religion and the Individual*, p. 329.

112. Putnam and Campbell, *American Grace*, p. 473; qtd. in Haidt, *The Righteous Mind*, p. 267.

113. John Jost and David Amodio, "Political Ideology as Motivated Social Cognition," *Motivation and Emotion* 36 (2012), p. 56.

114. For an overview, see Jeff Greenberg, Sheldon Solomon, and Tom Pyszczynski, "Terror Management Theory of Self-Esteem and Cultural Worldviews: Empirical Assessments and Conceptual Refinements," *Advances in Experimental Social Psychology* 29 (1997), pp. 61–139.

115. Brian Burke, Andy Martens, and Erik Faucher, "Two Decades of Terror Management Theory: A Meta-Analysis of Mortality Salience Research," *Personality and Social Psychology Review* 14 (2016), pp. 155–195.

116. Dan Kahan, "Three Models of Risk Perception and Their Significance for Self-Government," The Cultural Cognition Project, February 23, 2014, http://www.culturalcognition.net/blog/2014/2/23/three-models-of-risk-perception-their-significance-for-self.html.

117. Harris, *The End of Faith*, pp. 36–38.

118. Ara Norenzayan and Will Gervais, "The Origins of Religious Disbelief," *Trends in Cognitive Sciences* 17 (2013), pp. 20–25.

119. Emanuele Castano, Vincent Yzerbyt, Maria Paola Paladino, and Simona Sacchi, "I Belong, Therefore I Exist: In-group Identification, In-group Entitativity, and In-group Bias," *Personality and Social Psychology Bulletin* 28 (2002), p. 138.

120. Castano et al., "I Belong, Therefore I Exist," pp. 140–141.

121. Aaron Kay, Jennifer Whitson, Danielle Gaucher, and Adam Galinsky, "Compensatory Control," *Current Directions in Psychological Science* 18 (2009), p. 264.

122. Aaron Kay et al., "Religious Belief as Compensatory Control," *Personality and Social Psychology Review* 14 (2010), p. 37.

123. Kay et al., "Religious Belief as Compensatory Control," pp. 39–40.

124. Kay et al., "Religious Belief as Compensatory Control," p. 42.

125. Kay et al., "Religious Belief as Compensatory Control," p. 37.

126. Sigmund Freud, *The Future of an Illusion*, trans. W. D. Robson-Scott (London: Hogarth Press, 1949), pp. 26–27.

127. Freud, *The Future of an Illusion*, pp. 32–33.

128. Freud, *The Future of an Illusion*, p. 30.

129. Debora MacKenzie, "Living in Denial: Why Sensible People Reject the Truth," *New Scientist*, May 12, 2010, https://www.newscientist.com/article/mg20627606.100-living-in-denial-why-sensible-people-reject-the-truth/.

130. See Adam Gopnik, "Bigger than Phil," *The New Yorker*, February 17/24, 2014, http://www.newyorker.com/magazine/2014/02/17/bigger-phil.

131. Frank Minirth, Paul Meier, Richard Meier, and Dawn Hawkins, *The Healthy Christian Life* (Grand Rapids, MI: Baker Books, 1988), pp. 139–143.

132. See Ophelia Benson and Jeremy Stangroom, *Does God Hate Women?* (New York: Continuum, 2009).

133. See Zaid Jilani, "How Religious 'Liberty' Has Been Used to Justify Racism, Sexism and Slavery Throughout History," *Alternet*, April 6, 2016, http://www.alternet.org/belief/how-religious-liberty-has-been-used-justify-racism-sexism-and-slavery-throughout-history.

134. Chad Hovind, "Bible and Money: Why God Supports Free Market Capitalism," *Beliefnet*, n.d., http://www.beliefnet.com/columnists/godonomics/2011/06/bible-and-money-why-god-supports-free-market-capitalism.html.

135. Marshall, *Don't Even Think about It*, p. 3.

136. Jesse Preston and Nicholas Epley, "Science and God: An Automatic Opposition between Ultimate Explanations," *Journal of Experimental Social Psychology* 45 (2009), pp. 238–241.

137. George D. O'Clock, *Isaiah's Leper* (Lincoln, NE: iUniverse, 2005), p. 48.

138. Matt Pearce, "U.S. Rep. Paul Broun: Evolution a Lie 'from the Pit of Hell'," *Los Angeles Times*, October 7, 2012, http://articles.latimes.com/2012/oct/07/nation/la-na-nn-paul-broun-evolution-hell-20121007.

139. Matthew Arbuckle and David Konisky, "The Role of Religion in Environmental Attitudes," *Social Science Quarterly* 96 (2015), pp. 1244–1263; ctd. by Chris Mooney, "New Study Reaffirms the Link Between Conservative Religious Faith and Climate Change Doubt," *Washington Post*, May 29, 2015, https://www.washingtonpost.com/news/energy-environment/wp/2015/05/29/this-fascinating-chart-on-faith-and-climate-change-denial-has-been-reinforced-by-new-research/.

140. Charles Pierce, "Greetings from Idiot America," *Esquire*, November 1, 2005, p. 181.

141. Molly Worthen, "The Evangelical Roots of Our Post-Truth Society," *New York Times*, April 13, 2017, https://www.nytimes.com/2017/04/13/opinion/sunday/the-evangelical-roots-of-our-post-truth-society.html

142. Jelen and Lockett, "Religion, Partisanship, and Attitudes Toward Science Policy."

143. Dan Kahan, "ICT Eats RAT & CAT for Breakfast: More (and More Data on) Religiosity, Political Predispositions, and 'Anti-Science,'" The Cultural Cognition Project, November 17, 2014, http://www.culturalcognition.net/blog/2014/11/17/ict-eats-rat-cat-for-breakfast-more-and-more-data-on-religio.html.

144. Will Gervais and Ara Norenzayan, "Analytic Thinking Promotes Religious Disbelief," *Science* 336 (2012), pp. 493–496.

145. Norenzayan and Gervais, "The Origins of Religious Disbelief," p. 23.

146. See, for example, Pascal Boyer, *Religion Explained: The Evolutionary Origins of Religious Thought* (New York: Basic Books, 2002); Jesse Bering, *The Belief Instinct: The Psychology of Souls, Destiny, and the Meaning of Life* (New York: W. W. Norton, 2012); Robert McCauley, *Why Religion Is Natural and Science Is Not* (Oxford: Oxford University Press, 2011).

147. Norenzayan and Gervais, "The Origins of Religious Disbelief," p. 24.

148. Norenzayan and Gervais, "The Origins of Religious Disbelief," p. 23. See Gervais and Norenzayan, "Analytic Thinking Promotes Religious Disbelief."

149. Norenzayan and Gervais, "The Origins of Religious Disbelief," p. 23

150. Norenzayan and Gervais, "The Origins of Religious Disbelief," p. 23.

151. Marjaana Lindeman and Annika Svedholm-Häkkinen, "Does Poor Understanding of Physical World Predict Religious and Paranormal Beliefs?," *Applied Cognitive Psychology* 30 (2016), pp. 736–742.

152. Marjaana Lindeman, Annika Svedholm-Häkkinen, and Tapani Riekki, "Skepticism: Genuine Unbelief or Implicit Beliefs in the Supernatural?," *Consciousness and Cognition* 42 (2016), pp. 216–228.

153. Michaela Jarvis, "Conference Navigates Gap between Science and Government," *Science* 354 (2016), pp. 427–428.

154. Jeet Heer, "Conservatives Have Groomed the Perfect Suckers for Trump's Epic Scam," *The New Republic*, June 28, 2016, https://newrepublic.com/article/134667/conservatives-groomed-perfect-suckers-trumps-epic-scam.

155. From Louis Pojman and Michael Rea, *Philosophy of Religion: An Anthology* (Stamford, CT: Cengage Learning, 2015), p. 501.

156. David Hart, "Believe It or Not," *First Things*, May 2010, https://www.firstthings.com/article/2010/05/believe-it-or-not; qtd. in Kevin Drum, "Is God Dead? Or Merely Bored?," *Mother Jones*, April 25, 2010, http://www.motherjones.com/kevin-drum/2010/04/theology.

157. John Hick, *An Interpretation of Religion: Human Responses to the Transcendent*, 2nd ed. (London: Palgrave Macmillan, 2004), p. 240.

158. Hick, *An Interpretation of Religion*, p. 246.

159. Terry Eagleton, "Lunging, Flailing, Mispunching," *London Review of Books* 28 (2006), pp. 32–34.

160. Paul Zachary Myers, "The Courtier's Reply," *Science Blogs*, December 24, 2006, http://scienceblogs.com/pharyngula/2006/12/24/the-courtiers-reply/.

161. Anthony Clifford Grayling, "Apparently It's Emetic," *London Review of Books* 28 (November 2, 2006), http://www.lrb.co.uk/v28/n21/letters#letter5.

162. Sigmund Freud, *Civilization and Its Discontents* (Vienna: Internationaler Psychoanalytischer, 1931), p. 27.

163. Freud, *Civilization and Its Discontents*, pp. 27–28.

164. See Julian Baggini, "In God We Must," *Slate*, February 5, 2012, http://www.slate.com/articles/life/ft/2012/02/atheism_in_america_why_won_t_the_u_s_accept_its_atheists_.html.

165. David Bourget and David Chalmers, "What Do Philosophers Believe?," *Philosophical Studies* 170 (2014), pp. 465–500.

166. Edward Larson and Larry Witham, "Leading Scientists Still Reject God," *Nature* 394 (1998), p. 313; ctd. by John Messerly, "Religion's Smart-People Problem: The Shaky Intellectual Foundations of Absolute Faith," *Salon*, December 21, 2014, http://www.salon.com/2014/12/21/religions_smart_people_problem_the_shaky_intellectual_foundations_of_absolute_faith/.

167. Daniel Hungerman, "The Effect of Education on Religion: Evidence from Compulsory Schooling Laws," NBER Working Paper No. 16973 (2011); ctd. in Messerly, "Religion's Smart-People Problem"; and Naci Mocan, "Compulsory Schooling Laws and Formation of Beliefs: Education, Religion, and Superstition," NBER Working Paper No. 20557 (2014).

168. Norenzayan and Gervais, "The Origins of Religious Disbelief," pp. 23–24.

169. Norenzayan and Gervais, "The Origins of Religious Disbelief," p. 24.

170. See Ralph Hood Jr., Peter Hill, and Bernard Spilka, *The Psychology of Religion: An Empirical Approach*, 4th ed. (New York: Guilford Press, 2009), p. 114, for an overview of research on this point. See also Marjorie Gunnoe and Kristin Moore, "Predictors of Religiosity among Youth Aged 17–22: A Longitudinal Study of the National Survey of Children," *Journal for the Scientific Study of Religion* 41 (2002), pp. 613–622.

171. I credit (and resent) the authors of *Predisposed* for coming up with this line first. See Hibbing et al., *Predisposed*, p. 255.

Afterword

Directions for Science Communication

We have now seen that the fight for peace, justice, and good public policy puts us up not only against external vested interests but also our own psychology. We desperately need to make better decisions about energy and the environment, health, and political economy. Intergroup prejudice on the basis of religion, ethnicity, gender, sexual preference, et cetera continues to be the basis for many direct and indirect harms befalling a huge number of people. All these challenges stem in part from conscious self-interest and conscious mendacity, but they are massively exacerbated by the pernicious effects of implicit bias and self-deception. Our capacity for motivated reasoning in the face of contrary evidence is impressive, and the desire to affirm comforting factual claims—and to deny inconvenient truths—is deeply rooted in our nature. The result is individual misbehavior, poisonous public discourse, and bad public policy.

I conclude by saying a few brief words about the state of the discussion on what the research says about science communication in mitigating denialism. With the possible exception of a major nuclear exchange, climate change is the gravest existential threat to human civilization. Simply by maintaining our current trajectory, the Earth will almost certainly experience a 4–6 degrees Centigrade warmer atmosphere in the next hundred years. As British energy and climate change expert Kevin Anderson puts it: "A 4 degrees C future is incompatible with an organized global community, is likely to be beyond 'adaptation,' is devastating to the majority of ecosystems, and has a high probability of not being stable."[1] I shall therefore focus on climate change communication.

Positive proposals as to science denial remediation strategies divide roughly into (a) proposals about the *content* of science communication (i.e., we should push for better education, better access to information about expert consensus, and better appreciation for scientific reasoning), and (b) proposals about the *form* of science communication (i.e., we should focus on counteracting—or exploiting—motivated reasoning via manipulations of presentation or context).

A.1   More Information?

In a 2015 Pew survey of members of the American Association for the Advancement of Science, 98% described the public's limited knowledge of science as a problem, with 84% describing it as a "major problem."[2] There is plenty of evidence that Americans are poorly informed on a whole host of scientific issues. For example, over 40% believe that antibiotics are effective in treating viral infections.[3] In 2012, a National Science Foundation study revealed that only 55% knew both that the Earth orbits the Sun and that it takes a year to do so.[4] As noted in chapter 2, 73% of Americans deny evolution by natural selection.

At the same time—and despite the decades-long decline noted in chapter 2, in support for science among political conservatives—science remains overall relatively popular, and the generic "scientist" is a trusted figure. Seventy-six percent of U.S. adults have either a "great deal" or a "fair amount" of confidence in scientists to act in the public interest—a figure far outstripping their confidence in politicians, the media, and even religious leaders.[5] According to the aforementioned 2015 survey by Pew, "79% of adults say that science has made life easier for most people and a majority is positive about science's impact on the quality of health care, food and the environment."[6] Further, "About seven-in-ten adults say that government investments in engineering and technology (72%) and in basic scientific research (71%) usually pay off in the long run. Some 61% say that government investment is essential for scientific progress." These results might lead one to think that, if only the public were better informed about what the experts have to say, we could see a change in attitudes even about ideologically charged issues like climate change.

No doubt there are limits to one's resistance to facts. As Peter Ditto puts it, "Everyone will accept the validity of climate science once they're ankle-deep in ocean water."[7] Researchers optimistic about the power of information claim to have quantified a bias-overcoming "tipping point," demonstrating "that voters are not immune to disconfirming information after all, even when initially acting as motivated reasoners."[8] The challenge, of course, is achieving large-scale shifts in public opinion *before* terrible things happen. As we have exhaustively noted, resistance to inconvenient facts is the rule rather than the exception when it comes to ideology.

When it comes to civic issues like tax policy, Stanford communications professor James Fishkin believes in the corrective power of what he calls "deliberative democracy":

> The premise is simple: poll citizens on a major issue, blind; then see how their opinions evolve when they're forced to confront the facts. . . . [W]hile people start out with deep value disagreements over, say, government spending, they tend to agree on rational policy responses once they learn the ins and outs of the budget.[9]

"The problem is ignorance, not stupidity," political scientist Jacob Hacker agrees. "We suffer from a lack of information rather than a lack of ability."[10] Hibbing has something similar to say about prejudice against homosexuals, citing evidence that "people who believe that sexual orientation is biologically based are much more likely to be accepting of gay rights," and that "Americans became more accepting of gay lifestyles and gay rights because they started to accept the growing evidence that sexual orientation is less a moral choice than simply a part of people's biology."[11] On climate, it is not uncommon to hear the claim that wider knowledge of the scientific consensus would move public opinion on the need for action.[12] Researchers led by psychologist Sander van der Linden have conducted a series of studies, analysis of which, they say, reveals "robust and replicated evidence that communicating the scientific consensus on human-caused climate change leads to significant and substantial changes in perceived scientific agreement among conservatives, moderates, and liberals alike."[13] They claim that "conservatives and moderates are significantly less aware of the scientific consensus than liberals," suggesting that the discrepancy in acceptance of climate change between ideological groups is related to an informational asymmetry. In a 2017 study, they found that misinformation about climate can cancel out messages about scientific consensus on climate; however, they saw some success "inoculating" against climate misinformation simply by warning study participants about the existence of such misinformation before presenting information about the expert consensus.[14] Stephan Lewandowsky has claimed similar success in neutralizing polarization in conservatives simply by informing respondents about the consensus on AGW.[15]

Dan Kahan is not impressed with such studies, noting that the fact of a scientific consensus on the human contribution to climate change has been heavily advertised at least since 2004, while over this period of time, overall public acceptance of the claim that changes in global average temperature is primarily caused by humans has *decreased*.[16] The "real world" findings don't seem to bear out the "laboratory" findings. Measured change in view on the part of study participants is temporary. Rather, Kahan argues, the best real-world predictor of an individual's acceptance of scientific findings on various issues, such as climate, safe storage of nuclear waste, or the effects on crime of concealed carry laws, is simply whether the science is consistent or inconsistent with the respondent's cultural-ideological identifications. Further, as was noted in chapter 1, we know that the more scientifically literate an ideologue is, and thus the more likely he or she is in a position to appreciate the broad scientific consensus on an ideologically threatening issue, the more likely he or she is to reject the consensus.

We see something very similar when it comes to the data Hibbing cites on gay rights and acceptance of the science of sexual preference. Jeremiah Garretson and Elizabeth Suhay have shown that, while there has clearly been an overall generational shift on gay rights, political ideology makes a very big difference in whether someone accepts the science regarding the biological basis of sexual preference. There has been some movement on the part of conservatives since the 1990s, but widespread acceptance of the science is limited to liberals and moderates.[17]

We have discussed Nyhan and Reifler's research hinting at a "backfire effect," wherein the investigators saw ideological positions harden in response to evidence refuting the factual basis for that position (Hart and Nisbet found much the same thing, but called it the "boomerang effect"). Nyhan and Reifler even found that debunking myths can have a backfire effect on behavior as well: Correcting the myth that flu vaccines can cause the flu paradoxically *reduced* the intent to vaccinate among respondents with a prior high level of concern about vaccine safety.[18] A significant backfire effect probably crops up only in rather limited contexts, but a broad resistance to change in view across the ideological spectrum is indisputable. Further, being corrected on your rationalizations doesn't stop you from finding new ones. Even among those who look for reasons to think that new factual information can affect ideologues' policy preferences,[19] there is little dispute that, as Zaller and Kahan have argued, cues received about what positions characterize one's in-group identity have at least as much to do with such preferences as does knowledge of the facts.

The idea that more information leads straightforwardly to changes in attitude on emotionally charged issues looks like wishful thinking. The only results that have shown such a positive relation between information and opinion have been under artificial conditions, where the issues are raised in isolation from respondents' cultural context, peer identifications, and ideological matrices.

Factual knowledge does not inoculate us against denialist thinking any more than intellectual capacity does. We quoted Kahan earlier on the point that most people are not experts on climate, vaccines, economics, or cosmology. Where people "believe in" science, it is because they have chosen to trust scientific expertise (or elite cues about scientific expertise) in that area. Not "believing in," say, human evolution doesn't necessarily stem from a lack of knowledge about the theory. Certain religious literalists define themselves, in part, by a worldview that simply cannot incorporate evolution. As Kahan puts it, asking you whether you believe in evolution "doesn't measure science literacy, it measures whether you're religious. It's just an expression of identity."[20] Other kinds of ideologues cannot accept AGW for the same kind of reason. Even our greatest polymath intellectuals lack expertise in the vast majority of policy-relevant areas of expertise. We make most of our decisions on the basis of trust rather than personal expertise—and where we place that trust has to do with our background, our situation, our personality, our value identities, and the like. Our gut-level cognitive and emotional systems tell us to trust our established worldviews, and so in turn whatever spokespeople or "experts" we take to represent those worldviews.

Philosopher Heather Douglas agrees that focusing on information is not likely to be the most fruitful approach in addressing denialism. The public-school system is by far the biggest potential delivery system for any change in how science is understood by the public. Douglas proposes that the focus of the K-12 science curriculum shift from conveying *facts* to conveying *what science is and how it earns its authority*:

> The most important thing for the public to understand about science is not a set of scientific facts, but the nature of science, as empirical, inductive, and critical. Science is empirical because of the central importance of evidence gathered from interacting with the world (both social and natural). Scientists focus on gathering evidence to test the theories they develop to explain the evidence. . . . And because science is empirical and inductive it also must maintain a culture of critical interactions among scientists. Scientists have to be willing to challenge each other's work, to overturn long-standing views (if the evidence is there to do so), and to hold no claim above the critical fray. It is this critical culture, the social culture of science, combined with (and arising from) its evidential and inductive basis, that gives science its underlying epistemic authority.[21]

Some researchers have proposed early-childhood interventions aimed at evidence assessment and critical reasoning skills.[22] Researchers studying K-12 science education have produced some evidence that better educational techniques can bring about productive conceptual change in dealing with scientific claims.[23] Douglas hopes that a greater appreciation of science as a rigorous, evidence-based, self-correcting process would lead to a wider acceptance of scientific consensus on contentious issues. She wants schools to get kids involved in doing science; she also approves of programs that engage the public in "citizen science" projects, such as local water monitoring.[24] This engagement could inculcate an appreciation for how evidence is collected and analyzed, and how a finding has to stand up to peer review and further testing in order to be accepted. The more used a person is to scientific thinking and the "culture" of science, the more resistant he or she may be to motivated reasoning about science in the public interest. (There is as yet no evidence of the long-term efficacy of such interventions in counteracting denialist tendencies and external influences, however.)

In Kahan's research, he has found that the rules about how cultural and political identity determine beliefs about climate don't seem to apply to scientists (across disciplines) the way they do to the general public; he concludes that "scientists, unlike ordinary members of the public, are not meaningfully affected by cultural worldviews."[25] Recall Norenzayan and Gervais's observation that scientists are much less likely to be religious than the general public, and their speculation that "scientific training . . . cultivates habitual use of analytic thinking, possibly rendering it less cognitively effortful with practice."[26] So, perhaps, if ordinary citizens just thought more like scientists, they would be immune to science denial. Everyone agrees that people are *capable* of doing better in terms of accepting difficult truths; it's just that they don't do a good job of it most of the time.[27]

Douglas cites recent work by social scientists Caitlin Drummond and Baruch Fischhoff, who developed an "individual difference measure of *scientific reasoning skills*, defined as the skills needed to evaluate scientific findings in terms of the factors that determine their quality."[28] In three studies, they found that participants with superior scientific reasoning skills "are more likely to have beliefs consistent with the scientific consensus on potentially contentious issues, above and beyond education, political and religious beliefs, and scores on two widely used measures of scientific literacy." In other words, while scientific literacy (i.e., knowledge of *facts*) does not predict openness to scientific consensus in motivated contexts, an appreciation for the scientific *process* does. Another study found that "support for pro-environment policies is more strongly related to endorsement of scientific inquiry than to scientific literacy."[29] The idea is that a better understanding of how scientific reasoning works entails a better understanding of what makes for scientific expertise and scientific consensus, and for this reason a high scientific reasoning skills (SRS) proficiency helps counteract denialism in a way mere information cannot.

(And the benefits of getting people to start thinking more scientifically could apply not only to issues like AGW but also to social and
economic issues; like the natural sciences, the social sciences draw on
empirical evidence produced by controlled studies subject to peer criticism and replication.)

John Cook is a climate communication specialist at the University
of Queensland, and is well known for his climate denial–debunking
website, SkepticalScience.com. In his examination of the communication of scientific consensus on climate, he cites a number of studies that
support the notion of "inoculating" students against science denialism
through "misconception-based learning."[30] This sort of learning, he
explains,

> involves lessons that directly address and refute misconceptions as
> well as explain factual information, in contrast to standard lessons
> that teach the facts without explicitly addressing misconceptions.
> For example, one myth regarding the carbon cycle is that anthropo-
> genic carbon dioxide (CO_2) emissions are inconsequential because
> they are small in magnitude compared to natural CO_2 emissions.
> A misconception-based learning approach might explain the natural
> balance inherent in the carbon cycle, with natural CO_2 emissions
> roughly balanced by natural CO_2 absorptions, and how anthropo-
> genic CO_2 emissions have upset the natural balance. Thus the tech-
> nique employed by the myth is "cherry picking," failing to consider
> the role of natural CO_2 absorptions in the carbon cycle.[31]

Cook cites research showing that this approach to science education is effective in reducing misconceptions; that students are more
attracted to "refutational texts" than traditional textbooks; and that
misconception-based learning improves evidence assessment, argumentative skills, and critical thinking skills.

It is interesting to note in this context that some very recent studies
have indicated that (a) science literacy is not necessarily coextensive
with *curiosity* about science—as measured, say, by reported interest
in science books or interest in reading science articles reporting "surprising factors"; and (b) increased science curiosity is correlated with
greater openness to correction on polarizing science issues.[32] Being

intrigued by (surprising) corrections to misconceptions would seem to be a pretty good indicator of curiosity. Is science curiosity something that could be taught or encouraged? Misconception-based learning seems like a possible candidate for sparking greater curiosity. Indeed, as Kahan and colleagues have argued in a 2017 report, the data suggest the best counterbalance to ideological closed-mindedness is scientific curiosity.[33]

In his *Pensées*, Blaise Pascal observed that "People are generally better persuaded by the reasons which they have themselves discovered than by those which have come into the mind of others."[34] One really nice thing about an approach focusing on public engagement, and on understanding science as a process, is that it is not inherently political or ideological. No particular denial-triggering conclusions are pushed on the student or member of the public. In dealing with a denier, Douglas suggests asking the question "What evidence would change your mind?" Physicist Brian Cox, in debating AGW deniers, likes the question, "How would *you* test this hypothesis?"[35] One really nice thing about this sort of question is that it engages the respondent as a peer investigator, while redirecting the discussion toward evidence—and away from ideology. Respondents with good scientific reasoning skills should be all the more receptive to this kind of question and, it is hoped, more open to change in attitude as a consequence of considering it.

There are demonstrated merits to the idea of "solving" the science denial problem by inculcating scientific reasoning skills, and an appreciation for scientific practice, in K-12 students. But this approach has a couple of limitations. Whatever long-term benefits that could be gleaned from changes in K-12 education, this plan would require a massive shift in public education policy at the federal level, which is never easy to achieve. Further, it does not seem likely that enhancing scientific reasoning skills will be a priority for the current presidential administration and its Department of Education. (The 2012 official party platform for the Texas GOP specifically included its opposition to reasoning skills curricula: "We oppose the teaching of Higher Order Thinking Skills, . . . critical thinking skills, and similar programs . . . which focus on behavior modification and have the purpose of challenging the student's fixed beliefs and undermining parental authority."[36]) But even with a unified commitment to improved science education, this approach would take at least a generation to bear fruit. With climate change, and other pollution and resource-depletion issues, we don't have that kind of time to wait. In the meantime, vested in-group elites will continue to signal the unacceptability of certain policy positions, and citizens will continue to enjoy a range of expertise-undermining, bullshit sources (including the hired "merchants of doubt") that validate their dismissal of inconvenient warnings.

The second concern is that the professional researchers who have been shown to possess a special resistance to motivated reasoning belong to an intensely unrepresentative subgroup of the larger population. Indeed, their appreciation for the factors that lend modern science its authority exceed the average person's, but they additionally represent a unique set of people who chose to pursue a life of learning over any other kind of life. What scientifically literate climate change deniers may lack is not an appreciation of science but, rather, a particular orientation toward knowledge for its own sake. According to Plato (as famously argued in his *Republic*), the love of truth stems from a fundamental curiosity that he believed to derive at least in part from innate personality traits. Plato would call it part of one's *eros*—the personality makeup that determines one's interests and preferences. This is something he thought could be cultivated, but only up to a point. He noted that it was rather rare for an individual to be dominated by curiosity and a love of learning to the point that such drives could overcome the desire for comfort and consumption. Someone privileged enough to be able to attend a good college or university is presented with a wide range of options. The choice to pursue a career in research typically means a PhD or equivalent, and this decision involves a lot of delayed gratification: Quite typically these days you are talking about a training period consisting of eight to ten years of very long hours and subpoverty-level pay, as graduate teaching assistant, research assistant, and post-doc. *This* is the tiny, self-selected population that later demonstrates an unusual resistance to denial. Great athletes are successful because they have special motivations to train relentlessly for their chosen sport that others just don't have. The kinds of enthusiasms that would lead someone to make—and follow through on—a commitment to the life of the mind are not widely shared, even among the already economically and educationally privileged college population. Plato put a high priority on education, but he would likely be skeptical that, even with sufficient leisure time and opportunity, the masses could be enticed to develop a level of attachment to the scientific process sufficient to overcome their other motivations. In this respect, economic and cultural elites are just like everybody else, which is why they have been shown to be just as subject to denial as everybody else.

No student of ideology and motivated reasoning is *opposed* to better science education (including a better appreciation for scientific reasoning), better communication of scientific consensus, and improved public discourse on science and its findings. But none of these things is a proven cure for denial. Look at religion again. The large majority of Americans (a) have at least twelve years of formal education, including some contact with physics, biology, and world history; and (b) subscribe to a bronze-age mythology of invisible super-beings and miraculous events. If all that education cannot dislodge people from their commitment to such extravagant notions, how confident should we be that some adjustments in the science education curriculum would dislodge people from infinitely more plausible positions, such as the belief that vaccines cause autism or that climate change fears are overblown?

A.2   Message Framing and Delivery

These concerns—the immediacy of certain issues like climate change (or, say, systemic racial discrimination), together with the failure of the information deficit model—have led to a heavy emphasis on science communication framing informed by the research on denialism. In other words, the recommendation by many students of this issue is to focus on anti-denialist messaging that is designed to either *counteract* or, indeed, *utilize* the mechanisms of motivated reasoning. Pascal described "eloquence" as

> an art of saying things in such a way (1) that those to whom we speak may listen to them without pain and with pleasure; (2) that they feel

themselves interested, so that self-love leads them more willingly to reflection upon it.... It consists, then, in a correspondence which we seek to establish between the head and the heart of those to whom we speak on the one hand, and, on the other, between the thoughts and the expressions which we employ. This assumes that we have studied well the heart of man so as to know all its powers, and then to find the just proportions of the discourse which we wish to adapt to them.[37]

In the social sciences, "framing" is defined as the manner of communicating an idea or piece of information, where that manner of communication affects the emotional value of the information for the recipient.[38] A communicator can use devices like analogy or metaphor, or suggestive images, in an attempt to influence how information is contextualized—and thus what emotions are triggered. (Such techniques, obviously, are central to advertising; the art of advertising is basically about framing.) For example, communication intended to sway an audience in favor of nuclear power can use terms like "progress" or "modernization," while comparing it to particularly useful historical inventions like the light bulb or the internet. Communications intended to create doubt about nuclear power could include references to past environmental disasters, using terms like "risk" or "uncertainty." A politician might try to create a negative perception about, say, stronger environmental regulations, by giving reasons to think that this is an idea popular among "Hollywood elites" and despised by "regular Americans." Opponents of genetically modified (GM) crops might be more receptive to messages focusing on pesticide reduction, accompanied by images of lush vegetation and happy butterflies. A visual presentation about the proposal to open the borders to Muslim refugees might be accompanied by video clips of terrorist attacks; or, alternatively, images of a nice-looking refugee family gazing at us sadly from a tent.

The hope is that denialism about AGW can be circumvented by framing issues in ways that emphasize audience-specific values and that are less threatening (or even congenial) to individuals' group identities, system fealties, or worldviews.[39] For example, Matthew Nisbet suggests that communication about AGW focus on economic development ("green jobs") and the morality of preserving the biosphere for future generations.[40] There is some evidence that describing carbon dioxide and methane as "pollution" may be helpful in dealing with resistant audiences.[41] System justification theorists suggest framing designed to circumnavigate—or exploit—the tendency to system justification and status quo bias they see as peculiar to conservatives. Psychologist Erin Hennes, for example, has found that people are more accepting of climate science after being primed with thoughts of the strength of the underlying economic system.[42] As we have seen, system justification theory observes that personality types associated with conservatism exhibit bias in favor of social, political, and economic systems; and that people generally exhibit some such bias when they feel threatened. Some studies have indicated that framing conservation as a preservation of the status quo may help counteract AGW denialism in conservatives.[43] In targeting conservatives on AGW, advocates could stress potential system disruptions from climate-related refugee crises, political upheaval, and related security threats.

Moral foundations theory, popularized by Jonathan Haidt, is the view that moral judgments vary across cultures and subcultures, and that disagreements over ideology can derive from the priorities placed on different foundational moral concepts. Proponents argue that political liberals and conservatives are fundamentally distinguished by the different emphases they place on different moral concerns: Liberals, for example, are liberals because they are most motivated by concerns over fairness and harm to others, while conservatives manifest more interest in loyalty, respect for authority, and purity. According to moral foundations theory, the main reason that, say, liberals support the right to gay marriage is their overriding concern for fairness, while conservatives place a greater emphasis on concerns over the sanctity of marriage. According to this theory, a difference in moral concerns is not the *symptom* but, rather, the *cause* of ideological disagreement. Drawing on this theory, social psychologist Matthew Feinberg and sociologist Robb Willer tested how political messages tailored to different clusters of moral concern might resonate differently to different audiences. They found that, initially, only liberals view environmental issues in moral terms; however, when the issue of pollution is "reframed" for conservatives in reference not to harm but to purity and sanctity (say, with images of a landscape covered with disgusting garbage), differences between liberal and conservative concern are reduced or eliminated.[44] The conclusion is that persuasion on political issues is possible through framing that activates subgroup-specific moral concerns.

Cultural cognition theorists agree with the concept of framing, noting that issues can be framed in ways that resonate with, rather than threaten, an audience's group identity. Kahan calls this "identity-affirmative framing."[45] Noting that cultural "individualists" tend to approve of technological solutions to problems, he has found in studies that discussions of nuclear power and geoengineering as solutions to climate change "reduced cultural polarization over the *validity of scientific evidence on the consequences of climate change.*"[46] If rationalization of desired system- or identity-serving conclusions is inevitable, then maybe it's time to fight fire with fire; that is to say, to try to influence the facts people accept not by framing *problems* differently but, rather, by emphasizing *solutions* they find ideologically desirable. Discussing an experiment about framing strategies, psychologist Aaron Kay suggests that acceptance of the facts about AGW could be influenced by the nature of the proposed remediation strategy:

> Participants in the experiment, including both self-identified Republicans and Democrats, read a statement asserting that global temperatures will rise 3.2 degrees in the 21st century. They were then asked to evaluate a proposed policy solution to address the warming. When the policy solution emphasized a tax on carbon emissions or some other form of government regulation, which is generally opposed by Republican ideology, only 22 percent of Republicans said they believed the temperatures would rise at least as much as indicated by the scientific statement they read. But when the proposed policy solution emphasized the free market, such as with innovative green technology, 55 percent of Republicans agreed with the scientific statement.[47]

Indeed, our discussion in chapter 2 hypothesized that conservatives are more likely to be attracted to technological "production science" answers to environmental problems. This sort of framing hints at a sort of realpolitik bait-and-switch tactic, where denial of science is overcome by deliberately triggering motivated cognition. Advocates for climate change mitigation could limit themselves to publicly calling exclusively for industry-friendly "solutions" like large tax cuts and subsidies to energy producers. As we know, when the policy solutions are desirable enough, then positive perceptions of the reasons for those solutions will follow. Once the issue is sufficiently depolarized, we might hope that the denialist opposition will have fewer resources to resist real solutions.

Atmospheric scientist and evangelical Christian Katharine Hayhoe suggests that messages about protecting "God's Creation" (she proposes calling it "creation care") might appeal to religious conservatives.[48] In a 2016 study, social psychologists at Oregon State found that "conservatives shifted substantially in the pro-environmental direction after exposure to a binding moral frame, in which protecting the natural environment was portrayed as a matter of obeying authority, defending the purity of nature, and demonstrating one's patriotism to the United States."[49] (Some theorists caution, however, that "just-worlders"—a group that substantially overlaps with Christian conservatives—react badly to "apocalyptic messages" about AGW.[50])

Messages about impending environmental catastrophe immediately come up against the utterly predicable, instinctive response of avoiding or denying information that causes negative affect.[51] Hayhoe counsels against shaming and negativity in pro-environmental messages, warning that negative framing is likely to spur avoidance and backlash. Her advice also dovetails nicely with social identity theory (discussed in chapters 3 and 4). Social identity theory maintains that group identification is heavily tied up with self-esteem, and so threats to ideological identity may have the effect of hardening positions. This theory also predicts that priming individuals to feel a sense of individual identity affirmation will reduce identity-protective, group-serving bias. People who have been primed with thoughts affirming their own self-worth may be more open to appreciating the strength of opposing arguments;[52] people who have been encouraged to think positively about their most important personal values may be more open to compromise on unrelated partisan political issues.[53]

Is the combination of framing and identity-affirmative priming likely to be successful in changing minds? Some think so, especially when the argument is delivered by an in-group messenger like Hayhoe—an evangelical Christian talking to other evangelical Christians. Science communication researchers often stress the importance of friendly faces delivering the ideologically unwelcome message. Matthew Nisbet, for example, suggests "bringing to the conversation a greater diversity of trusted societal leaders who can frame the issue in a manner that resonates with the identity and cultural background of broader segments of the public."[54] This makes sense, given what we know about identity-protective cognition. Yet the challenges for this approach are clear: It is difficult to find convincing cultural group members who are actually allied with the other side—and even if they are, they have good reasons to suppress any politicized disagreements with their own tribe. The example of Bob Inglis—the conservative congressman who talked up climate and was promptly primaried out of office—is as rare as it is disheartening. In February 2017, leading conservative economists Martin Feldstein and N. Gregory Mankiw, joined by centrist Ted Halstead, published a much-discussed New York Times editorial entitled "A Conservative Case for Climate Change," in which they called for a federal tax on carbon emissions (which would be refunded as a dividend). Their supporters include conservative establishment heavies James Baker, Henry Paulson, and George Shultz. This sounds like a breakthrough, until you consider that not a single Republican actually in power publicly supports such an idea. Though this idea has been around a long time—and involves less government intervention than any other conceivable strategy—there is not a hint of a shadow of any prospect of support for any such plan in Republican-controlled branches of government. Indeed, in June 2016, Republicans in the House of Representatives prophylactically resolved, unanimously, to reject any carbon tax idea.

Even supposing many more in-group converts to climate reality, the fragmented media environment would still provide plenty of countering misinformation to choose from for a member of the public who is uncomfortable with dissonant messages. Further, those incentivized to deliberately sow doubt can—and do—employ their own framing (using their own media outlets) and have plenty of enthusiastic in-group messengers to choose from.

Studies examining the long-term effectiveness of framing on public opinion have had mixed results at best. Citing new research on the (in)efficacy of climate communication framing by political scientists Thomas Bernauer and Liam McGrath,[55] journalist David Roberts thinks that such tactics can't compete with the frames we already live in:

> Human beings are not freestanding reasoning machines. They are situated in the world, inheritors of particular socioeconomic conditions, worldviews, dispositions, and interpretive filters. They come complete with a strong set of overlapping, mutually reinforcing frames. To a great extent, those preexisting social and psychological commitments—which are outside the scope of any conceivable climate communication campaign—are going to determine how people assess a specific phenomenon like climate change. . . . A lifetime of baggage carries a lot of weight and momentum. Comparatively, a single exposure to a bit of framing is nothing, like blowing on the sails of a giant ship.[56]

Frames that work in the lab often do not translate to the messy, emotional, and polarized real world. As Dan Kahan would put it, framing has poor "operational validity."[57] Perhaps Feinberg and Willer can temporarily moralize environmental issues for their denialist test subjects. But what happens next, outside the lab? Our thought processes are permeated by motives vastly more powerful than can lastingly be overcome by some clever marketing. Thanks to social self-segregation and selective exposure, our social and media environment tends, rather, to reinforce the factual worldview that validates existing prejudices. As we have noted, public opinion is heavily influenced by elite signals (that is, cues from those politicians, media figures, religious leaders, and the like with whom one identifies ideologically); Zaller persuasively argued in *The Nature and Origins of Mass Opinion* that it is elite opinion that ultimately drives long-term public opinion. In their 2016 book *Democracy for Realists*, political scientists Christopher Achen and Larry Bartels remind us that most people, most of the time, are not paying much attention to policy debates, and consequently don't have much in the way of fixed ideas about policy;

rather, most voters identify parties that appear to be "on their side" and support policy proposals accordingly.[58] In fact, we see evidence of virtually immediate, top-down swings in public opinion, under the right conditions: The number of conservatives expressing a positive view of Russian leader Vladimir Putin jumped 20 percentage points immediately following Donald Trump's election; only one-third of Republicans accept the intelligence community consensus that Russia interfered in the U.S. 2016 presidential election.[59] (If Hillary Clinton had won in 2016 with evident Russian support, who would doubt that partisan assessment of Russian involvement in the election would look very different?) If we could get popular politicians, media figures, and denialist interest groups to support interventions on climate, a popular swing would likely follow. Unfortunately, deliberately mendacious, elite denialist messaging on climate is unlikely to be influenced by framing techniques. Partisans do quite poorly when called upon to explain the actual thinking behind favored policy positions on, say, raising the Social Security retirement age, universal health care, merit pay for teachers, or a cap-and-trade system for carbon emissions.[60] If the general public is just following elite cues about what to believe, then the framing of messages about scientific consensus is not going to have much effect.[61]

Heather Douglas adds that the whole strategy of audience-specific framing and delivery might wind up being counterproductive:

> It does not seem plausible that we can use such theories openly, as that seems insulting and disparaging of the public. Telling someone you are tailoring the message to their worldview and values because they will more likely accept it using motivated reasoning would not work, at least in the long run. And to use this work without acknowledgement is problematic as well. We don't want to just manipulate the public into accepting scientific consensus. Doing so would likely be self-defeating, as the public would probably notice that different science communication messages are tailored differently, and become suspicious of such communication efforts.[62]

Further, even if we decide the right strategy involves framing, priming audiences with self-affirming thoughts, and recruiting culturally appropriate communicators, who is going to be the central authority—the puppeteer? Even if the political elite were not already corrupted by self-interest and/or denial, any messaging coming from political representatives will automatically be interpreted as ideological. Scientists themselves—a more trusted group—might be a less polarizing choice. "STEM the Divide" is a new initiative with its own political action committee, "314action," which seeks to recruit scientists and others with scientific and technical backgrounds to run for office. The founder, a former cancer researcher turned politician, states that the goal is "electing more leaders to the US Senate, House, State Executive and Legislative offices who come from STEM backgrounds. We need new leaders who understand that climate change is real and are motivated to find a solution."[63] In theory, this sounds like a great plan. Yet I wonder if we will see a whole lot of candidates for office, or full-time activists, coming out of the physical and social sciences, despite, in many cases, strong feelings on the part of academics and researchers about these issues. That is to say, we might run into the Plato problem again. Scientists and researchers do what they do thanks to a unique set of motivations. With exceptions, they don't tend to go much for active involvement in politics, in large part because a life of political involvement calls for a different personality type—politicians need to be ambitious extroverts who find enough satisfaction in campaigning, fundraising, coalition-building, negotiating, and governing to devote their lives to politics. Further, scientists entering politics—most likely under the aegis of some political party—would immediately be identified as representing a particular ideology and tribe, and their declamations would no doubt be experienced by ideologues and identity groups through the same partisan filter as the positions of conventional politicians.

In a 2017 *New York Times* op-ed, coastal geologist Robert Young commented on the planned "March for Science," a political demonstration responding to the pervasive denialism of the Trump administration. He expressed the concern that this sort of activism will politicize science in general, turning "belief in" science into a polarizing identification. (The non–college-educated Trump supporters already express much less overall confidence in science and scientists than the college-educated voters who opposed him.[64]) Young suggests instead an approach of local engagement and personal contact:

> Rather than marching on Washington and in other locations around the country, I suggest that my fellow scientists march into local civic groups, churches, schools, county fairs and, privately, into the offices of elected officials. Make contact with that part of America that doesn't know any scientists. Put a face on the debate. Help them understand what we do, and how we do it. Give them your email, or better yet, your phone number.[65]

In a related vein, Kahan proposes an emphasis on the *normalization* of climate science as something communities already use—just as other science is used in local policy planning—to address matters of community concern, through a process heavy on community engagement.[66] He has written repeatedly about initiatives like the Southeast Florida Regional Climate Change Compact, wherein four politically diverse counties have joined together on over 100 action items on a variety of green issues, but pertaining mainly to seawater intrusion—an issue the community is very familiar with.[67] As he explains, a discussion about AGW is a discussion that forces one into an ideological corner. But citizens across the board approve of the general idea that the government should use the best available science in dealing with issues of immediate, local public interest. Despite the Southeast Florida region's ideological polarization on questions about the existence and severity of AGW, there is broad, bipartisan agreement on statements like "Local and state officials should be involved in identifying steps that local communities can take to reduce the risk posed by rising sea levels." The planners consciously focus on this point of agreement and shy away from forcing participants to take a position on the polarizing general issue of AGW. ("All politics is local," as House Speaker Tip O'Neill famously quipped—a description that may also serve as prescription.) The plan was developed through local forums organized and run, in many cases, by business owners, residential associations, and the like, thereby getting community members together with "people they trust and recognize as socially competent supporting the *use* of science in decision-making directly bearing on their lives."[68] The approach of the planners, as Kahan puts it, focuses on "what the community knows," rather than "whose side they are on." Citing similar success stories in New York, Virginia, Arizona, California, and elsewhere, he approvingly observes that:

> Ongoing political deliberations over adaptation are affecting people not as members of warring cultural factions but as *property owners, resource consumers, insurance policy holders,* and *tax payers*— identities they all share. The *people* who are furnishing them with pertinent scientific evidence about the risks they face and how to abate them are not the national representatives of competing political brands but rather their municipal representatives, their neighbors, and even their local utility companies. What's more, the sorts of issues they are addressing—damage to property and infrastructure from flooding, reduced access to scarce water supplies, diminished farming yields as a result of drought—are matters they deal with *all the time.* They are the issues they have *always dealt with* as members of the regions in which they live; they have a *natural* shared vocabulary for thinking and talking about these issues, the use of which reinforces their sense of linked fate and reassures them they are working with others whose interests are aligned with theirs. In *this* communication environment, people of diverse values are much more likely to converge on, rather than become confused about, the scientific evidence most relevant to securing the welfare of all.

Kahan calls this productive context for responding to climate change the "local adaptation science communication environment."[69] The liberal shop owner and the conservative farmer are likely to be equally concerned about an issue like local drinking-water contamination. In certain contexts, scientific know-how is a friend to all. Everybody wants his or her smartphone to be repaired by technicians who are familiar with electronics, everybody wants his or her doctor to know about human biology, and everybody wants the people who handle the local infrastructure to know something about engineering. Message framing has nothing to do with any of that. Residents of a rural agricultural community can likely all agree that government should use the best science available in planning local water-use policy in response to drought conditions; this action focus is likely to yield more productive public discourse than a politicized question like whether AGW is real or whether GM crops are dangerous. A recent article in *Mother Jones* discussed the Heritage Foundation's proposal to slash funding for the Federal Emergency Management Agency's Disaster Relief Fund, a proposal that was warmly received by the current presidential administration.[70] It notes that development in disaster-prone areas has mostly proceeded without regard for risk across the country; but without federal aid to rely on, states might have to take the (growing) risks of storms, flooding, wildfires, and tornadoes more seriously. This decision might thus accelerate the localization of AGW response.

Essential elements of the U.S. government have found compelling reasons to confront local AGW-related issues regardless of the politics.[71] Permafrost thawing threatens radar installations in Alaska, and wildfires have endangered the Marine Corps' Camp Pendleton and the Vandenberg Air Force base. Many other installations—including the U.S. Naval Academy—are dealing with increasing flood damage deriving from sea-level rise. The U.S. Navy has been forced to develop plans to manage regular flooding at its base in Norfolk, Virginia, simply because it has to, completely bypassing any top-down institutional decision on whether AGW is "real": "We don't talk about climate change," a base commander told visiting journalists, "we talk about sea-level rise. You can measure it."[72]

Public forums concerning generally agreed-upon local threats may help facilitate depolarizing cross-group contact effects like those proposed under the "contact hypothesis" (discussed in chapter 3); this sort of effect seems to be what Robert Young has in mind when he suggests scientists, instead of protesting in Washington, D.C., get out to communities and meet people face to face. This may also be helpful when talking about, say, health care policy or addressing racial or religious tensions: The most effective communication in such cases seems to involve community groups meeting in person, talking about local issues of mutual concern. As Kahan points out, such contexts emphasize citizens' *shared* identities as members of the same community, dealing with problems of mutual interest. Success at local climate change mitigation efforts, of course, will not prevent climate change. The hope is more that, over time, these small-scale interactions will defuse the polarization over

AGW science. (This may also be the most plausible route to depolarization with regard to racial and religious divides: Find ways to get people of different persuasions to work together on local issues of mutual interest.)

To summarize, in order to work around science denialism, we need communication in contexts that are less likely to trigger system justification and identity-defensive thinking. Make these contexts as affirmative as possible. Stress local concerns and shared identities. Talk about uses of science everyone can get on board with, rather than forcing everyone to take a position on the larger issue. Explain how climate change will affect the community, and stress technological solutions where possible. Avoid questions that polarize along political or cultural lines—and especially don't get people feeling defensive about their religious identity, the emotional commitment to which puts others to shame.* It is true that, in the case of AGW, local action is not enough. The crisis is fundamentally global, and international agreement on strategies for emissions control must be worked out as soon as possible. But national politicians have to feel they can push for things like this without committing political suicide. Perhaps the best bet to bring this about is the normalization of climate science through depolarizing local mitigation discussions—and, it is hoped, also some positive long-term developments in moving the emphasis in science education toward the development of scientific reasoning skills and scientific curiosity.

These suggestions don't seem remotely adequate given the scope and immediacy of the crisis, but, as David Roberts says, the situation is what it is, and "The thing to do is just keep plugging away at it."[73] This advice is not exceedingly hopeful, but it may be the best we can do with regard not only to climate but also to political economy, religious conflict, and all the rest.

Notes

1. Kevin Anderson and Alice Bows, "Beyond 'Dangerous' Climate Change: Emission Scenarios for a New World," *Philosophical Transactions*

---

* I suppose my chapter on religious belief may be a little counterproductive in this respect.

of the Royal Society A, November 9, 2010; qtd. in David Roberts, "The Brutal Logic of Climate Change," *Grist*, December 6, 2011, http://grist.org/climate-change/2011-12-05-the-brutal-logic-of-climate-change/.

2. Funk and Rainie, "Public and Scientists' Views on Science and Society."

3. Rebecca Carter, Jiayang Sun, and Robin Jump, "A Survey and Analysis of the American Public's Perceptions and Knowledge about Antibiotic Resistance," *Open Forum Infectious Diseases* 3 (2016), pp. 1–7.

4. "Science and Engineering Indicators of 2014," National Science Foundation, 2014, https://www.nsf.gov/statistics/seind14/index.cfm/overview.

5. Brian Kennedy, "Most Americans Trust the Military and Scientists to Act in the Public's Interest," Pew Research Center, October 18, 2016, http://www.pewresearch.org/fact-tank/2016/10/18/most-americans-trust-the-military-and-scientists-to-act-in-the-publics-interest/.

6. Funk and Rainie, "Public and Scientists' Views on Science and Society."

7. Qtd. in Wendee Holtcamp, "Flavors of Uncertainty: The Difference Between Denial and Debate," *Environmental Health Perspectives* 120 (2012), pp. 314–319.

8. David P. Redlawsk, Andrew Civettini, and Karen M. Emmerson, "The Affective Tipping Point: Do Motivated Reasoners Ever 'Get It'"? *Political Psychology* 31 (2010), pp. 563–593. See also Brendan Nyhan, Ethan Porter, Jason Reifler, and Thomas Wood, "Taking Corrections Literally But Not Seriously? The Effects of Information on Factual Beliefs and Candidate Favorability," *SSRN*, June 29, 2017, https://ssrn.com/abstract=2995128.

9. Andrew Romano, "How Ignorant Are Americans"? *Newsweek*, March 20, 2011, http://www.newsweek.com/how-ignorant-are-americans-66053.

10. Romano, "How Ignorant Are Americans"?

11. Hibbing et al., *Predisposed*, p. 253.

12. "Studies Show Scientists Agree Humans Cause Global Warming," *UQ News*, May 16, 2013, http://www.uq.edu.au/news/article/2013/05/study-shows-scientists-agree-humans-cause-global-warming; ctd. in Dan Kahan, "'Messaging' Scientific Consensus: Ruminations on the External Validity of Climate-Science-Communications Studies," The Cultural Cognition Project, June 17, 2014, http://www.culturalcognition.net/blog/2014/6/17/messaging-scientific-consensus-ruminations-on-the-external-v.html.

13. Sander van der Linden, Anthony Leiserowitz, and Edward Maibach, "Communicating the Scientific Consensus on Human-Caused Climate Change Is an Effective and Depolarizing Public Engagement Strategy: Experimental Evidence from a Large National Replication Study," *SSRN*, 2016. https://ssrn.com/abstract=2733956.

14. Sander van der Linden, Anthony Leiserowitz, Seth Rosenthal, and Edward Maibach, "Inoculating the Public Against Misinformation About Climate Change," *Global Challenges* 1 (2017), http://onlinelibrary.wiley.com/doi/10.1002/gch2.201600008/full.

15. Stephan Lewandowsky, Gilles E. Gignac, and Samuel Vaughan, "The Pivotal Role of Perceived Scientific Consensus in Acceptance of Science," *Nature Climate Change* 3 (2013), pp. 399–404.

16. Kahan, "'Messaging' Scientific Consensus."

17. Jeremiah Garretson and Elizabeth Suhay, "Scientific Communication About Biological Influences on Homosexuality and the Politics of Gay Rights," *Political Research Quarterly* 69 (2016), pp. 17–29.

18. "Does Correcting Myths About the Flu Vaccine Work? An Experimental Evaluation of the Effects of Corrective Information," *Vaccine* 33 (2015), pp. 459–464. Though, see also Kathryn Haglin, "The Limitations of the Backfire Effect," *Research and Politics*, July–September 2017, pp. 1–5.

19. See Martin Gilens, "Political Ignorance and Collective Policy Preferences," *American Political Science Review* 95 (2001), pp. 391–392.

20. Beck, "Americans Believe in Science, Just Not Its Findings."

21. Heather Douglas, "Science, Values and Democracy," 5th René Descartes Lectures, Tilburg University, The Netherlands, September 5–7, 2016.

22. See, for example, "Andy Oxman: Teaching Children Unbiased Testing, Can Professor Fair Help?," Nuffield Department of Medicine website, 2014, https://www.ndm.ox.ac.uk/andy-oxman-teaching-children-unbiased-testing.

23. Clark A. Chinn and Luke Buckland, "Model-based Instruction: Fostering Change in Evolutionary Conceptions and in Epistemic Practices," in *Evolution Challenges: Integrating Research and Practice in Teaching and Learning About Evolution*, ed. Karl S. Rosengren, Sarah K. Brem, E. Margret Evans, and Gale M. Sinatra (Oxford: Oxford University Press, 2012). See G. M. Sinatra, D. Kienhues, & B. Hofer, "Addressing Challenges to Public Understanding of Science: Epistemic Cognition, Motivated Reasoning, and Conceptual Change," *Educational Psychologist* 49 (2014), pp. 123–138.

24. See Darlene Cavalier and Jason Lloyd, "The Important Lesson Scientists Could Learn from Trump's Victory," *Slate*, December 22, 2016, http://www.slate.com/articles/technology/future_tense/2016/12/trump_s_victory_shows_that_scientists_need_to_engage_more_with_the_public.html.

25. Chelsea Harvey, "Yet Another Survey Suggests the Climate Change 'Debate' Is Settled Among Scientists," *Washington Post*, September 25,

2015, https://www.washingtonpost.com/news/energy-environment/wp/ 2015/09/25/yet-another-survey-shows-the-climate-change-debate-is-settled-among-scientists/.

26. Norenzayan and Gervais, "Origins of Religious Disbelief," p. 23.

27. In addition to the study by Redlawsk et al. ctd. in chapter 1 ("The Affective Tipping Point"), see also Brendan Nyhan's article summarizing recent work indicating that fact-checking can change minds: "Fact-Checking Can Change Views? We Rate That as Mostly True," *New York Times*, November 6, 2016, https://www.nytimes.com/2016/11/06/ upshot/fact-checking-can-change-views-we-rate-that-as-mostly-true.html.

28. Caitlin Drummond and Baruch Fischhoff, "Development and Validation of the Scientific Reasoning Scale," *Journal of Behavioral Decision Making* 30 (2017), pp. 23–38.

29. Aaron Drummond, Matthew A. Palmer, and James D. Sauer, "Enhancing Endorsement of Scientific Inquiry Increases Support for Pro-environment Policies," *Royal Society Open Science* 3 (2016), pp. 1–11.

30. John Cook, "Countering Climate Science Denial and Communicating Scientific Consensus," in *Oxford Research Encyclopedia of Climate Science*, ed. Hans Von Storch (Oxford: Oxford University Press 2016).

31. John Cook, "Countering Climate Science Denial," p. 18.

32. Dan Kahan, Asheley Landrum, Katie Carpenter, Laura Helft, and Kathleen Hall Jamieson, "Science Curiosity and Political Information Processing," *Political Psychology* 38 (2017), 179–199; ctd. in Brain Resnick, "There May Be an Antidote to Politically Motivated Reasoning, And It's Wonderfully Simple," *Vox*, February 7, 2017, http://www.vox.com/science-and-health/ 2017/2/1/14392290/partisan-bias-dan-kahan-curiosity.

33. Kahan et al., "Science Curiosity and Political Information Processing," pp. 179–199.

34. Blaise Pascal, *Thoughts*, in *The Harvard Classics*, ed. Charles Eliot (New York: P.F. Collier and Son, 1910), p. 48:11.

35. "Professor Brian Cox Explains Climate Science to Denier Australian Senator Malcom Roberts," *YouTube*, uploaded by Greenshack Dotinfo, August 15, 2016, https://www.youtube.com/watch?v=LxEGHW6Lbu8.

36. www.texasgop.org/wp-content/themes/rpt/images/2012Platform_ Final.pdf.

37. Pascal, *Thoughts*, pp. 12–13.

38. See Erving Goffman, *Frame Analysis: An Essay on the Organization of Experience* (New York: Harper & Row, 1974); and Matthew Nisbet, "Communicating Climate Change: Why Frames Matter for

Public Engagement," *Environment: Science and Policy for Sustainable Development* 51 (2009), pp. 12–23.

39. See Paul Voosen, "Striving for a Climate Change," *Chronicle Review*, November 3, 2014; and Mooney, "The Science of Why We Don't Believe Science."

40. Nisbet, "Communicating Climate Change."

41. David Roberts, "Your Vote in the 2016 Election Explains Almost Everything About Your Climate Beliefs," *Vox*, April 29, 2017, http://www.vox.com/science-and-health/2017/3/23/15032488/climate-beliefs-2016-election-votes.

42. Erin P. Hennes et al., "Motivated Recall in the Service of the Economic System: The Case of Anthropogenic Climate Change," *Journal of Experimental Social Psychology: General* 145 (2016), pp. 755–771.

43. See, for example, Irina Feygina, John Jost, and R. Goldsmith, "System Justification, the Denial of Global Warming, and the Possibility of 'System-Sanctioned Change,'" *Personality & Social Psychology Bulletin* 36 (2010), pp. 326–338; and Matthew Baldwin and Joris Lammers, "Past-focused Environmental Comparisons Promote Pro-environmental Outcomes for Conservatives," *Proceedings of the National Academy of Sciences of the United States of America* 113 (2016), pp. 14953–14957.

44. Matthew Feinberg and Robb Willer, "The Moral Roots of Environmental Attitudes," *Psychological Science* 24 (2013), pp. 56–62.

45. Dan Kahan, "Is Cultural Cognition a Bummer?," The Cultural Cognition Project, January 20, 2012, http://www.culturalcognition.net/blog/2012/1/20/is-cultural-cognition-a-bummer-part-1.html.

46. Kahan, "Is Cultural Cognition a Bummer?"; emphasis in original.

47. "Denying Problems When We Don't Like the Solutions," *Duke Today*, November 6, 2014, https://today.duke.edu/2014/11/solutionaversion. See Troy H. Campbell and Aaron C. Kay, "Solution Aversion: On the Relation Between Ideology and Motivated Disbelief," *Journal of Personality and Social Psychology* 107 (2014), pp. 809–824.

48. See Katharine Hayhoe and Andrew Farley, *A Climate for Change: Global Warming Facts for Faith-Based Decisions* (New York: Faithwords, 2009); qtd. in Holtcamp, "Flavors of Uncertainty."

49. Christopher Wolsko, Hector Ariceaga, and Jesse Seiden, "Red, White, and Blue Enough to Be Green: Effects of Moral Framing on Climate Change Attitudes and Conservation Behaviors," *Journal of Experimental Social Psychology* 65 (2016), pp. 7–19.

50. Matthew Feinberg and Robb Willer, "Apocalypse Soon? Dire Messages Reduce Belief in Global Warming by Contradicting Just-World Beliefs,"

Psychological Science 22 (2011), pp. 34–38; ctd. in Jost et al., " 'Hot' Political Cognition," p. 865.

51. Sweeny et al., "Information Avoidance." See also Marshall, *Don't Even Think about It.*

52. Joshua Correll, Steven Spencer, and Mark Zanna, "An Affirmed Self and an Open Mind: Self-Affirmation and Sensitivity to Argument Strength," *Journal of Experimental Social Psychology* 40 (2004), pp. 350–356.

53. See, for example, Cohen et al., "Bridging the Partisan Divide," pp. 415–430.

54. Matthew Nisbet, "Engaging in Science Policy Controversies: Insights from the U.S. Debate Over Climate Change," *Handbook of the Public Communication of Science and Technology,* ed. Massimiano Bucchi and Brian Trench (New York: Routledge, 2014), pp. 173–185. See also, for example, David Sleeth-Keppler, Robert Perkowitz & Meighen Speiser, "It's a Matter of Trust: American Judgments of the Credibility of Informal Communicators on Solutions to Climate Change," *Environmental Communication* 11 (2017), pp. 17–40.

55. Thomas Bernauer and Liam F. McGarth, "Simple Reframing Unlikely to Boost Public Support for Climate Policy," *Nature Climate Change* 6 (2016), pp. 680–683.

56. David Roberts, "Is It Worth Trying to 'Reframe' Climate Change? Probably Not," *Vox,* February 27, 2017, http://www.vox.com/2016/3/15/11232024/reframe-climate-change.

57. Dan Kahan, "The Politically Motivated Reasoning Paradigm," *Emerging Trends in Social & Behavioral Sciences,* November 2016, p. 18. https://onlinelibrary.wiley.com/doi/abs/10.1002/9781118900772.etrds0417

58. Christopher Achen and Larry Bartels, *Democracy for Realists* (Princeton, NJ: Princeton University Press, 2016).

59. James Kirchick, "How the GOP Became the Party of Putin," *Politico,* July 18, 2017, https://www.politico.com/magazine/story/2017/07/18/how-the-gop-became-the-party-of-putin-215387.

60. Philip Fernbach et al., "Political Extremism Is Supported by an Illusion of Understanding," *Psychological Science* 24 (2013), pp. 939–946.

61. See David Roberts, "Conservatives Probably Can't Be Persuaded on Climate Change. So Now What?," *Vox,* November 10, 2017, https://www.vox.com/energy-and-environment/2017/11/10/16627256/conservatives-climate-change-persuasion.

62. Douglas, "Science, Values and Democracy."

63. From the PAC website, http://www.314action.org/home; qtd. in Ed Yong, "Professor Smith Goes to Washington," *The Atlantic,* January 25, 2017,

https://www.theatlantic.com/science/archive/2017/01/thanks-to-trump-scientists-are-planning-to-run-for-office/514229/.

64. Daniel Engber, "The War on Science Is a Trap," *Slate*, February 6, 2017, http://www.slate.com/articles/health_and_science/science/2017/02/the_war_on_science_is_a_trap.html.

65. Robert S. Young, "A Scientists' March on Washington Is a Bad Idea," *New York Times*, January 31, 2017, https://www.nytimes.com/2017/01/31/opinion/a-scientists-march-on-washington-is-a-bad-idea.html.

66. Dan Kahan, "Five Theses on Climate Change Conversation," The Cultural Cognition Project, July 7, 2014, http://www.culturalcognition.net/blog/2014/7/7/five-theses-on-climate-science-communication-lecture-summary.html.

67. Dan Kahan, "What SE Florida Can Teach Us About the *Political* Science of Climate Change," The Cultural Cognition Project, June 27, 2014, http://www.culturalcognition.net/blog/2014/6/27/what-se-florida-can-teach-us-about-the-political-science-of.html.

68. Kahan, "What SE Florida Can Teach Us About the *Political* Science of Climate Change."

69. Dan Kahan, "The 'Local-Adaptation Science Communication Environment': The Precarious Opportunity," The Cultural Cognition Project, September 19, 2012, http://www.culturalcognition.net/blog/2012/9/19/the-local-adaptation-science-communication-environment-the-p.html.

70. Nathalie Baptiste, "Conservatives Want to Slash FEMA's Disaster Funding," *Mother Jones*, February 13, 2017, http://www.motherjones.com/environment/2017/01/fema-disaster-funding.

71. Laura Parker, "Who's Still Fighting Climate Change? The U.S. Military," *National Geographic*, February 7, 2017, http://news.nationalgeographic.com/2017/02/pentagon-fights-climate-change-sea-level-rise-defense-department-military/.

72. Parker, "Who's Still Fighting Climate Change? The U.S. Military."

73. Roberts, "Is It Worth Trying to 'Reframe' Climate Change? Probably Not."

Index

fake news, 42–3
false consciousness, 164
family dynamics, 193–4
fanaticism, 42
Feinberg, Matthew, 307, 311
Feldstein, Martin, 310
Festinger, Leon, 7–8
fine-tuning argument, 239, 240, 288n64
Fischhoff, Baruch, 301
Fishkin, James, 297
fluoridation, 98–9
framing, 82–3, 306–7, 311, 312, 315
Frank, Thomas, 160–1, 187
Frankfurt, Harry, 5
free-market capitalism, 178, 181, 273
Freud, Anna, 39
Freud, Sigmund, 73, 256, 269–70, 280
  and terror management, 265–72
Friedman, Milton, 178, 179, 186
Frijda, Nico, 18
fundamental attribution error (FAE),
  147–9, 152–3, 160, 168
fundamentalism, 213
future discounting, 79

Garretson, Jeremiah, 298
Garrett, R. Kelly, 95
Gasper, Karen, 18
Gauchat, Gordon, 103, 104, 107
Gendler, Tamar, 15–16
General Social Survey, 107
genetically modified (GM) foods, 97, 306
genocide, 12
Gerber, Alan, 89
Gervais, Will, 275–6, 282
"ghost helmet" experiments, 286n47
Gibbon, Edward, 257, 273
Giddens, Anthony, 85
Gilens, Martin, 159, 166
global warming, see anthropogenic global
  warming (AGW)
Gluckman, Peter, 277
Gopnik, Alison, 20–1
Gramm-Leach-Bliley Act, 142
Grayling, A. C., 279
group identification, 260
grouping, 168
group norms, 24
group polarization, 25, 42, 194

group-serving motivation, 24
gun control, 22–3
Guth, Alan, 239

Hacker, Jacob, 297
Haidt, Jonathan, 24–5, 92, 108, 253, 307
Halstead, Ted, 310
Hardin, Garrett, 110
Harman, Gilbert, 168
Harmon-Jones, Eddie, 7
Harris, Sam, 225, 227–8, 266, 273
Hart, David Bentley, 278, 280, 281, 298
Hart, P. Sol, 89
Hayek, Friedrich, 185, 186
Hayhoe, Katharine, 309–10
Heer, Jeet, 277
Hennes, Erin, 82, 307
heuristics, 7, 15, 39
Hibbing, John, 25, 26, 297, 298
Hick, John, 278, 279
hierarchicalism, 27–8, 41, 138–9, 140,
  192, 193, 281
  moral, 195
Hobbes, Thomas, 47
Hofstadter, Richard, 195
homosexuality, 105, 273
hot cognition, 30
human capital, 181
Hume, David, 14, 19, 21, 92, 222

identity:
  and beliefs, 34
  cultural, 28, 140, 220, 256, 265, 267,
    275, 301
  and group membership, 262
  political, 301
  racial, 154
  social, 220, 281
identity groups, 29, 112, 128
identity politics, 104
ideology, 10–11, 13, 26, 28, 29, 187
  anti-big government, 249
  anti-egalitarian, 249
  and conservatism, 104, 187
  libertarian, 171, 187
  moralizing, 258
  and partisanship, 24
  pathological, 44–9
  and peer group membership, 85